The United States Army War College

The United States Army War College educates and develops leaders for service at the strategic level while advancing knowledge in the global application of Landpower.

The purpose of the United States Army War College is to produce graduates who are skilled critical thinkers and complex problem solvers. Concurrently, it is our duty to the U.S. Army to also act as a "think factory" for commanders and civilian leaders at the strategic level worldwide and routinely engage in discourse and debate concerning the role of ground forces in achieving national security objectives.

The Strategic Studies Institute publishes national security and strategic research and analysis to influence policy debate and bridge the gap between military and academia.

The Center for Strategic Leadership contributes to the education of world class senior leaders, develops expert knowledge, and provides solutions to strategic Army issues affecting the national security community.

The Peacekeeping and Stability Operations Institute provides subject matter expertise, technical review, and writing expertise to agencies that develop stability operations concepts and doctrines.

The School of Strategic Landpower develops strategic leaders by providing a strong foundation of wisdom grounded in mastery of the profession of arms, and by serving as a crucible for educating future leaders in the analysis, evaluation, and refinement of professional expertise in war, strategy, operations, national security, resource management, and responsible command.

The U.S. Army Heritage and Education Center acquires, conserves, and exhibits historical materials for use to support the U.S. Army, educate an international audience, and honor Soldiers—past and present.

STRATEGIC STUDIES INSTITUTE

The Strategic Studies Institute (SSI) is part of the U.S. Army War College and is the strategic-level study agent for issues related to national security and military strategy with emphasis on geostrategic analysis.

The mission of SSI is to use independent analysis to conduct strategic studies that develop policy recommendations on:

- Strategy, planning, and policy for joint and combined employment of military forces;

- Regional strategic appraisals;

- The nature of land warfare;

- Matters affecting the Army's future;

- The concepts, philosophy, and theory of strategy; and,

- Other issues of importance to the leadership of the Army.

Studies produced by civilian and military analysts concern topics having strategic implications for the Army, the Department of Defense, and the larger national security community.

In addition to its studies, SSI publishes special reports on topics of special or immediate interest. These include edited proceedings of conferences and topically oriented roundtables, expanded trip reports, and quick-reaction responses to senior Army leaders.

The Institute provides a valuable analytical capability within the Army to address strategic and other issues in support of Army participation in national security policy formulation.

**Strategic Studies Institute
and
U.S. Army War College Press**

AVOIDING THE TRAP:
U.S. STRATEGY AND POLICY FOR COMPETING IN THE ASIA-PACIFIC BEYOND THE REBALANCE

**David Lai
John F. Troxell
Frederick J. Gellert
Project Editors**

February 2018

CONTENTS

Foreword ix

Acknowledgements xi

Summary xiii

Part I: Introduction..1

1. Forward From the Rebalance: Competing
    in the Asia-Pacific................................3
    David Lai, John F. Troxell, and
    Frederick J. Gellert

Part II: Regional Overview 27

2. China's Rise: What Does It Mean for the
    United States? 29
    William P. Donnelly

3. Developing a U.S.-led Multilateral Security
    Architecture for the Asia-Pacific.....................43
    Eric W. Young

4. The Largest Tiger: India in the U.S. Policy
    toward Indo-Asia-Pacific 83
    Todd D. Carroll

5. Japan's Strategic Renaissance: Implications
    for U.S. Policy in the Asia-Pacific 107
    Neil J. Owens

6. Curtail, Cooperate, or Compel in the South
    China Sea? 153
    Robert R. Arnold, Jr.

7. Philippine Ambivalence Toward the United
    States: Lessons Learned..................................189
    Romeo S. Brawner, Jr.

8. The United States and China in the Cyber Domain: Stop the Downward Spiral..............215
    Steven M. Pierce

Part III: Economic Instrument of Power....................255

9. U.S. Economic Rebalance to the Asia-Pacific Region: Is it Still Possible?...............................257
    Jeffrey M. Zaiser

Part IV: Military Instrument of Power....................285

10. A New U.S. Indo-Asia-Pacific Security Strategy...287
    Ryan M. Finn and David B. Moore

11. A Diplomatic Solution to the North Korea Problem..331
    Frazariel I. Castro

12. Korean Peninsula: Upgrading the Denuclearization Status Quo..........................361
    James L. Conner

Part V: Soft Power Considerations.............................377

13. People-Focused Activities: A Measure to Preserve American Strength...........................379
    Joel M. Buenaflor

14. Diplomacy Under The Strategic Rebalance and a Look Forward.....................411
    Sandra Minkel

About the Contributors..445

FOREWORD

This book is the product of a U.S. Army War College (USAWC) Integrated Research Project (IRP). It addresses a Chief of Staff, Army priority research topic and was sponsored by the U.S. Army Pacific and the Headquarters, Department of the Army, Directorate of Strategy, Plans, and Policy (HQDA G-35). The book resulted from a whole-of-War College effort. Core curriculum and regional elective studies augmented student research and facilitated analysis. Faculty from across the USAWC supported analytical discussions, mentored student participants, and reviewed the written contributions. Students and faculty met with Asia-Pacific policy experts in the U.S. Government from the Department of State, the Office of the U.S. Trade Representative, and the National Security Council. Researchers also traveled to the Asia-Pacific to meet with senior military leaders and security analysts in Japan and China, as well as the major U.S. military commands in Hawaii, to explore issues and develop recommendations on regional issues. Students, along with leading think tank subject matter experts from the Washington, DC, area, presented selected topics from this book at a round-table organized in conjunction with the Center for Strategic and International Studies.

In 2011, former U.S. Secretary of State Hillary Clinton provided a framework for the U.S. Government to refocus the instruments of national power — diplomatic, informational, military, and economic — toward the Asia-Pacific. She explained the importance of Asia-Pacific regional growth to the United States in the short-lived "pivot," and in 2012 former President Barack Obama formalized the U.S. Government effort with a commitment to "rebalance," which included negotiating a multilateral trade agreement, the Trans-Pacific Partnership (TPP) with 11 other nations, committing a larger portion of U.S. military forces to the region, and improving security agreements with allies and partners. However, President Donald Trump, shortly after taking office in January 2017, withdrew the United States from the TPP, and in March, the Acting Assistant Secretary of State, Bureau of East Asian and Pacific Affairs publicly declared the rebalance was over.

This book explores the validity of the U.S. rebalance to the Asia-Pacific; analyzes the ends, ways, and means of the strategy to meet U.S. and regional partner security objectives; and considers the effectiveness of the U.S. Government effort. This book focuses on the impact of China's increasing national power on U.S. objectives and those of Asia-Pacific nations. The instruments of national power are assessed to include hard power, economic, military, and diplomatic, along with providing recommendations for the United States' use of soft power. In addition to China, country specific chapters include an analysis and security recommendations concerning issues related to North and South Korea, Japan, and the Philippines. Analysis and recommendations in this book may provide insights for Trump's NSS and subsequent security documents and will inform security professionals across the U.S. Government, outside of government, and foreign governments as they modify their approaches to this critical region.

DOUGLAS C. LOVELACE, JR.
Director
Strategic Studies Institute and
 U.S. Army War College Press

ACKNOWLEDGEMENTS

This book is the product of an Integrated Research Project with 3 principal faculty advisors and 18 students. We would particularly like to recognize three International Fellows for their contributions to this project: Colonels Romeo S. Brawner, Jr., the Republic of the Philippines; Shigemi Sugimura, Japan; and Shu-wei Yang, Taiwan. While this faculty-student study team conducted the primary research and analysis, a number of other faculty members at the U.S. Army War College have also provided invaluable support, especially in advising the students on the writing of their individual chapters. We extend our sincere thanks to U.S. Army Colonel David W. DeTata, Professors Albert F. Lord and Grace Stettenbauer, U.S. Navy Captain Wade Turvold, and U.S. Army Lieutenant Colonel James V. Dicrocco III. Special thanks go to Ambassador Daniel Shields for his extensive engagement in this research project and his valuable insights in Asia-Pacific affairs.

During our research, we have also received tremendous support from a number of government and private institutions. We would like to extend our gratitude to the Bureau of East Asia and Pacific Affairs of the State Department, the Asia-Pacific Branch of the National Security Council, the Office of the U.S. Trade Representative, the U.S. Pacific Command, and the U.S. Army Pacific.

We are extremely grateful to the Center for Strategic and International Studies (CSIS) for its support to our project. We want to thank the subject matter experts there for helping with our student researchers and improving their reports. We also want to thank CSIS for organizing the roundtable for us to discuss our research results with noted analysts. We would like to thank in particular CSIS Senior Vice President Kathleen H. Hicks and Senior Advisor on Asia Bonnie S. Glaser for their whole-hearted support.

Finally, we want to thank the U.S. Army Attachés in Beijing, China, and the Defense Liaison Office in Shanghai for their support to our China field study group and the China Foreign Affairs University, the China Institute of Contemporary International Relations, the Shanghai Institute for International Studies, the Shanghai American Chamber of Commerce, the Shanghai Institute of International Relations of the Shanghai Social Sciences Academy, and Fudan University for hosting our roundtable discussions.

SUMMARY

The pivot to Asia is over, suggested Susan Thornton, Acting Assistant Secretary of State, Bureau of East Asian and Pacific Affairs, on the eve of Secretary of State Rex Tillerson's first visit to Asia on March 14, 2017.[1] This statement, though expected, begs many questions: Is this just a repeal of the bumper sticker "Strategic Rebalance," typical of administration change? If so, what is its replacement? Moreover, if this change is just in name but not in substance, will President Donald Trump stay the course? If not, what will be Trump's policy toward the Asia-Pacific? What should be the new focus and priorities? In short, given the enduring U.S. interests in the Asia-Pacific, what should be a sound and forward-looking U.S. strategy toward this region?

This research project began with two questions on the future of the U.S. rebalance to the Asia-Pacific: Was it the right thing to do, and have we done it right? Given the enormous expected growth in the region and thus the expected impacts in the world, the answer to the first question is a resounding yes. The answer to the second question is less clear. On the one hand, there have been several successes, not the least of which was the public pronouncement of the Obama administration's directive to pivot attention to the region and increase significant travel and engagement in the region by former President Obama and his senior officials. On the other hand, there have been limited effects in world affairs and murky plans for future U.S. endeavors in the region, complicated by growing financial and political challenges inside the United States. Perhaps the best answer to the second question is that there was a great start with an unclear follow-up. With the Trump administration now guiding U.S. foreign policy, it is time to move forward from the rebalance to a revitalized strategy and approach to the Asia-Pacific for the third decade of the 21st century.

The challenge now for the U.S. administration, and for policy experts writ large, is to build an effective strategy for whole-of-U.S. Government action in moving forward from the rebalance. In order to offer useful recommendations on the development of an effective U.S. strategy to address those challenges in the region, it is useful to establish an overarching concept with which to describe the wide-ranging strategic recommendations of the researchers in this project. To that end, we posit:

- **Strategic Goal**: Ensure American leadership, security, and prosperity.
- **Strategic Task**: Accommodate China's rise through competition without conflict.
- **Strategic Vision**: Economy by priority; enabled by military power; tempered by diplomacy.

The strategic goal has long been a foundation of American national policy. While it focuses on U.S. interests first, this does not mean to the exclusion of all others. American leadership will promote democratic values and preserve the successful international order. Partner nations want U.S. leadership in the region as a counter to China's rising power.

Long-range success in the Asia-Pacific region will only come from effective international cooperation. This cooperation must include China. In keeping with the 2015 U.S. *National Security Strategy*, we confirm the U.S. position to "welcome the rise of a stable, peaceful, and prosperous China."[2] To that end, the overarching strategic task for the United States is how to accommodate China's rise. America must not constrain the responsible rise of China in the region and globally, but at the same time should provide a check on Chinese power by protecting U.S. and partner national interests. This check will come through the effective use of a rules-based international order, but ultimately it will be empowered by a position of U.S. strength across the elements of national power.

Strategic change must have a vision to paint the picture of success but also to motivate and guide the efforts to achieve that success. The vision statement is intended to highlight the three strategic instruments the United States must use to lead in the region. The highest priority of effort must be economic, therefore the detailed American strategy for the region will need to chart a course for the future centered on economic cooperation and growth. Despite the primacy of economic considerations, the stark reality of the region is one of significant security concerns. Therefore, the strategy by necessity will require a strong, comprehensive plan for ensuring regional security through a revamped regional security architecture and military agreements and the interactions of capable, well trained, and professional armed forces to keep the peace. Finally, robust diplomatic efforts will enable the United States to resolve the many regional challenges without resorting to economic or armed conflict. This strategic concept frames the detailed recommendations of the project's researchers.

The subsequent chapters in this book, written by student researchers during their year at the U.S. Army War College, provide information and recommendations on topics regarding the instruments of national power, regional affairs, and key Asia-Pacific countries.

The key findings of this project can be distilled into four primary recommendations for the United States:

- Create a comprehensive Asia-Pacific strategy to guide whole-of-U.S. Government action plans.
- Improve U.S. national power across the instruments of national power to ensure the resources and capability exist to achieve the strategic goals.
- Create a "post-Trans-Pacific Partnership" (TPP) trade initiative as the cornerstone of the economic element of strategy.
- Create and lead a new Asia-Pacific regional security architecture that includes China; and modernize current alliances and partnerships.

ENDNOTES - SUMMARY

1. Ankit Panda, "Straight From the US State Department: The 'Pivot' to Asia Is Over," *The Diplomat*, March 14, 2017, available from *https://thediplomat.com/2017/03/straight-from-the-us-state-department-the-pivot-to-asia-is-over/*.

2. Barack Obama, *National Security Strategy*, Washington, DC: The White House, February 2015, p. 24.

PART I:
INTRODUCTION

CHAPTER 1

FORWARD FROM THE REBALANCE: COMPETING IN THE ASIA-PACIFIC

David Lai, John F. Troxell, and Frederick J. Gellert

The pivot to Asia is over, suggested Susan Thornton, Acting Assistant Secretary of State, Bureau of East Asian and Pacific Affairs, on the eve of Secretary of State Rex Tillerson's first visit to Asia on March 14, 2017.[1] This statement, though expected, begs many questions: Is this just a repeal of the bumper sticker "Strategic Rebalance," typical of administration change? If so, what is its replacement? Moreover, if this change is just in name but not in substance, will President Donald Trump stay the course? If not, what will be Trump's policy toward the Asia-Pacific? What should be the new focus and priorities? In short, given the enduring U.S. interests in the Asia-Pacific, what should be a sound and forward-looking U.S. strategy toward this region?

STRATEGIC REBALANCE: THE RIGHT THING TO DO

The most significant foreign policy undertaking of the Obama administration was the strategic rebalance toward the Asia-Pacific. Although it came as a surprise to many at a time when the nation was exhausted from the two wars in Iraq and Afghanistan and getting hard-hit by the 2008 global financial crisis, the strategic rebalance, officially announced in 2011, was the right thing for the United States to do.

The rise of China is the most significant event in the world in the last 20 years and probably for many years to come. According to former Secretary of State Hillary Clinton:

> The Asia-Pacific has become a key driver of global politics. . . . It boasts almost half the world's population. It includes many of the key engines of the global economy, as well as the largest emitters of greenhouse gases. It is home to several of our key allies and important emerging powers like China, India, and Indonesia. . . . One of the most important tasks of American statecraft over the next decade will therefore be to lock in a substantially increased investment — diplomatic, economic, strategic, and otherwise — in the Asia-Pacific region.[2]

The United States needed to focus more attention on this historic development and increasingly critical region. After all, the rise of China is not simply a change of national power distribution, but a phenomenon that influences the future of international relations. Concerning this necessary policy shift, Kurt Campbell, former Assistant Secretary of State for East Asian and Pacific Affairs, recalls:

> The central tenet of this bold policy shift is that the United States will need to do more with and in the Asia-Pacific to spur domestic revival and renovation as well as to keep the peace in the world's most dynamic region. If the larger Middle East can be described as the 'arc of instability,' then the region stretching from Japan through China and Southeast Asia to India can be seen as representing an 'arc of ascendance,' Asia's march on the future. American policy must heed this unrelenting feature of the future: that the lion's share of the history of the twenty-first century will be written in the Asia-Pacific region.[3]

It is former President Barack Obama who put the most significant touch on this huge undertaking:

U.S. economic and security interests are inextricably linked to developments in the arc extending from the Western Pacific and East Asia into the Indian Ocean region and South Asia, creating a mix of evolving challenges and opportunities. Accordingly, while the U.S. military will continue to contribute to security globally, *we will of necessity rebalance toward the Asia-Pacific region* [italics in original].[4]

STRATEGIC REBALANCE: NOT QUITE DONE RIGHT

Doing the right thing does not guarantee getting it done right. In retrospect, many of the Obama administration's approaches did not lead to the desired result. The United States wants to see China rise peacefully and become a responsible stakeholder; however, the rebalance to a large extent has driven China in the opposite direction. According to recent testimony from Secretary of Defense James Mattis, "a rising, more confident, and assertive China, places the international order under assault."[5]

Questionable Strategic Assumptions

The Center for Strategic and International Studies (CSIS) conducted several Department of Defense (DoD)-commissioned studies on the strategic rebalance. All of them categorically pointed out that the strategic rebalance lacks "a clear, coherent, or consistent strategy for the Asia-Pacific region, particularly when it comes to managing China's rise."[6]

Several questionable assumptions underlying U.S. policy toward the Asia-Pacific contributed to the lack of a coherent strategy. First, the rebalance builds upon an unwritten, yet long-held, U.S. foreign policy principle, put best by Kurt Campbell:

> a consistent feature of American Asia strategy has been to use diplomatic, economic, and military means to prevent the emergence of a dominating hegemon in Asia, thereby making the region safe for American pursuits like trade promotion, faith advocacy, democracy support, and territorial security.[7]

China's relentless rise, however, calls this principle into question. If the United States welcomes (or at least recognizes) the rise of China,[8] then it will need to accept this changing geostrategic reality and prepare to deal with an Asian hegemon. The nuance becomes reconciling acceptable degrees and understanding of "dominating regional hegemon." The focus should now be on preventing the emergence of a hostile regional hegemon.

Second, key architects of the rebalance, and many in the United States, opine that China is a threat. For example, General Mark Milley, U.S. Army Chief of Staff, in recent Congressional testimony identified China as a threat within the 4+1 threat construct.[9] However, China should not be viewed as a threat to the United States in the same vein as radical Islamic terrorists or even Russia. A heightened threat perception leads to over-militarizing the relationship with the tendency to generate spiraling security dilemmas and fulfilling Thucydides's Trap prophecies. Given the extensive economic interdependencies developed between these two powers, the United States should continue to deal with China mostly in diplomatic, economic, and sociocultural terms.

Finally, the designers of the strategic rebalance appeared to have argued against the centrality of China.

In Kurt Campbell's words, "China is the big story, no doubt. But for us to be successful, we're going to have to work with others more effectively. We've got to embed our China policy in a larger Asia strategy."[10] With this view came the repeated talking point: "It is not about China." Many in the Asia-Pacific understand that the rebalance is mainly, if not only, about China. After all, which other nation in the Asia-Pacific deserves such attention and effort from the superpower? The Obama administration's refusal to address the "elephant in the room" publicly as the main challenge resulted in a strategy that was not focused on the central issue of the rise of China.

Be that as it may, the rebalance, as Kurt Campbell puts it:

> would require bolstering alliances with states like Australia and Japan, working with new partners like India and Vietnam, strengthening our military and economic tools of statecraft, engaging multilateral institutions, and maintaining our democratic values, all while intensively engaging Beijing and seeking to shape the contours of China's rise.[11]

Despite the inherent soundness of each of these approaches, the problem is that when the United States does not focus its policy on China; no matter how much the United States has tried to shore up support from the other Asian nations; it is not enough to get China to behave in accordance with the existing rules-based international order. As a result, while it is good to strengthen relations with the allies and recruit more partners in the Asia-Pacific, the Obama administration's effort was not effective.

REVISITING THE POWER TRANSITION THEORY

Many in the United States are now aware of the Thucydides Trap and the danger of power transition between great powers. The Thucydides Trap is based on the ancient Greek historian's (Thucydides) account of the Peloponnesian War, in which he argues the inevitability of that war because of Sparta's fear of a rising Athens. The potential for conflict between the United States and China reflects a similar dynamic within the international system. Kenneth Organski, who first put forward the power transition theory, notes that accommodation is an alternative to the deadly Thucydides Trap. Indeed, in a power transition, the contending great powers, namely the extant stakeholders and the upstart, have basically two options: fight or accommodate. Organski suggests that if the rising power is unstoppable, accommodation should be the prudent policy.[12]

Figure 1-1 puts the power transition theory between the United States and China in perspective. Power transition between China and the United States has already passed the first stage where China has gone through the initial taking-off period. The transition is now in the initial part of the second stage where China continues to narrow its national power inferiority gap to that of the United States.[13]

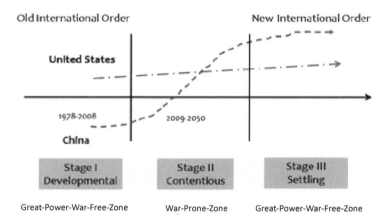

Figure 1-1. U.S.-China Power Transition.[14]

At this time, fear is no longer the defining factor. How the United States and China come to terms with the emerging realities in the two nations' relations is much more significant.

We can observe some typical behaviors at this stage of the power transition. The status quo leader is becoming more concerned as the rising power approaches parity with it in the two nations' national power capabilities. There is the temptation and danger of the status quo power launching a preventative attack to short-circuit the rising power. The rising power, on the other hand, emboldened by its growing power, can challenge the status quo power. Becoming more assertive is the typical recourse of the upstart.

In many respects, the relationship between the two in power transition is similar to a parent and teenager. The teenager has become a more independent actor and expects greater responsibility and control; yet the parent may not realize in time the changes and continues to demand acceptance of previous constraints and limitations. Holding firm to the rules and demanding obedience are typical on the parent side. The United States has been demanding that China behave in the rules-based order and become a responsible stakeholder. China, on the other hand, challenges U.S. rules and presses for changes.[15] The U.S. strategic rebalance is a typical act at this stage of the power transition. China's responses also fit many of the descriptions.[16]

There is widespread debate in the United States between the hawks and doves over what the United States should do about China. The hawks argue that the United States should stand firm and punish China for every wrongdoing, while the doves suggest accommodation should come into play in the U.S. policy toward China. Accommodation is by no means easy for the United States, especially at a time when it still enjoys a substantial upper hand in hard power. Yet it is not too early to prepare for it. Accommodation does not imply appeasement. In the case of China, such an approach would recognize a greater leadership role in international institutions and accept various Chinese initiatives, such as the Asia Infrastructure Investment Bank, but also insist that China adheres to reasonable boundaries as represented by the existing rules-based international order.

THE TRUMP ADMINISTRATION

On January 20, 2017, Donald J. Trump was sworn in as the 45th President of the United States. Determined to fix America's perceived domestic and international troubles, the new President put forward his policies:

> For many decades, we've enriched foreign industry at the expense of American industry; subsidized the armies of other countries, while allowing for the very sad depletion

of our military. We've defended other nations' borders while refusing to defend our own.

We assembled here today issuing a new decree to be heard in every city, in every foreign capital, and in every hall of power. From this day forward, a new vision will govern our land. From this moment on, it's going to be America first.[17]

Domestic issues aside, the President's call signaled a return to the realism of Presidents George Washington and Thomas Jefferson and the populist nationalism of President Andrew Jackson, from the idealism of President Woodrow Wilson that has been guiding U.S. foreign policy for much of the last 100 years. Under Trump, national interest—principally focused on the security and economic well-being of the American people—but not ideology will be the guiding principle for U.S. foreign policy.

Many find the President's call objectionable— because those Americans believe the liberal international order led by the United States shaping international institutions has significantly benefited U.S. economic development, national security, and international influence. Realists who focus on nationalism, such as Trump, argue that the United States must pursue a foreign policy with a viewpoint that anarchy is an enduring feature of the international system, with no permanent friends or enemies, but permanent interests; interactions tend to be conflictual because states compete for power and security.[18] Some argue this realist foreign policy vision is what the United States needs now. This is especially significant with respect to America's relations with China and the Asia-Pacific.

AN ASIA-PACIFIC STRATEGY BY DESIGN

This research project began with two questions on the future of the U.S. rebalance to the Asia-Pacific: Was it the right thing to do, and have we done it right? Given the enormous expected growth in the region and thus the expected impacts in the world, the answer to the first question is a resounding yes. The answer to the second question is less clear. On the one hand, there have been several successes, not the least of which was the public pronouncement of the Obama administration's directive to pivot attention to the region and increase significant travel and engagement in the region by former President Obama and his senior officials. On the other hand, there have been limited effects in world affairs and murky plans for future U.S. endeavors in the region, complicated by growing financial and political challenges inside the United States. Perhaps the best answer to the second question is that there was a great start with an unclear follow-up. With the Trump administration now guiding U.S. foreign policy, it is time to move forward from the rebalance to a revitalized strategy and approach to the Asia-Pacific for the 3rd decade of the 21st century.

Despite Trump's espoused "America First" priority, current reality for the Trump administration is dictating more, not less engagement for the United States in the Asia-Pacific region. Of note, the first trips by senior U.S. defense officials and diplomats in the new administration were to China and Northeast Asia. The first head of state visit received by Trump was from Japan's Prime Minister Shinzo Abe. Whether deliberately, or by circumstance, the Trump administration signaled the strategic importance of the Asia-Pacific region to the world. The challenge now for the U.S.

administration, and for policy experts writ large, is to build an effective strategy for whole-of-U.S. Government action in moving forward from the rebalance.

The Asia-Pacific region is fundamentally a set of diverse, complex challenges. In order to offer useful recommendations on the development of an effective U.S. strategy to address those challenges in the region, it is useful to establish an overarching concept with which to describe the wide-ranging strategic recommendations of the researchers in this project. To that end, we posit:

- **Strategic Goal**: Ensure American leadership, security, and prosperity.
- **Strategic Task**: Accommodate China's rise through competition without conflict.
- **Strategic Vision**: Economy by priority, diplomacy by necessity, enabled by military.

The strategic goal is straightforward and has long been a foundation of American national policy. While it focuses on U.S. interests first, this does not mean to the exclusion of all others. American leadership will promote democratic values and preserve the successful international order. Partner nations want U.S. leadership in the region as a counter to China's rising power. The United States is a Pacific nation with enormous power to do good works in the region. Long-range success in the Asia-Pacific region will only come from effective international cooperation.

This cooperation must include China. In keeping with the 2015 U.S. *National Security Strategy*, we confirm the U.S. position to "[welcome] the rise of a stable, peaceful, and prosperous China."[19] To that end, the overarching strategic task for the United States is how to accommodate China's rise. America must allow

China to rise in the region and globally, but at the same time provide a check on Chinese power by protecting U.S. and partner national interests. This check will come through the effective use of a rules-based international order, but ultimately it will be empowered by a position of U.S. strength across the elements of national power. Whether China rises through peaceful competition or through military and economic conflict may be determined solely by the fair and effective use of international rules.

Strategic change must have a vision to paint the picture of success and to motivate and guide the efforts to achieve that success. The vision statement here highlights the three strategic instruments the United States must use to lead in the region. The highest priority of effort must be economic, and therefore the detailed American strategy for the region will need to chart a course for the future centered on economic cooperation and growth. Despite the primacy of economic considerations for the region, the stark reality of the region is one of significant security concerns. Therefore, the strategy by necessity will require a strong, comprehensive plan for ensuring regional security through a revamped regional security architecture and military agreements and the interactions of capable, well trained, and professional armed forces to keep the peace. Finally, robust diplomatic efforts will enable the United States to resolve the many regional challenges without resorting to economic or armed conflict. This strategic concept then frames the detailed recommendations of the project's researchers.

The subsequent chapters in this book, written by student researchers during their year at the U.S. Army War College, provide information and recommendations on topics regarding the instruments of national power, regional affairs, and key Asia-Pacific countries. A summary of those chapters is presented here and can be distilled into four primary recommendations for the United States:

- Create a comprehensive Asia-Pacific strategy to guide whole-of-U.S. Government action plans.
- Improve U.S. national power across the instruments of national power to ensure the resources and capability exist to achieve the strategic goals.
- Create a "post-Trans-Pacific Partnership" (TPP) trade initiative as the cornerstone of the economic element of strategy.
- Create and lead a new Asia-Pacific regional security architecture that includes China; and modernize current alliances and partnerships.

Regional Overview

In Chapter 2, William Donnelly analyzes how the United States can get it right with China. First among U.S. strategic tasks is managing China's rise by understanding China's goals and intentions. A key will be to address China's concerns about containment. Thus, U.S.-China communication and cooperation must be robust and effective, including the difficult issue of military-to-military engagements.

A key for the future of relations in the region will be multilateral organizations. In Chapter 3, Eric Young discusses the need for a U.S.-led multilateral security architecture (MLSA). America must lead in the region while building multinational institutions. No other nation in the region can do so now or in the foreseeable future. While some nations may look to the United States as the ultimate protector in the region, the best long-term solution will be an effective multilateral security architecture of Asia-Pacific nations that includes China. This must not become a counter-China organization. Today, the largest and best-known multilateral organization in the Asia-Pacific is the Association of Southeast Asia Nations (ASEAN).

ASEAN expanded its initial writ of focusing on political and economic issues with the establishment of the ASEAN Regional Forum (ARF) in 1993 as the "first region-wide Asia-Pacific multilateral forum for official consultations on peace and security issues."[20] It has since added the annual ASEAN Defense Ministers' Meeting (ADMM), and regularly convenes the East Asian Summit (EAS). All of these entities are designed to address regional security challenges, but growing tensions in the region require moving beyond dialogue-based institutional arrangements to a MLSA that can actually resolve regional security issues. The MLSA must be able to respond quickly to military provocations and include enforcement mechanisms. The existing hub-and-spoke architecture for U.S. mutual defense treaties has served well as a deterrent for armed conflict. The challenge in the future will be to maintain security in a complex region, with emerging powers and gray zone actors, short of traditional war. A multilateral organization will offer the best method to address real challenges, manage competition, and avoid conflict.

Besides managing China's rise, the United States will need to manage the positive growth of other rising regional powers, notably India and Japan, as well as work with other Asia-Pacific nations in navigating difficult challenges such as the ongoing disputes in the South China Sea (SCS). Todd Carroll analyzes India in Chapter 4. India will likely have the largest population in the world by 2028 and an economy larger than the United States by 2050. This will require the U.S. strategy to include detailed goals and increased engagement with India in military, commercial, and diplomatic areas. Neil Owens analyzes Japan in Chapter 5. Japan is the world's third largest national economy and has embarked on a "strategic renaissance," seeking to assume a greater international leadership role, improve its bilateral and multilateral relationships, and increase its defense deterrent capabilities. These Japanese activities are strategically beneficial for the United States and should be encouraged. The Trump administration can assist Japan by encouraging its policy, facilitating a more cooperative Japan-South Korea relationship, deepening economic ties, reexamining the U.S.-Japan Base Realignment Plan, and encouraging continued public discussion on Japan's future international role.

Regarding the SCS, in Chapter 6, Robert Arnold, Jr., examines U.S.-China interactions in this volatile sub-region. Reviewing the U.S. options to curtail U.S. actions in the SCS, to cooperate with China in the SCS, or to compel China to change its activities within the SCS, his recommendation to cooperate with China is the most productive method to secure U.S. interests in the long term. Cooperation would focus on multilayered collaboration with China by building upon current U.S.-China military-to-military engagement and would necessitate the employment of all of the instruments of U.S. national power.

The Philippines is a key player in the SCS and in Chapter 7, Romeo Brawner, Jr., of the Philippine Army analyzes the current ambivalence of the Philippine leadership toward the United States and offers recommendations for U.S. interactions with Asia-Pacific nations from a unique third-country perspective. Because of its central geographic location, cooperation with the Philippines must remain a top priority for U.S. strategy. A key will be to acknowledge Philippine autonomy while meeting mutual needs in security, diplomacy, and economic realms.

An area of increasing importance in military and civilian domains is cyber. In Chapter 8, Steven Pierce finds cyber activities, good and bad, have the potential to enable or disrupt strategic goals, as what happens in the cyber domain increasingly does not stay solely in the cyber domain. Cyber cuts across diplomatic, information, military, and economic instruments in ways that we are only now beginning to understand. As nations interact and compete, cyber is becoming the ubiquitous medium through which all information flows. Without protected, resilient, and sufficient cyber-based capabilities, all strategic-level interactions become more difficult to conduct and less trustworthy. Because of the cyber domain's increasing power and influence at the national and international level, the U.S. strategy must produce effective U.S.-China cooperation regarding cyber activities. As a start, the United States and China should improve ongoing cooperation by developing actionable measures in the areas of commercial uses, intellectual property protection, and counter cyber-crime activities. This cooperation can then expand to other nations in the region and globally.

The Economic Instrument of Power

In Chapter 9, Jeffrey Zaiser argues that the top agenda item for U.S. economic strategy must be to seek a second best option to replace the TPP. As the former cornerstone to the U.S. economic strategy for the region, the TPP served as the instrument for U.S. economic leadership. Since the announcement of U.S. withdrawal from the agreement, the United States lacks a specified economic strategy for its participation in this critical economic region. The existing piecemeal system of trade agreements among the Asia-Pacific nations will not be sufficient to sustain and manage the significant economic growth in the coming decades. However, one key goal is to negotiate a free-trade agreement with Japan, thus recouping some of the effort put into the TPP negotiations. The United States should also consider formally joining the Asian Infrastructure Investment Bank (AIIB). A key lesson from the recent AIIB experience is that the United States cannot prevent nations from joining non-U.S. initiatives, and should not be seen as obstructing Chinese initiatives that meet legitimate needs and operate transparently within accepted international standards.

The Military Instrument of Power

Chapter 10 addresses the comprehensive military aspects of a future U.S. strategy. Ryan Finn and David Moore consider the transregional, multi-domain, and multifunctional (TMM) threats of today and make several recommendations. The United States should create a cohesive joint strategy for military forces in the region to impose multiple strategic dilemmas for China's growing military power. This will include maintaining the technological advantage, involving partner nations, and developing responses to gray zone activities.

Chinese military capabilities are a longer-term challenge for U.S. strategy. While China will take the path of least resistance as it seeks increasing hegemony,

China increasingly signals its willingness to showcase its growing military might. The United States must be open and direct with China to create a shared vision for the region. This vision must ensure that China, and the other 35 nations of the region, can only succeed by remaining inside the rules-based international order. The list of regional challenges and confrontations is long and growing, especially those involving resources such as in the SCS. Without strong encouragement and enforcement to settle disputes peacefully, the United States risks military involvement in conflicts not of its choosing. Thus, the United States, along with willing partners, will need to respond effectively and aggressively to negative behaviors by China, other states, and nonstate actors on American terms. There is a growing need to develop and conduct counter gray zone activities in whatever form or location they occur. This will require the United States to create a formal, written, and detailed whole-of-government strategy with supporting plans that can meet the growing variety of subtle and difficult challenges in the region.

The United States must seek frank dialogue with Chinese military and civilian leaders to foster transparency on both sides and avoid conflict by minimizing misunderstanding and miscalculation. A key component of frank dialogue will be effective engagements between Chinese and American military forces. Expanding Sino-American military exchanges, as part of the larger military engagement plans for the region, should be a part of the future U.S. strategy. Though constrained under the fiscal year (FY) 2000 National Defense Authorization Act, there remains much the two countries can do in furthering military exchanges. These partnerships foster transparency, legitimacy, expertise, partner capacity, and engage stakeholders.

This will result in negotiations that are more constructive during peace and improved mutual responses during crises.

Regarding U.S. military posture in the region, U.S. military forces and capabilities, currently centered in the Northeast Asia sub-region, should be redistributed across the whole region. This will transform the Cold War U.S. posture to current requirements in which security threats are more dispersed, military capabilities cover greater ranges, and challenges involve more nations than at any time in the past.

North Korean nuclear weapons and ballistic missile development is the key imminent security problem for the United States in the region. In Chapters 11 and 12, Frazariel Castro and James Connor, respectively, review the history and current situation on the Korean Peninsula and offer their recommendations for U.S. steps to combat a belligerent North Korea. Ensuring viable U.S. and partner military options are available to counter North Korean threats will continue to be essential. Castro argues that the international community has not succeeded, and will not succeed, in influencing Kim Jong Un to comply with United Nations Security Council Resolutions (UNSCR) to abandon completely, verifiably, and irreversibly North Korea's nuclear weapons and ballistic missile programs. As a counter-proposal, he posits that regional peace will best be achieved by the United States establishing diplomatic relations with North Korea without the pre-condition of North Korea abandoning its nuclear weapons program. The United States should then take nascent steps to limit Kim Jong Un's nuclear aims while maintaining U.S. military superiority as a deterrent against North Korean provocative actions.

Connor argues that the United States must persuade China to take a tougher stance with its policies toward North Korea to influence the country to comply with the UNSCRs regarding nuclear weapons and ballistic missile programs. In addition, the United States and South Korea should accelerate the transfer of wartime operational control (OPCON) from a U.S. lead to South Korean lead, and the international community must do more to stop the illicit flow of foreign currency into North Korea. Both sets of options generate significant counter arguments for further study. The first option of the United States establishing diplomatic relations with North Korea will raise concerns about the U.S. commitment to international institutions such as the UN Security Council and its resolutions, the Nuclear Non-Proliferation Treaty, and the International Atomic Energy Agency. Additionally, North Korea has a solid track record of violating bilateral and multilateral agreements. Through several multilateral diplomatic initiatives since the early 1990s, the United States has provided security commitments and economic incentives to North Korea with the U.S. assurance to normalize diplomatic relations if North Korea abandons nuclear weapons and ballistic missile development activities. North Korea agreed to these initiatives and then violated the agreements on every occasion. The second option of pressuring China to do more to influence North Korea to comply with the UNSCRs also has been unsuccessful, and might generate second- and third-order effects that would harm the China-North Korea relationship in ways that could increase instability on the peninsula.

Soft Power Considerations

An often under-appreciated power for U.S. influence in the Indo-Asia-Pacific is through people-to-people exchanges for scientific research, policy analysis, social and economic development, and education. Joel Buenaflor looks at people-focused activities in Chapter 13 and finds that people-focused activities provide tangible assurance of the benefits from a partnership with the United States. The U.S. strategy for the region should include methods and resources for a variety of people-focused activities throughout the various U.S. Government agencies. Commerce, agriculture, education, health, legal, energy, transportation, finance, and even military expertise are all areas in which the United States can exert enormous influence and build long-term good will. Proposed deep-cuts to funding for the U.S. Department of State and U.S. Agency for International Development (USAID) programs should be reversed. A robust program of education and development exchanges can provide significant results over the long term for relatively low cost.

In Chapter 14, Sandra Minkel reviews the major U.S. diplomatic efforts in the region as part of the rebalance and offers some lessons learned. The presence of senior U.S. officials, including the President, at high-level summits, dialogues, and forums has been very helpful in advancing U.S. plans in the region. A key diplomatic shortcoming was the long-delayed conclusion of the TPP agreement and the choice not to participate in the AIIB. The need to relay a consistent U.S. policy for the region through the numerous security, economic, and diplomatic forums will be critical to moving forward from the rebalance strategy. Finally, given the complex and long-range efforts that will be necessary in the region to achieve U.S. goals through a whole-of-government approach, there will be a need to maintain sufficient budgetary resources for Department of State and USAID activities.

ENDNOTES - CHAPTER 1

1. Ankit Panda, "Straight From the US State Department: The 'Pivot' to Asia Is Over," *The Diplomat*, March 14, 2017, available from *https://thediplomat.com/2017/03/straight-from-the-us-state-department-the-pivot-to-asia-is-over/*.

2. Hillary Clinton, "The American Century," *Foreign Policy*, October 2011.

3. Kurt Campbell, *The Pivot: The Future of American Statecraft in Asia*, New York: Twelve Hachette Book Group, 2016, p. 1.

4. Barack H. Obama, "Sustaining U.S. Global Leadership: Priorities for 21st Century Defense," Washington, DC: The White House, January 3, 2012.

5. James Mattis, Written Statement for the Record, testimony to the Senate Armed Service Committee, Washington, DC, June 13, 2017.

6. Michael Green et al., "Asia-Pacific Rebalance 2025: Capabilities, Presence, and Partnerships," Washington, DC: Center for Strategic and International Studies (CSIS) Report, January 2016, p. 4.

7. Campbell, *The Pivot*, p. 8.

8. Barack Obama, *National Security Strategy*, Washington, DC: The White House, February 2015, p. 24.

9. General Mark A. Milley, U.S. Army Chief of Staff, Posture Statement before the Senate Armed Services Committee, Washington, DC, April 7, 2016, available from *https://www.armed-services.senate.gov/imo/media/doc/16-40_4-07-16.pdf*. See also General Joseph Dunford, Chairman of the Joint Chiefs of Staff, Posture Statement before the Senate Armed Serves Committee,

Washington, DC, June 13, 2017, available from *https://www.armed-services.senate.gov/imo/media/doc/Dunford_06-13-17.pdf.* General Dunford identified the following major challenges: "In today's strategic environment, five key challenges — Russia, China, Iran, North Korea, and Violent Extremist Organizations — most clearly represent the challenges facing the U.S. military."

10. Hillary Clinton as quoted in Campbell, *The Pivot*.

11. Campbell, *The Pivot*, p. 12.

12. A. F. K. Organski, *World Politics*, 2d Ed., New York: Alfred A. Knopf, 1969. For additional information on power transition as it relates to the U.S.-China relations, refer to David Lai, *The United States and China in Power Transition*, Carlisle, PA: Strategic Studies Institute, U.S. Army War College, 2011.

13. United States DoD doctrine identifies the instruments of national power as: diplomatic, informational, military, and economic. U.S. Joint Chiefs of Staff, *Joint Publication 1, Doctrine for the Armed Forces of the United States*, Washington, DC: U.S. Joint Chiefs of Staff, March 25, 2013, pp. I-11–I-14.

14. Figure from Lai, *The United States and China in Power Transition*, p. 7.

15. David Lai and Fred Gellert, "Parenting China, the Teenage Power," *The Diplomat*, July 16, 2016.

16. David Lai, "The U.S.-China Power Transition: Stage II," *The Diplomat*, June 30, 2016.

17. President Donald J. Trump, Inaugural Address, January 20, 2017, Washington, DC, available from *https://www.whitehouse.gov/inaugural-address.*

18. See for example, H. R. McMaster and Gary D. Cohn, "America First Doesn't Mean America Alone," *The Wall Street Journal*, May 30, 2017. "The president embarked on his first foreign trip with a clear-eyed outlook that the world is not a 'global community' but an arena where nations, nongovernmental actors and businesses engage and compete for advantage."

19. Obama, *National Security Strategy*, p. 24.

20. Chung-in Moon, "ASEAN Regional Forum," *Encyclopedia Britannica*, December 7, 2001, available from *https://www.britannica.com/topic/ASEAN-Regional-Forum,* accessed January 15, 2017.

PART II:
REGIONAL OVERVIEW

CHAPTER 2

CHINA'S RISE: WHAT DOES IT MEAN FOR THE UNITED STATES?

William P. Donnelly

EXECUTIVE SUMMARY

China clearly wants to restore its rightful place as a world power. Its official statements confirm the desire to become a strong, economically prosperous society by 2049, and that it wishes to achieve this development peacefully. China will take the path of least resistance to achieve this and to protect its non-negotiable core interests, which include maintaining the Communist Party of China's (CPC) power. China will work within the rules-based international order when doing so furthers its aims. However, China will not accept being contained and will challenge the United States and the existing rules of the international order if it feels they are threatening its core interests. Increasingly, China questions the U.S.-led rules-based international order. What are the rules? Are they fair? Should the rules be modified and reformed? China's views and actions over South China Sea (SCS) issues and contests with the United States in those troubled waters have clearly borne this new Chinese character out. China clearly perceives the U.S. rebalance as a containment strategy.

U.S.-China communication and cooperation must continue, including military-to-military engagement when allowable, but the United States should be open and direct with its concerns about China's intentions. The United States must recognize that although China will pursue the path of least resistance, it will use whatever means necessary to achieve its goals, and the United States should be prepared to challenge China's statements and actions if they threaten U.S. or allied interests. The United States should do this constructively and from a position of strength—while there is still an opportunity to influence the relationship positively.

INTRODUCTION

Over the past several decades, numerous studies have attempted to decipher the strategic intentions of the People's Republic of China (PRC). Yet questions about this issue continue to emerge. The United States and its allies consistently express concerns about China's uncertain future.

What does China want? What does the rise of China mean for the United States and the world? Does the PRC desire to surpass the United States and replace the international order with one more favorable to China? Will China pursue its goals peacefully as promised or will it use force if necessary? What will it do if its goals are challenged? Has the United States correctly read China's strategic intentions—and can America still influence China and shape future U.S.-China relations?

In simple terms, China wants to return to what it perceives to be its rightful, historic place as a world power through growth, development, and modernization. China will take the path of least resistance to achieve this objective and to protect its core interests. In a 2011 National White Paper, titled "China's Peaceful Development," China identified its core interests as:

state sovereignty, national security, territorial integrity and national reunification, China's political system established by the Constitution and overall social stability, and the basic safeguards for ensuring sustainable economic and social development.[1]

The White Paper also expressed China's respect for other nations' rights and interests, and China's unwillingness to gain at the expense of another nation. However, China's actions reveal that it will not accept being contained and will challenge the United States and the rules-based international order if it feels its path to development is threatened.

Although U.S. intent is not to contain China directly, the Chinese perception is that most of the U.S. rebalance to the Asia-Pacific appears to be designed to encircle China. U.S. policy toward China over the past several decades has generally relied on a "principled position of strength."[2] However, because of China's development, the nature of U.S.-China relations has changed. The United States needs to adjust its approach toward China as well. It is important that the United States does this constructively and develops a shared vision with China about the future of U.S.-China relations—while the opportunity to influence the relationship positively still exists.

OPPOSING VIEWS ON CHINA'S INTENTION

There are numerous schools of thought on China's intentions, too many to examine in a study of this scope. However, two prominent opposing views are of particular significance. The first is the "Hundred-Year Marathon" approach advocated by Michael Pillsbury, a China observer with decades of experience in both government and professional research organizations.[3]

Pillsbury asserts that China's growth, ambitions, and intentions are based on a premeditated plan to surpass the United States and become the world's leading superpower by 2049. He argues that this has been China's intent all along, begun in earnest with Communist leader Mao Zedong and rooted in centuries of Chinese history. Deception is key to this strategy, and China uses it today as it did in centuries past. Now that the Soviet Union no longer poses a threat to China's ascendancy as a world power, China is focused on the United States and will use deception and whatever else is necessary to surpass it as the world's only superpower.

Pillsbury notes that the very use of the term "strong nation dream" by President Xi in one of his first speeches on the Chinese Dream is itself remarkable. He argues that no Chinese leader has ever used this type of language before and that it was a deliberate choice, specifically linked to Chinese publications that espouse China's intent to replace the United States as the world's leading superpower.[4] Pillsbury believes that China will reshape the world order in its image, to support its growth and expansion. He also suggests that the United States does not realize that this is happening and is behind in responding to this threat.

China's lack of transparency and recent aggressive actions certainly lend support to Pillsbury's argument. However, an opposing view of China's strategic intentions is articulated by Dr. David Lai, a professor and China expert at the U.S. Army War College (USAWC) in Carlisle, PA. Dr. Lai was born and raised in China and possesses a deep understanding of Chinese culture and history. Lai agrees that China has ambitions to become a world power, but disagrees with Pillsbury's primary thesis and argues that China's perceived aggressive expansion, including military activity, is simply a natural outgrowth of its incredibly rapid economic and increasing national power and capabilities. China is modernizing and growing at a rate that even Chinese leaders are struggling to grasp, and it must expand as a nation to meet the demands that this growth has put on its economy, resources, and population. This expansion naturally causes concern for China's immediate neighbors in the region, the international community, and the United States. However, Lai believes that China's actions cannot be ignored, and how the United States and the world respond to China directly affects future Chinese strategic actions.[5]

Dr. Lai notes that within the context of both of these viewpoints, there is a relevant axiom to consider—that a nation's strategic intentions depend on its capabilities.[6] In the same way that Carl von Clausewitz described an enemy's power of resistance as a product of the means at his disposal and the strength of his will, a nation's strategic intentions depend on its capabilities (means) and will to employ them (will)—and therefore naturally increase as capabilities increase.[7] This axiom can be applied to China's growth over the past 35 years. When China began to modernize in the 1970s under the leadership of Deng Xiaoping, the nation was underdeveloped and economically weak. Deng's modernization focused on four major areas: agriculture, industry, technology, and the military, with a goal of overall economic and social development.[8] Initially, the military had to accept being a lower priority in this development plan since the Chinese economy did not yet have the economic and technological engine to support it. It naturally follows that less ambitious Chinese strategic intentions accompanied this lack of economic and military capability. China's recent explosive growth has changed this dynamic.

If Pillsbury is correct that China desires to replace America as the world's most powerful superpower and will continue to use deception to carry out its strategy, then his thesis presents a worst-case scenario. Dr. Lai's premise is more optimistic. This book argues that both Pillsbury and Lai are partially correct. First and foremost, China's goals are to be a world power led by the CPC, maintain Chinese socialism, and ensure the betterment of the Chinese people. This is factual and openly stated by official Chinese documents and leaders. Next, China will achieve this by taking the path of least resistance (with the least amount of strategic risk), but will meet any resistance it encounters with whatever means necessary to overcome it. China will not accept being contained or encircled and will ensure that the CPC maintains its status and legitimate control of the PRC. China's statements and actions support this concept.

Does China harbor conscious intentions to replace the United States forcibly as a superpower and rewrite the international order in a manner favorable to China? China does not need an entirely new world order favoring its way of doing business. The level of effort involved with replacing the rules-based international order and the cost of the conflicts it might induce could actually arrest China's growth and impede its ability to achieve its goals. China has benefitted greatly from its inclusion in the existing world order established and led by the United States. China will continue to work within this order to achieve its goals when it is possible to do so.

However, China has demonstrated that when the international order hinders or precludes the achievement of its goals, it will ignore, amend, or uproot portions of it to protect its core interests. China simply will not be contained, and it considers its core interests to be non-negotiable. The United States must recognize this and be aware of the high potential for conflict and misunderstanding that exists where U.S. and Chinese interests overlap. Additionally, the United States must continue to emphasize that it welcomes China's peaceful and responsible rise, but not its rise at the expense of others and the existing international order.[9]

Has the United States read China's intentions correctly within the context of the rebalance to the Asia-Pacific? In some ways, it has. For example, U.S. leaders and policymakers have been adamant about communicating that the rebalance is not about containing China's rise.[10] The problem, however, is that China does not perceive this to be true and clearly believes the U.S. pivot to the Asia-Pacific is an attempt at containment. Recent Chinese military-to-military engagements between the United States and China confirm this.[11] The United States has interests other than China in the Asia-Pacific, but China is both a partner and a competitor in the region, and both nations see each other as such.

China is clearly the dominant regional power and is becoming more influential. The United States acknowledges this and should declare that its policies in the Asia-Pacific do largely concern China and its interests—some of which overlap with American interests. This can be done in a manner that allows for both cooperation and more frank discussions about points of friction, which will exist between an established and an emerging world power.[12] The new administration under President Donald Trump seems to be taking this approach, and should continue to do so.

At the same time, the United States is right to increase its military posture in the Asia-Pacific region, specifically in the maritime domain.[13] The United States and its allies must approach China's military growth and modernization, and its militarization of disputed territorial claims, with caution. China's military outposts in the SCS, its improved anti-access/area denial (A2/AD) and maritime capabilities, and its willingness to utilize the China Coast Guard and People's Liberation Army Navy in a coercive manner are concerning. These developments present potential challenges to interests of the United States and its allies in the region, including freedom of navigation, sovereignty, and a stable international order. China has repeatedly stated that it desires to pursue its core interests peacefully. However, if China feels that its interests are directly threatened and its use of measures short of conflict prove unsuccessful at protecting those interests, it has the ability and the potential will to use military force. The United States must maintain a hedge against this capability in order to protect U.S. interests, address threats to allies, and assist new partners in the region.

It is due to this growing capability that the United States must engage more with China now, while the balance of power is still in America's favor and China is willing to communicate. Can the United States still influence its relationship with China and persuade China to change? Recent engagements, though not without disagreements and some misunderstanding, suggest that the answer is yes. What remains to be seen is how the relationship between the two nations will develop and mature under Trump's administration. Although Trump has issued some tough rhetoric regarding China's behavior, his recent assurance that the United States will honor the "One China" policy demonstrates a potential for continued dialogue and engagement.[14] The relationship is dynamic and will continue to evolve, and will be tested if either nation openly challenges one of the others' core interests.

A recent positive development is the increased trade, military-to-military interaction, and memoranda of agreement between the United States and China. The two nations have demonstrated that there is still an opportunity for communication, cooperation, and resolution of disagreements. Military-to-military engagement is key to fostering this type of relationship. Regular interactions, even small ones, have proven to be fruitful and will be important going forward.[15] The United States should pursue more of these, as well as larger scale engagements such as the Rim of the Pacific exercise and fora involving senior defense officials.

U.S.-CHINA "ELBOW-RUBBING"

The relationship between the United States and China seems to have evolved into a series of back-and-forth actions and reactions. China takes actions to protect its interests, the United States objects and/or reacts, and China feels additional pressure to do even more to protect itself. Chinese officials have difficulty understanding why the United States and others cannot or will not respect China's claims or the actions taken to grow and to protect itself.[16] At times, it resembles the classic power transition struggle between an emerging and entrenched world power as described by Lai.[17] This dynamic was demonstrated by China's responses to recent U.S. rhetoric condemning China's militarization of territories in the SCS, the potential assignment of a U.S. Marine security detachment in Taiwan, and increased U.S. naval operations in the SCS—these U.S. actions elicited quick reaction from China.[18]

This is dangerous, but the onus is on China to slow down or stop this cycle. There is concern about provoking China, yet it is China that is expanding, coercing other nations, and disregarding international norms. Nobody wants a miscalculation or unnecessary escalation, and all nations should strive to avoid both. However, if China desires that the international community respect its interests—and wishes to honor its own words regarding peaceful development, respect for other nations rights, and rejecting expansion or hegemony—then it must demonstrate these intentions with credible actions.

Recently, China announced that its annual defense budget for 2017 will increase by only 7 percent—the lowest in 10 years—though Chinese officials still consider its defense spending "enough to protect its 'rights and interests' and prevent 'outside forces' from interfering in its territorial disputes."[19] While this reduced level of defense spending may not be a deliberate effort to slow down the action-reaction cycle, it does not accelerate it, and is at least a step in the right direction.

RECOMMENDATIONS

China is a rising power that wants to take its rightful place as a world power with a thriving economy, a strong military, and a prominent voice on the world stage by 2049. China will take the path of least resistance to achieve this position and protect its core interests while refusing to be contained or encircled. China will continue to be a contributing member of the rules-based international order, but will amend, add to, or ignore it as necessary to achieve its goals. This has a direct impact on the United States and the international community, neither of which can ignore the rapid growth or actions of the world's most populous nation.

The United States must be open about its intentions in the Asia-Pacific region regarding China and directly address areas where the two nations' interests intersect, and especially where those interests conflict. At the same time, the United States is right to increase its military presence in the region as China grows and modernizes its armed forces and expands its militarization of the region. This is necessary to ensure that the United States postures itself to support both allies and partners and maintain its interests in the Asia-Pacific. Additionally, both nations must continue, and ideally increase, military-to-military engagements with each other. These engagements offer opportunities for cooperation and lessen the probability of miscalculation from both sides.

Finally, it remains to be seen if China's strict adherence to one-party rule will be an inhibitor to its future growth and role as a world power, or if internal pressure from the Chinese population will ultimately prove too much to allow the CPC to rule as it chooses.

ENDNOTES - CHAPTER 2

1. Information Office of the State Council, The People's Republic of China, *China's Peaceful Development*, Beijing, China: Information Office of the State Council, September 6, 2011, available from *http://english1.english.gov.cn/official/2011-09/06/content_1941354. htm*, accessed January 13, 2017.

2. Orville Schell and Susan L. Shirk, *US Policy toward China: Recommendations for a New Administration Task Force Report*, New

York: Asia Society Center on US-China Relations, February 2017, p. 17.

3. Michael Pillsbury, *The Hundred-Year Marathon: China's Secret Strategy to Replace America as the Global Superpower*, New York: St. Martin's Press, 2016, p. 12.

4. Ibid., pp. 27-28.

5. David Lai, interview by author, Carlisle, PA, October 26, 2016. See also David Lai, "The United States and China in Power Transition: Stage II," *The Diplomat*, June 30, 2016, available from *http://thediplomat.com/2016/07/the-us-china-power-transition-stage-ii/*, accessed February 26, 2017; and David Lai, "China's Strategic Moves and Countermoves," *Parameters, Vol.* 44, No. 4, Winter 2014-15, pp. 12-25.

6. David Lai, interview by author, Carlisle, PA, October 26, 2016.

7. Carl von Clausewitz, *On War*, Michael Howard and Peter Paret, eds. and trans., Princeton, NJ: Princeton University Press, 1976, p. 77.

8. Pillsbury, p. 162.

9. Barack Obama, *National Security Strategy*, Washington, DC: The White House, February 2015, p. 24.

10. Hillary Clinton, "America's Pacific Century," *Foreign Policy*, October 11, 2011, available from *http://foreignpolicy.com/2011/10/11/americas-pacific-century*, accessed October 17, 2016; Barack Obama, "Remarks by President Obama and President Benigno Aquino III of the Philippines in Joint Press Conference," public speech, Malacañang Palace, Manila, Philippines, April 28, 2014, available from *https://obamawhitehouse.archives.gov/the-press-office/2014/04/28/remarks-president-obama-and-president-benigno-aquino-iii-philippines-joi*, accessed February 11, 2017.

11. "Between War and Peace: Reflections on U.S.-China Security Relations," 3rd Annual Mil-Mil Education and Research Exchange, forum, December 4-7, 2016, Carlisle Barracks, PA. This forum was a military-to-military engagement hosted by the U.S.

Army War College at both Bliss Hall and the Army Heritage and Education Center. Several senior officers from the People's Liberation Army attended the forum along with several senior officers and staff from the U.S. Army War College, U.S. Army, and the U.S. Department of State.

12. Lai, "The United States and China in Power Transition: Stage II."

13. U.S. Department of Defense, *The Asia-Pacific Maritime Strategy*, Washington, DC: U.S. Department of Defense, pp. 19-22.

14. Te-Ping Chen, "Beijing's Patience Pays Off with Trump's Reaffirmation of 'One-China' Policy," *The Wall Street Journal*, February 10, 2017, available from *https://www.wsj.com/articles/ beijings-patience-pays-off-with-trumps-reaffirmation-of-one-china- policy-1486737397*, accessed February 10, 2017.

15. "Between War and Peace: Reflections on U.S.-China Security Relations," 3rd Annual Mil-Mil Education and Research Exchange, forum, December 4-7, 2016, Carlisle Barracks, PA.

16. Ibid.

17. David Lai, "The United States and China in Power Transition: Stage II." Lai describes the dynamic of a dissatisfied emerging power (China) pushing against an established power (United States) and the world order it represents. As the emerging power grows, it becomes more assertive, and the danger of conflict increases.

18. Ministry of Defense, People's Republic of China, "Defense Ministry's Regular Press Conference," February 23, 2017, available from *http://eng.mod.gov.cn/Press/2017-02/24/content_4773551. htm*, accessed March 3, 2017. Colonel Ren Guoqiang, spokesperson for the Ministry of National Defense, answered reporters' questions during this conference. He specifically responded to questions about U.S. statements on China's potential militarization of islands in the South China Sea (SCS), and stated that China has indisputable sovereignty over these islands and has the right to deploy necessary defensive facilities on them. On the topic of U.S. Marines in Taiwan, Colonel Ren stated that China consistently opposes any form of official exchange and military contact

between the United States and Taiwan. On recent U.S. Navy operations in the SCS, Colonel Ren stated that China hopes the United States can respect the sovereignty and security concerns of regional countries, and that China respects the freedom of navigation and overflight that all countries enjoy in the SCS in accordance with international law.

19. Jeremy Page and Chun Han Wong, "China Eases Foot Off Gas on Military Spending," *The Wall Street Journal*, March 4, 2017, available from *https://www.wsj.com/articles/china-raising-military-budget-by-about-7-1488601110*, accessed March 4, 2017.

CHAPTER 3

DEVELOPING A U.S.-LED MULTILATERAL SECURITY ARCHITECTURE FOR THE ASIA-PACIFIC

Eric W. Young

EXECUTIVE SUMMARY

The Asia-Pacific region is viewed as the most consequential for America's security and prosperity. While five bilateral defense treaties demonstrate U.S. resolve for regional stability, the expanding Asia-Pacific security architecture, and increasing critical issues, demand greater U.S. engagement and leadership.

While the U.S. defense treaties provide large-scale conflict deterrence, shared responsibility for regional security threats below large-scale conflict is necessary and requires more than the dialogue-only solutions that existing regional forums provide. To remain the region's security leader, the United States must adapt to the evolving environment while capitalizing on existing organizations and infrastructures.

Strategically, such adaptation must recognize, but not succumb to, China's influence and perspectives as a rising regional power. As such, leading the development of a multilateral security architecture (MLSA) that includes but expands beyond the current "hub-and-spoke" defense treaty alliance system will increase regional capability and resolve to meet both long-term and emerging security challenges.

For strategic perspective, China has also indicated interest in developing a "win-win" regional security architecture of its own, providing itself opportunity to supplant the United States as the leader for regional security, especially if the United States decides to not act beyond its existing defense alliance obligations.

This chapter provides four specific recommendations for establishing a framework that enables shared responsibility for dealing with security threats below the level of large-scale conflict:

- The United States should lead the development of a MLSA that empowers existing regional forums and organizations, strengthens existing defense treaties and alliances, and encourages the development of new linkages between nations to advance regional stability and conflict prevention.
- Consider China as a potential partner in a MLSA in order to advance trust among regional participants while countering perceptions that a MLSA purposely contains China's rise; may also lessen observations of a U.S.-China power rivalry.
- Provide enforcement mechanisms not currently available in existing regional security structures.
- Utilize all instruments of national power for MLSA establishment and success—it is not a military-alone solution or requirement.

INTRODUCTION

While the nations in the Asia-Pacific strive for economic development, they are nevertheless troubled by unsettled territorial disputes and a wide range of other security issues. What should be the security mechanism to deal with these problems?

Since the end of World War II, the United States has taken upon itself as a provider and custodian for security in this region. The United States does this through a hub-and-spoke alliance system. For a variety of reasons, this system is increasingly inadequate for the growing security problems in the Asia-Pacific. Meanwhile, China is also pushing for a region-wide multilateral security architecture to replace the U.S.-led system.

Should the United States continue to rely on the existing alliance system to maintain order and resist China's moves? Should the United States cave in to China's pressure and let China create a new security system in the Asia-Pacific? Between these two opposing positions, is there a middle-ground approach for the United States to create a new security architecture to address regional challenges? The answer is straightforward: the United States has no choice but to take up the challenge to do so.

EXISTING U.S.-LED SECURITY ALLIANCE SYSTEM IN THE ASIA-PACIFIC

Centered around five bilateral mutual defense treaties with Japan, the Republic of the Philippines, Australia, Thailand, and the Republic of Korea, the U.S. security alliance system has contributed to regional security and stability since the early 1950s. These mutual defense treaties are commonly referred to as a hub-and-spoke system: the United States is at the center, and each bilateral treaty partner is a separate "spoke."[1] Each evolved from U.S. efforts to counter the spread of communism in Asia following World War

II, when the United States was unable to develop a "Pacific Ocean Pact" analogous to the North Atlantic Treaty in Europe.[2]

In his book, *Powerplay: The Origins of the American Alliance System in Asia*, Professor Victor Cha, former Director for Asian Affairs in President George W. Bush's National Security Council, notes that these exclusive and tightly-controlled bilateral hub-and-spoke alliances created a "'powerplay' in U.S. grand strategy," allowing it "to exert considerable political, military, and economic control over key countries in East Asia."[3] However, those alliances essentially guaranteed regional security, and arguably prosperity, by contributing to large-scale conflict deterrence during the Cold War era. Today they remain central to preventing large-scale regional conflict while also demonstrating continuing U.S. security commitment with each treaty partner.

OTHER ASIA-PACIFIC SECURITY CONFIGURATIONS

Twenty-seven years after the Cold War ended, Asia-Pacific regional challenges remain and are potentially becoming more volatile. The evolving security environment fosters insecurities that drive many countries to seek enhanced defense cooperation.[4] Existing defense alliances, partnership engagements, and security cooperation activities reassure allies and partners while simultaneously aligning U.S. regional strategy, resources, and capabilities. Further, regional security organizations and mechanisms also influence the existing security architecture.

The largest regional organization, the Association of Southeast Asian Nations (ASEAN), promotes the active collaboration and mutual support of 10 member states on issues including prosperity, economic development, regional peace and stability, agriculture, education, and industry.[5] For their specific relations with one another, ASEAN's Treaty of Amity and Cooperation in Southeast Asia (TAC) signed in 1976, requires signatories to settle differences or disputes peacefully, and renounce the threat, or use, of force.[6] Signatories must also mutually respect the independence of other states, their territorial integrity, and their national identity, while recognizing each state's right to exist free from external interference.[7]

In 1987, ASEAN amended the TAC, inviting non-Southeast Asia countries "to accede to the Treaty in order to build confidence, promote peace and security, and facilitate economic cooperation in the region."[8] Participating non-Southeast Asian countries and organizations (including China, India, South Korea, Russia, Australia, France, North Korea, and the European Union) reflect global interest in the region's security and prosperity. The United States signed the TAC in July 2009.[9] However, the TAC does not include enforcement provisions, which perhaps were not considered necessary in 1976 due to the significant U.S. military presence as well as the region's decentralized nature.

In 1993, ASEAN established the ASEAN Regional Forum (ARF) as the "first region-wide Asia-Pacific multilateral forum for official consultations on peace and security issues."[10] The ARF's objectives, identified in the First ARF Chairman's Statement in 1994, are:

> 1) to foster constructive dialogue and consultation on political and security issues of common interest and

concern; and 2) to make significant contributions to efforts towards confidence-building and preventive diplomacy in the Asia-Pacific region.[11]

Today, ARF membership includes the United States and 26 other regional and non-regional countries.[12] However, the ARF remains solely a security dialogue venue. For the United States, it is a "regional foreign minister-level forum for promoting security" through which the United States helps shape a regional rules-based order.[13]

In 2006, ASEAN convened the inaugural ASEAN Defense Ministers' Meeting (ADMM). Held annually, the ADMM:

is the highest defence consultative and cooperative mechanism in ASEAN . . . [aimed at promoting] mutual trust and confidence through greater understanding of defence and security challenges as well as enhancement of transparency and openness.[14]

As another, albeit high-level, dialogue forum, the ADMM's objectives include:

[promoting] regional peace and stability through dialogue and cooperation in defence and security; [giving] guidance to existing senior defence and military officials; dialogue and cooperation in the field of defence and security within ASEAN and between ASEAN and dialogue partners; [promoting] mutual trust and confidence through greater understanding of defence and security challenges as well as enhancement of transparency and openness; and [contributing] to the establishment of an ASEAN Security Community (ASC).[15]

As an ASEAN Dialogue Partner, the United States participates in the annual ADMM-Plus, which, since 2010, is a "platform for ASEAN and its eight Dialogue Partners to strengthen security and defence cooperation for peace, stability, and development in the region."[16] The ADMM-Plus objectives include building partner capacity among member countries to address shared security challenges, promote mutual trust and confidence, and enhance regional peace and stability through cooperation in defense and security.[17] Practical cooperation discussion areas, facilitated through Experts' Working Groups, include maritime security, counterterrorism, humanitarian assistance and disaster relief, peacekeeping operations, military medicine, and cyber.[18] As a practical matter, the ADMM-Plus provides the United States a conduit to engage with China, itself an ASEAN Dialogue Member, regarding security issues and concerns. Overall, ASEAN and its attendant sub-organizations are part of an inter-connected "web" of Asia-Pacific organizations (economic, diplomatic, and military) that bind regional and non-regional countries.

Notably, ASEAN's aims and purposes include promoting "regional peace and stability through abiding respect for justice and the rule of law in the relationship among countries of the region and adherence to the principles of the United Nations Charter."[19] As an active ASEAN Dialogue Partner (which includes an ambassadorship to ASEAN), the United States has a central role in "the evolving rules-based regional architecture that promotes regional peace, stability and prosperity."[20] The U.S.-ASEAN security dialogues focus on the U.S. role in "maintaining peace, security, and stability in the region through its participation in different ASEAN-led regional mechanisms such as the [ARF], the . . . ADMM-Plus, and the East Asia Summit (EAS)."[21]

For the United States, the EAS provides significant opportunity for strategic influence. At the conclusion of the first EAS meeting in 2005, the participating states agreed that the EAS "would continue to be a leaders'-led Summit for strategic discussions on key issues affecting the region and the evolving regional architecture."[22] Held annually, EAS strategic dialogues gained more prominence in recent years due to former U.S. President Barack Obama personally attending. While it originated with "a vision of community building," U.S. participation in the EAS, along with increasing strategic tensions, raised it to a "confidence building and conflict prevention mechanism" for addressing all regional security challenges, including threats arising from North Korea.[23] While it remains a dialogue opportunity, participating in the EAS advances U.S. leadership for regional security, influence, and conflict prevention.

An additional security and conflict prevention mechanism involves country-to-country dialogues on specific topics, such as the Six-Party Talks on ending North Korea's nuclear proliferation.[24] Although stagnant since 2009, the Six-Party Talks demonstrate multinational efforts to address and prevent regional conflict. Bilateral mechanisms also exist—most recently demonstrated in the 2017 Japan-Russia "two plus two" discussions between their respective foreign and defense ministers that were specially focused toward resolving long-standing disputes and urging North Korean restraint.[25]

Conflict prevention is defined as a:

> peace operation employing complementary diplomatic, civil, and, when necessary, military means, to monitor and identify the causes of conflict, and take timely action to prevent the occurrence, escalation, or resumption of hostilities.[26]

U.S. conflict prevention activities include reassuring allies and partners, conducting military and non-military engagements, supporting humanitarian assistance and disaster relief efforts, supporting ASEAN initiatives, undertaking confidence building measures, and reiterating international norms and law. Such activities involve various diplomatic, informational, military, and economic elements of national power that best enable regional stability and security.

Discussing conflict prevention's increasing role in the Asia-Pacific region, Dr. Frank Hoffman posits that:

> Declines in the preponderance of U.S. power in the Asia–Pacific theater have reduced conventional deterrence, and China's military expansion could accelerate instability. The United States is challenged to demonstrate that it retains the ability to conduct military operations in the Asia–Pacific region and fulfill its treaty obligations to its allies. This requires a military capacity—one that is growing increasingly suspect—to achieve two critical U.S. objectives: maintaining freedom of the commons (air, sea, space, and cyberspace) and limiting the potential for large-scale regional conflict through deterrence.[27]

Conflict prevention activities advance a key U.S. interest: supporting the rise of a peaceful China that adheres to international norms and law. For example, confidence building measures essentially lower the likelihood that conflict may occur between potential rivals by building interoperability and trust. U.S. military engagements with China's Peoples' Liberation Army (PLA) allow limited military-to-military confidence building discussions and exercises that contribute to decreasing mistrust while enabling regional stability and strategic interoperability.[28] Such an exercise is the U.S. Pacific Fleet's Rim of the Pacific (RIMPAC), held every 2 years, that includes China's

Peoples' Liberation Army-Navy (PLAN) participation.[29] Confidence building efforts facilitate conflict prevention by enabling allies and partners to align their security efforts to deter, or counter, future threats.

For all of their benefits, ASEAN (including its ADMM+ and ARF), the EAS, the Six-Party Talks, other regional security engagements, and bilateral and multilateral military-to-military security exchanges are limited in their ability to resolve regional security issues among participating nations. As the complex and uncertain security environment continually evolves, Asia-Pacific regional security requires more than dialogue, highly structured confidence building security engagements, or over-dependence on U.S. military presence. Further, the new U.S. administration, as discussed during Secretary of State Rex Tillerson's first trip to the region in March 2017, is distancing itself from previous dialogue efforts, most notably the Six-Party Talks.[30] In addition, whether the new U.S. President will personally participate in the ARF as his predecessor did also remains to be seen.

Based on existing security structures and the evolving U.S. foreign policy approach to the region, a gap exists for the United States between meeting bilateral mutual defense treaty provisions and enforcing decisions resulting from various multilateral regional forum discussions. Therein lies the weakness of the current system. As the 21st century unfolds, Asia-Pacific nations, including the United States, must be confident that threats to regional stability will be met with a clear, unified, region-wide resolve and response. It is within this gap between dialogue entities and mutual defense alliances that a U.S.-led MLSA takes shape.

CHINA'S PERSPECTIVES ON ASIA-PACIFIC SECURITY

While the:

> prevailing [U.S.]-led power structure has contributed to subdued levels of interstate conflict and war . . . that system and its attendant security are being challenged by major powers, abetted by a reduced [United States'] presence in key regions.[31]

In the Asia-Pacific, China's significant economic growth and rapid military modernization directly alter the balance of power, highlighting China's leadership against long-standing U.S. influence.[32] In this regard, the existing U.S. alliance system presents a significant concern for China: how to overcome this ostensibly Cold War relic while leading in the Asia-Pacific region. From the Chinese perspective, the U.S. "alliance system in the region surrounding China is a reality that will last for some time . . . [and an] important issue in China's rise is how Beijing will coexist effectively with U.S. alliances."[33] Recognizing that the:

> American centered alliance system in the Asia-Pacific region. . . . has critically influenced that region's security order [since World War II and] the recent implementation of the United States' 'rebalancing strategy' toward Asia and the strengthening American dominance over regional affairs has been interpreted by Beijing as a U.S. effort to enhance its alliance system in this part of the world and to strengthen its security partnerships with some countries in the region.[34]

While the United States consistently states that it welcomes a rising China that is peaceful, stable, prosperous, and a responsible player in international affairs,[35] assessing the Chinese view of the current U.S. security architecture and Pacific focus is essential.

Professor Zhou Fangyin, of the Guangdong University of Foreign Studies in China, articulates two schools of thought regarding China's views toward the U.S. alliance system. On one hand, the U.S. commitment to maintaining this system supports a "Chinese posture of 'peaceful development,' . . . which embodies a 'low profile' and generally nonconfrontational posture towards the United States and its alliance system in Asia."[36] Professor Zhou notes that:

> America's underwriting of this network meets some important security and political requirements of various U.S. allies such as Japan, South Korea, and Australia. Mitigating allied anxiety by the United States extending deterrence guarantees has traditionally contributed to regional stability by, for example, 'capping the bottle' of Japanese militarism or maintaining a conflict threshold on the Korean Peninsula. This has been especially true in the absence of an effective or efficient macrosecurity architecture to solve the security problems faced by East Asian countries. In this context, those in China who have acknowledged this situation have concluded that the U.S. alliance system in Asia has played a fundamental role in regional security, even though its indefinite survival might not be welcomed as the preferred outcome by most Chinese policymakers.[37]

Challenging the "peaceful development" school of thought is the view that the U.S. alliance system is a "security impediment" rather than facilitator.[38] In December 2016, the United States Pacific Command (USPACOM) commander reiterated the U.S. position that "[in] Asia, there's not that compelling, single, focused enemy."[39] Those in China believing that the U.S. alliance system is a security impediment do not hold the same view. Rather, they view the formerly named Rebalance, and resulting emphasis on the existing alliance system, as a direct response to China's rapid rise. It is:

> the obvious catalyst behind Washington's decision to reinforce its strategic influence and presence in the Asia-Pacific region . . . [and the] U.S. pivot strategy, according to this faction, is nothing less than a U.S. effort to contain [China].[40]

While the United States openly supports China becoming an increasingly capable and active partner in addressing regional and global challenges, the Chinese view the U.S. legacy alliance system as increasingly resembling an "offensive realist strategy directed against China that impedes the realization of a great rejuvenation of the Chinese nation."[41] An interesting opinion-perspective is that China has never conceived of a foreign nation "as more than a tributary to it," and China's current rise arguably appears to retain this hubris.[42] Reinforcing this perspective is Chinese President Xi Jinping's proclamation that "it is for the people of Asia to run the affairs of Asia, solve the problems of Asia and uphold the security of Asia"—with an ascending China as the leader.[43] As Professor Zhou notes, coexisting with the U.S. alliance system while China's "own strength and influence are rising" is a significant challenge.[44]

In June 2016, Chinese Assistant Foreign Minister Kong Xuanyou noted, "when compared with economic cooperation, the security architecture construction in East Asia lags behind."[45] As such, he further identified that constructing "a security architecture that complies with the regional reality and meets the needs of all sides is a major strategic task for regional states."[46] Such comments reinforce Xi's proposal for a Chinese-led counter to the U.S. alliance system. At the

2014 Conference on Interaction and Confidence Building Measures in Asia (CICA), Xi stated:

> One cannot live in the 21st century with the outdated thinking from the age of Cold War and zero-sum game. We believe that it is necessary to advocate common, comprehensive, cooperative and sustainable security in Asia. We need to innovate our security concept, establish a new regional security cooperation architecture, and jointly build a road for security of Asia that is shared by and win-win to all.[47]

Xi's vision is already taking shape, at least in public Chinese government rhetoric. At the 2016 Xiangshan Forum in Beijing, China's Vice Foreign Minister Liu Zhenmin identified five existing security mechanisms in the Asia-Pacific:

- The United States-led alliance system and relevant bilateral and multilateral arrangements;
- The ASEAN-centered security dialogue and cooperation frameworks such as the ARF and ADMM+;
- Special mechanisms on hotspot issues such as the Six-Party Talks on Korean Peninsular Nuclear Issue and the Quartet on Afghanistan;
- Regional security cooperation mechanisms including the Shanghai Cooperation Organization (SCO) and the Conference on Interaction and Confidence Building Measures in Asia (CICA); and,
- Track 1.5 or Track 2 security dialogues such as the Shangri-La Dialogue, the Xiangshan Forum, and the Asia-Pacific Roundtable.[48]

Rather than identifying how any, or all, of these existing structures might best enhance 21st century security, Vice Minister Liu instead noted that they "reflect underlying disconnects in our region: problems left by the cold war, lack of coordination among sub-regions, and differences on security concepts."[49] Therefore, in order to best deal with existing, and emerging, regional security challenges, China's view is that a new, Chinese-led security architecture is necessary.

China's proposed architecture is based on its concept of common, comprehensive, cooperative, and sustainable security, advocating "consultation and dialogue, openness, inclusiveness, and win-win cooperation."[50] Essentially, China desires replacing the U.S.-led alliance system with a China-led and promoted "partnership" community, perhaps mirroring the Shanghai Cooperation Organization.[51] Within this community, Xi advocates employing the Five Principles of Peaceful Co-existence (mutual respect for sovereignty and territorial integrity, mutual nonaggression, noninterference in each other's internal affairs, equality and mutual benefit, and peaceful coexistence) as the baseline for interaction among Asia-Pacific nations.[52] Further, Xi notes that "China stays committed to seeking [the] peaceful settlement of disputes with other countries over territorial sovereignty and maritime rights and interests."[53]

Although advocating a "win-win" security environment, China's actions in the disputed East Sea and South China Sea areas demonstrate otherwise. While China's rise and corresponding increase in national strength arguably shifted the world's economic center of gravity to the Asia-Pacific, "[it] is not surprising, then, that as China's economic might has grown, so has its ability and inclination to use national power and influence to advance its geopolitical ends."[54] For example, as a party to the United Nations Convention on the Law of the Sea (UNCLOS), China specifically reserved and declared that it:

> will effect, through consultations, the delimitation of the boundary of the maritime jurisdiction with the States with coasts opposite or adjacent to China respectively on the basis of international law and in accordance with the principle of equitability.[55]

While China's domestic laws claim certain named (and "other") islands as belonging to China, other coastal nations (including the Philippines, Japan, and Vietnam) also claim several of the same islands, creating multiple disputes that should be resolved equitably on the basis of international law, which the Philippines attempted to do through its 2016 UNCLOS arbitration case.[56] However, China's aggressive island building in the South China Sea in the midst of these unsettled maritime claims arguably indicates, and certainly so perceived by the other regional states, that the principle of "mutual respect for sovereignty and territorial integrity" is not a reciprocal requirement where China's interests are concerned.[57]

U.S. LEADERSHIP FOR 21ST CENTURY ASIA-PACIFIC SECURITY

Charting the initial course for his administration, President Donald Trump recently stated that U.S. "foreign policy calls for a direct, robust and meaningful engagement with the world," which involves "American leadership based on vital security interests that we share with our allies all across the globe."[58] Further,

> America is willing to find new friends, and to forge new partnerships, where shared interests align. We want harmony and stability, not war and conflict. We want

peace, wherever peace can be found. America is friends today with former enemies. Some of our closest allies, decades ago, fought on the opposite side of these terrible, terrible wars. This history should give us all faith in the possibilities for a better world.[59]

This U.S. foreign policy vision preserves the open, stable, and rules-based international order that has underpinned Asia-Pacific peace, prosperity, and stability since World War II. Formalized ties throughout and external to the region create a web of engagements (diplomatic, economic, and military) that demonstrate regional interests are more common, and combined, than believed possible when the United States first entered into its bilateral defense treaties.

As Asia-Pacific nations look to the United States for security reassurance and rules-based stability, it is in the U.S. national interest to share that responsibility beyond the existing bilateral security alliance structure. Incorporating existing bilateral security alliances (without terminating them) into an interconnected, regional security architecture will reinforce Asia-Pacific security resilience, strengthen regional diplomatic and economic endeavors, and enable shared conflict prevention. Professor Cha identifies such a scenario as a "'complex patchwork' of bilaterals [sic], trilaterals [sic], and other plurilateral configurations," which inevitably includes already-existing security mechanisms. Such an interconnected and dependent geometry between states results in "a useful tool for muting regional security dilemmas" through shared responsibility and mutual security interests.[60] For the United States, developing and leading such a "complex patchwork" MLSA that builds on existing relationships while strengthening bilateral security alliances, is a feasible, acceptable, and suitable means for sustaining regional security. Reinforcing this approach is the observation that "US-centered bilateralism and Asia's emerging regional institutions (both ASEAN-centered and China-based . . .) [do not] operate at odds with one another."[61] To retain this important dynamic, a U.S.-led MLSA should recognize, and build on, the region's complex nature, economic inter-dependence, and already-existing security mechanisms.[62]

While a U.S.-led MLSA could take many forms, the chosen form cannot trump substance; as a precondition, it must work in concert with existing U.S. defense treaties. The MLSA must define regional security requirements, establish responsibilities and relationships among participating states, and implement national contribution procedures (such as funding, personnel, equipment, and logistics). Basic, guiding principles such as resolving disputes peacefully, uniting to counter emerging threats to regional security, allowing countries to make their own security decisions free from intimidation, preserving the rules of international law pertaining to air and sea navigation, and acting in recognition of each country's own constitutional processes, must be addressed and resolved. Further, a MLSA must include implementation mechanisms (e.g., consultation among member nations, special discussion processes, support to existing regional security mechanisms) and enforcement procedures (when and how to act—including using force—beyond dialogue exchanges) in order to be effective and viable for conflict prevention.

While existing regional security dialogue venues provide many of the baseline principles outlined above, establishing when and how participating nations actively align against emerging threats must be developed. Fortunately, other non-Asia-Pacific organizations are instructive in this matter. The Organization for Security and Cooperation in Europe (OSCE) is one such organization. While not a perfect template, the OSCE demonstrates an architecture that has evolved from the challenges of the Cold War to addressing "the present era of regional conflict, arms proliferation, terrorism and other emerging threats by combining a uniquely comprehensive definition of security with flexibility and innovation of response."[63]

Membership is key to gaining regional support, and a U.S.-led MLSA must welcome and incorporate new partners and opportunities. While the existing defense treaties provide the greatest deterrence against large-scale regional conflict, all regional nations should be invited and encouraged to participate in the MLSA to their fullest individual potential. The MLSA will enable those nations to go beyond dialogue to resolve actively lesser threats and challenges on the conflict spectrum (e.g., through partnered maritime domain awareness), essentially altering existing regional security dynamics. Further, as a MLSA builds on existing relationships (creating linkages within linkages), a new security forum similar to the North Atlantic Treaty Organization's (NATO) North Atlantic Council, while not precluded, may not be needed if the EAS or ARF grows into this role.

Finally, U.S. leadership must accomplish three goals. First, reassure allies and partners that entanglement or entrapment for U.S. regional gain (including countering China) is not the MLSA's purpose. Second, advocate that mutually supporting and regionally responsible security protects against current and future threats. Third, retain the existing bilateral defense treaties while not precluding new U.S. security relationships.[64] Working toward these goals will help the United States avoid alienation while also shaping regional expectations for responding to security threats.

Implications and Options for the New U.S. Administration.

For the United States, an important decision includes whether to advance the prior administration's principled security network efforts in the Asia-Pacific region. The danger for the decision maker is that policy becomes so geared to satisfying the vigorously communicated needs of those close at hand that insufficient account is taken of the needs of those more distant and less salient. The hierarchy of concerns on the foreign policy agenda will reflect hierarchies within national political systems and salient alliances and international organizations.[65]

For the new U.S. administration developing its Asia-Pacific policies, the following MLSA strengths, weaknesses, opportunities, and risks should be considered. Leading a MLSA provides the means to achieve lasting influence and shared security responsibility that ultimately supports diplomatic, economic, and informational efforts within, and external to, the Asia-Pacific region. Further, a MLSA enables pan-regional military-to-military engagement and modernization while reassuring allies, partners, and neighbors through conflict prevention activities. A MLSA also provides a strategic opportunity for the U.S. military (principally the USPACOM) to plan and conduct engagements within a web of interconnected security partners who each have diverse regional economic and diplomatic interests.[66]

The region's previously discussed security dynamics risk escalation and conflict, most notably on the Korean Peninsula and in the South China and East Seas. However, diversifying security relationships, modernizing existing alliances, enhancing interactions among new partners, strengthening regional institutions to reinforce rules and norms, and developing collective responses to shared challenges all define ways in which the United States can achieve its regional objectives.[67] Further, MLSA "burden sharing" potentially lowers overall U.S. costs in both money and personnel as a web of interconnected nations is empowered (with U.S. support rather than dependence) to prevent conflict and respond collectively when required. Most significantly, a MLSA provides a different, evolving approach to regional security that adapts to the changing security environment and pits, interdependently with allies and partners, "our enduring strengths against the vulnerabilities of our adversaries."[68]

Further, MLSA legitimacy under international law adds credibility. Article 52 of the United Nations' Charter provides that:

> regional arrangements for dealing with such matters relating to the maintenance of international peace and security as are appropriate for regional action [are not precluded] . . . provided that such arrangements are consistent with the Purposes and Principles of the United Nations.[69]

For example, NATO is such a regional security arrangement.[70] Establishing a MLSA, whether formal or informal, that complies with international law and reinforces "rules-based order" for the Asia-Pacific region provides legitimacy; doing otherwise risks both international acceptance and respected U.S. leadership.

The biggest potential weakness is a lack of regional resolve to participate actively in a MLSA that advocates and advances conflict prevention activity. While a MLSA would buttress existing arrangements through an interconnected enforcement web of shared-interest nations, participating nations would be expected to contribute more than dialogue for conflict prevention.

Further, China likely will view a U.S.-led MLSA as a direct threat to its regional leadership: "China has all along taken the advancement of regional prosperity and stability as its own responsibility."[71] According to its January 2017 "White Paper" on Asia-Pacific Security Cooperation, China is:

> [c]ommitted to pushing forward the building of regional security mechanisms . . . [while shouldering] greater responsibilities for regional and global security, and [providing] more public security services to the Asia-Pacific region and the world at large.[72]

The U.S.-China competition for regional security leadership, arguably the most difficult issue to address, risks regional states having to choose between their closely-located economic trading partner (China) and more distantly-located security provider (United States), potentially weakening a U.S.-led MLSA.[73]

Mitigating these weaknesses requires an approach that the United States should openly consider: invite China's participation as a welcome and necessary partner in order to utilize both U.S. and Chinese regional security leadership. Doing so establishes the single-largest confidence building mechanism for both countries, as transparency will be necessary for both nations to work together for common security goals. Finally, including both nations (perhaps someday as co-equal participants) in a single MLSA requires strategic patience; simply bringing both nations into the same U.S.-led security architecture will not happen quickly. Underlying, long-standing security issues and differences remain unresolved and must be addressed before a U.S.-China MLSA could be considered or even implemented.

A U.S.-led MLSA presents two notable opportunities. First, achieving long-term regional security presents an opportunity for the United States and China to work together for a common security purpose, even if they are not MLSA partners. Strategically, and with a nod toward China's economic growth and rapid military modernization, the United States generally considers China an emerging, or already existing, "near-peer competitor."[74] Henry Kissinger recently noted that the United States should try to make Chinese President Xi's objective to "turn adversaries into partners . . . the dominant theme of U.S.-China relations." Changing the analysis from "near-peer competitor" to "near-peer partner" clearly alters regional security dynamics. Doing so should not make the United States beholden to China, or require the United States to compromise its values and interests. Rather, removing a potential near-peer competitor by finding common ground for security engagement will change the region's conflict prevention security dynamic. However, such a change requires significant action by both nations, which for the United States includes re-looking the NDAA 2000 limits on military-to-military engagement.

Second, developing a U.S.-led MLSA that overlaps existing regional economic and security forums demonstrates U.S. understanding of, and commitment to, the evolving region. It also provides enforcement mechanisms, or "teeth," that existing security dialogues do not. Further, and unlike the existing bilateral U.S.

treaty alliances, a MLSA presents opportunities to welcome all states interested in working together to maintain regional security. Granted, creating a MLSA, and encouraging states to exercise the strategic patience to let it develop, will take time. However, ever-evolving Asia-Pacific dynamics present the United States a significant opportunity for regional security leadership.

The most significant risk is inaction. Although China has not yet established a regional security architecture that does not mean the United States should not do so. Strategically, the United States must determine whether silence regarding or inaction toward China advocating for its own regional security architecture potentially signals that 21st century Asia-Pacific security leadership belongs to China. Abdicating such leadership potentially threatens U.S. stature and influence within the region, arguably validating a power transition perception that China's rise is at the expense of a declining United States. A further potential risk is whether extending "linkages among the spokes" beyond the current hub-and-spoke alliance system, (e.g., a Philippines-Japan-South Korea "link" where the United States is individually connected to each participant) increases the possibility that the United States may be pulled into a regional conflict "without any additional security benefits [of its own]."[75] Addressing these risks within the MLSA is essential for mitigating their impact on U.S. security leadership and regional resolve.

CONCLUSION

The United States should lead the development of an Asia-Pacific multilateral security architecture that empowers existing regional forums and organizations, strengthens existing defense treaties and alliances, and encourages the development of new linkages between nations to advance regional stability and conflict prevention. Carefully considering China as a potential partner is essential, as doing so will advance trust among regional participants and counter perceptions that such an architecture purposely contains China's rise. At the same time, gaining China's participation may lessen observations of, and challenges inherent to, a great power rivalry between a rising China and an established United States. Ultimately, effective Asia-Pacific regional conflict prevention—a significant reason for developing a multilateral security architecture that evolves beyond mutual defense treaties—requires a joint U.S.-China partnership from the beginning. Doing so necessitates changed behaviors and expectations by both nations, as well as strategic patience to adjust to a near-peer partner environment. Simultaneously, an effective MLSA will provide enforcement mechanisms not currently available in existing regional security structures. Finally, developing a MLSA requires all instruments of national power—it is not a military-alone solution or requirement. Patience and trust will be necessary, especially since a U.S.-led MLSA is not intended, at least currently, to counter or oppose a specific threat, but instead to meet the complex security challenges facing the Asia-Pacific region in the 21st century.

ENDNOTES - CHAPTER 3

1. Victor D. Cha, *Power Play: The Origins of the American Alliance System in Asia*, Princeton, NJ: Princeton University Press, 2016, p. 3. See also Victor D. Cha, "Complex Patchworks: U.S. Alliances as Part of Asia's Regional Architecture," *Asia Policy*, No. 11, January 2011, p. 29, available from *www.nbr.org/publications/*

asia_policy/Preview/AP11_US_Alliance_preview.pdf, accessed February 20, 2017.

2. Cha, *Power Play*, p. 184. Essentially, the United States determined that "multilateralism was out . . . bilateralism, in." For a background discussion on the Australia-New Zealand-U.S. council preparations and post-World War II U.S. efforts at multilateral Asia-Pacific regional security, see Christopher Van Hollen, "Background Paper: References in the Negotiation of the ANZUS Treaty To Broader Security Arrangements Affecting the Pacific Area," Washington, DC: U.S. Department of State, Division of Historical Research, July 24, 1952, available from *https://www. trumanlibrary.org/whistlestop/study_collections/achesonmemos/view. php?documentVersion=both&documentid=70-6_26&documentYear=1 952&pagenumber=1*, accessed December 23, 2016. By the beginning of 1951, however, the United States had decided that it was desirable to take a more active role in building a security system in the Pacific area. With this in mind, John Foster Dulles, Consultant to the Secretary of State, was sent to the Far East early in 1951 on a special mission, with the rank of Ambassador, with instructions to discuss a security arrangement to which the parties would be the United States, Japan, the Philippines, Australia, New Zealand, and perhaps Indonesia—in other words, all the nations exercising sovereignty over the so-called island chain stretching from the Aleutians to New Zealand, excluding Formosa (although in Manila, Dulles mentioned the possibility of including Formosa in the security arrangement under discussion).

3. Cha, *Power Play*, p. 3.

4. Recommended Talking Points—China (U), November 29, 2016.

5. For a detailed listing of ASEAN's aims and purposes, see *Overview, Association of Southeast Asian Nations*, available from *http://asean.org/asean/about-asean/overview/*, accessed March 19, 2017.

6. Treaty of Amity and Cooperation in Southeast Asia Indonesia, February 24, 1976, available from *http://asean.org/treaty-amity-cooperation-southeast-asia-indonesia-24-february-1976/*, accessed January 15, 2017. Article 2 provides: In their relations with one another, the High Contracting Parties shall be guided by the following fundamental principles:

a. Mutual respect for the independence, sovereignty, equality, territorial integrity and national identity of all nations;
b. The right of every State to lead its national existence free from external interference, subversion or coersion [sic];
c. Non-interference in the internal affairs of one another;
d. Settlement of differences or disputes by peaceful means;
e. Renunciation of the threat or use of force;
f. Effective cooperation among themselves.

7. Ibid.

8. U.S. Department of State, "United States Accedes to the Treaty of Amity and Cooperation in Southeast Asia," Washington, DC: Bureau of Public Affairs, July 22, 2009, available from *https://2009-2017.state.gov/r/pa/prs/ps/2009/july/126294.htm,* accessed January 15, 2017.

9. U.S. Department of State, "Association of Southeast Asian Nations (ASEAN)," available from *https://www.state.gov/p/eap/regional/asean/,* accessed February 13, 2017. See also U.S. Department of State, "United States Accedes to the Treaty of Amity and Cooperation in Southeast Asia." According to then-Secretary of State Hillary Clinton, "we believe that the United States must have strong relationships and a strong and productive presence here in Southeast Asia."

10. Chung-in Moon, "ASEAN Regional Forum," *Encyclopedia Britannica,* December 7, 2001, available from *https://www.britannica.com/topic/ASEAN-Regional-Forum,* accessed January 15, 2017. The ARF was established at the 26th ASEAN Ministerial Meeting and Post Ministerial Conference in 1993, and its inaugural meeting was held on July 25, 1994. See also ASEAN Regional Forum, "About the ASEAN Regional Forum," available from *http://aseanregionalforum.asean.org/about.html,* accessed January 15, 2017. Note: As perspective on regional security, by 1993 the large U.S. military presence in the Philippines had ended. For a general discussion on the U.S. military withdrawal from the Philippines, see David Sanger, "Philippines Orders U.S. to Leave Strategic Navy Base at Subic Bay," *The New York Times,* December 28, 1991, available from *www.nytimes.com/1991/12/28/world/philippines-orders-us-to-leave-strategic-navy-base-at-subic-bay.html,* accessed January 28, 2017. During treaty negotiations to keep the bases open, "the Philippine Senate rejected the treaty . . . after an

impassioned debate in which the American military presence was assailed as a vestige of colonialism and an affront to Philippine sovereignty."

11. ASEAN Regional Forum, "About the ASEAN Regional Forum."

12. Ibid. Current ARF participants include: Australia, Bangladesh, Brunei Darussalam, Cambodia, Canada, China, Democratic People's Republic of Korea, European Union, India, Indonesia, Japan, Lao People's Democratic Republic, Malaysia, Mongolia, Myanmar, New Zealand, Pakistan, Papua New Guinea, Philippines, Republic of Korea, Russia, Singapore, Sri Lanka, Thailand, Timor-Leste, United States, and Vietnam.

13. U.S. Department of State, "U.S. Engagement in the 2015 ASEAN Regional Forum," Washington, DC: Bureau of Public Affairs, August 6, 2015, available from *https://2009-2017.state. gov/r/pa/prs/ps/2015/08/245759.htm*, accessed January 15, 2017.

14. ASEAN Defence Ministers Meeting, "About the ASEAN Defence Ministers' Meeting (ADMM)," February 6, 2017, available from *https://admm.asean.org/index.php/about-admm/about-admm.html*, accessed February 13, 2017.

15. Ibid.

16. ASEAN Defence Ministers Meeting, "About the ASEAN Defence Ministers' Meeting (ADMM-Plus)," February 6, 2017, available from *https://admm.asean.org/index.php/about-admm/about-admm-plus.html*, accessed February 13, 2017.

17. Ibid. The ADMM-Plus Objectives, as outlined in the ADMM-Plus Concept Paper, adopted by the Second ADMM, Singapore, November 13-15, 2007, are:

- To benefit ASEAN member countries in building capacity to address shared security challenges, while cognisant of the differing capacities of various ASEAN countries;

- To promote mutual trust and confidence between defence establishments through greater dialogue and transparency;

- To enhance regional peace and stability through cooperation in defence and security, in view of the transnational security challenges the region faces;

- To contribute to the realization of an ASEAN Security Community which, as stipulated in the Bali Concord II, embodies ASEAN's aspiration to achieve peace, stability, democracy and prosperity in the region where ASEAN member countries live at peace with one another and with the world at large;

- To facilitate the implementation of the Vientiane Action Programme, which calls for ASEAN to build a peaceful, secure and prosperous ASEAN, and to adopt greater outward-looking external relation strategies with our friends and Dialogue Partners.

18. Ibid.

19. *Overview, Association of Southeast Asian Nations.*

20. Chairman's Statement of the 4th ASEAN-United States Summit, "Turning Vision into Reality for a Dynamic ASEAN Community," Vientiane, LAO PDR, September 8, 2016, p. 1, available from *http://asean.org/storage/2016/09/Chairmans-Statement-of-the-4th-ASEAN-US-Summit1.pdf*, accessed January 15, 2017.

21. ASEAN Secretariat's Information Paper, "Overview of ASEAN-U.S. Dialogue Relations," January 4, 2016, available from *www.asean.org/wp-content/uploads/2016/01/4Jan/Overview-of-ASEAN-US-Dialogue-Relations-(4-Jan-2016).pdf*, accessed December 4, 2016.

22. The Honourable Dato' Seri Abdullah Ahmad Badawi, "Chairman's Statement of the First East Asia Summit Kuala Lumpur, December 14, 2005," Association of Southeast Asian Nations, available from *http://asean.org/?static_post=chairmans-statement-of-the-first-east-asia-summit-kuala-lumpur-14-december-2005-2*, accessed March 19, 2017. The first EAS was attended by "Heads of State/Government of ASEAN, Australia, the PRC, the Republic of India, Japan, the Republic of Korea, and New Zealand. Russia was invited as Guest of the Government of Malaysia." Malaysia hosted and chaired this Summit.

23. John Pang, NTU, "The East Asia Summit: a platform for confidence building," East Asia Forum, November 12, 2016, available from *www.eastasiaforum.org/2016/11/12/the-east-asia-summit-a-platform-for-confidence-building/*, accessed March 8, 2017.

> The EAS is by design a flexible forum for strategic dialogue and cooperation on the key issues facing the region. The leaders can shape the agenda with their personal interventions. The role of the United States is all the more prominent because the president attends, while China and Russia only send their premiers.

See also Kang Seung-woo, "East Asia Summit urges NK to abandon nuclear program," *The Korea Times*, September 8, 2016, available from *www.koreatimes.co.kr/www/news/nation/2016/09/116_213780.html*, accessed March 19, 2017.

24. For a detailed discussion on the Six-Party Talks, see Jayshree Bajoria and Beina Xu, "The Six Party Talks on North Korea's Nuclear Program," *CFR Backgrounders*, Washington, DC: Council on Foreign Relations (CFR), September 30, 2013, available from *www.cfr.org/proliferation/six-party-talks-north-koreas-nuclear-program/p13593*, accessed March 19, 2017. "Launched in 2003, the Six Party Talks are aimed at ending North Korea's nuclear program through negotiations involving China, the United States, North and South Korea, Japan, and Russia." Essentially, the talks have met with little success.

25. For a discussion on the Japan-Russia "two-plus-two" talks, see Elaine Kurtenbach, Associated Press, "Japan, Russia bolster cooperation, urge NKorean restraint," *AP News*, March 20, 2017, available from *https://www.apnews.com/f565f6d2dffa4782919c c98368dd7c6a*, accessed November 30, 2017.

26. *Joint Publication 1-02, Department of Defense Dictionary of Military and Associated Terms*, November 8, 2010 (as amended through February 15, 2016), p. 46, available from *www.dtic.mil/doctrine/new_pubs/jp1_02.pdf*, accessed February 18, 2017.

27. Frank G. Hoffman, "The Contemporary Spectrum of Conflict: Protracted, Gray Zone, Ambiguous, and Hybrid Modes of War," *2016 Index of U.S. Military Strength: Assessing America's Ability to Provide for the Common Defense,* Washington, DC: The

Heritage Foundation, available from *http://index.heritage.org/ military/2016/essays/contemporary-spectrum-of-conflict/*, accessed February 18, 2017.

28. National Defense Authorization Act for Fiscal Year 2000, Public Law 106-65, 106th Congress, Washington, DC, October 5, 1999, §1201. Section 1201(a) provides that the:

> Secretary of Defense may not authorize any military-to-military exchange or contact described in subsection (b) to be conducted by the armed forces with representatives of the People's Liberation Army of the People's Republic of China if that exchange or contact would create a national security risk due to an inappropriate exposure specified in subsection (b).

Section 1201(c) provides that the limitations in subsection (a) do not apply to "any search-and-rescue or humanitarian operation or exercise." See also Matthew Cox, "General Warns of North Korean Missile Threat, Talks China Visit," Military.com, January 25, 2017, available from *www.military.com/daily-news/2017/01/25/ general-warns-north-korean-missile-threat-talks-china-visit.html*, accessed February 19, 2017. Lieutenant General Robert Brown, U.S. Army Pacific commander, participated in a "visit to China as Army units took part in a disaster management exchange exercise there." He said he met with many leaders during that trip. "We concentrated on what we had in common . . . [we] talked about Ebola and many [humanitarian assistance, disaster relief] and peacekeeping operations—other things we had in common."

29. For an overview on the RIMPAC exercise and participants, see generally Commander, U.S. Pacific Fleet, "RIMPAC improves international cooperation," available from *www.cpf.navy.mil/ rimpac/*, accessed March 28, 2017. See also Commander Naval Surface Force, U.S. Pacific Fleet, *RIMPAC 2016*, available from *www. public.navy.mil/surfor/Pages/RIMPAC-2016.aspx*, accessed March 28, 2017.

> Held every 2 years by Commander, U.S. Pacific Fleet (PACFLT), and executed by Commander, U.S. 3rd Fleet (C3F), RIMPAC is a multinational maritime exercise that takes place in and around the Hawaiian Islands. [RIMPAC 2016] is the 25th in the series that began in 1971.

30. For an overview on Tillerson's first trip to Asia, see Eli Watkins, "Nikki Haley on North Korea talks: US has 'been there, done that'," CNN, March 16, 2017, available from *www.cnn.com/2017/03/16/politics/nikki-haley-north-korea/index.html*, accessed March 19, 2017. "We don't want to get back into the six-party talks," [UN Ambassador Nikki] Haley said, referring to the previous negotiating structure. "We're not willing to do that. Been there, done that." During this trip, Tillerson "derided the US approach to [North Korea] during the past 2 decades and pledged a new path."

31. Hoffman, "The Contemporary Spectrum of Conflict: Protracted, Gray Zone, Ambiguous, and Hybrid Modes of War."

32. Ibid.

33. Zhou Fangyin, "The U.S. Alliance System in Asia: A Chinese Perspective," *Asian Politics & Policy*, Vol. 8, Issue 1, Version of Record online: January 16, 2016, p. 207, available from *http://onlinelibrary.wiley.com/doi/10.1111/aspp.12231/pdf*, accessed December 22, 2016.

34. Ibid., p. 208.

35. Recommended Talking Points—China (U), November 29, 2016.

36. Fangyin, "The U.S. Alliance System in Asia: A Chinese Perspective," p. 208.

37. Ibid.

38. Ibid.

39. Aaron Mehta, "A NATO to Contain China? Key US Commander Doesn't See it," *DefenseNews*, December 7, 2016, available from *www.defensenews.com/articles/a-nato-to-contain-china-pacom-head-doesnt-see-it*, accessed January 15, 2017.

40. Fangyin, "The U.S. Alliance System in Asia: A Chinese Perspective," p. 208.

41. Ibid., p. 209.

42. Jeffrey Goldberg, "The Lessons of Henry Kissinger," *The Atlantic*, December 2016, available from *www.theatlantic.com/magazine/archive/2016/12/the-lessons-of-henry-kissinger/505868/*, accessed January 10, 2017.

43. President Xi Jinping, "New Asian Security Concept For New Progress in Security Cooperation," Remarks at the Fourth Summit of the Conference on Interaction and Confidence Building Measures in Asia, Shanghai, China, May 21, 2014, available from *www.fmprc.gov.cn/mfa_eng/zxxx_662805/t1159951.shtml*, accessed January 16, 2017.

44. Fangyin, "The U.S. Alliance System in Asia: A Chinese Perspective," p. 212.

45. MFA News, "Assistant Foreign Minister Kong Xuanyou Attends 5th EAS Workshop on Regional Security Architecture," June 29, 2016, available from *www.fmprc.gov.cn/mfa_eng/wjbxw/t1376789.shtml*, accessed February 20, 2017.

46. Ibid.

47. Xi, "New Asian Security Concept for New Progress in Security Cooperation."

48. Liu Zhenmin, "Work together to improve regional security architecture and address common challenges," public speech, 1st Plenary Session of The 7th Xiangshan Forum, Beijing, China, October 12, 2016, available from *www.fmprc.gov.cn/mfa_eng/wjdt_665385/zyjh_665391/t1405158.shtml*, accessed January 16, 2017. For a discussion on the SCO, see Eleanor Albert, "The Shanghai Cooperation Organization," Washington, DC: Council on Foreign Relations, March 2009, available from *www.cfr.org/china/shanghai-cooperation-organization/p10883*, accessed January 16, 2017. Founded in 2001, the SCO is composed of six member states, two ascending members, four observer nations, and six dialogue partners. Originally formed as a confidence building forum to demilitarize borders, the organization's goals and agenda have since broadened to include increased military and [counterterrorism] cooperation and intelligence sharing. The SCO has also intensified its focus on regional economic initiatives like the recently announced integration of the China-led Silk Road Economic Belt and the Russia-led Eurasian Economic Union.

While some experts say the organization has emerged as an anti-U.S. bulwark in Central Asia, others believe frictions among its members effectively preclude a strong, unified SCO. For a discussion on the Conference on Interaction and Confidence Building Measures in Asia, see *About CICA*, available from *www.cica-china.org/eng/gyyx_1/*, accessed March 19, 2017. China currently holds the CICA presidency, and there are 26 member states; the United States is an observer.

> CICA follows the principle of consensus . . . [and] is a forum for dialogues and consultations on regional security issues in Asia, with the main objective and purpose of enhancing cooperation through multilateral confidence-building measures towards promoting peace, security and stability in Asia.

49. Zhenmin, "Work together to improve regional security architecture and address common challenges."

50. Ibid.

51. For a counter viewpoint/observation that China is essentially establishing its own hub-and-spoke system with "partner" countries through its "One Belt, One Road" and other initiatives, see Cha, *Power Play*, pp. 200-204.

52. For a discussion on the Five Principles, see Consulate-General of the People's Republic of China in Houston, "The Five Principles of Peaceful Co-existence," June 28, 2004, available from *http://houston.china-consulate.org/eng/nv/t140964.htm*, accessed January 16, 2017. See also President Xi Jinping, "New Asian Security Concept for New Progress in Security Cooperation," Remarks at the Fourth Summit of the Conference on Interaction and Confidence Building Measures in Asia, Shanghai, China, May 21, 2014, available from *www.fmprc.gov.cn/mfa_eng/zxxx_662805/t1159951.shtml*, accessed January 16, 2017.

53. Xi, "New Asian Security Concept for New Progress in Security Cooperation."

54. Scott A. Carpenter, "Limits to U.S.-China Mil-to-Mil Engagements Under the 2000 National Defense Authorization Act," *Small Wars Journal*, August 16, 2015, available from *http://*

smallwarsjournal.com/print/27181, accessed February 20, 2017. The author further notes that:

> While China forecasts that 'the international situation will remain generally peaceful,' they also predict profound changes in the security environment caused by intensifying international competition for the redistribution of power, rights, and interests and the threat of local wars due to regional conflicts.

55. United Nations, Division for Ocean Affairs and the Law of the Sea, China Declaration upon Ratification, June 7, 1996, available from *www.un.org/depts/los/convention_agreements/convention_declarations.htm#China after ratification*, accessed January 16, 2017.

56. AsianLII, "Law of the People's Republic of China on the Territorial Sea and Contiguous Zone," The Standing Committee of the People's Republic of China, No. 55, Article 2, February 25, 1992, available from *www.asianlii.org/cn/legis/cen/laws/lotprocottsatcz739/*, accessed March 26, 2017. For an overview of the July 2016 UNTLOS decision, see Award Decision, PCA Case N° 2013-19, "In the Matter of the South China Sea Arbitration, before An Arbitral Tribunal Constituted under Annex VII to the 1982 United Nations Convention on the Law of the Sea, between The Republic of the Philippines and the People's Republic of China, Permanent Court of Arbitration," July 12, 2016, available from *https://pca-cpa.org/wp-content/uploads/sites/175/2016/07/PH-CN-20160712-Award.pdf*, accessed January 16, 2017.

57. To be fair, China's actions are not surprising or without precedent. As Graham Allison noted prior to the Permanent Court of Arbitration (PCA) issuing its 2016 award in the Philippines' case against China, "none of the five permanent members of the [United Nations] Security Council have ever accepted any international court's ruling when (in their view) it infringed their sovereignty or national security interests." Further, China ultimately rejecting the 2016 PCA decision reflects, "what the other great powers have repeatedly done for decades." Graham Allison, "Of Course China, Like All Great Powers, Will Ignore an International Legal Verdict," *The Diplomat*, July 11, 2016, available from *https://thediplomat.com/2016/07/of-course-china-like-all-great-powers-will-ignore-an-international-legal-verdict/*, accessed March 26, 2017. As an additional outside viewpoint, China's actions also present

a cautionary observation for how China might administer its own MLSA: less "win-win" and more "China first" may become the mantra.

58. "Trump's Speech to Congress: Video and Transcript," *The New York Times*, February 28, 2017, available from *https://www. nytimes.com/2017/02/28/us/politics/trump-congress-video-transcript. html?_r=1*, accessed March 9, 2017.

59. Ibid.

60. Cha, "Complex Patchworks: U.S. Alliances as Part of Asia's Regional Architecture," p. 29. Professor Cha notes that from a multilateral security viewpoint, "previous U.S. disinterest in regional architecture at the end of the Cold War stemmed from an 'if it ain't broke, don't fix it' mentality. Initially, there were concerns that regional initiatives were meant to undermine U.S. leadership."

61. Cha, *Power Play*, p. 204.

62. For a general discussion of, and the U.S. Pacific Command commander's observations on, Asia-Pacific security structures, see Mehta, "A NATO to Contain China? Key US Commander Doesn't See it." According to Admiral Harry Harris, "I do not believe we're ever going to see a NATO in Asia."

63. U.S. Helsinki Commission, "The Security Dimension," Commission on Security and Cooperation in Europe, available from *https://www.csce.gov/about-csce/helsinki-process-and-osce/security-dimension*, accessed March 19, 2017.

64. For a discussion on the U.S. alliance system as an "organic part of Asia's . . . security landscape," see Cha, *Power Play*, p. 205.

65. Lawrence Freedman, *Deterrence*, Cambridge, UK: Polity Press, 2004, p. 50.

66. See Bernard FW Loo, "China, the South China Sea, and ASEAN: Are we witnessing the impending end of multilateral security?" *Military Studies at RSIS*, July 14, 2012, available from *https://rsismilitarystudies.wordpress.com/2012/07/14/896/*, accessed February 18, 2017. Note: This paper's author envisions a MLSA

"bubble" for visual reference as an example of an overarching MLSA that encompasses and overlays the existing Asia-Pacific organizations shown on the graphic in Loo's article "The Security Architecture of the Asia-Pacific," including several not previously mentioned in this paper: Asia Pacific Economic Council (APEC), US-Lower Mekong Initiative, the Pacific Island Forum (PIF), the South Asian Association for Regional Cooperation (SAARC), and ASEAN +3. His figure identifies the primary roles for each organization.

67. See generally Barack Obama, *National Security Strategy*, Washington, DC: The White House, February 2015, p. 24, available from *https://www.whitehouse.gov/sites/default/files/docs/2015_national_security_strategy.pdf*, accessed December 23, 2016. The author notes that, while the new administration has not yet published its own national security strategy (NSS), the 2015 NSS is instructive as it aligns regional security with U.S. leadership and resolve to support allies and partners.

68. Bob Work, "The Third U.S. Offset Strategy and its Implications for Partners and Allies," public speech, Willard Hotel, Washington, DC, January 28, 2015.

69. United Nations, Charter, 1 UNTS XVI, art. 52, para. 1, October 24, 1945.

70. North Atlantic Treaty, 34 UNTS 243 (No. 541), Washington, DC, April 4, 1949, available from *www.nato.int/cps/en/natolive/official_texts_17120.htm*, accessed December 4, 2016. Article 1 provides that:

> the Parties undertake, as set forth in the Charter of the United Nations, to settle any international dispute in which they may be involved by peaceful means in such a manner that international peace and security and justice are not endangered, and to refrain in their international relations from the threat or use of force in any manner inconsistent with the purposes of the United Nations.

71. The State Council Information Office of the People's Republic of China, "China's Policies on Asia-Pacific Security Cooperation," January 2017, available from *news.xinhuanet.com/*

english/china/2017-01/11/c_135973695.htm, accessed February 20, 2017.

72. Ibid.

73. For a discussion on Asia-Pacific countries "hedging" between the United States and China, see Van Jackson, "Asian Security after US Hegemony: Spheres of Influence and the Third Wave of Regional Order," *The Asian Forum*, October 14, 2016, available from *www.theasanforum.org/asian-security-after-us-hegemony-spheres-of-influence-and-the-third-wave-of-regional-order/#17*, accessed February 20, 2017. Citing Van Jackson, "Power, Trust, and Network Complexity: Three Logics of Hedging in Asian Security," *International Relations of the Asia-Pacific, Vol.* 14, No. 3, September 2014, pp. 331-356, the author notes that:

> . . . military modernization represents only one indicator that Asian states—even those openly aligned with the United States—are adopting hedging strategies in their foreign policies. The hedging trend has been documented thoroughly elsewhere, but it is sufficient for purposes here to note that other indicators of hedging include: states simultaneously relying primarily on China for economic prosperity and the United States for security; a conspicuous absence of overt balancing or bandwagoning; and attempts to multilateralize security cooperation without taking on costly commitments or subscribing to rule enforcement mechanisms.

74. Dr. Greg Austin, telephone interview by author, October 27, 2016. Dr. Austin is a Professor in the Australian Centre for Cyber Security at the University of New South Wales, Canberra, Australia, and concurrently serves as a Professorial Fellow with the EastWest Institute (EWI) in New York. As a counterpoint, Dr. Austin noted that being a peer-competitor is how one assesses relative power, and that China does not think that they are as close a competitor as some in the United States believe. He offered that by 2050, China may be a "2nd tier power, but not at U.S. level." Impacting U.S. strategic analysis is the likelihood that U.S. confidence in its own power is perhaps not as high as other nations' confidence in U.S. power, which, in turn, impacts the near-peer competitor analysis.

75. Cha, *Power Play*, p. 184. See also Richard Haass, "Desert Storm, the Last Classic War," Op-Ed, Council on Foreign Relations, July 31, 2015, available from *www.cfr.org/defense-and-security/desert-storm-last-classic-war/p36857*, accessed March 10, 2017. The author notes that:

> multilateralism constrains the U.S., but it can yield big dividends. Broad participation ensures a degree of burden-sharing. . . . Multilateralism [in the example of the first Gulf War] can also generate political support within the U.S. and around the world; it supplies a source of legitimacy often judged missing when the U.S. acts alone.

CHAPTER 4

THE LARGEST TIGER:
INDIA IN THE U.S. POLICY TOWARD
INDO-ASIA-PACIFIC

Todd D. Carroll

EXECUTIVE SUMMARY

India is the world's most populous democracy and shares many western values and political institutions with the United States. While it has been a rocky relationship for many years since India gained independence in 1947, the trend has been improving for the past decade and a half. This chapter explores ways in which the United States can best support the development of India while coaxing it to play a bigger role in the Indo-Asia-Pacific (IAP). India is especially well suited to check China's assertiveness, as no one can claim India is an outsider meddling in Asian affairs. With a population poised to become the world's largest in 2028, and an economy that could surpass that of the United States by 2050, India will be the most important player in the decades to come in maintaining cooperation, stability, and security in the IAP. To guide India's rise as a great power that respects and defends the rules-based international order, the United States should engage India along four lines of effort: military, diplomatic, commercial, and people-to-people.

INTRODUCTION

India is the world's most populous democracy and a rising power. Although it shares many western values and political institutions with the United States, the U.S.-India relationship had been rocky for many years since the latter gained independence in 1947. The past 15 years, however, have witnessed an impressive improvement in the two nations' relations. With a U.S.-friendly Prime Minister in Narendra Modi, the time is ripe for the United States to do everything possible to assist India in harnessing the power of its growing population and guide its path toward becoming a responsible great power that respects and defends the rules-based international order.

Perhaps the best indication of the rising importance of India is its economic turnaround since the liberalization of its economy in 1991. Since these reforms went into effect, the gross domestic product (GDP) of India has more than quadrupled, growing at an average rate of 7 percent a year.[1] Economists expect this trend to continue, predicting that India's GDP will rise from $7.28 trillion in 2014 in terms of purchasing power parity (PPP, or real GDP adjusted for price level differences across countries) to $42.21 trillion in 2050, and likely displacing the United States as the world's second largest economy.[2]

With a political and judicial system developed during the British colonial period, India shares many western values with the United States. One might assume this would make the two powers natural allies, but for much of India's post-independence history, this has not been the case. During the Cold War, India was the leader of the Non-Aligned Movement, which was a group of third-world countries that refrained from siding with either the United States or the Soviet Union. However, as this movement gradually weakened, India drifted closer to the Soviet Union while the United States built stronger strategic relations with Pakistan and China.[3] Much of India's foreign policy calculus is focused on what is happening in Pakistan, with which India has gone to war four times. There are still extremely high tensions over the disputed Kashmir region. As recently as September 2016, 18 Indian soldiers were killed by armed militants in the garrison town of Uri. High-ranking Indian officials, including the Home Minister, have accused the Pakistani government of being complicit in the attacks.[4] India had a brief war with China as well in 1962 over their disputed boundary in the Himalayas, which remains problematic to this day. Sino-Indian relations were further strained due to China's assistance to Pakistan in the development of its nuclear weapons program and continued aid to Pakistan's civil nuclear program.[5]

Indo-American relations declined further as a result of India's underground nuclear test program. In 1998, the Clinton administration responded with economic sanctions,[6] even encouraging Beijing to play a bigger role in ensuring peace and security in the South Asian region.[7]

Former President George W. Bush took a different approach toward India. His administration was more suspicious of a rapidly rising China than the Clinton administration. Feeling that China was trying to alter Asia's balance of power in its own favor,[8] Bush engineered a lower-key pivot to Asia. Part of this effort was to engage India. His former National Security Advisor and Secretary of State Condoleezza Rice wrote, "India is an element in China's calculation, and it should be in America's, too."[9] President Bush lifted sanctions against India because they were "not in the national security interests of the United States."[10] The strategic relationship was furthered with the announcement of the U.S.-India Civil Nuclear Cooperation Initiative in 2005 (approved by the International Atomic Energy Agency [IAEA] in 2008).[11]

Following former President Barack Obama's inauguration, Indo-U.S. relations began to drift as the new administration pursued a closer relationship with China. Obama made early important concessions to China in the realm of human rights in the hope of developing a closer partnership, perhaps even a "G2" aimed at stabilizing global issues.[12] Indian sensitivities were further rattled as the former President did not include Prime Minister Manmohan Singh in his first wave of introductory phone calls to other foreign leaders, including Pakistani President Asif Ali Zardari.[13] In November 2009, in a major policy speech in Asia, Obama vowed to "strengthen old alliances and build new partnerships" in the IAP but failed to include India on the list of countries to which he was referring.[14]

By mid-2010, once again India became a part of the U.S. strategic calculus. William J. Burns, the Under Secretary of State for Political Affairs, affirmed this when he stated, "India's strength and progress on the world stage is deeply in the strategic interest of the United States." Michele Flournoy, the Under Secretary of Defense for Policy, added "India's success is very much in America's national interest" and that "increasingly our specific security interests are converging."[15] In November of that year, Obama delivered a very well received address to the Indian Parliament, in which he endorsed India's bid for a permanent United Nations (UN) Security Council seat. Prior to the speech, most Indians felt Obama placed their interests behind those of regional rivals Pakistan and China. Afterwards, very few held the same opinion.[16]

In 2011, the Obama administration rolled out the "Pivot to Asia" or Strategic Rebalance, a long-term U.S. effort to spur domestic revival and renovation as well to keep peace in the world's most dynamic region.[17] India figured to play a prominent role in the rebalance. With these actions, Indo-U.S. relations were back on a positive track. The Bharatiya Janata Party (BJP) considers India and the United States to be natural allies, whose relations "constitute the key element in the architecture of tomorrow's democratized world order."[18] With the BJP rising to power in 2014 under the leadership of Modi, the Obama administration wanted to redouble the efforts toward consolidating gains and taking the relationship to the next level.

To guide India's rise as a great power that respects and defends the rules-based international order, the United States should engage India along four lines of effort: military, diplomatic, commercial, and people-to-people. Each of these lines of effort is discussed in more detail.

MILITARY LINE OF EFFORT

Former Secretary of Defense (SECDEF) Ashton Carter played a critical role in advancing this line of effort. Carter devoted more personal attention to his Indian counterpart, Defense Minister Manohar Parrikar, than any previous SECDEF. During regular meetings in both India and the United States, the two developed a very strong personal relationship.[19] In an encouraging sign of how the new SECDEF will treat the relationship, James Mattis, in his testimony before the Senate Armed Services Committee, stated that "The U.S. policy should continue to pursue a long-term strategic relationship with India" and he "will focus on what steps can be taken to bolster the overall defense relationship."[20]

Some of Ash Carter's most important work has included the Defense Technology and Trade Initiative (DTTI) and the status of India as a "Major Defense Partner." In 2012, as Deputy SECDEF, Carter undertook an initiative to provide increased senior-level engagement to get beyond the legal and bureaucratic obstacles to defense technology and trade with India.[21] This initiative became the DTTI, which incorporated the ability to co-produce weapons in India, along with the transfer of technology. Carter's efforts also paved the way for naming India a Major Defense Partner in June of 2016, further easing technology sharing "at a level commensurate with that of its closest allies and partners."[22]

While the DTTI is an incredible step in the right direction of improving the military relationship and meshes nicely with Modi's "Make in India" campaign, more can be done. While relaxing the standards for technology exchange is beneficial, the current levels of sharing impede greater sales and undermine the potential of the relationship. Russia, which provides 70 percent of India's defense imports, provides strategically sensitive technology in hardware ranging from missiles, to ships, to nuclear submarines, to fifth-generation fighter aircraft.[23] As of now, co-production efforts between the United States and India are limited to only low-end weapons such as the Raven unmanned aerial vehicle (UAV) and reconnaissance modules for the C-130J aircraft.[24] The Trump administration should work with Congress to remove barriers in order to allow for greater transfer and sharing of technology without intrusive end-use monitoring agreements, something India will absolutely not accept.[25] Until this happens, Russia will remain India's main defense supplier. This is important as co-production and technology sharing accelerate Indian development, and as a partner with the United States, interoperability is key to the effectiveness of multinational military operations.

As India builds its capabilities through advanced systems acquired from either the United States or Russia, bilateral defense cooperation could be furthered by allowing Indian service members access to U.S. training. Teaching India's warfighters the knowledge the U.S. military has gained over time in some of their recently gained technologies, such as UAV or airborne anti-submarine warfare (ASW) employment, and synchronizing tactics, techniques and procedures (TTP) would make an enormous difference to India's ability to use these new capabilities effectively.[26] By providing more advanced warfighting systems and training India's operators in U.S. service schools, the United States will exponentially increase India's ability to be a net provider of security in the Indian Ocean and Western Pacific. An economically vibrant and militarily strong India will be more inclined to look after its interests regionally, the foremost of which is peace and stability. Beyond technology sharing, improving interoperability, and synchronizing procedures, there is one other significant area in which the United States could do more to enhance the bilateral security relationship.

Joint military exercises have become a common occurrence between the United States and India. The United States has been a long-time participant with India in the Malabar Naval Exercise and India has contributed warships to the U.S. Navy-led Rim of the Pacific (RIMPAC) exercise since 2014. In fact, the United States cooperates with India in more military exercises than it does with any other country, and across all five military branches.[27] This provides outstanding training for both sides as it is not often that U.S. military units are able to interact with Russian hardware. These exercises not only strengthen Indian forces, they also help identify shortcomings in U.S. employment procedures. At Cope India in 2004, some U.S. Air Force tactics were exposed as ineffectual and forced revisions in the way the Air Force fights.[28] The incorporation of other friendly regional countries such as Japan and Australia only magnifies the benefits. However, exercises are for the most part still relatively simple and often times overly scripted. To maximize effectiveness, these exercises must become more complex and involve the best combatant capabilities on both sides.[29] As defense analyst Ashley Tellis notes, "taking the gains from familiarization and common TTPs," as discussed above, "and applying them in combined operations represents the acme of defense cooperation."[30]

DIPLOMATIC LINE OF EFFORT

Diplomacy is another area where inroads could be made to aid India's development and strengthen the bilateral relationship. India's older statesmen, insistent upon state intervention in the economy, a "nonaligned" stance to world affairs, and a distrust of close relations with the United States, are giving way to a younger generation that is friendlier toward the West due to the two nations' many cultural ties and a wish for India to play a greater role in world affairs.[31] A window has opened for greater opportunity to expand connections.

There are multiple areas in which the United States can support India's rise, facilitating the dream of India's younger generation that the country play a larger role, while providing the additional voice of a great power with common, shared values on international affairs.

As was previously mentioned, since 2010, former President Obama supported India's bid for a permanent seat on the UN Security Council. This was a very successful, trust-building move, and the United States should continue to push for it.

Since the early 1990s, India has sought membership in the Asia-Pacific Economic Cooperation (APEC) forum as part of its "Look East" policy, in which it tries to integrate further with Pacific Rim and East Asian economies, but has been repeatedly denied.[32] The United States invited India as an observer for the 2011 APEC meetings hosted by the United States in Hawaii and has supported India's accession to membership.[33] The United States needs to continue to press for Indian membership here and in other groups such as the Missile Technology Control Regime (MTCR), which would allow for greater exchanges of defense technology, and the Nuclear Supplier Group (NSG), which would enable India to expand its civilian atomic energy sector.

In addition, the United States could offer assistance to the Indian government with expertise and programs for combating corruption, alleviating poverty, homeland security, improving agricultural practices and women's empowerment. Corruption is rampant in India; by some estimates, India's underground economy could be half of the country's GDP.[34] In fact, on the World Bank's Ease of Doing Business scale, India ranks 130 out of 190 nations.[35]

Technical assistance could also be offered to support Indian programs to fight corruption, such as Modi's attempts at a cashless society to combat exploitative middlemen from collecting fees on monies intended for the poor. To attract the investment and manufacturing required to employ India's vast population, corruption has to be reduced. Poverty is pervasive in India, and has only increased with globalization, providing another reason why the country so badly needs investment.[36] Creating jobs through investment is how India harnesses the power of its population dividend and would greatly reduce poverty, lessen instability, and help eliminate the barriers and special interests that paralyze the central government. Breaking down the caste system and improving education and health care could diminish the crushing effects of poverty. Homeland security and terrorism are among the top concerns of the Indian citizenry, and these are certainly areas where the United States has much expertise to offer.

Agriculture in India is notoriously underdeveloped and forms a massive protectionist-voting bloc that stifles reform. Over half of India's total employment is involved in agriculture (in 2010, India was 51 percent compared to just 2 percent in the United States);[37] by enhancing agricultural productivity and competitiveness, India could overcome political resistance to free trade and build the type of economy it needs to grow. Enlarging opportunities for women and bringing them into the labor force could raise India's GDP growth by as much as two percentage points a year.[38] For India to grow into the world-class economy it wishes to be, these factors need to be addressed.

COMMERCIAL LINE OF EFFORT

To advance and broaden the bilateral economic relationship between the two countries, an emphasis should be placed on cooperation at the level of individual companies and states while waiting for progress on cooperation between the national governments.[39] Some Indian state governments provide more business-friendly environments than the national government. Notably, Gujarat, where Modi was the chief minister, realized annual GDP gains of 10 percent during his tenure from 2001-2012.[40] Other business-oriented states, such as Maharashtra and Tamil Nadu, have been success stories, while less open states have languished. Indian states can neutralize national trade barriers with incentives, and many have the size to qualify by themselves as high-priority customers for American companies.[41] The U.S. Government could help facilitate greater investment in India by lessening the burden of taxation on U.S. companies that repatriate profits. This would encourage companies to do business in India while keeping more earnings to reinvest at home, benefitting both countries. The large market and incredible potential has many companies hoping to gain a foothold in a burgeoning India; proper incentives could give U.S. companies an advantage over fierce international competitors.

If India can develop and take advantage of its population dividend, it will be the world's largest free market, and a critical one for sustaining the American economic engine. Creating barriers to the greater foreign investment required for India to become an economic powerhouse are its rampant corruption, complex and lengthy investment and business approval processes, antiquated land acquisition and labor laws, poor contract enforcement, and protectionist policies for its manufacturing and agriculture sectors.[42] The protectionist policies and other trade barriers harken back to the time of India's independence, when Indians felt the need to support their fledgling industries.[43] What would be most beneficial to both the United States and India would be a free-trade agreement (FTA) and a high-quality bilateral investment treaty (BIT). An FTA would significantly enhance the present unimpressive trade numbers between two economies of such size, valued at only $66 billion in 2015.[44] A high-quality BIT, one that included intellectual property rights as investors look for transparency and rule of law,[45] would bring massive investment and new companies to India. These investments and the jobs they will bring are required for India's economy to develop and sustain fiscal health for the long term. Talks on these initiatives will ebb and flow due to poorly-conceived existing policy and reticence within parliament, but Modi urgently wants these measures. The United States should continue to press on these reforms but give the Prime Minister the space, time, and technical assistance he requires as he works to convince the opposition of the benefits of such agreements.

PEOPLE-TO-PEOPLE LINE OF EFFORT

People-to-people ties, much like military-to-military cooperation, can be of great benefit to advancing cooperation between the United States and India. Over time, as Indians and Americans interact and gain greater appreciation for each other's cultures, the relations between the two nations should improve, fostering understanding and communication.[46] While we have a strong and vibrant Indian immigrant population of 2.4 million[47] in the United States, the second largest immigrant population behind Mexico, the U.S. Government can facilitate greater human contacts between our two nations to enhance the partnership and aid India's development.

While programs are in place to improve educational and worker exchanges, improvements could be made. The U.S.-India Education Foundation (USIEF) is an outstanding program that has provided 19,000 students from the United States and India the opportunity to study in the other country since program inception in 1950.[48] Every effort should be made to continue and expand programs such as this to increase people-to-people ties. When it comes to worker exchanges, much more can be done, which will be explored further below. It is imperative that people be allowed to travel between the countries to provide the innovations and cultural and economic ties both need to compete and thrive in an increasingly connected and competitive world.

In recent years, stories highlighting the horrors of outsourcing have come out in the press and have taken hold of the American consciousness. In turn, constituents have pressed their representatives to take action that in some cases have hurt the advancement of human ties between the United States and India. The progression of these crucial relations is most damaged once policy and law impose barriers to H-1B and L-1 visas, which Indians use far more than any other nationality to live and work in the United States. Both visas are nonimmigrant visas that allow companies to temporarily employ foreign workers.

H1-Bs require a bachelor's degree or equivalent and are issued for those going to work in a specialty field. L-1s require no specific skill, but the worker must work for a multinational company and have been employed by that company for 1 year in their home nation.[49] H-1B and L-1 visas normally work on a reciprocity schedule, meaning if a foreign government charges a U.S. citizen a fee for a visa, the U.S. Government will charge the same fee.[50] Rhetoric about outsourcing has turned into more frequent visa application rejections and increased fees, which exceedingly affect information technology (IT) firms due to their significant international presence.[51] The IT field is a top Indian industry generating over $150 billion annually, more than half of which results from business being done with North America.[52] American fees and rejection rates for Indian visas have both risen sharply, in contrast to treatment of workers of other nationalities.[53]

Some of the anger is warranted, because some U.S. companies, such as Disney, have been accused of replacing American workers with immigrants to save money and are responsible for the rise of "body shops."[54] Body shops are contracting companies that sponsor workers on H-1B visas and illegally subcontract the workers out to other companies using doctored resumes.[55] The body shop can then report it never displaced American workers since the sub-contracting employer does not need to report it hired any H-1B workers.[56]

This policy should extend to those with degrees in science, technology, engineering, and math (STEM) or other defined fields where the United States is lacking trained people. About a quarter of all start-up companies in engineering and technology are founded by foreign-born entrepreneurs, and of those, 33.2 percent were from India. In fact, Indians founded more engineering and technology firms than immigrants born in the next nine immigrant-founder countries combined.[57] Keeping opportunities open for immigrants is key to maintaining a vibrant and growing economy while advancing relations by building cultural affinity between the United States and India. While some good legislation, such as the Stopping Trained in America Ph.D.s From Leaving the Economy Act of 2015 (STAPLE Act), have been proposed, they have not been enacted. The U.S. Government needs to pass such legislation while encouraging India to liberalize its labor laws to bring in the global talent it desperately needs to expand Indian corporations and provide additional jobs to employ its burgeoning youth population.

It may seem counterintuitive for India to send its most talented innovators to the United States, but in the long run, such a move greatly assists Indian development. The talent networks remaining in India will gain access to valuable knowledge and technological networks abroad.[58] Additionally, many expatriates will eventually return home, empowered by new ideas, experience, and connections to play a direct role in India's development.[59]

Those individuals with people-to-people ties or simply a strong interest in furthering the partnership between the United States and India can do their part by pressing government officials on the need to revise policies, which restrict this critical exchange. As Richard Boucher, Assistant Secretary of State for South and Central Asian Affairs, noted in 2008:

> We've had periods of excitement between the United States and India before. The bubbles burst, the enthusiasm is turned to disappointment. What's to make this different? And, for those of us in government, how do we make it different this time? My answer to the first question is: YOU. You're the ones who make it different: the students, the trans-oceanic families, the academics, the doctors, the business people. You are the foundation and the dynamic between the United States and India. And, what can

governments do to help you? Listen to you, please tell us how to open doors and remove obstacles. We'll help you find even more exciting opportunities.[60]

CONCLUSION

A strong and thriving India is in the best long-term interest of the United States. As traditional allies and partners in the West see their relative power decline, the United States will need new partners with strong voices that are willing to defend the existing international rules-based order and to reinforce acceptable norms. No single country has an advantage or potential that is even close to that of India. By focusing on these four lines of effort—military, diplomatic, economic, and people-to-people—the United States can best assist Indian development and guide India's path toward becoming a responsible world power. India's rise can be exemplary to other developing nations, demonstrating that democracy and open societies will work better than authoritarian alternatives. Additionally, India's extensive connections with China will help encourage them to work within the rules-based system rather than outside of it. For now, the United States should encourage India to do more as a partner in maintaining regional security, for in the long-term, India may be the strongest guarantor of peace and prosperity in the Indo-Asia-Pacific. It will be an extensive and challenging process—relationships take a long time to build, and the United States cannot be dissuaded by short-term disagreements that will inevitably arise. In the end, a strong bilateral relationship will pay dividends far greater than any sacrifice either country will have to make to achieve it.

ENDNOTES - CHAPTER 4

1. "One more push," *The Economist*, July 21, 2011, available from *http://www.economist.com/node/18988536*, accessed November 26, 2016.

2. John Hawksworth and Danny Chan, "The World in 2050," London, UK: Economics and Policy Team, PricewaterhouseCoopers, February 2015, available from *https://www.pwc.com/gx/en/issues/the-economy/assets/world-in-2050-february-2015.pdf#page3*, accessed November 26, 2015.

3. Kurt M. Campbell, *The Pivot: The Future of American Statecraft in Asia*, New York: Hachette Book Group, 2016, p. 251.

4. Ravi Agrawal, "Could India and Pakistan go to war?" CNN, September 29, 2016, available from *www.cnn.com/2016/09/21/asia/india-pakistan-kashmir-conflict/index.html*, accessed November 24, 2016.

5. Rohan Joshi, "China, Pakistan, and Nuclear Non-Proliferation," *The Diplomat*, February 16, 2015, available from *https://thediplomat.com/2015/02/china-pakistan-and-nuclear-non-proliferation/*, accessed November 27, 2016.

6. "U.S. imposes sanctions on India," CNN, May 13, 1998, available from *www.cnn.com/WORLD/asiapcf/9805/13/india.us/*, accessed December 1, 2016.

7. Mohammad Samir Hussain, "India-United States Strategic Relations: China as a Factor," *Journal of Political Studies*, Vol. 19, Iss. 2, 2012, p. 86.

8. Condoleezza Rice, "Promoting the National Interest," *Foreign Affairs*, January/February 2000, p. 56.

9. Ibid.

10. "US lifts India and Pakistan sanctions," BBC News, September 23, 2001, available from *http://news.bbc.co.uk/2/hi/americas/1558860.stm*, accessed December 1, 2016.

11. "U.S.-India: Civil Nuclear Cooperation," U.S. Department of State Archive, 2001-2009: Bureau of South and Central Asian Affairs, October 2008, available from *https://2001-2009.state.gov/p/sca/c17361.htm,* accessed November 27, 2016.

12. Peter Feaver and Inonut Papescu, "Is Obama's Foreign Policy Different From George W. Bush's?" E-International Relations, August 3, 2012, available from *www.e-ir.info/2012/08/03/is-obamas-foreign-policy-different-to-bushs/,* accessed December 1, 2016.

13. David J. Karl, "U.S.-India Relations: The way Forward," *Orbis*, Vol. 56, Iss. 2, 2012, p. 313.

14. Speech of President Barack H. Obama at Suntory Hall, Tokyo, Japan, November 14, 2009, trans. by Office of the Press Secretary, "Remarks by President Barack Obama," The White House, President Barack Obama, November 14, 2009, available from *https://obamawhitehouse.archives.gov/the-press-office/remarks-president-barack-obama-suntory-hall,* accessed November 30, 2016.

15. Karl, pp. 313-314.

16. Scott Wilson and Emily Wax, "Obama endorses India for U.N. Security Council seat," *The Washington Post*, November 8, 2010, available from *http://www.washingtonpost.com/wp-dyn/content/article/2010/11/08/AR2010110807129.html,* accessed November 27, 2016.

17. Campbell, p. 1.

18. Karl, p. 316.

19. Ryan Browne, "Carter looks to boost India ties as China rises," CNN, December 7, 2016, available from *www.cnn.com/2016/12/07/politics/india-military-ties-ash-carter-china-trump/index.html,* accessed December 10, 2016.

20. Press Trust of India, "US' relationship with India of utmost importance: General James Mattis," *The Economic Times*, January 12, 2017, available from *https://economictimes.indiatimes.com/news/defence/us-relationship-with-india-of-utmost-importance-general-james-mattis/articleshow/56504083.cms,* accessed January 14, 2017.

21. "U.S.-India Defense Technology and Trade Initiative (DTTI)," Office of the Under SECDEF for Acquisition, Technology and Logistics International Cooperation, n.d., available from *www.acq.osd.mil/ic/DTTI.html,* accessed December 2, 2016.

22. Joe Gould, "US Names India 'Major Defense Partner'," *Defense News,* June 7, 2016, available from *www.defensenews. com/story/defense/2016/06/07/us-names-india-major-defense-partner/85571518/,* accessed December 5, 2016.

23. Vivek Raghuvanshi, "India, US Advance Strategic Relations," *Defense News,* January 28, 2015, available from *www. defensenews.com/story/defense/policy-budget/industry/2015/01/28/ india-obama-modi-dtti-us-agreement-weapons-coproduce-bilateral-russia/22457599/,* accessed December 5, 2016.

24. Ibid.

25. Sunjoy Joshi, C. Raja Mohan, Vikram Sood, Rajeswari Pillai Rajagopalan, James J. Carafano, Walter Lohman, Lisa Curtis, and Derek Scissors, "Beyond the Plateau in U.S.-India Relations," The Heritage Foundation, April 26, 2013, available from *www.heritage. org/research/reports/2013/04/beyond-the-plateau-in-us-india-relations,* accessed December 1, 2016.

26. Ashley J. Tellis, "Back to First Principles: Realizing the Promise of U.S.-Indian Defense Ties," Carnegie Endowment for International Peace, December 10, 2015, available from *http:// carnegieendowment.org/2015/12/10/back-to-first-principles-realizing-promise-of-u.s.-indian-defense-ties-pub-62245,* accessed December 5, 2016.

27. U.S. Department of Defense, "Report to Congress on U.S.-India Security Cooperation," Washington, DC: U.S. Department of Defense, November 2011, available from *https://www. defense.gov/Portals/1/Documents/pubs/20111101_NDAA_Report_on_ US_India_Security_Cooperation.pdf,* accessed November 30, 2016.

28. Dario Leone, "Cope India: When India's Russian Jets Achieved a Surprising 9:1 Kill Ratio Against U.S. F-15s," *The Aviationist,* May 2, 2014, available from *https://theaviationist. com/2014/05/02/cope-india-2004-results/,* accessed December 4, 2016.

29. Tellis.

30. Ibid.

31. Anja Manuel, *This Brave New World: India, China, and The United States*, New York: Simon & Schuster, 2016, pp. 36, 171.

32. Ankit Panda, "Is India's APEC Membership on the Table at this Year's Summit?," *The Diplomat*, September 8, 2015, available from *https://thediplomat.com/2015/09/is-indias-apec-membership-on-the-table-at-this-years-summit/*, accessed December 8, 2016.

33. Ibid.

34. Liz Zuliani, "The Cost of Corruption in India," *Economy Watch*, April 18, 2011, available from *www.economywatch.com/economy-business-and-finance-news/the-cost-of-corruption-in-india.19-04.html*, accessed December 13, 2016.

35. "Doing Business: Ease of Doing Business in India," The World Bank, n.d., available from *www.doingbusiness.org/data/exploreeconomies/india*, accessed December 13, 2016.

36. "Poverty in India: Causes, Effects, Injustice & Exclusion," October 15, 2013, Poverties, available from *www.poverties.org/blog/poverty-in-india*, accessed December 11, 2016.

37. International Labour Organization, ILOSTAT database, "Data: Employment in agriculture (% of total employment)," The World Bank, March 2017, available from *https://data.worldbank.org/indicator/SL.AGR.EMPL.ZS?view=chart*, accessed December 4, 2017.

38. Manuel, p. 150.

39. Laveesh Bhandari, Jeremy Carl, Bibek Debroy, Michelle Kaffenberger, Pravakar Sahoo, and Derrick Scissors, "Unleashing the Market in the India-U.S. Economic Relationship, Part 1," Washington, DC: The Heritage Foundation, January 7, 2013, available from *www.heritage.org/research/reports/2013/01/unleashing-the-market-in-the-india-us-economic-relationship-part-1*, accessed December 17, 2016.

40. "The Gujarat model," *The Economist*, January 8, 2015, available from *www.economist.com/news/finance-and-economics/21638147-how-modi-nomics-was-forged-one-indias-most-business-friendly-states*, accessed December 14, 2016.

41. Bhandari et al.

42. Bureau of Economic and Business Affairs, "2013 Investment Climate Statement," Washington, DC: U.S. Department of State, February 2013, available from *https://www.state.gov/e/eb/rls/othr/ics/2013/204659.htm*, accessed December 14, 2016.

43. Manuel, p. 213.

44. "Foreign Trade: Trade in Goods with India," United States Census Bureau, n.d., available from *https://www.census.gov/foreign-trade/balance/c5330.html#2015*, accessed December 13, 2016.

45. Sachin Parashar, "India, US agree to restart talks on bilateral investment treaty," *The Times of India*, January 12, 2015, available from *https://timesofindia.indiatimes.com/india/India-US-agree-to-restart-talks-on-bilateral-investment-treaty/articleshow/45846021.cms*, accessed December 20, 2016.

46. David W. Kearn, Jr., "Toward Alliance or Ambivalence: A Theoretical Assessment of U.S.-India Relations," *India Review*, Vol. 13, No. 2, 2014, p. 138.

47. "Largest U.S. Immigrant Groups over Time, 1960-Present," Migration Policy Institute, n.d., available from *www.migrationpolicy.org/programs/data-hub/charts/largest-immigrant-groups-over-time*, accessed December 11, 2016.

48. "About the Fulbright Program," United States-India Educational Foundation, 2011, available from *http://www.usief.org.in/About-USIEF/About-the-Fulbright-Program.aspx*, accessed February 4, 2017.

49. "Working in the United States: Temporary (Nonimmigrant) Workers," U.S. Citizenship and Immigration Services, n.d., available from *https://www.uscis.gov/working-united-states/temporary-nonimmigrant-workers*, accessed March 7, 2017.

50. "U.S. Visa: Reciprocity and Civil Documents by Country," Travel.State.Gov, n.d., available from *https://travel.state.gov/ content/travel/en/us-visas/Visa-Reciprocity-and-Civil-Documents-by-Country.html*, accessed March 8, 2017.

51. Margherita Stancati, "India to Escalate U.S. Visa Row," India Real Time, blog of *The Wall Street Journal*, April 27, 2012, available from *https://blogs.wsj.com/indiarealtime/2012/04/27/india-to-escalate-u-s-visa-row/*, accessed February 5, 2016.

52. Ananya Bhattacharya, "Will the H-1B be worth it for Indian IT firms if the US overhauls its work-visa programs?" Quartz India, January 31, 2017, available from *https://qz.com/899306/will-the-h-1b-be-worth-it-for-indian-it-firms-if-the-us-overhauls-its-work-visa-programs/*, accessed March 8, 2017.

53. Bhandari et al.

54. Julia Preston, "Lawsuits Claim Disney Colluded to Replace U.S. Workers With Immigrants," *The New York Times*, January 25, 2016, available from *https://www.nytimes.com/2016/01/26/ us/lawsuit-claims-disney-colluded-to-replace-us-workers-with-immigrants.html?_r=0*, accessed December 22, 2016.

55. Alessandria Masi, "The Companies Scamming America's H-1B Worker Visa System," Vocativ, February 3, 2014, available from *www.vocativ.com/money/business/theyll-sponsor-american-dream-might-cost-soul/*, accessed December 22, 2016.

56. Shari B. Hochberg, "United States-India Relations: Reconciling the H-1B Visa Hike and Framework for Cooperation on Trade and Investment," *Pace International Law Review,* January 1, 2012, pp. 244-245.

57. Vivek Wadhwa, Anna Lee Saxenian, and F. Daniel Siciliano, "America's New Immigrant Entrepreneurs: Then and Now," Kansas City, Missouri: Ewing Marion Kauffman Foundation, October 2, 2012, available from *www. kauffman.org/what-we-do/research/immigration-and-the-american-economy/americas-new-immigrant-entrepreneurs-then-and-now*, accessed December 18, 2016.

58. Ajay Agrawal, Devesh Kapur, and John McHale, "Brain Drain or Brain Bank? The Impact of Skilled Emigration on Poor-Country Innovation," NBER Working Paper No. 14592, Cambridge, MA: The National Bureau of Economic Research, December 2008, available from *www.nber.org/papers/w14592*, accessed December 18, 2016.

59. Karl, p. 326.

60. Assistant Secretary for South and Central Asian Affairs Richard A. Boucher, "Remarks at the Annual Convention of the American Association of Physicians of Indian Origin, Las Vegas, Nevada," U.S. Department of State 2001-2009 Archive, June 27, 2008, available from *https://2001-2009.state.gov/p/sca/ rls/2008/106476.htm*, accessed December 23, 2016.

CHAPTER 5

JAPAN'S STRATEGIC RENAISSANCE: IMPLICATIONS FOR U.S. POLICY IN THE ASIA-PACIFIC

Neil J. Owens

EXECUTIVE SUMMARY

Japan has responded to what it sees as an increasingly unfavorable strategic situation by implementing a "Proactive Contribution to Peace" policy. As the Trump administration develops its new Asia-Pacific policy, how should the United States approach the U.S.-Japan alliance?

The Japanese perspective is that it needs to assume a greater international leadership role, strengthen its alliance with the United States, and improve the Joint Self Defense Force's deterrent effect. Japan's increased international role will present some risk to the United States, but the biggest risk would be to allow the U.S.-Japan alliance to atrophy.

The United States should continue to encourage Japan to assume an increased international role and pave the way for Japan's new policy by facilitating a closer Japan-South Korea relationship. The United States and Japan should also renegotiate the 2006 Realignment Roadmap that would result in the reduction of U.S. combat power in Japan. A successful renegotiation would result in a plan that reduces the impact of U.S. bases on the Okinawa community, thus maintaining the long-term political viability of a forward-deployed U.S. military posture while maintaining the current level of deterrence. Finally, the United States should encourage Japan to continue its existing public discussion on the regional security environment and on the appropriate role for the United States-Japan alliance to play within it. The ability of the Japanese public to identify the link between the U.S. military presence and Japan's national security will likely serve to strengthen public support for the alliance.

INTRODUCTION

In November 2016, Donald Trump shocked American political culture by securing an upset electoral victory over Democratic nominee Hillary Clinton.[1] Former Secretary of State Clinton held views representative of those within the U.S. foreign policy establishment and was expected to continue former President Barack Obama's strategic "Rebalance" to the Asia-Pacific region. Of the many questions that have emerged from Trump's unexpected victory, some of the most important involve what his presidency will mean for U.S. Asia-Pacific policy. What policy approach will the new administration take? What part will Japan play within it?

Japan is a major power in the Asia-Pacific. An advanced industrial nation that has been on the forefront of cutting-edge technological development and design for decades, it possesses the world's third largest economy and exports advanced manufactured items worldwide.[2] Japan is a successful liberal democracy and shares U.S. views on the importance of democracy, human rights, and the existing rules-based international system. Although it has traditionally followed a modest approach to foreign and defense policy, there is ample evidence that Japan is willing to do more in these areas.

The United States should understand the international environment from Japan's perspective, identify the major elements of Japan's policy response, and highlight the benefits that the U.S.-Japan alliance can provide to the United States.

THE VIEW FROM ICHIGAVA

Japanese strategists see an international environment that is becoming increasingly unstable and decidedly less safe.[3] A palpable shift of global power away from the West and toward the Asia-Pacific brings with it uncertainty and an unwelcome weakening in international leadership and resolve.[4] "Gray zone" situations, in which states employ carefully calibrated levels of force to advance their interests incrementally, while being careful to remain below the threshold that would trigger a military response—are on the rise in the Asia-Pacific.[5] Japan, a self-described maritime nation economically reliant on seaborne trade, is confronting a world in which the principle of freedom of navigation is being challenged by a growing number of states.[6] The international rules and norms that have enabled Japan to navigate its way from post-war ruin to economic ascendancy are increasingly under threat.

This is a significant concern for a state that identifies itself as a "peace-loving nation" and which has rigorously adhered to international rules and norms for over 70 years. Conscious of its early 20th-century history and restrained by a constitution that limits its ability to employ military force abroad, Japan is careful to operate as a responsible international actor. It maintains a defense-oriented, nonthreatening military posture and its "Three Non-Nuclear Principles," which forbid possession, use, and third-party storage of nuclear weapons, demonstrates its deep-seated opposition to nuclear weapons.[7]

Japan views North Korea as the greatest threat to its national security. North Korea's ballistic missile and nuclear weapons development programs appear to be accelerating, and it is currently capable of ranging nearly all Japanese territory.[8] North Korean behavior is provocative and destabilizing, and its aggressive rhetoric is frequently aimed at Japan. North Korea's bizarre Japanese abduction program, in which it kidnapped Japanese citizens and brought them to North Korea in an apparent attempt to improve the quality of its intelligence services, remains a high-profile political issue in Japan.[9]

While North Korea constitutes an immediate threat, China poses a more long-term strategic challenge to Japan's interests. China's economic ascendency has been swift: since the early 1970s, it has undergone "the fastest sustained expansion by a major economy in history." It now boasts the world's second largest economy, is the world's largest manufacturer, and exports more than any other country.[10] Over the past decade, it has placed an increasing emphasis on building a modern, capable military: its defense budget is the world's second largest and is six times larger than that of Japan. Japan estimates that China's military spending has increased by over 300 percent in the years between 2006 and 2016.[11] Most observers believe that China's defense spending is significantly higher than its official documents indicate; the lack of reliable information on China's military budget makes it difficult to determine how it prioritizes its spending or to identify the capabilities that it is trying to develop.[12] Japan maintains that this lack of transparency is troubling because it obscures China's long-term strategic intentions.[13] Even more troubling is that, as China's economic and military power have grown, so too has the aggressiveness with which it pursues its expansive maritime territorial claims. China's behavior in the East China Sea has resulted in significantly increased Japan-China tension.

Japan and China are involved in three closely related East China Sea disputes. The first dispute involves the maritime boundary between Japan's and China's Exclusive Economic Zones (EEZs); although there was a 2008 agreement to negotiate a boundary settlement and to develop hydrocarbon resources jointly in the disputed region, negotiations broke down in 2010 and have yet to restart.[14]

The second dispute involves sovereignty of the resource-rich Senkaku/Diaoyu Islands.[15] The Senkaku Islands — eight uninhabited features claimed by Japan, China, and Taiwan — have been in the possession of Japan for over a century. Although the United States does not take a position on the territorial dispute, it recognizes that Japan "administers" the islands and that they are covered by U.S.-Japan security guarantees.[16] In 2010 and again in 2012, the Senkaku dispute became a flash point between China and Japan. These crises caused significant diplomatic, political, and economic friction, and drove China to increase its civilian Coast Guard patrols dramatically in the disputed waters.[17] Japan views China's Senkaku activity as a "gray zone" attempt to challenge Japan's territorial integrity using non-military means.[18] Japanese and

Chinese Coast Guard vessels now regularly engage each other in tense encounters, and, while both sides behave professionally, the likelihood of a crisis-inducing miscalculation remains uncomfortably high.[19]

The third dispute began in November 2013 when China established an Air Defense Identification Zone (ADIZ) over part of the East China Sea.[20] Japanese military aircraft operating within the declared ADIZ are often intercepted by Chinese military aircraft; meanwhile, the Japan Air Self-Defense Force (JASDF) is regularly forced to scramble to intercept Chinese intrusions into its own ADIZ (see Figure 5-1).[21] Not only does China's military regularly operate within Japan's ADIZ, but many of its flights also violate Japan's territorial airspace over the Senkakus.[22]

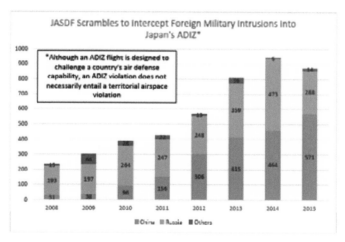

*Although an ADIZ flight is designed to challenge a country's air defense capability, an ADIZ violation does not necessarily entail a territorial airspace violation.

Figure 5-1. JASDF Scrambles to Intercept Foreign Military Intrusions into Japan's ADIZ.[23]

China's actions during these disputes fuel the concern with which Japan views China's rise. China has consistently displayed a willingness to employ every instrument at its disposal to pressure its neighbor and advance its interests; many of the methods used seem escalatory and disproportionate. The de facto embargo of rare earth minerals, the sanction—if not outright encouragement—of violent anti-Japanese protests, the use of heavily-armed maritime craft to challenge disputed maritime boundaries and territorial claims, and the willingness to treat international waters and airspace as its own territory raise troubling questions about China's judgment and its dedication to adhering to the existing rules-based international system.[24]

Japan also has a contentious relationship with Russia.[25] The main area of disagreement is the fate of Japan's four Northern Territories, which Russia seized at the end of World War II and of which both countries claim ownership.[26] Despite some recent optimism that Prime Minister Shinzo Abe of Japan and President Vladimir Putin of Russia would be able to negotiate a settlement, it appears now that the negotiations fell victim to the larger dispute between Russia and the West over Russia's actions in Crimea and Ukraine.[27] Although Russia and Japan cooperate on economic issues, and in particular on hydrocarbon exploration, the Japanese-Russian relationship is tempered by the continuation of Russian military activities in Japanese airspace as well as by Russian unabated efforts to modernize its military capabilities on the disputed islands.[28]

Even Japan's relationship with the Republic of Korea (ROK), a neighbor which shares many of the same security concerns and with which it shares a major ally, is troubled. Despite close economic ties and the recent signing of some modest security agreements, political and diplomatic relations between the two countries are marred by a continuing dispute over the highly-charged legacy of the Korean "comfort women" issue and by a territorial dispute over Takeshima/Dokdo Island.[29] Polling indicates that a sizeable majority of Koreans oppose the 2016 "final" agreement on the comfort woman controversy that the Abe government negotiated with ROK President Park Geun-hye's government.[30] Moon Jae-in, recently elected to replace the impeached President Park, has stated that he thinks the agreement should be revised, and a recent comfort women flare-up has caused Japan to withdraw its ambassador to Korea.[31] These disputes effectively reduce the likelihood of meaningful bilateral security cooperation, complicate the strategic landscape, and serve as an unwelcome reminder to Japan that the legacy of its behavior in World War II can still be difficult to overcome.

Finally, Japan faces major economic and demographic challenges. After 45 years of rapid expansion, Japan's economic growth slowed considerably in the early 1990s and has remained sluggish ever since.[32] A long period of deflation acted as a further drag on the economy, and Japan's government debt is the highest in the world.[33] Japan cannot rely on population growth to alleviate these economic problems, as its population is aging rapidly and is expected to enter a period of steep decline.[34] The prospects of successfully turning these long-term systemic trends around appear dim.

The one bright spot on the horizon for Japanese strategic planners is Japan's alliance with the United States, the undisputed "cornerstone of Japan's security" since the end of World War II.[35] At the heart of the U.S.-Japan alliance is the U.S.-Japan Treaty of Mutual Cooperation and Security, in which the United

States committed itself to Japan's security.[36] By basing its military forces in Japan and extending its nuclear deterrence, the United States enabled Japan to focus on economic development, while de-prioritizing the development of its self-defense forces.[37] At the same time, the U.S.-led security architecture maintained regional stability, enabling a remarkable period of region-wide economic growth. As regional challenges have increased, the United States-Japan alliance has kept pace, and the United States is now heavily involved in Japan's maritime surveillance and ballistic missile defense.[38]

Yet, even the U.S.-Japan relationship is experiencing uncertainty. During his election campaign, Trump implied that Japan should acquire its own nuclear weapons and complained that Japan's funding for U.S. military basing is inadequate.[39] More significantly, he withdrew from the Trans-Pacific Partnership (TPP), a free-trade agreement that the Obama administration viewed as central to its Rebalance to the Pacific policy and which many observed as an essential element of Washington's attempt to maintain its competitive strategic advantage over China.[40] The TPP would have improved economic ties between members and would have further cemented the U.S. leadership role in the Asia-Pacific. Abe's allies in the Japanese Parliament (the Diet) had supported the TPP despite the substantial political risks involved.[41] Although Defense Secretary James Mattis's visit to Tokyo and Abe's trip to Washington in early 2017 provided much needed reassurance, the events of the presidential campaign and of the early days of the Trump administration demonstrated Japan's vulnerability to the whims of American politics.[42] It is likely that profound unease remains in Tokyo.

JAPAN'S RESPONSE: PROACTIVE CONTRIBUTION TO PEACE

Under the leadership of Prime Minister Abe, Japan has instituted an ambitious and multi-faceted approach to confront the challenges. Entitled the "Proactive Contribution to Peace" policy, Japan's new strategic approach will enable it to exert its international influence more effectively.[43] Abe's first step was to establish a National Security Council, which immediately released a *National Security Strategy* (NSS) establishing the foundation of the new policy.

The 2013 *National Security Strategy* articulates Japan's three national security objectives: to increase deterrence, to improve regional security by strengthening the U.S.-Japan alliance and improving Japan's regional ties, and to strengthen the rules-based international order while adopting a leading international role.[44] While it insists that its policy orientation is peaceful in nature, it emphasizes "the international community expects Japan to play a more proactive role for peace and stability in the world, in a way commensurate with its national capabilities."[45] The NSS goes on to describe how, in order to fulfill its international role and safeguard its national interests, Japan must embark upon a series of broad strategic approaches.

The first approach is to both "strengthen and expand" Japan's defense and diplomatic capabilities. This requires Japan to pursue an increased international leadership role aggressively so that it possesses "the power to take the lead in setting the international agenda."[46] This also involves increasing the deterrent effect of the Japan Self-Defense Forces (JSDF) by improving warfighting capabilities, particularly in ways suited to protecting Japan's territorial integrity and maritime security. The JSDF must be integrated into a whole-of-government security architecture that includes law enforcement agencies and local governments, thus enabling Japan to respond seamlessly to a full spectrum of security challenges, from gray zone activities to natural disasters.[47] The *National Defense Program Guidelines for FY2014 and beyond* (NDPG) provides amplifying guidance. It calls for the development of an integrated and more agile "Dynamic Joint Defense Force" capable of deterring potential aggressors; responding to and defeating any attack; and otherwise contributing to regional and global stability.[48] The NDPG prioritizes the development of air and maritime capabilities to enable Japan to monitor and defend its dispersed island territories and defend against the North Korean nuclear threat; areas targeted for improvement include persistent maritime and aerial intelligence, surveillance and reconnaissance, strategic and operational lift, amphibious forces, and ballistic missile defense. While most of the modernization effort is focused on the Air and Maritime Self-Defense Forces, the Ground Self-Defense Force is directed to reduce its reliance on heavy conventional forces in favor of lighter, more agile ones.[49] The NDPG also calls for greater interoperability with the United States and for enhanced joint training.[50]

In order to implement this approach, the Abe government has increased defense spending and loosened the rules prohibiting the export of defense technologies. Japan's defense budget has increased for each of the last 5 years, and its fiscal year (FY) 2017 defense budget is the world's seventh largest.[51] In 2014, the government modified a long-standing prohibition on arms exports, authorizing exports to allies and partners under limited circumstances.[52] This policy is meant to create a more competitive defense industry, increase cooperation with the United States, and reduce per-unit costs for the self-defense forces.[53] Japan now offers major systems for export, increasing the prospect for closer defense ties with regional partners. Its Soryu submarines and Shin Maywa seaplanes are attractive to regional militaries, while the SM-3 Block IIA ship-launched anti-ballistic missile — developed jointly with the United States and an integral part of their combined ballistic missile defense plans — is a candidate for third party sales.[54] Although Japan recently failed in a bid to obtain a contract to build submarines for Australia, its status as a finalist is evidence of the increasing competitiveness of Japan's defense industry.[55]

The second NSS approach is to strengthen the U.S.-Japan alliance to ensure that the United States remains committed to upholding Japan's security requirements. This involves expanding and deepening defense cooperation, ensuring the continued presence of U.S. bases in Japan, and tightening economic ties.[56] The periodic U.S.-Japan secretary-level Security Consultative Committee conference has subsequently gained an increased prominence and formalized alliance defense arrangements. The resulting *Guidelines for Japan-U.S. Defense Cooperation* of 2015 clarifies each state's responsibilities in the event of armed attack, identifies areas in which to improve military interoperability, and establishes a standing "Alliance Coordination Mechanism" (ACM) to improve operational coordination.[57] The ACM is particularly important because it enables the United States and Japan to respond to contingencies without having to establish an ad hoc coordinating framework as they did when responding to the 2011 Great East Japan earthquake and tsunami.[58]

The highly controversial Security Legislation of 2014 was specifically designed to improve the U.S.-Japan alliance; it removed legal restraints, which would potentially have prevented the Japanese from providing military assistance to the United States while it was actively involved in the defense of Japan. This legislation authorized the use of "collective self-defense" in circumscribed circumstances, modestly increased the circumstances in which Japan could provide logistic assistance during United Nations (UN)-led operations, and broadened rules of engagement for certain peacekeeping operations.[59]

The final NSS approaches are designed primarily to strengthen security and diplomatic cooperation with other regional allies, with regional multi-lateral institutions, and with organizations and countries outside of the Asia-Pacific. The Abe government has aggressively undertaken this approach, and in particular, it has emphasized Japan's "special relationship" with Australia and its budding relationship with India.[60] At the same time, Japan has increased its profile within regional institutions such as the Association of Southeast Asia Nations (ASEAN) Regional Forum, the East Asian Summit, and the ASEAN Defense Ministerial Meeting-Plus.[61] Cognizant of the challenge posed by China's aggressive defense of its territorial claims in the South China Sea, Japan has provided several ASEAN nations—including the Philippines, Vietnam, and Indonesia—with funding and equipment to improve their maritime patrol capabilities.[62] These diplomatic initiatives will gradually help build Japan's profile and regional leadership role.

IT'S NOT ALL GOOD NEWS FOR THE UNITED STATES

As the Trump administration develops its Asia-Pacific policy, it should recognize the extraordinary strategic importance of the U.S.-Japan alliance. The United States accrues enormous benefits from the U.S.-led Asia-Pacific security and economic system, and its alliance with Japan constitutes the "cornerstone" of the system.[63] For more than 60 years, the robust U.S. military presence in Japan has ensured regional peace and stability. Japan possesses significant economic clout; the alliance between two of the world's three largest economies is greater than the sum of its parts. Japan is the United States' closest Asian ally and has proven to be a reliable partner. U.S. and Japanese interests align in all major policy areas; Japan shares U.S. liberal values and is dedicated to increasing its role in upholding the U.S.-led international system and the rule of law. Japan cooperates closely with the United States on virtually every issue of significance in the Asia-Pacific, and the importance of this cooperation will only increase as Japan's diplomatic clout grows. The impact of this relationship is global in scope, as the United States and Japan cooperate on economic, diplomatic and security issues such as countering terrorism, providing assistance to developing economies, advancing global health initiatives and fighting infectious diseases, implementing G7 sanctions on Russia, and working toward UN reform.[64] Japan has accommodated the forward basing of U.S. troops for decades, and pays approximately 70 percent of the associated financial costs.[65] Simply put, the U.S.-Japan alliance is a fundamental component of U.S. efforts to safeguard its national interests in the Asia-Pacific and around the world.

The U.S.-Japan alliance is as important as ever due to the deterioration of the security situation in Northeast Asia and in the Asia-Pacific. As challenges mount, it is critical for the United States to ensure it maintains a close relationship with like-minded allies. The United States has consistently stated that it "welcomes the rise of a stable, peaceful, and prosperous China," and while it appears likely that China's relative power will continue to grow, it is unclear if it will develop into a country that respects and adheres to existing international rules and norms.[66] A U.S.-Japan alliance is essential to ensure continued deterrence of North Korea, to serve as an effective bulwark against any Chinese attempt to dominate the region, and to help guarantee the continued existence of a security and economic framework that provides peace and prosperity for the Asia-Pacific.

Japan's strategic renaissance poses some risks to U.S. national interests: one risk is that Japan, emboldened by U.S. security guarantees, may escalate the East China Sea conflicts; a second is that others in the Northeast Asia — particularly South Korea and China — may resist Japan's attempts to pursue a more active role in regional affairs.[67] Although these risks should not be discounted entirely, they can be mitigated and are outweighed by the benefits that Japan's new policy provides.

The greatest risk is that Japan, knowing that the United States is committed to backstopping Japan's national security, would escalate the Senkakus dispute in an attempt to demonstrate conclusively its sovereignty and permanently resolve the dispute in its favor. This could result in an armed conflict between the United States and China over a few uninhabited islands. This risk is unlikely to develop, however, because it would not be in keeping with Japan's over-whelmingly non-aggressive approach to foreign policy. It is unlikely that Japan would choose an aggressive course because it would significantly damage its security interests were it to be unsuccessful. Moreover, as the stronger power in the alliance, the United States has enough leverage over Japan to ensure that it does nothing that the United States would consider overly provocative.

The second risk is that other states in Northeast Asia would actively resist Japan's efforts to implement its new policy approach. Neither the Korean nor the Chinese people have forgotten the atrocities that Imperial Japan inflicted during the 20th century, and those memories color their views of modern Japan. The ill will that these memories generate is exacerbated by the well-publicized behavior of Japanese nationalists and some members of the Abe government.[68] There is a risk that either South Korea or China — or both — could use these issues as justification to challenge the legitimacy of Abe's policy approach and of Japan's efforts to increase its international role. This could reduce the scope of Japan-ROK cooperation, complicate efforts to resolve East China Sea disputes or respond to North Korean provocations, and reduce the willingness of either the ROK or China to cooperate with the United States on other issues.

To mitigate this risk, Japan will need to work to convince its neighbors of its benign intent. As Japan's relationship with the ROK demonstrates, this will be neither quick nor easy. Japan can point to its 70-year tradition of adhering to international rules and norms, and in the case of the ROK, can point to shared interests. The United States can assist in this effort. While it is unlikely that China will recognize that Japan's policy is purely defensive, it is not clear that Japan's new approach will dramatically change the status quo of the difficult Japan-China relationship.

The biggest risks to U.S. national interests are not associated with Japan's new policy; rather, they are related either to the United States weakening the alliance itself deliberately or through inaction. Twenty years ago, Zbigniew Brzezinski wrote that, unmoored from its only alliance, "A disoriented Japan would be like a beached whale, thrashing helplessly but dangerously"; such a scenario "would spell the end of the American role in the Asia-Pacific."[69] Ultimately, Japan has other options available to it, as unpalatable as those options may be to both Japan and the United States. Were Japan to doubt the inviolability of U.S. security guarantees, or were it to determine that there was no place for a U.S.-Japan alliance in an "America First" policy, then there is a real possibility that Japan would have to develop a security strategy that does not involve the United States. Japan would have three options: it could develop an East Asian security system which did not involve the United States but which was able to balance against China; it could develop an independent method of maintaining its own security and deterring potential adversaries; or it could learn to accommodate China's regional interests. The first two options seem unlikely: as a major economic and military power, China would be difficult for East Asian states to balance against; moreover, China has proven its ability to disrupt any regional consensus that runs counter to its interests.[70] It is unlikely that Japan could develop sufficient conventional military power to effectively deter North Korea and, if necessary, China. Although Japan possesses the capability to develop a nuclear deterrent, it is unlikely that it would overcome its overwhelming, deep-seated political and cultural resistance to doing so. Which leaves accommodation of China.

Despite the historical antagonism between Japan and China, there is a logic to such an approach: why balance against Asia's ascending major power when Japan can gain a measure of security by bandwagoning with it instead? After all, China has significant leverage over North Korea should it decide to use it, so China could significantly reduce the severity of the threat that North Korea poses to Japan. Moreover, China would also be more likely to negotiate over the Senkakus if to do so would enable it to drive a wedge between Japan and the United States or to draw Japan into its orbit. Should the Japanese come to view the United States as unreliable, Japan may reluctantly decide that its safest course is to reconcile itself to the inevitability of Chinese regional hegemony and to accommodate China's supplanting of the United States.

Barring the emergence of a domestic political or economic crisis that derails China's continued growth or internal stability, such a policy would increase the likelihood of China's ascendance to regional hegemony from a mere possibility to a virtual certainty. The United States would find that its influence in Northeast Asia and in the greater East Asian region would be greatly diminished. Japan and other Asia-Pacific nations would have to subordinate their interests to those of China in order to maintain harmonious relations. Slowly but surely, China would reshape established rules and norms of regional behavior to fit its interests. Although China has benefitted tremendously from the existing international system, it is not wedded to it, and if it were in a position to set the rules it would likely do so in a way that undermined U.S. values and weakened U.S. economic and security interests.[71]

Fortunately, the likelihood of this occurring is low; Japan shows little interest in foregoing its liberal values or in subordinating its interests to China's. Japan has amply demonstrated that it is wedded to a rules-based international approach grounded in liberal values. It also shares a long, conflict prone history with China, and the associated historical baggage decreases the likelihood of cooperation.[72] Although the possibility is low, it is not non-existent. The Proactive Contribution to Peace policy makes clear that "Japan cannot secure its own peace and security by itself," so if the United States should demonstrate indifference to Japan's security interests, then it may be forced to seek help elsewhere.[73] There is recent precedence for such an approach. During his short-lived 2009-2010 administration, Prime Minister Yukio Hatoyama had intended to prioritize Japan's relationship with China over its relationship with the United States.[74] Although Hatoyama's approach did not represent a full formal repudiation of the U.S.-Japan alliance, it is hard to see how the United States would have fit into the integrated East Asian system that Hatoyama envisioned.[75] The Hatoyama administration should be seen as a cautionary tale that demonstrates the U.S.-Japan alliance is not something that the United States should take for granted.

RECOMMENDATION FOR U.S. POLICY

So what policy approaches should the new Trump administration take toward Japan? First and foremost, the Trump administration should continue to encourage Japan as it develops and implements its new policy. Japan's strategic renaissance can bring tremendous benefits to the United States. As one former U.S. official said of the Abe administration's policies, "As far as we're concerned it's all good news."[76] The more Japan assumes a leadership role in the Asia-Pacific, the more it is able to advance shared Japanese-U.S. interests. As Japan develops closer relationships with other U.S. allies such as Australia, its actions will serve to reinforce the U.S.-led security and economic order. Japan will also be in a better position to use its heightened diplomatic profile to assist the United States in improving its relationship with important regional states such as Vietnam.[77] Although the occasionally cautious and incremental nature of Japan's policy changes may lead to some frustration in Washington, a stronger Japan will strengthen U.S. ability to safeguard its own national interests in the long run.

The United States should also help pave the way for Japan's new policy by facilitating a closer Japan-ROK relationship. Both Japan and South Korea play a critical role in ensuring stability in Northeast Asia, but their difficult relationship complicates regional security. The United States should facilitate the improvement of the Japan-South Korea relationship by employing what Mark Manyin from the Congressional Research Service refers to as the "Commissioner" method of managing the dispute. In this model, the United States would focus on advancing the South Korea-Japan-U.S. trilateral relationship, thereby providing a mechanism for Japanese and South Korean officials to work together to advance common interests without allowing ongoing disputes to derail cooperation.[78] Even if this trilateral relationship is focused exclusively on security issues, it can serve as a foundation for a more comprehensive political and diplomatic relationship.

Japan has recent experience in this regard: Japan's relationship with Australia began as a pragmatic military relationship but has since blossomed into a successful strategic partnership.[79] Ultimately, successful U.S. efforts to improve the Japan-South Korea relationship would significantly advance the national security interests of all three states.

At the same time, the United States should continue to communicate its disapproval when members of the Abe cabinet appease or otherwise support Japanese nationalists and ultra-nationalists. The statements and actions of Abe and his cabinet members, which include trips to the controversial Yasukuni shrine, attempt to obscure Japanese responsibility for the Pacific war. Statements that seek to minimize the depravity of—or simply deny the existence of—wartime atrocities inflicted by Imperial Japan are not only historically inappropriate, they are also damaging to Japan's efforts to improve regional relationships and to increase its diplomatic leadership role.[80]

The United States should reciprocate Japanese efforts to strengthen the alliance. One way to do this is to deepen U.S.-Japan economic ties. Although the Trump administration has chosen to pull out of the TPP, the administration has indicated that it is interested in pursuing a bilateral Free Trade Agreement (FTA) with Japan in its place.[81] Such an agreement would deliver net benefits to both countries by reducing barriers to trade and anti-competitive subsidies. Although Japan is the fourth largest U.S. trading partner, it maintains steep import tariffs and quotas to protect its agricultural industry; the United States provides the largest share of Japan's agricultural imports, so it has much to gain if an FTA reduces Japan's protectionist policies.[82]

The United States should also work with Japan to renegotiate the 2006 Realignment Roadmap. Although the Roadmap was an appropriate response to the political and security situation of 2006, it is no longer suited to fulfill the policy goals of either the United States or Japan in the new, more challenging security environment. The Realignment Roadmap, which reduces the U.S. military footprint in Okinawa by rebasing some U.S. units elsewhere in the Pacific, was designed to "maintain deterrence and to mitigate the impact of U.S. forces on the local communities."[83] Yet, while it successfully reduces the impact of U.S. forces on some Okinawan communities, it fails to maintain, and indeed weakens, deterrence. In light of increased Asia-Pacific security challenges, it is counterproductive for the United States to reduce its combat power in Japan and disperse it westward and eastward across the Pacific. As one senior U.S. military officer commented while looking at a map that depicted the planned realignment, "All the arrows are moving in the wrong direction."[84] It reduces military capability and signals a weakening of U.S. resolve, thus reducing deterrence during an uncertain and increasingly unstable time.[85]

Advocates for the current plan argue that, while the plan is far from ideal, reducing the impact of the U.S. military presence on Okinawa is critical in order to maintain the "long-term political viability" of the U.S.-Japan alliance.[86] Yet, it is possible to do this without reducing deterrence. The United States and Japan should continue with the elements of the existing Roadmap that reduce the military footprint on Okinawa but rebase the displaced units elsewhere in Japan. This would fulfill the original intent of the Roadmap: it would reduce the impact of U.S. basing on Okinawa, maintain deterrence, signal U.S. resolve, and reassure Japan of U.S. commitment.[87]

Finally, the United States should encourage Japan to continue its existing public discussion on the regional security environment and on the appropriate roles for Japan and for the U.S.-Japan alliance to play within it.[88] Recent polling demonstrates that the Japanese consider the United States a reliable partner, and that a majority of Japanese support the U.S.-Japan alliance.[89] This support is crucial for the continued political viability of a robust U.S. military presence in Japan; the ability of the Japanese public to identify the link between U.S. basing and Japan's security will strengthen public support for the alliance. Japan is facing an increasingly challenging security environment, and Japanese citizens are well served by an informed public discussion on the challenges that exist and on the options available to Japan. In the long run this will not only increase the popular consensus that underlies Japanese decision making, it will also help to improve the U.S.-Japan alliance by increasing the public's understanding of the important role that the United States plays, and that U.S. military bases and forces play, in Japan's defense.

CONCLUSION: GETTING READY FOR THE ASIAN CENTURY

Although it is notoriously difficult to determine the shape of the future international environment, current economic and demographic trends indicate that the Asia-Pacific region will continue to grow in importance. The United States will want to ensure that it is positioned properly to take advantage of the opportunities that these trends bring, while ensuring that it can continue to safeguard its national interests. The U.S.-Japan alliance is sure to play a vital role in those efforts. Yet, as Japan evaluates its regional environment, it has recognized that the policy approaches that have served it so well over the past half-century are no longer suited to the challenges that it faces. Japan recognizes that the security situation in Northeast Asia is gradually deteriorating, so its response has been to reinvigorate its foreign and defense policies to enable it to increase its contribution to regional and global stability. Ultimately, this new policy approach serves the interests of both Japan and the United States. As the Trump administration designs and implements its own Asia-Pacific policy, it should seek to ensure that it remains firmly anchored upon the hugely beneficial U.S.-Japan alliance.

ENDNOTES - CHAPTER 5

1. The author would like to thank the following for generously agreeing to meet for interviews: Hideshi Tokuchi, Senior Fellow, National Graduate Institute For Policy Studies; Taro Yamato, Director, Japan-U.S. Defense Cooperation Division, Defense Policy Bureau, Ministry of Defense; Daisuke Aoyama, National Security Policy Division, Foreign Policy Bureau, Ministry of Foreign Affairs, Tomohiko Satake, Senior Research Fellow, Policy Studies Department, National Institute for Defense Studies;

Colonel Makino JGSDF, Commander Okasaki JMSDF, Lieutenant Colonel Ogawa, and Lieutenant Colonel Kasai from the Joint Staff Office/J5, Ministry of Defense, and Lieutenant Colonel Otsuka from the Ground Staff Office G5, Ministry of Defense. I would also like to thank the following for helping set up interviews: Colonel Kei Sekiguchi, Director, Japan Peacekeeping Training and Research Center; Etsuko Kanno from the National Institute of Defense Studies; Kumiko Horimoto from the Japan-U.S. Defense Cooperation Division, Bureau of Defense Policy, Ministry of Defense; Colonel Shigemi Sugimura, a fellow student at the U.S. Army War College: Miho Higashi from the Tohoku Defense Bureau; Lieutenant Colonel Paula Marshall, the U.S. Marine Attaché; and Major Daniel Benson, Marine Forces Pacific Liaison Officer to the Ground Staff Office. I'd also like to thank the following personnel from the Supply, Services and Support Division at the Bureau of Local Cooperation, Ministry of Defense, for their generous hospitality during my visit: Mayu Inoue, Hisanao Ohara, Tomoko Otsu, and Yoko Yamamoto. Finally, I would like to thank Mr. Nicholas Szechenyi, from the Center for Strategic and International Studies, for his assistance and advice.

2. The European Union is often listed ahead of Japan, but is excluded from these rankings because it represents a group of states. See World Bank, "Gross domestic product 2016," April 17, 2017, World Development Indicators database, available from *databank.worldbank.org/data/download/GDP.pdf*, accessed December 1, 2017; Central Intelligence Agency, "Japan," *The World Factbook*, Washington, DC: Central Intelligence Agency, updated November 14, 2017, available from *https://www.cia.gov/library/publications/the-world-factbook/geos/ja.html*, accessed December 1, 2017.

3. Ichigaya is the neighborhood in which the Japan Ministry of Defense (MOD) is located. The author has heard it referred to by MOD employees as "Ichigaya Prison" due to the surprisingly long hours that MOD employees are expected to work while the Diet is in session. It is not unusual for MOD civilian employees to work until 2 or 3 a.m.

4. Office of the Prime Minister of Japan, *National Security Strategy*, Provisional Translation published on Official Website of the Prime Minister of Japan and His Cabinet, December 17, 2013, p. 6, available from *https://japan.kantei.go.jp/96_abe/*

documents/2013/__icsFiles/afieldfile/2013/12/18/NSS.pdf, accessed September 15, 2016; also Office of The Cabinet Secretariat, "Cabinet Decision on Development of Seamless Security Legislation to Ensure Japan's Survival and Protect its People," Provisional Translation published on Official Website of The Cabinet Secretariat, July 1, 2014, p. 1, available from *www.cas.go.jp/jp/gaiyou/jimu/pdf/anpohosei_eng.pdf*, accessed September 15, 2016.

5. Office of the Prime Minister of Japan, *National Security Strategy*, p. 11.

6. Ibid., pp. 2, 8-9. For information on Japan's dependence on trade, see Observatory of Economic Complexity (OEC) at the Massachusetts Institute of Technology Media Lab, "Japan," OEC, n.d., available from *https://atlas.media.mit.edu/en/profile/country/jpn/*, accessed February 19, 2017; Central Intelligence Agency, "Japan."

7. Ministry of Foreign Affairs of Japan, "Japan: Path of 60 Years as a Nation Striving for Peace (Fact Sheet)," published on Website of the Ministry of Foreign Affairs, July 2005, available from *www.mofa.go.jp/policy/postwar/60th.html*, accessed February 12, 2017; also Ministry of Foreign Affairs of Japan, *60 Years: The Path of a Nation Striving for Global Peace*, published on Website of the Ministry of Foreign Affairs, July 2005, p. 3, available from *www.mofa.go.jp/policy/postwar/pamph60.pdf*, accessed February 12, 2017; Office of the Prime Minister of Japan, *National Security Strategy*. Although many criticize Japan for failure to address its World War II behavior fully, Japan's foreign policy has clearly been shaped by a recognition of its wartime activities. While "nonthreatening" is in the eye of the beholder, a persuasive case can be made that Japan has adopted a nonaggressive, defense-oriented posture.

8. Between January 6 and October 20, 2016, there were two nuclear tests and 15 ballistic missile/satellite launches, while between May 1993 and the end of 2015, there were three nuclear tests and 14 satellite/missile launches. Most analysts believe that North Korea's Nondong and Taepodong-1 missiles are nuclear-capable; these missiles can range nearly the entirety of Japan. Daisuke Aoyama, National Security Policy Division, Ministry of Foreign Affairs, "Japan's greater contribution to peace, security and stability in Asia," briefing slides and interview by author,

Tokyo, Japan, Ministry of Foreign Affairs, January 12, 2017. See also David E. Sanger and Choe Sang-Hun, "As North Korea's Nuclear Program Advances, U.S. Strategy Is Tested," *The New York Times*, May 6, 2016, available from *https://www.nytimes. com/2016/05/07/world/asia/north-korea-nuclear-us-strategy.html*, accessed February 17, 2017; Scott A. Snyder, Darcie Draudt, and Sungtae "Jacky" Park, *The Korean Pivot: Seoul's Strategic Choices and Rising Rivalries in Northeast Asia: A Council on Foreign Relations Discussion Paper*, Washington, DC: Council on Foreign Relations Press, February 2017, p. 5, Council on Foreign Relations website, available from *https://www.cfr.org/sites/default/files/pdf/2017/01/ Discussion_Paper_Snyder_Draudt_Park_Korean_Pivot_OR.pdf*, accessed February 17, 2017.

9. Shinzo Abe championed the abduction issue early on, enabling him to increase his public profile and accelerate his political career. See Choe Sang-Hun, "North Korea Cancels Investigation Into Abductions of Japanese Citizens," *The New York Times*, February 13, 2016, available from *https://www.nytimes. com/2016/02/14/world/asia/north-korea-japan-abductions.html?_r=1*, accessed February 13, 2017; also Elizabeth C. Economy, "Podcast: The True Story of North Korea's Abduction Project," *Asia Unbound,* blog of the Council on Foreign Relations, November 15, 2016, available from *https://www.cfr.org/blog/podcast-true-story-north-koreas-abduction-project*, accessed February 13, 2017.

10. World Bank, "The World Bank In China: Overview," updated March 28, 2017, World Bank webpage, available from *http://www.worldbank.org/en/country/china/overview*, accessed December 1, 2017; Central Intelligence Agency, "China," *The World Factbook*, Washington, DC: Central Intelligence Agency, updated November 14, 2017, available from *https://www.cia.gov/library/ publications/the-world-factbook/geos/ch.html*, accessed December 1, 2017; World Bank, "Gross domestic product 2016."

11. Ian E. Rinehart, *The Chinese Military: Overviews and Issues for Congress*, Washington, DC: Congressional Research Service, U.S. Library of Congress, March 24, 2016, p. 21, available from *https://fas.org/sgp/crs/row/R44196.pdf*, accessed September 17, 2016; Aoyama, "Japan's greater contribution to peace, security and stability in Asia," briefing slides. It is difficult to obtain accurate information on Chinese defense expenditures; most observers

believe that actual expenditures exceed those published by official Chinese sources. "Actual" budget data is subject to debate; for instance, the U.S. Department of Defense estimated China's 2012 defense budget increase at 10.7 percent, while some observers estimated that the increase was as high as 18-20 percent. For more on China's defense spending, see David Helvey, "Department of Defense Press Briefing on the 2013 DoD Report to Congress on Military and Security Developments Involving the People's Republic of China in the Pentagon Briefing Room," press release, U.S. Department of Defense Information/Federal Information and News Dispatch, May 6, 2013; see also Office of the Secretary of Defense, *Annual Report to Congress: Military and Security Developments Involving the People's Republic of China 2015*, Washington, DC: U.S. Department of Defense, May 2016, pp. 49-50, U.S. Department of Defense website, available from *https://www.defense.gov/Portals/1/Documents/pubs/2015_China_Military_Power_Report.pdf*, accessed February 18, 2017. For information on Japan's 2016 military budget, see Fanz-Stefan Gady, "Japan Approves Record Defense Budget," *The Diplomat*, December 28, 2015, available from *https://thediplomat.com/2015/12/japan-approves-record-defense-budget/*, accessed February 18, 2017.

12. China Power Team, "What does China really spend on its military?" China Power, December 28, 2015, updated August 4, 2017, available from *chinapower.csis.org/military-spending/*, accessed December 1, 2017.

13. Office of the Prime Minister of Japan, *National Defense Program Guidelines for FY2014 and beyond (Summary)*, December 17, 2013, published on Official Website of the Prime Minister of Japan and His Cabinet, available from *https://japan.kantei.go.jp/96_abe/documents/2013/__icsFiles/afieldfile/2013/12/27/NDPG(Summary).pdf*, accessed September 15, 2016; also Ministry of Foreign Affairs of Japan, *Diplomatic Bluebook*, published on Website of the Ministry of Foreign Affairs, 2016, pp. 2-4, 156, available from *http://www.mofa.go.jp/policy/other/bluebook/index.html*. The *Bluebook* mentions China's lack of military spending transparency 10 times.

14. According to the United Nations Convention on the Law of the Sea (UNCLOS), which both China and Japan are a party to, an Exclusive Economic Zone (EEZ) extends 200 nautical miles (NM) from a state's shores and provides exclusive rights to the

fishing and minerals/hydrocarbons located within and beneath it. Unfortunately, not all of the East China Sea is wide enough to accommodate two 200 NM EEZs. Japan's position is that the EEZ boundary lies along the half-way point between Japan and China, while China maintains that, due to the existence of a continental shelf extending from its coast, the EEZ boundary lies at the edge of Japan's territorial waters 12 NM west of Okinawa. In 2015, Japan accused China of extracting oil and gas near the disputed boundary in violation of the joint agreement, while China argued that its drilling activities are well within its EEZ. This dispute is about more than just sovereignty; both Japan and China depend on imported energy and view the hydrocarbon resources under the East China Sea as a way to mitigate their energy dependence. To further complicate matters, China's position that it has the authority to regulate foreign military activity within its EEZ, a position which, when China attempts to enforce it, further increases tension for all military forces that operate in the area, including the United States. Most states explicitly reject China's position because EEZs are considered international waters for purposes not involving resource management. For more on EEZs and international law, see National Oceanic and Atmospheric Administration (NOAA) Office of General Counsel, "Maritime Zones and Boundaries," NOAA, last updated May 19, 2017, available from *www.gc.noaa.gov/gcil_maritime.html*, accessed December 1, 2017. For more on the details of the Japan-China EEZ dispute, see Shelia A. Smith, "Japan and the East China Sea Dispute," *Orbis,* Summer 2012, pp. 381-382. For more on Japan's argument that China is extracting resources in the disputed area in violation of the 2008 agreement, see Nicholas Szechenyi, "Platforms of Mistrust: Natural Resource Development in the East China Sea," Analysis, Asia Maritime Transparency Initiative, August 5, 2015, available from *https://amti.csis.org/platforms-of-mistrust-natural-resource-development-in-the-east-china-sea*, accessed January 20, 2017. For the importance that both countries place on the hydrocarbon and fishing resources, see Ronald O'Rourke, *Maritime Territorial and Exclusive Economic Zone (EEZ) Disputes Involving China: Issues for Congress,* Washington, DC: Congressional Research Service, U.S. Library of Congress, May 31, 2016, pp. 2-3, available from *https://fas.org/sgp/crs/row/R42784.pdf*, accessed January 20, 2017; Andrew Stocking and Terry Dinan, "China's Growing Energy Demand: Implications for the United States," *Working Paper Series*, Washington, DC: Congressional Budget Office, June

2015, pp. 2-4, Congressional Budget Office website, available from *https://www.cbo.gov/sites/default/files/114th-congress-2015-2016/ workingpaper/50216-China_1.pdf*, accessed January 28, 2017. For more on China's claims regarding its authority within its EEZ, see O'Rourke, *"Maritime Territorial and Exclusive Economic Zone (EEZ) Disputes Involving China,"* pp. 10-14.

15. The islands are known by the Japanese as the "Senka-ku-shoto," by the Chinese as the "Diaoyu Dao," and by the Tai-wanese as the "Diaoyutai Lieyu." The term "Senkaku Islands" or "Senkakus" will be used throughout this book. It is unclear if the features would be recognized as "islands" under interna-tional law. Geologists estimate that there are significant hydrocar-bon resources in the immediate area. The United States actually administered the islands for an 18-year period after World War II. Taiwan and Japan have successfully managed their compet-ing territorial claims in the Senkakus. In 2013, Taiwan and Japan came to an agreement over fishing rights in the vicinity of the Senkakus, and while the agreement does not address issues of sovereignty, it succeeded in effectively reducing the likelihood of a dispute. See Mark E. Manyin, *The Senkakus (Diaoyu/Diaoyu-tai) Dispute: U.S. Treaty Obligations,* Washington, DC: Congressio-nal Research Service, U.S. Library of Congress, October 14, 2016, pp. 1, 2-4, 9, available from *https://fas.org/sgp/crs/row/R42761.pdf*, accessed December 29, 2016.

16. Ibid., pp. 5-8; Ankit Panda, "Obama: Senkakus Covered Under US-Japan Security Treaty," *The Diplomat*, April 24, 2014, available from *https://thediplomat.com/2014/04/obama-senkakus-covered-under-us-japan-security-treaty/*, accessed December 29, 2016; Manyin, *The Senkakus*, pp. 6-8; Shelia A. Smith, "Behind Japan, 100%," *Asia Unbound,* blog of the Council on Foreign Rela-tions, February 13, 2017, available from *https://www.cfr.org/blog/ behind-japan-100*, accessed February 19, 2017.

17. In September 2010, the Japan Coast Guard arrested a Chi-nese fishing boat captain in the Senkakus, sparking a diplomatic crisis that quickly took on an economic hue when China imposed an "unofficial" restriction on Japan-bound mineral exports. In China, there were anti-Japanese protests and Japanese businessmen were arrested; while in Japan, the crisis led to increased political acri-mony and accusations of diplomatic mismanagement. Although

the immediate crisis passed when Japan released the Chinese captain without charge, the underlying tensions remained. In 2012, a second crisis erupted when, in order to prevent the nationalist Mayor of Tokyo from taking ownership of some of the Senkakus, the Japanese government purchased several of the islands from its private Japanese owners (the Japanese government had already owned the remaining five islands). This crisis was significantly more severe, and, like the first crisis, involved widespread and often violent anti-Japanese protests that negatively affected Japanese companies. China has subsequently declared that the waters around the Senkakus are Chinese territorial waters. Chinese Coast Guard ships now frequently enter Japanese waters around the Senkakus: in the 2 years between November 2014 and November 2016, Chinese Coast Guard vessels entered Japanese contiguous waters—24 nautical miles (NM) around the Senkakus—every 2 days on average, while entering Japan's 12 NM territorial waters an average of three times a month. Chinese vessels entered Japanese territorial waters five times in the first 45 days of 2017. See Smith, "Japan and the East China Sea Dispute," pp. 374-380; Paul J. Smith, "The Senkaku/Diaoyu Island Controversy: A Crisis Postponed," *Naval War College Review*, Vol. 66, No. 2, Spring 2013, pp. 27-28, available from *https://www.usnwc.edu/getattachment/bfa92a47-1f5f-4c23-974c-f92e1ed27be4/the-Senkaku-Diaoyu-Island-Controversy--A-Crisis-Po.aspx*, accessed January 1, 2017. The Council on Foreign Relations website provides a good overview of the disputes in both the South and East China Seas. See Council on Foreign Relations, "China's Maritime Disputes: A CFR InfoGuide Presentation," available from *https://www.cfr.org/interactives/chinas-maritime-disputes#!/*, accessed December 29, 2016. For information on Chinese territorial intrusions, see Aoyama, "Japan's greater contribution to peace, security and stability in Asia," briefing slides; NHK World, "China vessels enter Japanese waters near Senkakus," NHK World News, February 18, 2017; Council on Foreign Relations, "China's Maritime Disputes"; "Beijing submits East China Sea claims to the UN," *Taipei Times*, December 12, 2012.

18. Many of these Coast Guard vessels are converted Chinese People's Liberation Army Navy (PLAN) ships, and some of them are larger than conventional destroyers. China's use of heavily armed "law enforcement" Coast Guard craft, which can outgun and out power Japan Coast Guard craft (significant when

encounters occasionally involve deliberate ramming), can be viewed as a deliberate attempt to blur the line between the civilian and military sphere. On the one hand, Japan's Coast Guard vessels are underpowered to respond effectively to China's Coast Guard vessels, but on the other, China could accuse Japan of escalating tensions if it were to use Maritime Self-Defense Force vessels against Chinese "civil law enforcement" craft. Asia Maritime Transparency Initiative, "East China Sea Tensions: Approaching a Slow Boil," Analysis, Asia Maritime Transparency Initiative, April 14, 2016, available from *https://amti.csis.org/east-china-sea-tensions/*, accessed January 4, 2017.

19. Ibid.

20. The ADIZ boundaries closely mirror the boundaries of China's claimed EEZ, and include the airspace over the Senkaku Islands. This particular ADIZ is unusual in that it places burdensome requirements on commercial aircraft—even those that are not bound for China—that are customarily only imposed over territorial airspace. Although Japan and many other countries refuse to recognize the ADIZ, some 60 commercial carriers now submit flight plans with the Chinese government for flights which transit the ADIZ, even if those flights will never enter into Chinese airspace. See Matthew Waxman, "China's ADIZ At One Year: International Legal Issues," Analysis, Asia Maritime Transparency Initiative, November 25, 2014, available from *https://amti.csis.org/chinas-adiz-at-one-year-international-legal-issues*, accessed January 1, 2017; NOAA; Zhu Feng, "China's First ADIZ Decision: One Year Later," Analysis, Asia Maritime Transparency Initiative, November 25, 2014, available from *https://amti.csis.org/chinas-first-adiz-decision-one-year-later/*, accessed January 1, 2017.

21. In 2015, the Japan Air Self-Defense Force (JASDF) scrambled 571 times to meet Chinese military aircraft violating Japanese territorial airspace. The JASDF also frequently had to scramble to meet Russian military aircraft that regularly violated its airspace. Aoyama, "Japan's greater contribution to peace, security and stability in Asia," briefing slides; see also Feng; Shelia A. Smith, *Japan's New Politics and the U.S.-Japan Alliance,* Council on Foreign Relations Special Report, Washington DC: Council on Foreign Relations Press, 2014, p. 19, available from *https://www.cfr.org/report/japans-new-politics-and-us-japan-alliance,* accessed January

1, 2017; Asia Maritime Transparency Initiative, "East China Sea Tensions: Approaching a Slow Boil."

22. Japan Ministry of Defense, "Organizations Responsible for the Defense of Japan, and Effective Deterrence and Handling (Part III, Section 1, Chapter 2)," in *Defense of Japan 2016,* Defense White Paper, pp. 285-287, Ministry of Defense, available from *www.mod.go.jp/e/publ/w_paper/pdf/2016/DOJ2016_3-1-2_web.pdf,* accessed March 25, 2017.

23. Aoyama, "Japan's greater contribution to peace, security and stability in Asia," briefing slides. This figure is a variation on one of the slides in the presentation.

24. News reports indicate that these protests were encouraged by state-run media and sanctioned by Chinese authorities. For information on China's sanctioning of protests, see "Anti-Japan protests across China over islands dispute," BBC News, August 19, 2012, available from *www.bbc.com/news/world-asia-19312226,* accessed February 18, 2017; "Anti-Japan protests hit China cities amid island row," BBC News, September 15, 2012, available from *www.bbc.com/news/world-asia-china-19609945,* accessed February 18, 2017; N.D., Shanghai, "Anti-Japan protests: Outrage, to a point," Analects China blog of *The Economist,* September 17, 2012, online, available from *www.economist.com/blogs/analects/2012/09/anti-japan-protests,* accessed February 18, 2017. For information on the mineral embargo, see Smith, "Japan and the East China Sea Dispute," pp. 375-376.

25. Despite a functioning diplomatic and economic relationship, the two countries are not technically at peace because Russia never signed the 1951 San Francisco Peace Treaty that ended World War II in the Pacific.

26. The four islands extend from Hokkaido toward the Kuril Islands; the United States recognizes Japanese sovereignty over the islands. Mira Rapp-Hooper, "A Treaty To End WWII For Russia And Japan?" Analysis, Asia Maritime Transparency Initiative, December 3, 2014, available from *https://amti.csis.org/a-treaty-to-end-wwii-for-russia-and-japan/,* accessed February 18, 2017.

27. An attempt to sign a treaty in 1956, which would have returned the two southern-most islands to Japan, failed over

the fate of the remaining two islands. See Ibid.; Shelia A. Smith, "Putin's Japan Visit," Asia Unbound, blog of the Council on Foreign Relations, December 19, 2016, available from *https://www.cfr.org/blog/putins-japan-visit*, accessed February 18, 2017.

28. Ibid.; Ministry of Foreign Affairs, *Diplomatic Bluebook*, pp. 122-124; Aoyama, "Japan's greater contribution to peace, security and stability in Asia," briefing slides.

29. Japan and the ROK are each other's third largest trading partner. In 2016, the two countries joined with their common ally, the United States, to develop a trilateral intelligence sharing mechanism and to participate in a trilateral missile defense exercise. Although these are positive developments, they are overshadowed by the continued legacy of the "comfort women," who the Japanese forced into prostitution during its brutal Imperial-era occupation of the Korean peninsula. Emotions regarding Takeshima—which Japan claims but which the ROK occupies—run high, and one observer notes that for the South Korean public, "attachment to Dokdo has assumed a quasi-religious tenor." See Ministry of Foreign Affairs, *Diplomatic Bluebook*, pp. 31-32, 35, 37, 40; also Scott A. Snyder, "Japan-South Korea Relations in 2016: A Return to the Old Normal," Asia Unbound, blog of the Council on Foreign Relations, September 23, 2016, available from *https://www.cfr.org/blog/japan-south-korea-relations-2016-return-old-normal*, accessed February 19, 2017. For information on Takeshima/Dokdo, see Krista E. Wiegand, "The South Korean-Japanese security relationship and the Dokdo/Takeshima islets dispute," *The Pacific Review*, Vol. 28, No. 3, July 2015, pp. 349-350, 353-356; also Mark E. Manyin, "Managing Japan-South Korea Tensions," Council on Foreign Relations Discussion Paper, December 2015, p. 10, available from *https://www.cfr.org/sites/default/files/pdf/2015/12/Discussion_Paper_Korea_Japan_Manyin.pdf*, accessed January 10, 2017.

30. Kenichi Yamada, "South Korean still firmly oppose 'comfort women' deal," *Nikkei Asian Review*, December 31, 2016, online, available from *https://asia.nikkei.com/Politics-Economy/International-Relations/South-Koreans-still-firmly-oppose-comfort-women-deal*, accessed March 21, 2017.

31. Kyodo News, "Park's downfall muddles Japan's options on 'comfort women' agreement, North Korea," *The Japan*

Times, March 11, 2017, available from *www.japantimes.co.jp/ news/2017/03/11/national/politics-diplomacy/parks-downfall-muddles- japans-options-comfort-women-issue-north-korea/#.WNl3ek3yncs*, accessed March 21, 2017; Choe Sang-Hun and Motoko Rich, "Japan Recalls Ambassador to South Korea to Protest 'Comfort Woman' Statue," *The New York Times*, January 6, 2017, available from *https://www.nytimes.com/2017/01/06/world/asia/japan-south- korea-ambassador-comfort-woman-statue.html*, accessed February 19, 2017; for Moon's lead in the polls, see Kanga Kong, "Moon Leads the Pack as South Korea Prepares for Special Election," Bloomberg, March 9, 2017, available from *https://www.bloomberg. com/politics/articles/2017-03-10/meet-the-top-contenders-to-replace- park-as-south-korea-s-leader*, accessed March 21, 2017.

32. Central Intelligence Agency, "Japan."

33. Government debt stands at 234 percent of GDP, which is the highest level in the world (for comparison, Greece's government debt is 181 percent of GDP. For more information on deflation, see Simon Kennedy, "Deflation: The Trouble With Falling Prices," Bloomberg, March 10, 2016, available from *https://www. bloomberg.com/quicktake/deflation*, accessed February 27, 2017; for information on the debt, see Central Intelligence Agency, "Japan"; also Central Intelligence Agency, "Country Comparison: Public Debt," *The World Factbook*, Washington, DC: Central Intelligence Agency, updated November 14, 2017, available from *https://www. cia.gov/library/publications/the-world-factbook/rankorder/2186rank. html*, accessed December 1, 2017.

34. Japan's population is projected to fall by nearly 30 percent within the next 5 decades. D.M., "Japan's demography: The incredible shrinking country," Banyon, blog of *The Economist*, March 25, 2014, available from *www.economist.com/blogs/ banyan/2014/03/japans-demography*, accessed February 27, 2017.

35. Office of the Prime Minister of Japan, *National Security Strategy*, p. 20.

36. Beina Xu, "The U.S.-Japan Security Alliance," Council on Foreign Relations Backgrounder, July 1, 2014, available from *www.cfr.org/japan/us-japan-security-alliance/p31437*, accessed September 15, 2016.

37. Ibid.

38. Ministry of Foreign Affairs of Japan, "Joint Statement of the Security Consultative Committee: Toward a More Robust Alliance and Greater Shared Responsibility," October 3, 2013, pp. 3-4, Ministry of Foreign Affairs, available from *www.mofa.go.jp/files/000016028.pdf*, accessed January 10, 2017; Ministry of Foreign Affairs of Japan, "Joint Statement of the Security Consultative Committee: A Stronger Alliance For A Dynamic Security Environment," Ministry of Foreign Affairs, April 27, 2015, p. 4, available from *www.mofa.go.jp/files/000078186.pdf*, accessed January 10, 2017.

39. Shelia A. Smith, "Abe's Trump Test," *Asia Unbound,* blog of the Council on Foreign Relations, November 18, 2016, available from *https://www.cfr.org/blog/abes-trump-test*, accessed November 20, 2016.

40. Emma Chanlett-Avery, Mark E. Manyin, Rebecca M. Nelson, Brock R. Williams, and Taishu Yamakawa, *Japan-U.S. Relations: Issues for Congress*, Washington, DC: Congressional Research Service, U.S. Library of Congress, February 16, 2017, p. Summary, available from *https://fas.org/sgp/crs/row/RL33436.pdf*, accessed February 25, 2017. For an explanation on how the TTP increased the United States competitive security advantage over China, see Ashley J. Tellis, "The geopolitics of the TTIP and the TTP," in Sanjaya Baru and Suvi Dogra, eds., *Power Shifts and New Blocs in the Global Trading System*, London, UK: Adelphi Books, 2015, pp. 93-120.

41. The TPP was seen by Prime Minister Abe as a central component of his plans to improve the U.S.-Japan alliance by deepening economic ties between the two countries. Chanlett-Avery et al.; Scott A. Snyder, "SecDef Mattis's Mission in Northeast Asia: Provide Reassurance from the Trump Administration," *Asia Unbound,* blog of the Council on Foreign Relations, February 2, 2017, available from *https://www.cfr.org/blog/secdef-mattiss-mission-northeast-asia-provide-reassurance-trump-administration*, accessed February 19, 2017; Elizabeth C. Economy, "When the United States Abdicates the Throne, Who Will Lead?" *Asia Unbound,* blog of the Council on Foreign Relations, February 6, 2017, available from *https://www.cfr.org/blog/when-united-states-abdicates-throne-who-will-lead*, accessed February 19, 2017. For more on the TTP's

role in Abe's plans to improve the U.S.-Japan alliance, see Ministry of Foreign Affairs, *Diplomatic Bluebook*, pp. forward, 91, 257-258; James McBride and Beina Xu, "Abenomics and the Japanese Economy," Council on Foreign Relations Backgrounder, February 10, 2017, available from *https://www.cfr.org/backgrounder/abenomics-and-japanese-economy*, accessed February 21, 2017.

42. Smith, "Behind Japan, 100%"; Michael R. Gordon and Choe Sang-Hun, "Jim Mattis Seeks to Soothe Tensions in Japan and South Korea," *The New York Times*, February 5, 2017, available from *https://www.nytimes.com/2017/02/05/us/politics/jim-mattis-south-korea-japan.html?_r=0*, accessed February 19, 2017.

43. Office of the Prime Minister of Japan, *National Security Strategy*, p. 1.

44. The three national interests are: the protection of Japan's sovereignty, independence, and the lives and property of its citizens; the pursuit of "the prosperity of Japan and its nationals through economic development"; and the maintenance of a values-based international order in which the rule of law is respected. Ibid., pp. 4-5.

45. Ibid., pp. 3-4.

46. Ibid., pp. 14-20.

47. Ibid., p. 15.

48. Office of the Prime Minister of Japan, *National Defense Program Guidelines*, pp. 3-4, 6-7.

49. Ibid., pp. 7, 13. See footnote on bottom of p. 13 for a discussion on the reduction in Ground Self-Defense Force conventional equipment.

50. Ibid., pp. 4-5, 7-8.

51. At $43 billion, the budget is still a modest 0.97 percent of GDP, which ranks 102nd in the world. Tim Kelly, "Japan's government approves record military spending," Reuters, December 21, 2016, available from *www.reuters.com/article/us-japan-defense-budget-idUSKBN14B01C*, accessed February 20, 2017; also, see Central Intelligence Agency, "Japan."

52. Ministry of Foreign Affairs of Japan, "Three Principles on Transfer of Defense Equipment and Technology," Ministry of Foreign Affairs, April 1, 2014, available from *www.mofa.go.jp/files/000034953.pdf*, accessed September 16, 2016. The three principles are: Transfers are prohibited when they would violate Japanese treaties, UN resolution or when the purchasing country is party to a conflict; transfers are authorized when they contribute to peace and security or when the transfer "contributes to Japan's security"; and finally transfers will ensure that Japan has control regarding a subsequent transfer to third parties.

53. Mina Pollman, "The Trouble With Japan's Defense Exports," *The Diplomat*, October 02, 2015, available from *https://thediplomat.com/2015/10/the-truth-about-japans-defense-exports/*, accessed September 16, 2016; also Taisuke Hirose, "Japan's New Arms Export Principles: Strengthening United States-Japan Relations," *Center for Strategic & International Studies Newsletter*, October 14, 2014, available from *https://www.csis.org/analysis/japan%E2%80%99s-new-arms-export-principles-strengthening-us-japan-relations*, accessed February 21, 2017.

54. Hirose; Kyle Mizokami, "Japan's Emerging Defense Export Industry," *U.S. Naval Institute News*, February 23, 2015, available from *https://news.usni.org/2015/02/23/japans-emerging-defense-export-industry*, accessed February 21, 2017; Arthur Herman, Hudson Institute, "The Awakening Giant: Risks And Opportunities For Japan's New Defense Export Policy—Analysis," *Eurasia Review*, December 21, 2016, available from *www.eurasiareview.com/21122016-the-awakening-giant-risks-and-opportunities-for-japans-new-defense-export-policy-analysis/*, accessed February 21, 2017.

55. Tim Kelly, Cyril Altmeyer, and Colin Packham, "How France sank Japan's $40 billion Australian submarine dream," Reuters, April 29, 2016, available from *https://www.reuters.com/article/us-australia-submarines-japan-defence-in/how-france-sank-japans-40-billion-australian-submarine-dream-idUSKCN0XQ1FC* accessed February 21, 2017.

56. Ibid., pp. 20-22.

57. Japan-U.S. Security Consultative Committee, *The Guidelines for Japan-U.S. Defense Cooperation*, published on Official

Website of the Ministry of Foreign Affairs of Japan, April 17, 2015, pp. 1-23, available from *www.mofa.go.jp/files/000078188.pdf*, accessed January 6, 2017.

58. Taro Yamato, Director Japan U.S. Defense Cooperation Division, Defense Policy Bureau, Ministry of Defense, interview by author, Tokyo, Japan, January 12, 2017.

59. According to Hideshi Tokuchi, former Vice-Minister of Defense for International Affairs, this legislation was very much about alliance management: "'Collective self-defense' is more important in peacetime than it is during times of conflict" because it demonstrates Japan's commitment to participate in the alliance and reduces the asymmetric nature of the security relationship. See Office of The Cabinet Secretariat; also Ministry of Foreign Affairs of Japan, "Japan's Legislation for Peace and Security," briefing slides, March 2016, Ministry of Foreign Affairs, available from *www.mofa.go.jp/files/000143304.pdf*, accessed September 15, 2016; Hideshi Tokuchi, Senior Fellow, National Graduate Institute for Policy Studies (GRIPS), interview by author, Tokyo, Japan, January 13, 2017.

60. Ministry of Foreign Affairs, *Diplomatic Bluebook*, pp. 63-64, 68-69; Michael Auslin, "Japan's New Realism," *Foreign Affairs*, Vol. 95, No. 2, March/April 2016, p. 132.

61. Ministry of Foreign Affairs, *Diplomatic Bluebook*, p. 167.

62. Ibid., p. 166; also Auslin, p. 132; Renato Cruz de Castro, "Philippines and Japan Strengthen a Twenty-First Century Security Partnership," Analysis, Asia Maritime Transparency Initiative, December 17, 2015, available from *https://amti.csis.org/philippines-and-japan-strengthen-a-twenty-first-century-security-partnership/*, accessed February 21, 2017.

63. The term "cornerstone" is ubiquitous in discussions and writings about the U.S.-Japan Alliance. For just one example, see U.S. Department of State, "Fact Sheet: U.S. Relations With Japan," Washington, DC: Bureau of East Asian and Pacific Affairs, U.S. Department of State, January 25, 2017, available from *https://www.state.gov/r/pa/ei/bgn/4142.htm*, accessed February 22, 2017.

64. Ibid; The White House Office of the Press Secretary, "U.S.-Japan Joint Statement: The United States and Japan: Shaping the Future of the Asia-Pacific and Beyond," Obama White House Archives, April 25, 2014, available from *https://obamawhitehouse. archives.gov/the-press-office/2014/04/25/us-japan-joint-statement-united-states-and-japan-shaping-future-asia-pac*, accessed March 21, 2017.

65. Kazuya Sakamoto, "What Is The Strengthened Japan-U.S. Alliance for? Defending and Advancing the Liberal World Order," *Strategic Japan Working Papers*, Washington, DC: Center for Strategic & International Studies, 2016, p. 4, available from *http:// csis-prod.s3.amazonaws.com/s3fs-public/160401_What_Strengthened_ Japan_US_Alliance.pdf*, accessed March 5, 2017. The government of Japan's fiscal year (FY) 2016 budget for U.S. basing was approximately ¥581B. Ministry of Foreign Affairs, *Diplomatic Bluebook*, p. 165.

66. Barack Obama, *National Security Strategy*, Washington, DC: The White House, February 2015, p. 24.

67. There is a third risk, but the likelihood of it coming to fruition is so small that it is not worth mentioning in the main text: there is the risk that Japan would revert back to its Imperial, expansive past. This is nearly unimaginable for several reasons. First, Japan's modern political climate and popular culture has been shaped by the devastation of World War II and 70 years of a purely defensive, non-aggressive foreign policy, so the Japanese people are highly unlikely to support any military aggressiveness that falls outside of a purely self-defense situation. Another reason is that Japan no longer possesses the overwhelming power advantages over its neighbors that it did in the early part of the 20th century, so it is unlikely that an aggressive military policy would achieve success. Finally, the international environment has changed, and imperialism is no longer an acceptable model for a modern state to follow.

68. Visits to the Yakusuni shrine — in which several class A criminals are enshrined — are considered particularly provocative; Defense Minister Tomomi Inada visited the shrine soon after Prime Minister Abe's visit to Pearl Harbor. See Nobuhiro Kubo, "Japan minister visits controversial shrine honoring was dead after Pearl Harbor trip," Reuters, December 29, 2016, available from *www.*

reuters.com/article/us-japan-shrine-inada-idUSKBN14I025, accessed March 22, 2017.

69. Zbigniew Brzezinski, "A geostrategy for Eurasia," *Foreign Affairs,* Vol. 76, No. 5, September/October 1997, pp. 50-64. Thanks go to Colonel Doug Winton, USA, for suggesting the quote.

70. In 2012, ASEAN was unable to issue a joint communique after China apparently pressured Cambodia to reject language about China's behavior in the South China Sea; and in 2016, it was able to convince Greece, Hungary, and Croatia — all of which are recipients of Chinese "One Belt, One Road" investment — to neuter language in a European Union communique on a Permanent Court of Arbitration decision, which ruled against China. See Ernest Z. Bower, "Commentary: China Reveals Its Hand on ASEAN in Phnom Penh," Center For Strategic & International Studies, July 20, 2012, available from *https://www.csis.org/analysis/ china-reveals-its-hand-asean-phnom-penh*, accessed March 21, 2017; Theresa Fallon, "The EU, The South China Sea, and China's Successful Wedge Strategy," Analysis, Asia Maritime Transparency Initiative, October 13, 2016, available from *https://amti.csis.org/ eu-south-china-sea-chinas-successful-wedge-strategy*, accessed March 21, 2017.

71. For China's ambivalence toward the existing international economic system, see Robert D. Blackwill and Ashley J. Tellis, "Revising U.S. Grand Strategy Toward China," Council on Foreign Relations Special Report No. 72, Washington, DC: Council on Foreign Relations Press, 2015, p. 16, *https://www.cfr.org/sites/ default/files/pdf/2015/04/China_CSR72.pdf*, accessed September 1, 2016.

72. China and Japan have been rivals for centuries; for a quick discussion on their conflicts during the late 19th-century conflict, see Henry Kissinger, *On China*, New York, NY: Penguin, 2012, pp. 77-88.

73. Ministry of Foreign Affairs, *National Security Strategy*, p. 3.

74. Smith, *Japan's New Politics*, p. 5; see also Yukio Hatoyama, "A New Path for Japan," *The New York Times*, August 26, 2009, available from *www.nytimes.com/2009/08/27/opinion/27iht-edhatoyama.html?pagewanted=1&_r=1*, accessed March 7, 2017;

Carolyn Leddy, "The Widening U.S.-Japan Security Divide," *The Wall Street Journal*, October 22, 2009, available from *https://www.wsj.com/articles/SB10001424052748704597704574486272405220200*, accessed March 7, 2017.

75. Hatoyama.

76. U.S. official during a discussion with U.S. Army War College students, November 2016.

77. Tokuchi, interview by author.

78. Manyin, "Managing Japan-South Korea Tensions," pp. 11-12.

79. Tomohiko Satake, Senior Research Fellow, Policy Studies Department, National Institute for Defense Studies, interview by author, January 13, 2017, Tokyo, Japan.

80. Chanlett-Avery et al., pp. 8-10.

81. David Brunnstrom and Matt Spetalnick, "Trump to seek quick progress with Japan's Abe on replacement trade deal," Reuters, January 27, 2017, available from *www.reuters.com/article/us-usa-trump-japan-idUSKBN15A33Q*, accessed February 25, 2017; see also Ibid., p. 31.

82. U.S. Census Department, "Top Trading Partners - December 2016: Year-to-Date Total Trade," U.S. Census Department, December 2016, available from *https://www.census.gov/foreign-trade/statistics/highlights/top/top1612yr.html*, accessed February 22, 2017. See also Economic Research Service, United States Department of Agriculture, "Japan: Trade," Economic Research Service, United States Department of Agriculture, October 6, 2017, available from *https://www.ers.usda.gov/topics/international-markets-trade/countries-regions/japan/trade/*, accessed December 4, 2017. The United States exports high quality manufactured goods to Japan such as optical/medical equipment, aircraft, machinery, agricultural products, and commercial services. For its part, the Japan exports vehicles and machinery to the United States. For more information, see Office of the U.S. Trade Representative, "Japan," Office of the U.S. Trade Representative, Executive Office of the

President, n.d., available from *https://ustr.gov/countries-regions/ japan-korea-apec/japan*, accessed February 22, 2017.

83. Japan-U.S. Security Consultative Committee, "Joint Statement of the Security Consultative Committee," Ministry of Foreign Affairs of Japan, April 27, 2012, p. 1, available from *www. mofa.go.jp/region/n-america/us/security/scc/pdfs/joint_120427_en.pdf*, accessed January 10, 2017; also Ministry of Foreign Affairs, *Diplomatic Bluebook*, p. 162.

84. This comment was made by a senior commander to the author in 2016.

85. The current U.S. Pacific Command (USPACOM) Commander described deterrence as the product of "Capability x Resolve x Signaling," but under the current plan, two elements of the equation — capability and signaling — decrease significantly. I would argue that dispersing the 3d Marine Division in disaggregated elements to bases as distant from each other as California, Hawaii, Guam and Australia unquestionably weakens warfighting capability. Forward basing in Okinawa provides significant benefits: specialized training facilities such as the Jungle Warfare Training Center; consolidated command and control of III Marine Expeditionary Force (MEF) units; coordination between III MEF units; shorter response times for regional contingencies; and offset basing funding from Japan. Under the current realignment plan, all of those advantages are lost. The operational disadvantages associated with the current Okinawa basing scheme — namely the lack of on-island combined-arms training areas and the insufficient quantity of inter-theater lift — exist to varying degrees at many of the proposed future basing locations. And while the Japanese government mitigates Okinawa training area shortfalls by coordinating and funding "relocation exercises" in which U.S. units train on Japan Self-Defense Forces (JSDF) installations in mainland Japan, the United States will be fully responsible for coordinating and funding similar exercises to overcome training shortfalls at the proposed basing locations. The political costs associated with forward basing are likely to continue even after the plan is executed, they are simply transferred to Guam or Australia, both of which are home to opponents of U.S. basing. For USPACOM Commanders views on deterrence, see Admiral Harry Harris, "Address to the Lowy

Institute for International Policy," public speech, Sydney, Australia, December 14, 2016, available from *www.pacom.mil/Media/Speeches-Testimony/Article/1029173/address-to-the-lowy-institute-for-international-policy/*, accessed January 25, 2017. For opposition to U.S. basing in Guam, Australia, and California, see Jon Letman, "Proposed US military buildup on Guam angers locals who liken it to colonization," August 1, 2016, *The Guardian*, available from *https://www.theguardian.com/us-news/2016/aug/01/guam-us-military-marines-deployment*, accessed February 27, 2017; Avani Dias, "No support for US military base in NT from Chief Minister Adam Giles," ABC [Australian Broadcasting Corporation] News, January 26, 2016, available from *www.abc.net.au/news/2016-01-25/no-support-for-us-military-base-in-nt-from-chief-minister-adam-/7114054*, accessed February 27, 2017; Steven Cuevas, "In Joshua Tree, Marine Base Expansion Faces Strong Opposition," *The California Report*, October 14, 2013, KQED California Public Radio, available from *https://ww2.kqed.org/news/2013/10/14/in-joshua-tree-marine-base-expansion-faces-strong-opposition/*.

86. Tokuchi, interview by author; Yamato, interview by author.

87. While rebasing Okinawa-based units elsewhere in Japan may appear to substitute a new set of political problems for an old one, this is not necessarily the case: increasing the U.S. military footprint elsewhere in Japan can be accomplished with a relatively low amount of local controversy, as the recent relocation of KC-130J refuelers from Futenma Air Station in Okinawa to Iwakuni Air Station in southern Honshu demonstrates. This rebasing effort could involve existing U.S. installations such as the Combined Arms Training Center Mt. Fuji, or it could involve existing Japanese training bases, such as the Yausubetsu Maneuver Area in eastern Hokkaido. While there would potentially be a need to increase the family-support infrastructure (schools, housing, facilities) in some locations to accommodate this realignment, this is mitigated by the fact that many of the Marine units which would be moved are rotational units which deploy without families, significantly reducing the amount of family support required. If the U.S. units adopted a system similar to the one used by some U.S. units in South Korea — in which military families live on existing U.S. installations with family support services already available, while the service member commutes to and

150

from a more austere work installation on the weekend — it would further reduce the requirement to increase family support service infrastructure.

88. Japan's political culture has historically been opaque when it comes to issues of national security policy, and the strategic decision making process is often controlled by bureaucrats whose institutional memory is longer than that of oft-changing political leadership. The result was that the rationale behind security policy decisions often remained unexplained, making it difficult to have an informed public discussion about national security issues. This historical lack of public discourse has had negative practical ramifications; when the Democratic Party of Japan (DPJ) took power from the Liberal Democratic Party (LDP) in 2009, it did not understand some aspects of Japan's security policy or the policy making process because its members had never been exposed to the dynamics which influenced LDP decisions. For more, see Smith, *Japan's New Politics*, pp. 4-5, 24-26, 31, 33.

89. For information on the United States as a reliable partner, see Genron NPO, "Poll 2016: The Future of Northeast Asia and Public Opinions," Genron NPO, March 23, 2017, p. 13, available from *http://www.genron-npo.net/en/opinion_polls/archives/5342. html*. For information on the January 2016 Yomiuri Shimbun poll showing Japan public support for the alliance, see Craig Kafura, "Public Opinion and the US-Japan Alliance at the Outset of the Trump Administration," The Chicago Council on Global Affairs, February 8, 2017, available from *https://www.thechicagocouncil. org/publication/public-opinion-and-us-japan-alliance-outset-trump-administration#_ftn8*, accessed March 29, 2017. The article has a link to the poll, but the results are written in kanji. Thanks to Mr. Nicholas Szechenyi from the Center for Strategic & International Studies for suggesting these polls.

CHAPTER 6

CURTAIL, COOPERATE, OR COMPEL IN THE SOUTH CHINA SEA?

Robert R. Arnold, Jr.

EXECUTIVE SUMMARY

The United States and China are currently in direct conflict over each other's actions in the South China Sea. Chinese acts include aggressive behavior to further territorial aspirations and excessive maritime claims, harassment of U.S. military-led Freedom of Navigation Operations (FONOPS), significant reclamation on disputed land features, and construction of new infrastructure that serves both military and non-military purposes.

The United States is concerned that China's activities challenge the existing international order and are a violation of international law. Maintaining military freedom of navigation is also a vital U.S. interest. The U.S. interpretation of freedom of navigation is the most contentious issue for China.

Although China declared it respects commercial freedom of navigation and has taken no steps to limit it, the United States is concerned that China "may change its mind" and restrict commercial freedom of navigation in the future despite the negative impacts it might have on both China's and U.S. economic interests. The United States takes no position on territorial and maritime claims, but wants to see a peaceful resolution, thereby sustaining regional stability. U.S. actions consist of maintaining a strong military presence in the area, engagement with allies and partners, and freedom of navigation operations near disputed areas to support United Nations Convention on the Law of the Sea (UNCLOS). China's main assertion is that U.S. military freedom of navigation operations are intrusions into its sovereignty and a breach of China's territorial integrity. China views state sovereignty and territorial integrity as core interests. China stated it is committed to upholding international law, maintaining freedom of navigation in and flight over the South China Sea, and to preserving peace and stability by cooperating with partners throughout the region.

While a proposal to cooperate with China seems counterintuitive and is likely to be unpopular with many audiences in the United States, it is the most productive method to resolve this issue for the following reasons. First, it is the truly pragmatic choice. Second, this plan has the best chance for long-term success because it involves China as a willing participant. Third, no matter how hard it tries, the United States cannot stop the rise of China, short of going to war. Fourth, if the United States wants a peaceful and responsible China, it must guide the process. Fifth, cooperation with China would bring greater international respect and legitimacy for U.S. global leadership efforts. Finally, the Trump administration's willingness to accept nontraditional solutions and modifications to the existing international system will enable the success of this policy.

INTRODUCTION

The United States and China are currently in direct conflict over each other's actions in the South China Sea. Chinese acts include aggressive behavior toward its neighbors to further territorial aspirations and excessive maritime claims, harassment of FONOPS, significant reclamation on disputed land features, and construction of new infrastructure that serves both military and nonmilitary purposes.[1] The primary U.S. concern is that China's activities challenge the existing international order and are a violation of international law. Since the United States is the leader of the global system, it views Chinese opposition to the rules and norms associated with this structure as an attempt to increase China's regional and international influence at U.S. expense. Maintaining freedom of navigation is also a vital U.S. interest for two reasons. First, the United States desires assured access for its military forces throughout the maritime global commons, to include the South China Sea. This aspect of freedom of navigation is the most contentious for China. Second, although the Chinese have stated they respect commercial freedom of navigation and have taken no steps to limit it, the United States has a very real concern that China "may change its mind" and restrict commercial freedom of navigation in the future, despite the negative impacts it might have on both China's and U.S. economic interests. Finally, the United States takes no position on territorial and maritime claims, but wants to see a peaceful resolution thereby sustaining regional stability.[2] U.S. actions consist of maintaining a strong military presence, engagement with allies and partners, and FONOPS near disputed areas to support UNCLOS.

China's main assertion is that U.S. military FONOPS are intrusions into Chinese sovereignty and a breach of China's territorial integrity. China holds state sovereignty and territorial integrity so dear that it views them as core interests.[3] In addition, China stated it is committed to upholding international law, maintaining freedom of navigation and overflight in the South China Sea, and to preserving peace and stability throughout the region.[4] Upon examination of China's affirmed principles, it would seem the United States and China share common interests in the South China Sea. If so, why are the two counties involved in such a contested dispute? To answer this question, this chapter will address the following four points: 1) the background behind this problem and the contemporary issues surrounding this issue; 2) U.S. national interests and China's core interests; 3) the official government positions of both nations on the South China Sea; and 4) the current actions of the United States and China in the area. Lastly, three options will be provided for review, culminating with a final recommendation for the current administration to consider as the U.S. response to China's actions in the South China Sea.

BACKGROUND

For centuries, China maintained sporadic contact with South China Sea islands and other land features. The most frequent use of the area was by Chinese fisherman.[5] As China's power waned, European colonial nations increased their influence throughout the region. However, they also generally maintained freedom of navigation for all parties transiting the South China Sea. The region was administered by Imperial Japan during World War II, and although Japan was forced to relinquish all "stolen" land features in the

Western Pacific, including the South China Sea, as a part of the post-war settlement, it did not surrender the "spoils" to any clearly designated recipient country.

In 1946, the Republic of China sent two destroyers to the South China Sea to "recover" the islands and land features.[6] In the following year, the Republic of China government proclaimed a vast majority of the South China Sea with the infamous 11-dash line. The Chinese claim was through an official map depicting the area in the South China Sea.[7] The Republic of China did not have the time and effort to take effective control of its claimed properties in the South China Sea, since China had become engulfed in a civil war between the government and Communist forces.

The Nationalist government lost the war and sought shelter in Taiwan in 1949. The Communists founded the People's Republic of China (PRC) on the mainland. With respect to the South China Sea, the PRC continued to claim it by using the 11-dash line, yet for a variety of reasons did not exercise much actual control. In 1953, China removed two lines in the Gulf of Tonkin as a friendly gesture to North Vietnam,[8] creating China's Nine-Dash Line.[9]

CONTEMPORARY ISSUES

The most contentious territorial claims include three main areas: Paracel Islands, Spratly Islands, and Scarborough Shoal. The Paracels are claimed by China, Taiwan, and Vietnam, but have been occupied and administered by China since 1974 after a successful armed struggle with South Vietnam. Brunei, China, Malaysia, the Philippines, Taiwan, and Vietnam all have claims within the Spratlys. All claimants, except for Brunei, hold land features there. There has been friction among nations in this area for nearly 30 years, as best illustrated by the military conflict between China and Vietnam in 1988. The Scarborough Shoal is disputed by China, the Philippines, and Taiwan and was the site of a stand-off between China and the Philippines in 2012. Although the Sino-Philippine relationship has become more positive since October 2016, when Philippine President Rodrigo Duterte stated his desire to move his country closer to China, their discord has yet to be fully resolved.[10] A good illustration of this rift occurred in February 2017 when the Philippines alleged that China might be building on a reef near the Scarborough Shoal to solidify its claim there.[11] Finally, less controversial claims include the Pratas Islands that is contested by China and Taiwan, but occupied by Taiwan and the Macclesfield Bank, which is claimed by China, the Philippines, and Taiwan.[12]

The conflicting maritime disputes are caused by two major issues: overlapping Economic Exclusion Zones (EEZ) that, in accordance with UNCLOS, can extend 200 nautical miles (NM) from internationally recognized landmasses; and China's Nine-Dash Line which has no clear definition and has been officially and successfully debunked. The Nine-Dash Line was challenged by the Philippines in 2013 when it filed an arbitration case with the Permanent Court of Arbitration against China over 15 counts of maritime disagreements, the most significant of which was the Nine-Dash Line.[13] A year later, China tested one of its maritime assertions within the Nine-Dash Line by emplacing an oil-drilling platform near the Paracel Islands within Vietnam's EEZ. This was the first time the Chinese drilled in an EEZ that was contested with another nation. It sparked stern reaction by both the Vietnamese government and its people. Violent protests broke out, causing damage to Chinese businesses in Vietnam and resulting in the death of two of China's citizens. During the conflict,

Chinese and Vietnamese vessels were seen colliding at sea. China eventually removed the oil rig, 1 month earlier than originally planned.[14] The Permanent Court of Arbitration released its results on July 12, 2016, and all of its rulings were against China. Most significant was its decision that "there was no legal basis for China to claim historic rights to resources within the sea areas falling within the 'nine-dash line'."[15] China rejected the whole arbitration act, did not participate in the hearings, and disavowed the ruling. There is a certain bit of irony in China's reaction, given its status as a signatory to UNCLOS since 1996.[16] See Figure 6-1.

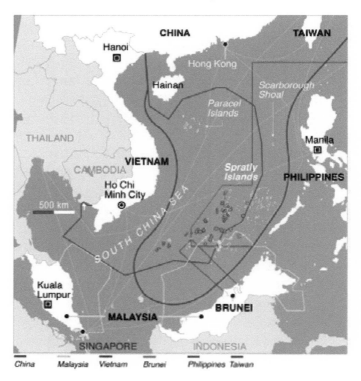

Figure 6-1. Maritime Claims in South China Sea.[17]

In late 2013, China started land reclamation in the Spratlys. In less than 2 years, China reclaimed over 2,900 acres of land at seven of its eight outposts and built multiple artificial structures on six of its controlled land features in the Spratly Islands. The speed and scale shocked the United States, the disputants, and the rest of the world.[18] China also stated its territories in the Spratlys would be used for military and nonmilitary tasks like search and rescue, disaster relief, scientific research, fishing production, conservation, and maritime safety.[19] Previously, in 1993, China built a military capable airfield and upgraded Woody Island in the Paracels with "an artificial harbor with a concrete dock 500-m long and capable of accommodating destroyer and frigate class vessels."[20] In February 2016, China deployed surface-to-air missiles to Woody Island.[21]

INTERESTS

According to the *National Security Strategy* (NSS), vital U.S. national interests are to maintain global leadership to promote security, prosperity, values, and international order.[22] The specific plan to address interests in the Asia-Pacific, officially called the "Strategic Rebalance," had been nested with broader priorities contained in the NSS. In October 2011, then-Secretary of State Hillary Clinton introduced the idea of shifting U.S. focus to the region that became known as the pivot to the Pacific.

> We need to be smart and systematic about where we invest time and energy, so that we put ourselves in the best position to sustain our leadership, secure our interests, and advance our values. One of the most important tasks of American statecraft over the next decade will therefore be to lock in substantially increased investment-diplomatic,

economic, strategic, and otherwise-in the Asia-Pacific region.[23]

The next month, former President Barack Obama clarified his intent during a speech to the Australian Parliament.

> We seek security, which is the foundation of peace and prosperity. We stand for an international order in which the rights and responsibilities of all nations and all people are upheld. Where international law and norms are enforced. Where commerce and freedom of navigation are not impeded. Where emerging powers contribute to regional security, and where disagreements are resolved peacefully.[24]

During his inaugural remarks in January 2017, President Donald Trump prioritized domestic concerns such as employment, internal investment, national unity, and the transfer of power back to the population. However, he also addressed international affairs focused primarily on the NSS priorities of security, prosperity, and values. The President's comments supported the need for security through strength and revealed his desire for greater economic prosperity. Although important, U.S. values should not be forced.[25] The United States would instead "shine as an example" for other nations to emulate.[26] In a true realist approach, which stresses an international order that is guided by states focused on attaining interests through the accumulation of power, Trump proclaimed all countries have the right to seek their own interests.[27] This statement reveals that the Trump administration may be more accepting of other nations working to achieve their own interests, likely so long as they do not compete with U.S. national interests. In the future, such a perspective may lead to a more multipolar system instead of the current U.S.-driven unipolar international order.[28] Even though Trump's inaugural address did not specifically mention his position on continued engagement in the Asia-Pacific, his pledge to "reinforce old alliances and form new ones"[29] seems to imply that maintaining current bilateral hub-and-spoke[30] alliances with Japan, South Korea, Australia, New Zealand, Thailand, and the Philippines is a priority. Additionally, it is likely that Trump would be open to engaging new partners in this region and elsewhere in the world.

Based on China's claims in the area, it is clear that their core values are truly held sacred and guide their every action.

> China is firm in upholding its core interests which include the following: state sovereignty, national security, territorial integrity and national reunification, China's political system established by the Constitution and overall social stability, and the basic safeguards for ensuring sustainable economic and social development.[31]

Chinese territorial and maritime assertions in the East and South China Seas highlight the importance of state sovereignty, territorial integrity, and the desire for national reunification. However, the emphasis on Taiwan is the clearest example of the value of national reunification. China supports its core interest of national security by the reform and buildup of its military, the stated desire for a nuclear-free Korean peninsula, and by its territorial and maritime claims, land reclamation, military infrastructure construction, and by actions within the East and South China Seas. Although not often mentioned internationally, the bolstering of Chinese military capabilities also strengthens its internal stability.[32] China's increase in economic prosperity directly supports its core interest to achieve sustainable economic and social development. China created and distributed its specific vision for the future of the Asia-Pacific in a recent white paper.

> China has all along taken the advancement of regional prosperity and stability as its own responsibility. China is ready to pursue security through dialogue and cooperation in the spirit of working together for mutually beneficial results, and safeguard peace and stability jointly with other countries in the region.[33]

The Chinese focus on being responsible and enhancing peace and stability through dialogue and cooperation with regional partners should be especially enticing to the Trump administration since these goals are in line with overall U.S. interests and could be used to foster a better and closer relationship with China.

OFFICIAL POSITIONS

In reference to the South China Sea, the four main themes expressed in the NSS include maintaining freedom of navigation, deterring aggression, resolving disputes peacefully, and respecting international law and order.[34] First, perceived threats to freedom of navigation within the South China Sea are a major security concern for the United States because open trade routes remain absolutely critical to the economic well-being of the United States, China, and the greater world community. Prosperity is also touted as a key priority in both the NSS and in statements by Trump. In addition to accounting for "more than 10 percent of global fisheries production"[35] and billions of gallons of oil and gas reserves,[36] "almost 30 percent of the world's maritime trade transits the South China Sea annually, including approximately $1.2 trillion in ship-borne trade bound for the United States."[37] While economic protection remains a genuine concern for the United States, there is another, often unexpressed, aspect that is crucial for the United States: unimpeded military access to the Asia-Pacific region. Since the United States is the pre-eminent military power with global operational reach, it must preserve its ability to project military force anywhere in the world, with unopposed access being preferred. China's military presence in the South China Sea remains a real threat to U.S. power projection capabilities. Second, the United States is committed to deterring aggression in the area. Major global conflict has been averted for over 70 years because of continued U.S. presence, its relationship with allies and partners, and the inherent security that brings. Third, the United States would ultimately like to see all disputes worked out in a peaceful manner that will help sustain regional stability.[38] Finally, international law and order must be reinforced. This has been facilitated by several methods. First, sustaining freedom of navigation is inextricably linked to bolstering international law since it supports UNCLOS. Although the United States has not ratified UNCLOS, it follows its tenets, considering them world norms. Second, deterring aggressive acts sustains the international order by preserving peace and stability. Finally, and significantly, strengthening the rules-based international system supports the leadership and influence the United States enjoys globally.

In December 2016, then President-elect Trump stated China was building a "massive military complex in the middle of the South China Sea."[39] Beyond that, he has not professed an official position on the South China Sea. However, both Secretary of State Rex Tillerson and Secretary of Defense James Mattis made clear and direct statements on the U.S. official position there. Unfortunately, their comments were not mutually supporting. This led to ambiguity on the actual U.S. position regarding the South China Sea. At his confirmation hearing in January 2017, Tillerson stated, "We're going to have to send China a clear signal that, first, the island-building stops and, second, your access to those islands also is not going to be allowed."[40] His words seemed to indicate the Trump administration was planning to take a strong military approach to Chinese actions in the region. However, in early February 2017, Secretary of Defense Mattis contradicted Tillerson when he declared, "What we have to do is exhaust all efforts, diplomatic efforts, to try to resolve this properly, maintaining open lines of communication."[41] He went on to add, "and certainly our military stance should be one that reinforces our diplomats."[42] Such discord indicates there is no clear U.S. policy on the South China Sea. Given this fact, the Trump administration may be open to considering a wide variety of recommended options.

China has consistently stated its position on the South China Sea emphasizing four main points: being a regional leader, maintaining peace and stability, following international law, and its dedication to cooperating with partners.

> China is an important force for maintaining peace and stability in the South China Sea. It abides by the purposes and principles of the Charter of the United Nations and is committed to upholding and promoting international rule of law. It respects and acts in accordance with international law. While firmly safeguarding its territorial sovereignty and maritime rights and interests, China adheres to the position of settling disputes through negotiation and consultation and managing differences through rules

and mechanisms. China endeavors to achieve win-win outcomes through mutually beneficial cooperation.[43]

First, it is significant for the United States to recognize and welcome the message in the first sentence of China's posture statement. Simply stated, China is telling the world it longs to be an important player in regional affairs. This desire is a critical first step for influencing China to become a responsible partner of the United States. Two of China's other points were also noteworthy: peace and cooperation. Given this promise, it can be inferred that those two particular themes are important to China. The second point, preserving peace and stability, is imperative to broadening China's economic progress — that is its main source of strength.

Additionally, any military action, especially against the United States, would hamper China's development and is not something the Chinese would welcome, at least for now. Despite its increasing military capability, China is still no military match for the United States.[44] Another aspect of maintaining peace and stability is China's stated dedication to the peaceful settlement of disputes. This assertion also supports international law and order.

The third point is that China is committed to international law. Although most people in the United States would likely question this fact, there is a certain truth to this argument. In spite of China's poor behavior in the region demonstrated by its bullying actions in response to territorial ambitions and extreme maritime claims, increased reclamation, and continued military capable construction, the Chinese have not blocked commercial vessel freedom of navigation in the South China Sea. China's rationale for respecting this aspect of freedom of navigation is simple: ensuring the free flow of commercial goods through this vital trade route is critical to sustain China's economic prosperity, so it is within its interest. As previously mentioned, the real concern for China regarding freedom of navigation is the U.S. military FONOPS, which China views as provocative. For that reason, China continues to harass, shadow, and impede U.S. warships conducting this mission. Although not precisely in the manner the United States would desire, China has also followed the guidelines of UNCLOS in two ways. It abides by Article 310, which says signatory states can provide a declaration or statement upon acceding to UNCLOS. A small percentage of nations have done so, with China being one of them. During the ratification process, China stated the desire "to obtain advance approval from or give prior notification"[45] to foreign military vessels transiting its EEZ which China considers territorial waters. What China fails to recognize is that "declarations or statements do not purport to exclude or to modify the legal effect of the provisions of" UNCLOS.[46] In other words, all UNCLOS signatories can make official statements, but doing so will not alter the rights or precepts guaranteed by the convention.[47] China also subscribes to Article 298 of UNCLOS that allows signatory nations to opt out of certain provisions concerning the resolution of disputes, without prejudice. This is what China did when it rejected the ruling of the Permanent Court of Arbitration that held that China's "Nine-Dash Line" was inconsistent with UNCLOS.[48]

The last Chinese pledge pertains to cooperation with partners. When coupled with peaceful claim settlement, the Chinese method to achieve both is best addressed by what it calls a "dual track approach."

China proposed this idea to the Association of Southeast Asian Nations (ASEAN) which emphasized territorial and maritime dispute resolution through bilateral negotiations while concurrently working together to maintain regional security and stability multilaterally.[49]

> China's dual-track approach means specific disputes are to be peacefully solved through bilateral negotiations and consultations by countries directly involved on the basis of observing historic facts and international law; in the meantime, peace and stability in the region should be jointly protected by China and ASEAN countries.[50]

It is abundantly clear that this method leaves out the United States, who is not a claimant to South China Sea territorial or maritime disputes. Actions such as this are meant to increase China's regional influence at the expense of the United States. Given this fact, the United States must remain engaged in the South China Sea or its regional influence will be steadily diminished.

ACTIONS

U.S. actions in the South China Sea consist of three components: a substantial physical military presence, military exercises and exchanges with allies and partners, and unilateral FONOPS. Forward deployed U.S. military forces are meant to bolster regional stability and security. Military exchanges with allies and emerging partners serve two purposes: to improve the security capacity of traditional allies; and to engage new partners, including China and important regional organizations like ASEAN, in a cooperative manner mitigating future conflict. The Rim of the Pacific (RIMPAC) is one such exercise that meets those parameters.

The exercise's objectives are to enhance the interoperability of the combined RIMPAC forces as well as to integrate new participants in the employment of multinational command and control at the tactical and operational levels. In 2014, China participated for the first time.[51]

U.S. FONOPS have been conducted near contested territories and excessive maritime claims made by China, but have been ineffectual in altering China's behavior since the execution of FONOPS have not been aligned with the intended purpose. The United States proclaims that, within the South China Sea, it "will continue to fly, sail, and operate in accordance with international law."[52] However, in many cases, when it actually performed FONOPS, it constrained itself by operating as if it was in China's territorial waters by purposely sailing beyond 12 NM of disputed land features. Doing so actually legitimized China's assertions since its "territorial waters" were being respected. Additionally, U.S. vessels would often execute innocent passage within 12 NM of the contested land. Again, such actions supported the very same claims that the FONOPS were originally meant to challenge, because innocent passage is only required to be performed within territorial waters.[53]

China has continued to engage in a number of procedures that supported its territorial and maritime contentions to include hostile actions against other claimants, countering U.S. FONOPS, enhancing land reclamation efforts, and building infrastructure to support military and nonmilitary functions.[54] China prefers to employ a mixture of civilian and military assets to enforce its assertions in the South China Sea. These include civilian fishermen, Chinese Coast Guard, militia, other maritime law enforcement units, and the

People's Liberation Army Navy who support their actions.[55]

> Maritime militias may escalate their operations and even clash with other nations' ships. They did just that in 2011, when they harassed PetroVietnam vessels near the Vietnamese coast; in 2012, when they became embroiled in a standoff with the Philippines over Scarborough Shoal; and in 2014, when they protected China's Haiyang Shiyou 981 oil rig from Vietnamese reprisals. Chinese militias also impeded U.S. vessels that were conducting freedom of navigation patrols in waters claimed by China in 2015.[56]

Using civilians and other nonmilitary assets to conduct asymmetrical tactics keeps the conflict below the threshold to be considered an act of war. Neither the United States nor any South China Sea claimant will likely go to war with China over its militia ramming a fishing boat, its quiet land reclaiming actions on a small reef in the middle of the ocean, or its building of dual-purpose airports on such features. China knows this reality very well and is following the teachings of ancient Chinese theorist Sun Tzu who stated, "to subdue the enemy without fighting is the acme of skill."[57] These "gray zone" tactics are China's attempts to "win without fighting."[58] China's opposition to U.S. FONOPS and overflight operations has also been executed using conventional methods. In October 2016, the USS *Decatur* conducted FONOPS outside the 12 NM range of the Paracels. China reacted by dispatching three ships to follow the U.S. vessel.[59] More recently, China responded to a U.S. aircraft near Scarborough Shoal where:

> on Feb. 8 (local), an interaction characterized by U.S. Pacific Command as 'unsafe' occurred in international

airspace above the South China Sea between a Chinese KJ-200 aircraft and a U.S. Navy P-3C aircraft.[60]

It is not readily apparent if this was an accident or an intentional encounter, but it is clear that China will continue resisting U.S. efforts to ensure freedom of navigation using military assets.

OPTIONS

Three alternatives for changing U.S. policy in the South China Sea were constructed within the general framework of curtail, cooperate, and compel. The curtail option would involve the United States halting FONOPS in the South China Sea, but continuing to maintain military presence in the region. Additionally, engagement with China using diplomatic and economic methods would increase. There are three opportunities present with this choice. First, stopping FONOPS would provide the United States with the flexibility to use its economic instrument of national power to focus on other priorities within the Asia-Pacific, other hotspots around the world, or on domestic issues. During his inauguration, Trump declared the United States had prioritized the needs of other nations before its own for too long, creating negative economic impacts. This might be a chance to invest in the homeland and elsewhere.

> For many decades, we've enriched foreign industry at the expense of American industry; subsidized the armies of other countries, while allowing for the very sad depletion of our military. We've defended other nations' borders while refusing to defend our own. And spent trillions of dollars overseas while America's infrastructure has fallen into disrepair.[61]

171

Easing the national debt, which in mid-February 2017 amounted to over $19 trillion, would also be an economic benefit of the curtail alternative since there would be some cost savings with discontinuing FONOPS, although this would admittedly be a drop in the bucket.[62] Second, just as stated with the economic resources, some military assets could be diverted and refocused on other areas of tension like the Korean peninsula, the fight against the Islamic State in Iraq and Syria (ISIS), and the deterrence of Russia in Europe. Finally, removing the friction of FONOPS and concentrating more closely with China on diplomatic and economic collaboration may lead to a better relationship between the two nations. This could, at some point in the future, result in even stronger economic interaction and China's support for other U.S. security interests like future UN Security Council initiatives, defeating ISIS, dissuading Russian aggression, rebuking North Korean belligerence, influencing Iranian actions in the Middle East, and prohibiting global nuclear proliferation.

There are three risks inherent in this option. First, choosing to discontinue FONOPS may signal a weakening of U.S. global leadership and resolve. This could send a negative message to U.S. allies and partners and to near-peer competitors and adversaries, initiating new challenges to U.S. interests if not properly explained. Second, this action could be politically risky for the Trump administration for appearing weak on China. As in the first risk, the rationale of this policy would need to be clarified for Congress and for the U.S. public. Finally, diplomatic and economic cooperation may not be compelling enough to influence China to discontinue its aggressive actions in the South China

Sea. Building a solid relationship with China may partially mitigate this risk.

The cooperate alternative would focus on collaboration with China on multiple levels and would consist of executing procedures by employing all instruments of U.S. national power. Start by communicating with several audiences, using varied messages. The Chinese government would need to understand why the United States was seeking greater cooperation. The plan would be to use China's own message emphasizing the mutual benefits of cooperation or its "win-win process."[63] Next, reiterate the respect and affinity the American and Chinese people have for one another. The Chinese-American diaspora should be used to support this theme. The dissemination of U.S. pop culture or "soft power" may also be very appealing to Chinese youth. Congress and the U.S. populace would need to comprehend why cooperating with China was necessary. This collaboration must be viewed as a positive undertaking that would result in greater security, stability, and economic prosperity for the United States. The objective to exert greater influence on China in the long term also must be explained, primarily to Congress. The international community must recognize the benefit of this approach and believe that this will facilitate peace, stability, and prosperity. As equal partners, the United States and China would be able to maintain and further develop their military and economic strength. Each nation would be able to cooperate with the other from a position of strength. Diplomatically, given China's current interest in military-to-military engagement and exercises with the United States which focus on common interests and challenges such as antiterrorism, counterterrorism, antipiracy, humanitarian assistance disaster relief (HADR), search and rescue, and maritime navigational safety, would be the best place to begin efforts. In this case, the U.S. military would be used to further diplomacy.

The current U.S. military maritime strategy empha-sized both opportunities and risks in working with China's rising military, but welcomed the chance to do so.

> China supports counter piracy operations in the Gulf of Aden, conducts humanitarian assistance and disaster response missions enabled by its hospital ship, and participates in large-scale, multinational naval exercises. . . . However, China's naval expansion also presents challenges when it employs force or intimidation against other sovereign nations to assert territorial claims.[64]

Similarly, the Chinese military echoed a desire to work with U.S. military forces.

> China's armed forces will continue to foster a new model of military relationship with the US armed forces that conforms to the new model of major-country relations between the two countries, strengthen defense dialogues, exchanges and cooperation, and improve the CBM (confidence-building measures) mechanism for the notification of major military activities.[65]

As the relationship between the United States and China developed, the level of cooperation would be expanded to include improved diplomatic, economic, and military collaboration such as support for critical U.S. short-term security interests like resolving fric-tion in the East and South China Seas in accordance with UNCLOS. The United States would first need to ratify UNCLOS. Later, both countries could work together on long-term security issues like defeating ISIS, neutralizing terrorists, stopping the prolifera-tion of nuclear weapons, and deterring the aggressive behaviors of North Korea, Russia, and Iran. China's Vice Foreign Minister, Liu Zhenmin, supported cooperation with the United States in January 2017 when he proclaimed, "China is committed to working with the US to build relations featuring no conflict, non-confrontation, mutual respect, and win-win cooperation, and achieve positive interaction and inclusive coordination in the Asia-Pacific."[66] Another aspect of engagement would be facilitating the nascent relationship between China and ASEAN, initially regarding the completion of the code of conduct that will govern the interaction of China and its neighbors. This effort is ongoing and scheduled to be completed by the middle of 2018.[67] However, the enduring relationship between China and ASEAN could be based on China's dual-track approach that stresses bilateral negotiations between South China Sea claimants with multilateral cooperation on regional security.[68]

There are three risks associated with this alternative. First is the chance that those receiving the messaging, the Chinese government and people and the U.S. Congress and people, would not accept the information being provided. Second, this action will not be successful if China refused to participate, thinking this was simply an attempt to contain it. Both of these risks could be reduced by clearly and frequently communicating the intent of this increased engagement. Finally, there is the risk that China may join forces with the United States only to build its power and challenge the United States in the future when China becomes economically and militarily stronger. Strengthening the relationship with China could help minimize this risk.

With the compel option, more coercive actions would be taken toward China by utilizing all instruments of U.S. national power. The United States would publicly and frequently chastise China for bullying its weaker neighbors and for refusing to accept the July 2016 decision by the Permanent Court of Arbitration. Diplomatically, concentrate efforts on isolating China politically and on building international coalitions to pursue economic and military action against China if required. Economically, lead and impose multilateral economic sanctions on China to weaken its financial power base. This would also limit China's ability to further reform and equip its military forces with advanced materiel. Militarily, increase U.S., allied, and partner military presence in the area and lead a multinational coalition to patrol the South China Sea to enforce international law according to UNCLOS. To maintain legitimacy during this process, the United States should ratify UNCLOS. The two major opportunities with this plan would be exhibiting very strong U.S. leadership and vigorous support of international law and order.

However, this option would also clearly be extremely high risk since it could lead to armed conflict with China, as it would be seen as an overt challenge to Chinese state sovereignty and territorial integrity that are viewed as "core interests."[69] Pursuing this more aggressive procedure could push the United States into what has been termed a "Thucydides Trap." Former Chairman of the Joint Chiefs of Staff General Martin Dempsey explained this as: "Thucydides, the Greek historian, described what he called the 'Thucydides Trap,' and it goes something like this: It was Athenian fear of a rising Sparta that made war inevitable."[70] The United States would gain little from a military struggle with China unless the result was a total defeat of China which would be difficult to achieve and would expend plenty of U.S. "blood and treasure." Additionally, such an event would likely cause economic ruin for the United States and the rest of the world. Other risks include: economic sanctions would negatively impact the United States, its allies, and partners; enhanced U.S. actions in the South China Sea would be costly and require an increase in U.S. military forces, and it would be politically risky since it could lead to a war that neither the Congress nor the American people would likely support. The risks could only be partially diminished by explaining expectations to China and by gaining full consensus on action by the coalition, the U.S. Congress, and the American people.

RECOMMENDATION

While the suggestion to cooperate with China in the South China Sea runs counter to the current mainstream American view and is likely to be unpopular among U.S. national decision makers, it should be adopted for several reasons. First, it is the most practical of choices. Based on ongoing economic interaction and the participation of China in U.S. military exchanges and exercises, a positive baseline for further cooperation has already been set. It simply needs to be expanded by working initially on non-contentious common interests until the relationship matures. Once this occurs, both parties would then be able to work together on solving tougher issues. Second, this proposal has the most likely chance for enduring success because it would involve China in the process as a willing and equal participant. It is easy to see from current Chinese behavior and statements that their nation longs for the international recognition of its greater status in the world. Cooperating with the United States will afford China the opportunity to achieve this without limiting its development. As the Chinese so aptly say, this would truly be a win-win situation. Third, no matter how much effort the United States puts behind this aim, it will not be able to stop the rise of China unless it is willing to go to war to do so. Although, this will require a mind shift to accept, the reality of the situation is that China has "come of age." It wants to do more in the world, and it is capable of doing more in the world, so why not let it? This revelation also comes with the understanding that it would be far easier to influence China by example than by coercion or through military conflict. It is probable that most of the American people would not believe an armed struggle with China to maintain control of the South China Sea would be worth the effort. Fourth, the United States declared it "welcomes the emergence of a peaceful, stable, and prosperous China that plays a responsible role in and contributes to the region's security network."[71] If this statement is true, then the United States must assist China in doing so. The best way to accomplish this is to provide China with a solid example by employing collaborative measures.

Fifth, working together with China would raise the international standing of the United States and improve respect for its leadership and legitimacy globally since this action would show a willingness to work with other nations to achieve regional peace and stability. Finally, although this proposal may appear difficult for the Trump administration to accept, it is actually more possible now than under the previous administration. Trump has demonstrated the ability to consider unconventional methods and ways of thinking. In his inauguration speech, he set the stage for nontraditional policy by proclaiming the United States was still committed to cooperating with other countries, but that it would now be more accepting of other nations' interests. The desire to collaborate implies the United States does not always have to lead and that it can work with others to develop solutions to difficult issues. It also indicates a readiness to allow a more multipolar world where other countries can contribute more robustly. Furthermore, the President stated U.S. values would not be forced and the United States would lead by example. The option to cooperate with China is just that, an opportunity for the United States to lead by example.

> We will seek friendship and goodwill with the nations of the world, but we do so with the understanding that it is the right of all nations to put their own interests first. We do not seek to impose our way of life on anyone, but rather to let it shine as an example. We will shine for everyone to follow.[72]

The United States has nothing to lose, but much to gain, by pursuing the option to cooperate with China. Once given the choice to play, the ball will be in China's court, and it will be up to China to accept or decline such a gracious offer.

ENDNOTES - CHAPTER 6

1. U.S. Department of Defense, *The Asia-Pacific Maritime Security Strategy: Achieving U.S. National Security Objectives in a Changing Environment,* Washington, DC: U.S. Department of Defense, 2015, pp. 6-8, 14-17; Clarence J. Bouchat, *The Paracel Islands and U.S. Interests and Approaches in the South China Sea,* Carlisle, PA: Strategic Studies Institute, U.S. Army War College, June 2014, pp. 1-5; Christopher L. Daniels, *South China Sea: Energy and Security Conflicts,* Lanham, MD: Scarecrow Press Inc., 2014, pp. 2-11; Bernard D. Cole, *Sea Lanes and Pipelines: Energy Security in Asia,* Westport, CT: Praeger Security International, 2008, pp. 102-103.

2. National Security Advisor Susan E. Rice, "National Security Advisor Susan E. Rice's As Prepared Remarks on the U.S.-China Relationship at George Washington University," Washington, DC: George Washington University, September 21, 2015, p. 6; Michael McDevitt, "The South China Sea: Assessing U.S. Policy," *American Foreign Policy Interests*, Vol. 37, No. 1, April 8, 2015, pp. 25-26, available from *http://www.tandfonline.com/doi/full/10.1080/10 803920.2015.1006519*, accessed December 19, 2016.

3. The State Council Information Office of the People's Republic of China, "III. China's Foreign Policies for Pursuing Peaceful Development," September 6, 2011, pp. 1-4, available from *www. scio.gov.cn/zfbps/ndhf/2011/Document/1000031/1000031_3.htm*, accessed December 15, 2016; McDevitt, p. 24.

4. Ibid.

5. Zhiguo Gao and Bing Bing Jia, "The Nine-Dash Line in the South China Sea: History, Status, and Implications," *The American Journal of International Law*, Vol. 107, No. 98, 2013, p. 98.

6. David Lai, *The United States and China in Power Transition*, Carlisle, PA: Strategic Studies Institute, U.S. Army War College, 2011, pp. 126-132; Bouchat, pp. 1-5, 13-16; U.S. Department of Defense, p. 6; Gavin Briggs, "Geography Matters in the South China Sea," *Asia & The Pacific Policy Society*, July 23, 2015, available from *www.policyforum.net/geography-matters-in-the-south-china-sea/*, accessed November 6, 2016.

7. Chris P. C. Chung, "Drawing the U-Shaped Line: China's Claim in the South China Sea, 1946–1974," *Modern China*, Vol. 42, No. 1, 2016, pp. 38-39.

8. Erik Franckx and Marco Benatar, "Dots and Lines in the South China Sea: Insights from the Law of Map Evidence," *Asian Journal of International Law*, Vol. 2, Iss. 1, January 2012, pp. 89-118, quoted in Chung, p. 57.

9. Chung, p. 62.

10. Lai, *The United States and China in Power Transition*, pp. 126-132; Bouchat, pp. 1-5, 13-16; U.S. Department of Defense, p. 6; Briggs; Katie Hunt, Matt Rivers, and Catherine E. Shoichet, "In

China, Duterte Announces Split with US: 'America has Lost'," CNN, October 20, 2016, available from *www.cnn.com/2016/10/20/ asia/china-philippines-duterte-visit/*, accessed February 18, 2017.

11. Nandini Krishnamoorthy, "South China Sea: Philippines sees Chinese Attempt to Build on Reef near its Coast," *International Business Times*, February 8, 2017, available from *www.ibtimes.co.uk/ philippines-sees-chinese-attempt-build-reef-near-its-coast-1605358*, accessed February 12, 2017.

12. Lai, *The United States and China in Power Transition*, pp. 126-132; Bouchat, pp. 1-5, 13-16; U.S. Department of Defense, p. 6; Briggs.

13. U.S. Department of Defense, pp. 6-8; Bert Chapman, "China's Nine-Dashed Map: Continuing Maritime Source of Geopolitical Tension," *Geopolitics, History, and International Relations*, Vol. 8, No. 1, 2016, pp. 146-150; United Nations Convention on the Law of the Sea (UNCLOS), December 10, 1982, pp. 43-53, 129-132; Max Fisher, "The South China Sea: Explaining the Dispute," *The New York Times*, July 14, 2016, available from *www.nytimes. com/2016/07/15/world/asia/south-china-sea-dispute-arbitration-explained.html*, accessed October 19, 2016; Hannah Beech, "Just Where Exactly Did China Get the South China Sea Nine-Dash Line From?" *Time*, July 19, 2016, available from *http://time.com/4412191/ nine-dash-line-9-south-china-sea/*, accessed November 7, 2016; Permanent Court of Arbitration, "The South China Sea Arbitration: The Republic of the Philippines v. The People's Republic of China," Press Release, The Hague, July 12, 2016, available from *https://assets.documentcloud.org/documents/2990864/Press-Release-on-South-China-Sea-Decision.pdf*, accessed March 24, 2017.

14. Ankit Panda, "1 Year Later: Reflections on China's Oil Rig 'Sovereignty-Making' in the South China Sea," *The Diplomat*, May 12, 2015, available from *https://thediplomat.com/2015/05/1-year-later-reflections-on-chinas-oil-rig-sovereignty-making-in-the-south-china-sea/*, accessed February 5, 2017; Andrew Chubb, "China-Vietnam clash in the Paracels: History still Rhyming in the Internet Era?" May 7, 2014, available from *https://southseaconversations.wordpress. com/2014/05/07/china-vietnam-clash-in-the-paracels-history-still-rhyming-in-the-internet-era/*, quoted in Shinji Yamaguchi, "Strategies of China's Maritime Actors in the South China Sea," *China Perspectives 2016*, No. 3, 2016, p. 27.

15. Permanent Court of Arbitration. p. 2.

16. Fisher; Beech, "Just Where Exactly Did China Get the South China Sea Nine-Dash Line From?"; Zheng Wang, "China and UNCLOS: An Inconvenient History," *The Diplomat*, July 11, 2016, available from *https://thediplomat.com/2016/07/china-and-unclos-an-inconvenient-history/*, accessed February 6, 2017; Hannah Beech, "China Will Never Respect the U.S. Over the South China Sea. Here's Why," *Time*, July 7, 2016, available from *http://time.com/4397808/south-china-sea-us-unclos/*, accessed March 24, 2017; United Nations Oceans & Law of the Sea, Division for Ocean Affairs and the Law of the Sea, "China's Declarations and Statements," June 7, 1996, available from *www.un.org/depts/los/convention_agreements/convention_declarations.htm#China after ratification*, accessed March 25, 2017.

17. Map courtesy of Wikimedia Commons contributor, "File:-South China Sea claims map.jpg," Wikimedia Commons, the free media repository, last revised July 3, 2017, available from *https://commons.wikimedia.org/w/index.php?title=File:South_China_Sea_claims_map.jpg&oldid=250120981*.

18. U.S. Department of Defense, pp. 15-17; David Lai, email message to author, March 19, 2017.

19. U.S. Department of Defense, pp. 15-17.

20. Central Intelligence Agency, "Paracel Islands," *The World Factbook*, Washington, DC: Central Intelligence Agency, updated November 14, 2017, available from *https://www.cia.gov/library/publications/the-world-factbook/geos/pf.html*, accessed December 4, 2017; Andrei Chang, "Analysis: China's air-sea buildup," Space War, September 26, 2008, available from *www.spacewar.com/reports/Analysis_Chinas_air-sea_buildup_999.html*, accessed February 18, 2017; D. Collins, "China counters U.S. Asia-Pivot Strategy: Fortifies island military base," The China Money Report, August 13, 2012, available from *www.thechinamoneyreport.com/2012/08/13/china-counters-u-s-asia-pivot-strategy-fortifies-island-military-base/*, accessed February 18, 2017, quoted in Bouchat, p. 18.

21. Katie Hunt, Jim Sciutto and Tim Hume, "China said to deploy missiles on South China Sea island," CNN, February 17,

2016, available from *www.cnn.com/2016/02/16/asia/china-missiles-south-china-sea/*, accessed February 18, 2017.

22. Barack Obama, *National Security Strategy*, Washington, DC: The White House, February 2015, pp. 1-35.

23. Hillary Clinton, "America's Pacific Century," *Foreign Policy*, October 11, 2011, p. 1, available from *foreignpolicy.com/2011/10/11/americas-pacific-century/*, accessed October 17, 2016.

24. U.S. President Barack H. Obama, "Remarks By President Obama to the Australian Parliament," public speech, Parliament House, Canberra, Australia, released by The White House, Office of the Press Secretary, November 17, 2011, p. 4.

25. Aaron Blake, "Donald Trump's full inauguration speech transcript, annotated," *The Washington Post*, January 20, 2017, p. 5, available from *https://www.washingtonpost.com/news/the-fix/wp/2017/01/20/donald-trumps-full-inauguration-speech-transcript-annotated/?utm_term=.5a37ad7689fe*, accessed January 20, 2017.

26. Ibid.

27. Russell Bova, *How the World Works: A Brief Survey of International Relations*, 2nd ed., Boston, MA: Longman, 2012, pp. 8-19; Hans J. Morgenthau, *Politics Among Nations: The Struggle for Power and Peace*, 6th ed., New York: McGraw-Hill Publishing Company, 1985, pp. 5, 31-32; Robert C. Nation, "Introduction to International Relations: Seminar 14, USAWC, AY 2017 Introduction to Political Realism," Carlisle Barracks, PA, U.S. Army War College, September 6, 2016, notes; Blake, p. 5.

28. Blake, pp. 1-9; Obama, *National Security Strategy*, pp. 1-35; Nation, notes.

29. Blake, p. 5.

30. Victor D. Cha, "Complex Patchworks: U.S. Alliances as Part of Asia's Regional Architecture," *Asia Policy*, Vol. 11, January 2011, pp. 27-31, available from *www.nbr.org/publications/asia_policy/Preview/AP11_US_Alliance_preview.pdf*, accessed January 22, 2017.

31. The State Council Information Office of the People's Republic of China, "III. China's Foreign Policies for Pursuing Peaceful Development," p. 2; David Lai, "The United States and China in Power Transition, Stage II," manuscript prepared for the 4th International Conference on Economics, Politics, and Security of China and the United States, July 2016, p. 9.

32. The State Council Information Office of the People's Republic of China, *China's Policies on Asia Pacific Security Cooperation*, January 11, 2017, file received through email, available from *www.scio.gov.cn*, accessed January 18, 2017; Lai, "The United States and China in Power Transition, Stage II," pp. 9-22; Chinese Ministry of Defense, *China's Military Strategy*, Beijing, China: Chinese Ministry of Defense, May 26, 2015, pp. 1-26.

33. The State Council Information Office of the People's Republic of China, *China's Policies on Asia Pacific Security Cooperation*, p. 2.

34. Obama, *National Security Strategy*, p. 13.

35. US Department of Defense, p. 5.

36. Ibid.

37. U.S. Energy Information Administration data quoted in U.S. Department of Defense, p. 1.

38. Rice, p. 6; McDevitt, p. 25.

39. Jethro Mullen, "Trump attacks China on trade but misses the mark," CNN, December 5, 2016, available from *http://money.cnn.com/2016/12/05/news/economy/trump-china-yuan-dollar-currency-taxes/*, accessed February 11, 2017.

40. CNBC, "Trump secretary of state nominee: China should be denied access to South China Sea islands," Reuters, January 11, 2017, available from *www.cnbc.com/2017/01/11/trump-secretary-of-state-nominee-china-should-be-denied-access-to-south-china-sea-islands.html*, accessed February 11, 2017.

41. Phil Stewart, "Mattis says no need for dramatic U.S. Military moves in South China Sea," Reuters, February 3, 2017, available from *www.reuters.com/article/*

us-usa-trump-southchinasea-mattis-idUSKBN15J061, accessed February 11, 2017.

42. Ibid.

43. The State Council Information Office of the People's Republic of China, "V. China's Policy on the South China Sea Issue," in The State Council Information Office of the People's Republic of China, *China Adheres to the Position of Settling Through Negotiation the Relevant Disputes Between China and the Philippines in the South China Sea*, July 13, 2016, p. 6, available from *http://www.scio.gov.cn/zfbps/32832/Document/1483616/1483616_5.htm*, accessed December 13, 2017.

44. Lai, *The United States and China in Power Transition*, pp. 75-99; Chinese Ministry of Defense. pp. 6-23.

45. United Nations Oceans & Law of the Sea.

46. UNCLOS, p. 140.

47. United Nations Oceans & Law of the Sea; UNCLOS, p. 140.

48. UNCLOS, pp. 136-137; Fisher; The State Council Information Office of the People's Republic of China, "V. China's Policy on the South China Sea Issue."

49. "A New Solution To an Old Issue: The dual-track approach emphasizes peace for resolving the South China Sea disputes," *Beijing Review*, May 28, 2015, p. 1, available from *https://search.proquest.com/docview/1683024482?accountid=4444*, accessed December 20, 2016; Wang Junmin, "Dual track right approach to South China Sea," *China Daily*, April 22, 2015, p. 9.

50. "A New Solution To an Old Issue."

51. U.S. Department of Defense, p. 25.

52. Ibid, p. 19.

53. U.S. Secretary of Defense Ash Carter, "The Rebalance and Asia-Pacific Security," *Foreign Affairs*, Vol. 95, No. 6, November/December 2016, pp. 74-75; Idress Ali and Matt Spetalnick,

"U.S. warship challenges China's claims in South China Sea," Reuters, October 21, 2016, available from *www.reuters.comarticle/us-southchinasea-usa-exclusive-idUSKCN12L1O9*, accessed October 26, 2016; Lieutenant Michael S. Proctor, U.S. Navy Reserve, "Check China," *Proceedings Magazine*, Vol. 142/12/1,366, December 2016, pp. 18-20; UNCLOS, pp. 27-33.

54. U.S. Department of Defense, pp. 6-8, 14-17; Bouchat, pp. 1-5; Daniels, pp. 2-11; Cole, pp. 102-103.

55. "Navigating Conflict in the South China Sea," *STRATFOR Global Intelligence*, pp. 29-31.

56. Ibid, p. 31.

57. Sun Tzu, *The Art of War*, Samuel Griffith, trans., New York: Oxford University Press, 1963, p. 77.

58. David Barno and Nora Bensahel, "Fighting and Winning in the 'Gray Zone'," War on the Rocks, May 19, 2015, available from *https://warontherocks.com/2015/05/fighting-and-winning-in-the-gray-zone/*, accessed February 12, 2017.

59. Ali and Spetalnick.

60. Mike Yeo, "US, Chinese aircraft in 'unsafe' encounter in South China Sea," *DefenseNews*, February 9, 2017, available from *www.defensenews.com/articles/us-chinese-aircraft-in-unsafe-encounter-in-south-china-sea*, accessed February 12, 2017.

61. Blake, p. 3.

62. "U.S. National Debt Clock: Real Time," U.S. Debt Clock. org, cont. updating, available from *www.usdebtclock.org/*, accessed February 17, 2017.

63. The State Council Information Office of the People's Republic of China, "III. China's Foreign Policies for Pursuing Peaceful Development," p. 1.

64. Ray Mabus, Admiral Jonathan W. Greenert, General Joseph F. Dunford, Jr., Admiral Paul F. Zukunft, "A Cooperative Strategy for 21st Century Seapower," Washington, DC: The Government Printing Office, March 2015, pp. 3-4.

65. Chinese Ministry of Defense. p. 24.

66. Liu Zhenmin, "China's Policies on Asia-Pacific Security Cooperation," press conference, January 11, 2017.

67. Li Xiaokun, "Code of conduct framework taking shape," *China Daily*, January 12, 2017, available from *usa.chinadaily.com.cn/epaper/2017-01/12/content_27936031.htm*, accessed March 26, 2017; Manuel Mogato and Michael Martina, "Philippines hopes South China Sea 'conduct code' ready this year," Nick Macfie, ed., Reuters, January 11, 2017, available from *https://in.reuters.com/article/myanmar-rohingya-un/myanmar-forces-may-be-guilty-of-genocide-against-rohingya-u-n-says-idINKBN1DZ143*, accessed March 26, 2017.

68. "A New Solution to an Old Issue," p. 1; Junmin, p. 9.

69. The State Council Information Office of the People's Republic of China, "III. China's Foreign Policies for Pursuing Peaceful Development," pp. 1-4; McDevitt, p. 24.

70. General Martin Dempsey, "A Conversation with General Martin Dempsey," interview by Jessica Tuchman Mathews, Carnegie Endowment for International Peace, Washington, DC, May 1, 2012, pp. 15-16, transcript available from *carnegieendowment.org/files/050112_transcript_dempsey.pdf*, accessed February 17, 2017; Lai, "The United States and China in Power Transition, Stage II," p. 1; Robert B. Strassler, ed., *The Landmark Thucydides: A Comprehensive Guide to the Peloponnesian War*, New York: The Free Press, 1996, p. 49.

71. Carter, pp. 69-70.

72. Blake, p. 5.

CHAPTER 7

PHILIPPINE AMBIVALENCE TOWARD THE UNITED STATES: LESSONS LEARNED

Romeo S. Brawner, Jr.

EXECUTIVE SUMMARY

Newly elected Philippine President Rodrigo Duterte announced his intention to cut military and economic ties with the United States, the Philippines' long-time ally, during his state visit to China in 2016. This caught the international community by surprise and seems to be a significant setback to the U.S. rebalance effort in the Indo-Asia-Pacific (IAP). For the Philippines, the rift is based on perceptions of mistreatment by and inequality with its long-standing ally. The good news, however, is that there seems to be a strong opportunity for the Trump administration to mend fences going forward. With a little political and cultural astuteness, the United States should be able to restore its friendship with the Philippines and count on a strong partnership as both countries pursue their interests in the IAP.

The Philippines' discontent with its current relationship with the United States is the product of the following three factors. First, the Filipino identity of being a fighter for independence makes them staunch advocates for Philippine sovereignty. Second, the Philippine centralized political culture places great power on the President to formulate the country's domestic and foreign policies and thus expects respect and political independence. Third, the Filipino resilience to natural and international challenges makes the Philippines a fair and rules-abiding player in the international arena and therefore expects reciprocity from its allies and international partners.

In order to mend fences and to engender a more amicable and stable relationship, the United States should intervene less with the domestic affairs of the Philippines based on the international law principle of non-interference. The United States should respect the leadership of the Philippines by considering closely the country's political culture and respecting its leadership. This is referenced on the principle of mutual trust. It is also important for the United States to assure the Philippines and its other allies that they will abide by their obligations in accordance with their agreements. They should also bolster their credibility in the international world order by agreeing to, ratifying, and complying with the provisions of international conventions and agreements. This lesson is based on the international relations principle of reciprocity.

The future holds a lot of promise for the reestablishment of a good U.S.-Philippine relationship under the Trump-Duterte administrations. Both leaders have displayed a personal liking for each other but more importantly, both have stated their desire to find common areas of cooperation. After all, it is all of humanity that benefits from a peaceful and harmonious world.

INTRODUCTION

> Your honors, in this venue, I announce my separation from the United States, both in military and economics.
> — Philippine President Rodrigo Duterte

The U.S.-Philippine relationship was rocked in 2016 with the pronouncement of then newly elected Philippine President Rodrigo Duterte that he would cut ties with the United States of America, the Philippines' long-time ally. He further announced that he would build stronger ties with China and Russia. He made these statements during his state visit to Beijing in October 2016.[1]

What led to this pronouncement? Is this merely the rhetoric of an independent-thinking statesman or is this a shared sentiment among the Filipino people? What lessons can we learn from this?

This chapter examines this unexpected policy change by the Philippines toward its long-standing ally, the United States. It aims to answer two main questions—first, what factors contributed to the ambivalence of the Philippine government toward the United States under the administration of Philippine President Duterte, and second, what lessons in international relations can we derive from this phenomenon. The Analytical Cultural Framework for Strategy and Policy (ACFSP) developed by the Strategic Studies Institute of the U.S. Army War College in 2008 was used in the analysis.[2]

This chapter argues that the change of heart by the Philippines, following a rekindled romance with the United States during the previous administration of Philippine President Benigno Aquino III, is the product of three factors: 1) the Filipino identity of being a fighter for independence makes them staunch advocates for Philippine sovereignty; 2) the Philippine centralized political culture places great power on the President to formulate the country's domestic and foreign policies and thus expects respect and political independence; and 3) the Filipino resilience to natural and international challenges makes the Philippines a fair and rules-abiding player in the international arena and therefore expects reciprocity from its allies and international partners.

From these factors above, the three lessons in international relations that may be derived are: 1) nations should intervene less in the domestic affairs of another; 2) an understanding of the political culture of a country and the respect for its political leadership are imperative to good bilateral relations; and, 3) a country should be clear and resolute in reassuring its allies and partners that it will comply with the obligations under their treaties and agreements.

THE ANALYTICAL CULTURAL FRAMEWORK FOR STRATEGY AND POLICY

The Analytical Cultural Framework for Strategy and Policy (ACFSP) is a systematic and analytical tool that may assist strategists and policymakers "view the world through many lenses."[3] It provides a framework that analyzes the interests of other players in the international arena through the cultural lens, and then considers these interests in the formulation of strategies and international policies. A country becomes more effective in dealing with other state or nonstate players by using this framework.

The ACFSP identifies three basic cultural dimensions. These are identity, political culture, and resilience. The identity of a people comes from their shared values, principles, norms, and practices, which are traceable from its history. The most important dimension is identity because this is where the people draw their purposes and interests, which in turn, determine their policies and strategies.[4]

The political culture of a country is determined from its structure of power and decision-making. The structure of power and decision-making determines where the political power of a country resides, as well as the extent to which this power is centralized or distributed. By understanding this dimension, a country can formulate strategies that will enable it to deal constructively with the political leadership of friendly or hostile nations.[5]

Finally, resilience is the capacity or ability to resist, adapt, or succumb to pressures from the external world. It is determined from its response to globalization, global environmental issues, and international institutions. This dimension would tell the world how a particular country would react to international pressures such as economic sanctions or troop contributions to coalitions. It also gives a glimpse as to how a country would interact with other countries and how it would act within or outside international organizations.[6]

FACTORS LEADING TO THE AMBIVALENCE

The following sections will present an application of the Analytical Cultural Framework for Strategy and Policy to determine the factors that led to the ambivalence of the Philippines toward the United States.

Identity: The Filipino Fighting Spirit

Perhaps the best way to determine the identity of the Filipino people is to look at their history. One striking aspect of the history of the Philippines is that it is comprised of a compendium of a peoples' struggle for independence. This struggle may be categorized into three eras: Spanish colonialism, American occupation, and post-independence neo-colonialism. In 1892, strong patriotic sentiments among the Filipino elite began a movement for independence that threatened to end more than 3 centuries of Spanish rule. This was the first nationalist movement in Southeast Asia.[7] This movement led to a bloody revolution that nearly won the independence for Filipinos. However, the ceding of the Philippines to the United States by Spain in 1899 dashed the Filipino dream for self-rule. The American occupation of the islands followed this period. Another revolt by the Filipinos greeted the new colonizers, but the Americans quickly repelled this through military and diplomatic maneuvers.

The colonization of the Philippines by the United States was met with dissention from some lawmakers in the mainland because it went against the very principles that make up the core of American society—freedom and independence. Nonetheless, the arguments for the spread of democratic values and the need for economic expansion of American goods prevailed over the dissenting views.[8]

In 1935, the United States gave conditional independence to the Filipinos as the Philippines transitioned to full independence. The Japanese cut this short with the attack on Manila, a few hours after their attack on Pearl Harbor, Hawaii. Finally, on July 12, 1946, the United States granted full independence to the Philippines.

Some Filipinos felt this newfound independence was not a total independence. Sentiments of skepticism and continued oppression were manifest across Philippine society. Some scholars called this the "Era of Neo-Colonialism."[9] The continued presence of American military bases contributed to this growing sentiment. In 1991, it was this same feeling of independence from American neo-colonialism that drove the Philippine Senate to vote against the renewal of the U.S.-Philippine Bases Agreement.[10]

On the other hand, the presence of American forces brought a cover of security to a country strategically situated in the Asia-Pacific region. It was only in the past decade, however, that Philippine sovereignty was actually threatened with intrusions into the Philippine exclusive economic zone by China. These aggressive actions by China spurred debates within the Philippine congress and judiciary on whether or not U.S. forces should be allowed to come back to Philippine shores on a more permanent status and with larger numbers.

Neo-colonialism may also come through economic ways. Critics of U.S. economic influence on the Philippines stated that:

> The ensuing years [after World War II] were characterized by political manipulations, through the exploitative maneuverings of U.S. hegemony, that began to hurt the country's economic foundation and put in place the conditions that later pulled the Philippines down the path of political decadence and, more seriously, economic retardation.[11]

Many of these critics believe that the Philippines is still at the mercy of international lending institutions such as the World Bank and the International Monetary Fund. Some sectors of Philippine society see this as anti-development because of the restrictive economic and financial policies imposed by these financial institutions.[12]

Coming out of this colorful history, it is evident that Filipinos have always had a strong desire to be fully independent, not just from an occupying power, but also from neo-colonialist influences. Thus, national pride is engrained in the Filipino identity. This, therefore, results in the Filipinos' enduring interest for self-determination and sovereignty.

Political Culture: Centralized Presidential System

The Philippines follows a democratic system of government that has three branches: the executive, the legislative, and the judiciary. Among these three branches, however, it is the executive branch, led by the president, which is the most influential. This form of government is that of a unitary government with power centralized in the Office of the President.[13] The president determines the national vision, the national priorities, and the general policies of the state, including its foreign policies.

The incumbency of former President Ferdinand Marcos from 1966 to 1986 demonstrates how a Philippine president can have great political power. In 1972, President Marcos declared martial law and took control of almost all facets of government, including control of key industries and businesses. His political reign ended after 2 decades, with a bloodless revolution called the "People's Revolution" when millions of people gathered in the nation's capital calling for his resignation. Marcos went into exile with his family to Hawaii.[14]

Because of this experience under a dictatorship, the newly formed government under former President Corazon Aquino instituted reforms to limit the powers of the president. The 1987 Philippine Constitution embodies these limitations to presidential power.[15] Despite the delimiting constitutional provisions, however, the Philippine president still exercises great political powers and the incumbency of Duterte manifests this trend.

When Duterte took over the seat of power in the Philippine government, he placed a premium on the resolution of domestic issues over international concerns. One of his top priorities was to get rid of the drug menace and criminality that plagued most of Philippine society. This "war on drugs and crime" has resulted in the death of thousands of drug pushers and users as well as other criminals. However, it also produced critics, both domestic and international.

In August 2016, a rift between Duterte and former U.S. President Barack Obama sent ripples in the international media. This came about after Obama made statements criticizing the human rights violations and extrajudicial killings resulting from Duterte's war on drugs and crime. This statement was not taken well by Duterte and it prompted him to announce that he was abrogating ties with the United States.[16] He further said Russia could be a very important ally of the Philippines because "they do not insult people, they do not interfere."[17] Obama was not the only recipient of the tirade from Duterte. United Nations (UN) Secretary General Ban Ki-moon, the European Union, and the Catholic Church also received similar remarks from the Philippine president for contrary opinions against the manner of conduct of the "war on drugs and criminality."[18]

From the instances mentioned above, it is clear that because of the centrality of political power inherent on the Philippine president, personality and experiences play an important role. A study made on former U.S. Presidents demonstrates that the personality of the national leader played a big role in determining his vision and priorities for his country, as well his effectiveness as a leader.[19] Another study made at the U.S. Army War College in 2010, argues that the personality and leadership style of the American Chief Executive strongly influences the relationship of the United States with the Philippines.[20]

What was it in Duterte's experience and personality that led to his change in policy toward the United States? In several fora, the president admitted to being "left-leaning," having been a student of the Communist Party of the Philippines founder, Jose Maria Sison. This inclination toward the left has instilled in the president anti-American and anti-colonial sentiments early on in his life.[21] This anti-American sentiment was fueled further by several not-so-pleasant experiences with the United States. He claimed that the United States once denied him a visa, and in another instance, airport officials detained him at the Los Angeles airport while he was in transit to South America. Perhaps the more serious matter is his claim that the United States was behind the bombing of Davao City when he was still its mayor. He also claims that alleged agents of the Central Intelligence Agency rescued the bombing suspect who was a U.S. citizen.[22]

Looking at recent events, it is evident that the president has a disdain for criticism of his policies, but a liking for anyone or any nation that approves of his domestic war on drugs. For instance, Duterte made public his appreciation of two countries in the region, China and Japan, that declared their support for his drug and crime policies. On September 29, 2016, Chinese Foreign Ministry spokesperson Geng Shuang said in a press briefing, "Under the leadership of President Duterte, the new Philippine government enacted policies that prioritize combating drug-related crimes. China understands and supports that."[23] On the other hand, during Japanese Prime Minister Shinzo Abe's visit to the Philippines in January 12, 2017, he declared his support for Duterte's war on drugs saying, "on countering illegal drugs, we want to work together with the Philippines to think of relevant measures of support."[24]

These series of statements and incidents certainly reflect the centralization of political power in the seat of the Philippine presidency, which, in turn, depends to a great deal on the personality and experiences of the president. Consequently, this results in an expectation that the international community will recognize this Philippine political culture and respect its national leadership.

Resilience: The Philippine's Position in the International Order

Perhaps Filipinos are some of the more resilient people on this planet considering the number of natural calamities that affect the Philippines annually. An average of 20 typhoons hit the country per year because of its geographical location along the Pacific Rim of Fire. In addition, several earthquakes shake the country, claiming thousands of lives and millions of dollars' worth of properties. Despite these natural calamities, the Filipino people have risen repeatedly to recover from destruction to normalcy within a short period of time.[25]

This realization of the vulnerability of mankind against natural disasters led the Philippine government to set up an extensive network with local and international organizations in order to mitigate the effects of these disasters. There have been several instances when this collaborative effort of the Philippine government with international humanitarian institutions has been demonstrated and proven effective, contributing to the strengthening of the resilience of the Filipino people.

Aside from resilience to natural calamities, resilience is also defined as the ability of a nation to resist, adapt, or succumb to pressures from the external world. It is determined from its response to globalization.[26] Thus, the resilience of a nation is measured not only by how it reacts to international issues, but also by how it deals with other nations in the international community.

In the international realm, the Philippines is seen as one of the pioneering countries that has supported globalization through the establishment of international institutions. This is manifested in the fact that the Philippines is one of the first countries to join the UN. Manila was also the venue in the establishment of the South East Asian Treaty Organization (SEATO). Currently, aside from the UN, the Philippines is a member of the Association of South East Asian Nations (ASEAN), the ASEAN Regional Forum, and the Asia-Pacific Economic Cooperation (APEC), among others.

The Philippines also has bilateral relations with other countries, but its biggest diplomatic relation is with its only ally, the United States. This alliance is clearly established in the Mutual Defense Treaty that was signed in 1951, but is still in effect today. It stipulates that the two parties should go to the aid of the other in the event of an attack on its territory or people, whether on land or on a ship in the Pacific. More than just a defense agreement, however, the Mutual Defense Treaty emphasizes the peaceful resolution of international disputes, the development of the capacity, either separately or jointly, to resist or counter an attack, and the necessity for collaboration in other areas such as law enforcement, counterterrorism, and humanitarian assistance and disaster relief.[27]

During his visit to the Philippines in April 2014, Obama said, "[the U.S.] commitment to defend the Philippines is ironclad and the United States will keep that commitment, because allies never stand alone."[28]

It was also during this visit where Obama and Aquino signed the Enhance Defense Cooperation Agreement (EDCA). The EDCA would allow an increased U.S. military presence in the Philippines on a rotational basis, thus enhancing the defense capabilities of both nations as well as improving the maritime security situation in the region.[29]

Despite this new defense agreement, however, there is still the lack of assurance that the United States will come to the aid of its ally in the event of an attack by China. According to Pacifico A. Agabin, a former dean of the College of Law of the University of the Philippines:

> our reliance to the Mutual Defense Treaty and assurance of U.S. is purely illusory. The treaty, which guarantees mutual support in the event of an attack on either the Philippines or the U.S., has its limits. For one, the U.S. has no automatic participation since the U.S. Congress has yet to pass an operating law for the treaty.[30]

Another factor to be considered is the perceived lack of credibility of the United States in its desire to establish a rules-based order in the region. While the United States insists that the countries in the region should adhere to the United Nations Convention on the Laws of the Sea (UNCLOS), the U.S. Senate has not ratified this international convention. This does not speak well of a global power that considers the establishment of a rules-based international order as one of its enduring interests. On the contrary, ratification of the UNCLOS would strengthen the U.S. position as a global power.[31]

From these analyses, we deduce that Filipinos are very resilient as a people, particularly when dealing with natural disasters as well as when dealing with globalization and the international challenges and issues that go with it. As a member of the international community, Filipinos are fair and just players, who honor the rule of international law and thus expect reciprocity from their international allies and partners.

LESSONS LEARNED

Considering the factors mentioned above, what then could we learn? The following lessons can be gleaned from the ambivalence of the Philippines to the United States: first, states should respect the culture and identity of other countries and interfere less in their domestic affairs; second, countries should ascertain the power culture of the target country and deal with its political leadership in an appropriate manner; and third, countries should assure their allies and partners that they will abide by their obligations as stipulated in the agreements they may have, while establishing their credibility as fair and resolute international players. These lessons are discussed, drawing foundational references from principles in international relations and international law.

Less Intervention

History is replete with examples of a people's victory following a struggle for freedom and independence. The American independence story is one excellent example. At the end of the struggle, the American people got what they desired—freedom and independence from Great Britain. However, in modern times, countries may still struggle for independence, not from an occupying power but from a dominant country trying to impose its will on the other through intervention.

As such, the international law principle of non-interference was developed. This principle was also written into the UN Charter. The Charter states, "every State has an inalienable right to choose its political, economic, social and cultural systems, without interference in any form by another State."[32] Thus, a nation-state acting independently from any external intervention is able to chart its own course and follow this in the best way it sees fit. It does this to pursue fully its national interests in consideration of its culture and resources.[33]

The newly elected U.S. President Donald Trump seemed to share this point of view when he said during his inaugural speech on January 20, 2017:

> We will seek friendship and goodwill with the nations of the world, but we do so with the understanding that it is the right of all nations to put their own interests first. We do not seek to impose our way of life on anyone, but rather to let it shine as an example.[34]

The principle of non-interference is also explicitly written in the charter of the ASEAN. International theorists share the view that the principle of absolute non-interference in the internal affairs of states is a central pillar of Southeast Asian regionalism.[35]

During the formal launching of the Philippine chairmanship of the ASEAN for 2017, Duterte called on ASEAN Dialogue Partners to:

> renew their dedication to the valued purposes and principles stated in the Treaty of Amity and Cooperation—including non-interference—in promoting regional peace and stability through abiding respect for the rule of law.[36]

The Treaty of Amity and Cooperation in Southeast Asia is a peace treaty among Southeast Asian countries, signed by the founding members of the ASEAN (Indonesia, Malaysia, the Philippines, Singapore, and Thailand) on February 24, 1976. Today, there are 30 signatories to the Treaty of Amity and Cooperation in Southeast Asia, including the United States, the European Union, and China.

Article I of the Treaty states its purpose as "to promote perpetual peace, everlasting amity, and cooperation among their peoples which would contribute to their strength, solidarity and closer relationship." Article 2 enumerates its fundamental principles as follows:

a. Mutual respect for the independence, sovereignty, equality, territorial integrity, and national identity of all nations;
b. The right of every State to lead its national existence free from external interference, subversion or coercion;
c. Non-interference in the internal affairs of one another;
d. Settlement of differences or disputes by peaceful means;
e. Renunciation of the threat or use of force;
f. Effective cooperation among themselves.[37]

This brings to light the differences in the way the West views intervention in contrast to how the East views it: "Western global governance norm of interventionism is being challenged by East Asian norm of non-interference and territorial integrity." The West views interventionism as a way to implement their role as the governor of the world affairs. On the other hand, the East translates this seemingly benign act as an affront to their sovereignty and an act of absolute intervention.[38]

Hence, from the discussion above, one lesson that we could draw is that countries should interfere less into the domestic issues of another.

Respect for Political Culture and National Leadership

In the previous section, one of the factors that contributed to the ambivalence of the Philippines to the United States is the centralized political culture that places much power in the Office of the President. Because of this, the personality and experiences of the president play a big role in the shaping of national policies. Therefore, a lesson that we can draw from this is that if a country wishes to have an effective bilateral relation with another, it has to consider the political culture of that country and try to deal with its national leadership in an appropriate manner.

This lesson is based on the principle of mutual respect. A study made by Reinhard Wolf argues that the "peoples' fundamental interest in self-respect makes them insist on receiving from other people a proper respect and recognition of their equality."[39] Wolf also claims that when:

> U.S. President Barack Obama promised numerous nations new relationships based 'on mutual respect', many foreign leaders had already begun to insist on being 'duly respected' by the United States and other (mostly Western) countries.[40]

This principle was deemed violated by the U.S. President, the U.S. Ambassador to the Philippines, and the Secretary General of the UN, from the point of view of Duterte, when the former high officials criticized the latter's war on drugs and crime. Considering the political culture of the Philippines, as well as the personality of Duterte, a more appropriate response to the Philippine's war on the drugs and crime would have been an offer of assistance through legally accepted means on this campaign to eradicate the drug menace and the culture of crime from the country.

Assurance for Allies and Partners

The third factor that was identified as contributing to the ambivalence of the Philippines to the United States is the resilience or ability to adapt to globalization by the Filipino people. History has proven that Filipinos have embraced globalization even in its infancy as a nation by joining international organizations, abiding by their norms, and respecting international law. It is therefore natural for the Philippines to expect the same from its ally, partners, and friends.

Unfortunately, the current sentiment in the Philippines is that the United States will not abide by its obligations under the Mutual Defense Treaty. Therefore, a lesson learned from this factor is that countries should be resolute in their relationships with their allies and partners and should give assurances that they will abide by obligations as stipulated in their treaties and agreements. This lesson is based on the principle of reciprocity.

Generally, reciprocity in international relations is the appropriate form of behavior of sovereign states that creates cooperation between them. The principle of reciprocity as it relates to treaties and agreements is known as specific reciprocity. It states that a country that has entered into a treaty or agreement with another must abide by its obligations as it expects the latter to abide by its obligations as well.[41]

Another kind of reciprocity is the diffuse reciprocity where a body of norms dictates how nations should act within alliances, coalitions, and international organizations. One such norm is the expectation that nations would comply with its obligations, even if carried in the future.[42] Therefore, an assurance that a nation will respect and will comply with its obligation is important. An incentive for such an assurance is the maintenance of its reputation as a responsible player in the international arena.[43]

The United States should likewise establish its credibility as a global power by ratifying the UNCLOS. This will give credence to the pursuit of its enduring interest of promoting a rules-based international order. While it could be argued that the United States has been honoring and adhering to the provisions of the UNCLOS even without ratification by the U.S. Congress, a formal approval of the convention will send the signal to the world that the United States means business when it comes to protecting the global commons.

CONCLUSION

A lot can be learned from the controversy that was created by the surprising statements made by Philippine President Duterte. Although dismissed by some as merely the rhetoric of a strong-minded national leader, his statements may have wisdom that could remind nations of some basic principles or concepts in international relations.

It is useful for a country to consider not only its own interests but the interests of the other nations as well, especially when it is formulating its foreign policies and strategies. This is why it is essential to view the world from the other nation's lens.

Using the ACFSP, this chapter argues that the change of policy by the Philippines toward the United States is the product of decades long of colonialization and neo-colonialization, a centralized Philippine political culture, and the resilience of the Filipino people to national and international challenges. From these factors, the following lessons can be learned: First, nations should intervene less with the domestic affairs of another nation. This is based on the principle in international law of non-interference. Second, states should respect the leadership of other countries by considering closely the political culture of the target country. This is referenced on the principle of mutual trust. Third, it is important for nations to assure their allies and partners that they will abide by their obligations in accordance with their agreements. They should also establish their credibility in the international world order by agreeing to, ratifying, and complying with the provisions of international conventions and agreements. This lesson is based on the international relations principle of reciprocity. In the end, it all boils down to how well one nation treats another.

The future holds a lot of promise for the reestablishment of the U.S.-Philippine relationship under the Trump-Duterte administrations. Both leaders have displayed a personal liking for each other but more importantly, both have stated their desire to find common areas of cooperation. After all, all of humanity benefits from a peaceful and harmonious world.

ENDNOTES - CHAPTER 7

1. Daxim L. Lucas, "Duterte announces military, economic split with US," *Philippine Daily Inquirer*, October 20, 2016, available from *https://globalnation.inquirer.net/147293/duterte-announces-military-economic-split-with-us*, accessed December 21, 2016.

2. Jiyul Kim, *Cultural Dimensions of Strategy and Policy*, Carlisle, PA: Strategic Studies Institute, U.S. Army War College, May 2009.

3. Ibid.

4. Ibid.

5. Ibid.

6. Ibid.

7. Nicolas Tarling, *Southeast Asia: A Modern History*, Oxford, UK: Oxford University Press, 2001, p. 364.

8. Colin Mason, *A Short History of Asia*, 3rd Ed., New York: Palgrave Macmillan, 2014, p. 289.

9. William J. Pomeroy, *American Neo Colonialism: Its Emergence in the Philippines and Asia*, New York: International Publishers, 1970, p. 83.

10. Philip Shenon, "Philippine Senate Votes to Reject U.S. Base Renewal," *The New York Times*, September 16, 1991, available from *www.nytimes.com/1991/09/16/world/philippine-senate-votes-to-reject-us-base-renewal.html*, accessed March 20, 2017.

11. "How US Neocolonial Development Failed the Philippines — Part I," News Junkie Post, October 30, 2013, available from *newsjunkiepost.com/2013/10/30/how-us-neocolonial-development-failed-the-philippines*, accessed January 3, 2017. For further on News Junkie Post's view of U.S. hegemony see "US Hegemonic Empire and Culture of Death: State Terrorism on a Global Scale," News Junkie Post, June 1, 2013, *newsjunkiepost.com/2013/06/01/us-hegemonic-empire-and-culture-of-death-state-terrorism-on-a-global-scale*.

12. Sandra Nicolas, "IMF-WB in the Philippines: Half-Century of Anti-Development," Bulatlat, Vol. IV, No. 11, April 18-24, 2004, available from *www.bulatlat.com/news/4-11/4-11-imf.html*, accessed January 21, 2017.

13. D. R. SarDesai, *Southeast Asia: Past and Present*, 5th Ed., Boulder, CO: Westview Press, 2003, p. 209.

14. Mason, p. 292.

15. "The Constitution of the Republic of the Philippines," *The Philippine Official Gazette*, 1987, available from *http://www.officialgazette.gov.ph/constitutions/1987-constitution/*.

16. Euan McKirdy and Kathy Quiano, "Philippines' Duterte to US: 'Do not make us your dogs'," CNN, October 25, 2016, available from *www.cnn.com/2016/10/25/asia/duterte-us-comments/*, accessed December 21, 2016.

17. Associated Press, "Philippines' Duterte to U.S. on aid issue: 'Bye-bye America'," *Politico*, December 17, 2016, available from *www.politico.com/story/2016/12/philippines-duterte-to-us-over-aid-issue-bye-bye-america-232776*, accessed December 21, 2016.

18. Nandini Krishnamoorthy, "Philippine President Duterte slams UN for criticizing his war on drugs," *International Business Times*, August 19, 2016, available from *www.ibtimes.co.uk/philippine-president-duterte-slams-un-critcising-his-war-drugs-1576746*, accessed February 3, 2017.

19. Robert J. House, William D. Spangler, and James Woycke, "Personality and Charisma in the U.S. Presidency: A Psychological Theory of Leader Effectiveness," *Administrative Science Quarterly*, Vol. 36, No. 3, September 1991, pp. 364-396.

20. Colonel Paterno Reynato C. Padua, *Republic of the Philippines-United States Defense Cooperation: Opportunities and Challenges, A Filipino Perspective*, Strategy Research Project, Carlisle Barracks, PA: U.S. Army War College, May 17, 2010, p. 15.

21. Ryan Pickrell, "Why Duterte Really Hates the USA," The Daily Caller, October 31, 2016, available from *http://dailycaller.com/2016/10/31/why-duterte-really-hates-the-usa/*, accessed March 20, 2017.

22. Ibid.

23. Patricia Lourdes Viray, "China backs Duterte's drug war," *The Philippine Star*, September 30, 2016, available from *www.philstar.com/headlines/2016/09/30/1629007/china-backs-dutertes-drug-war*, accessed January 20, 2017.

24. Agence France-Presse, "Japan PM offers Philippines drug war support," The Philippine Rappler, January 12, 2017, available from *www.rappler.com/nation/158169-japan-pm-abe-philippines-drug-war-support*, accessed January 20, 2017.

25. Justin Goldman, "Resilience in the Philippines in the Face of Natural Calamities," Diplomatic Courier, May 21, 2014, available from *www.diplomaticourier.com/resilience-in-the-philippines-in-the-face-of-natural-calamities/*, accessed January 14, 2017.

26. Kim, p. 2.

27. Eleanor Albert, "The U.S.-Philippines Defense Alliance," *Backgrounder*, Washington, DC: Council on Foreign Relations, October 21, 2016, available from *www.cfr.org/philippines/us-philippines-defense-alliance/p38101*, accessed February 1, 2017.

28. Carmela Fonbuena, "Obama: U.S. commitment to PH 'ironclad'," The Philippine Rappler, April 29, 2014, available from *www.rappler.com/nation/56690-obama-ironclad-support-philippines*, accessed January 14, 2017.

29. CNN Philippines Staff, "What You Need to Know About EDCA," CNN Philippines, April 14, 2016, available from *http://cnnphilippines.com/news/2016/01/13/what-you-need-to-know-about-edca.html*, accessed January 21, 2017.

30. Noemi M. Gonzales, "US assistance not immediate under Mutual Defense Treaty," Business World Online, June 29, 2011, available from *http://www.bworldonline.com/content.php?section=Nation&title=us-assistance-not-immediate-under-mutual-defense-treaty&id=33858*, accessed December 5, 2017.

31. Leon Panetta, "UNCLOS Accession Would Strengthen US Global Position," *Hampton Roads International Security Quarterly*, July 1, 2012, p. 23.

32. Maziar Jamnejad and Michael Wood, "The Principle of Non-intervention," *Leiden Journal of International Law*, June 2009, p. 345.

33. James E. Dougherty and Robert L. Pfaltzgraff, Jr., *Contending Theories of International Relations: A Comprehensive Survey*,

4th Ed., New York: Addison-Wesley Educational Publishers Inc., 1996, p. 30.

34. "FULL TEXT: of President Donald Trump's Inauguration Speech," *ABC News*, January 20, 2017, available from *abcnews. go.com/Politics/full-text-president-donald-trumps-inauguration-speech/story?id=44915821*, accessed January 21, 2017.

35. Lee Jones, "ASEAN's unchanged melody? The theory and practice of 'non-interference' in Southeast Asia," *The Pacific Review*, Vol. 23, Iss. 4, August 11, 2010, p. 479.

36. CNN Philippines Staff, "Duterte leads launch of PH chairmanship of ASEAN 2017," *CNN Philippines*, January 15, 2017, available from *http://cnnphilippines.com/news/2017/01/15/duterte-leads-asean-2017-launch.html*, accessed January 16, 2017.

37. "Treaty of Amity and Cooperation in Southeast Asia Indonesia, 24 February 1976," Association of Southeast Asian Nations, February 24, 1976, available from *http://asean.org/treaty-amity-cooperation-southeast-asia-indonesia-24-february-1976/*, accessed January 16, 2017.

38. Lauren Dunn, Peter Nyers, and Richard Stubbs, "Western interventionism versus East Asian non-interference: competing 'global' norms in the Asian century," *The Pacific Review*, Vol. 23, Iss. 3, July 5, 2010, p. 295.

39. Reinhard Wolf, "Respecting foreign peoples: the limits of moral obligations," *Journal of International Relations and Development*, Vol. 19, Iss. 1, January 2016, available from *search.proquest.com/docview/1750884197?pq-origsite=summon*, accessed February 17, 2017.

40. Ibid.

41. Robert O. Keohane, "Reciprocity in International Relations," *International Organization*, Vol. 40, No. 1, Winter 1986, available from *www.jstor.org/stable/2706740*, accessed March 20, 2017.

42. Ibid.

43. Jon Hovi, *Games, Threats and Treaties: Understanding Commitments in International Relations*, London, UK: Pinter, 1998, p. 103.

CHAPTER 8

THE UNITED STATES AND CHINA IN THE CYBER DOMAIN: STOP THE DOWNWARD SPIRAL

Steven M. Pierce

EXECUTIVE SUMMARY

The cyber domain has the potential to profoundly influence other domains such as land, maritime, and space and, consequently, the way nations employ national power in and across those domains. What happens in the cyber domain does not stay in the cyber domain. This is especially significant for U.S.-China relations. For better or worse, the United States and China have a contentious cyber relationship. There is ample evidence that actions taken by the two nations have affected broader U.S.-China relations negatively and intensified distrust between the two nations. It is imperative that the United States and China take measures to stop the downward spiral in cyber space and find ways to cooperate within the cyber domain to ensure stability across the other domains. Specifically, the United States and China should:

- Focus early on cooperation in areas that both the United States and China view as harmful or criminal but that are not politically charged. Examples include cybercrime, protection of critical infrastructure, supply chain security, intellectual property theft, and prevention of proliferation of cyber capabilities to violent extremist organizations and other nonstate actors.

- Follow-up on the September 2015 U.S.-China Cyber Espionage Agreement with specific and actionable measures aimed at curbing cyber-enabled commercial espionage, theft of intellectual property, and cybercrime.
- Increase people-to-people exchanges between the two countries. Exchanges of U.S. and Chinese citizens in academia and technology related industries could help build shared understanding and trust at the lowest levels.
- Further discussion of "red lines" in the cyber domain. The discussion of red lines is essential to avoid miscalculation and misjudgment during crises that could lead to unintended escalatory actions on both sides.

INTRODUCTION

Why is it important that the United States and China get along? While no two nations always agree completely on every issue, it is important for the world's two greatest powers to find common ground upon which to anchor their relationship because, ultimately, that relationship will have implications for the other nations of the world. As Travis Tanner and Wang Dong of the National Bureau of Asian Research asserts:

> Given that the global challenges facing the world today cannot be resolved without both the United States and China, calculations in the cyber, maritime, nuclear, and space domains are increasingly consequential and carry implications for other nations.[1]

Even though the relationship between the United States and China is currently "stronger than it has ever been," there exists an:

> increasing number of sources of tension and disagreement. . . . In addition, general strategic mistrust plagues the relationship and carries the potential...to quickly exacerbate tensions and bring about a harmful deterioration of the relationship or even conflict.[2]

CYBER DOMAIN STRATEGIC ENVIRONMENT

As is the case with many emerging, immature technologies, cyber is a domain that can be at once an opportunity and a vulnerability. As Sven Sakkov, Director of the NATO Cooperative Cyber Defense Centre of Excellence, explains it:

> Everything that is good and everything that is bad in human nature have their manifestations in cyberspace. The ultra-rapid advancement of technology has challenged and outpaced the development of the normative frameworks that should limit malicious activities—be it crime, hacktivism or state-sponsored activities.[3]

Albert Einstein's observation that "All our lauded technological progress—our very civilization—is like the axe in the hand of the pathological criminal" could be as true today with respect to the cyber domain as it was 100 years ago when he penned it in a letter to a colleague.[4] This idea of the duality of the domain—that it can be both an opportunity and a vulnerability—is explored in more detail in the analysis of how the U.S. and China view the domain differently.

The description and characteristics section begins with a definition of the cyber domain. The 2006 *National Military Strategy for Cyberspace Operations* defines it as "a domain characterized by the use of electronics and the electromagnetic spectrum to store, modify and exchange data via networked systems and associated physical infrastructures."[5] As Viktor Nagy of the National University of Public Service in Budapest, Hungary, notes, even though the domain is relatively new when compared to the other strategic domains, it "has evolved enough to significantly affect geostrategy."[6] The cyber domain is the first man-made domain and while it exists primarily as a virtual world, nation-states and nonstate actors interact in it in much the same way as they do in the other physical domains, and those interactions often result in "very real effects. Similarly to the advent of human activity in the other domains, cyberspace is now strongly contested."[7]

While much of the domain exists in a virtual space, there are critical physical infrastructure and nodes that enable operations, and much of that infrastructure resides within the United States. Adam Segal and Tang Lan of the National Bureau of Asian Research explain the structure this way: "A small number of Internet providers carry the bulk of data over the backbone, and a majority of Internet data is drawn in and routed through the United States, even if it makes little geographic sense."[8] Because of the U.S. commitment to maintaining an open internet and the free flow of information, the result is that "American cyberspace is one of the least secure online realms."[9] A major reason for this is simply the sheer number of users connected to the internet.

> The United States has so many computers and so much of the Internet's underlying infrastructure — with perhaps 500 million hosts compared to 20 million for China — it is not surprising that so many criminal attacks originate or pass through here.[10]

The sheer numbers of connected devices in the United States is a measure of America's dependence on the cyber domain and increases U.S. vulnerability to attacks in the domain.

Another challenge is the anonymity that the domain provides. As one expert writes:

> it is virtually impossible to differentiate legitimate Internet traffic from traffic with a malicious purpose. Information that has been stolen from somewhere, or that contains commands that will 'flip a switch' in such a way as to cause severe damage to a critical infrastructure system, is extremely difficult to identify.[11]

Unlike the other physical domains where actions can be observed to a great degree with existing systems:

> We have no early warning radar system or Coast Guard to patrol the borders in cyberspace . . . [and] information of an attack will come first from those being attacked. Therefore it is highly unlikely that a government organization, unless it is actually the target of a cyber-attack, will have greater situational awareness.[12]

Although many countries interact in the cyber domain, there are three primary nations that possess the majority of cyber capability and cyber power: the United States, China, and Russia.[13] This concentration of power is an interesting characteristic for a domain with the potential to connect billions of people around the world. In a speech given in Seoul, South Korea, in 2015, then-U.S. Secretary of State John Kerry stated, "Roughly three out of every five people in the world today remain without internet access—and in the poorest countries that figure can top 95 percent."[14]

Another characteristic of the cyber domain, not unlike the other domains, is the number of stakeholders with an interest in it. A key attribute of the domain is that "states, organizations, corporations, and even individuals can have major, global impact."[15] The reality is that "a variety of nongovernmental actors are significant players in each country's use of and deliberations about the cyber realm."[16] Due to the nascent and ever-evolving nature of the domain, "it is hard to set boundaries between the responsibilities of civilian and military agencies, creating the need for intense coordination between all actors involved."[17] Complicating the multi-stakeholder environment is the fact that these stakeholders do not all share a common vision of what "security" or "openness" within the domain means, even though these concepts affect both developed and developing countries interdependently.[18]

The cyber domain is also characterized by its dual nature of providing immense opportunities, while at the same time allowing nefarious actors to take advantage of its vulnerabilities. One researcher explained it this way:

> In a way, the world has become a victim of its own developmental successes. Over the last two decades, we have seen an incredible amount of openness in commerce and the exchange of ideas. However, with openness comes much vulnerability.[19]

On the same topic, former U.S. Secretary of State Kerry remarked, "obviously, the internet is not without risk—but at the end of the day, if we restricted all technology that could possibly be used for bad purposes, we'd have to revert to the Stone Age."[20] While actors in all the strategic domains continue to evolve their actions to gain advantage, nowhere is this evolution more pronounced than in the cyber domain where new opportunities and vulnerabilities seem to emerge daily. James Clapper, the former Director of National Intelligence, described one such evolution at a U.S. Congressional hearing in September 2015:

> The next frontier in cyberspace will feature the manipulation of data, rather than theft or destruction. Such tools could be used to alter decision making, and prompt business executives and others to question the credibility of information they receive.[21]

Another key aspect of the cyber domain is that it:

> enables a new sphere for great powers to carry out conflicts directly among each other (and any other power for that matter). Previously, their behavior was frozen at a certain level due to the strategic nuclear stalemate.[22]

However, the domain is not just occupied by great powers. While it may be true that "the overwhelming advantage of developed countries can also be reflected in distribution and management mechanism of physical facilities of key infrastructures that ensure operation of global cyberspace," there are also possibilities for smaller countries to develop significant cyber capabilities that can offset comparative advantages held by larger powers.[23] As one national security author noted, "Because of its ability to render long-established positions in other domains irrelevant, and the chance to operate with only the slightest risk of detection, cyberspace is now . . . at the center of global geostrategic struggle."[24] This duality of the cyber domain is analyzed in relation to U.S. and Chinese views of the domain.

DOMAIN'S INFLUENCE ON THE INSTRUMENTS OF NATIONAL POWER

Unlike actions in some of the other strategic domains, what happens in the cyber domain does not remain there. Actions taken in the cyber domain and, more importantly, their effects, spill over into and can influence all other domains. The result is that cyber domain operations influence all of the instruments of national power, and can do so almost instantaneously. For that reason, cybersecurity is not only the responsibility of the military but also the civilian national security agencies.[25] As Kenneth Lieberthal and Wang Jisi of the John L. Thornton China Center at Brookings noted in a 2012 study, "Recent years have witnessed the dramatic transformation of economic, military, and social activities in a way that makes the digital world increasingly critical to all three."[26]

The United States operates in the cyber domain to further its interests across all the instruments of power. As U.S. Assistant Secretary of Defense Eric Rosenbach stated recently regarding the U.S. cyber operations:

> The place where I think it will be most helpful to senior policymakers is what I call 'the space between'. What is the space between? . . . You have diplomacy, economic sanctions . . . and then you have military action. In between there's this space . . . [and] there are a lot of things that you can do in that space . . . that can help us accomplish the national interest.[27]

Just as the United States operates in the domain to further its national interests, so do other nations. As Nagy asserts, "cyberspace is now vital for maintaining national power at its entirety and thus for national security."[28] He points out that currently the United States, China, and Russia account for the majority of world cyber power and defines cyber power as "the ability to use cyberspace to create advantages and influence events in other operational environments and across the instruments of power."[29] He states that the reason for the United States and its adversaries to build up their cyber capabilities is simple: "Whereas China's and Russia's incentive for building national cyber power was to counterweigh overall Western power and to catch up, the West's is to defend that very power."[30] To do that, China and Russia took advantage of U.S. dependencies on information technologies:

> in increasing areas of the economy, society, politics, and the military . . . and for a time they managed to turn their greatest disadvantage—lack of advanced information infrastructure—to an effective weapon and tool against the West.[31]

They did not just focus their efforts on military power, but across all instruments of national power by "accessing and copying highly sensitive data of direct military, diplomatic, and economic importance."[32]

This strategy of near-simultaneously disrupting or degrading all instruments of power pursued by our adversaries is no secret. As Segal and Tang reveal:

> Chinese open-source writings discuss the importance of seizing information dominance early in a conflict through cyberattacks on command-and-control centers. Follow-up attacks would target transportation, communications, and logistics networks to slow down an adversary.[33]

It is important to remember that the cyber domain is still relatively young and that:

> In the near future, the size of the international cyber stage and the number of actors upon it will grow. Governments will both want and need to flex their digital muscles in

order to gain a comparative advantage in political and
military affairs.[34]

This analysis of the cyber domain's influence on the
instruments of national power will now highlight some
examples across the diplomatic, information, military,
and economic instruments of power.

Domain's Influence on the Instruments of Diplomatic Power

The United States uses the cyber domain to enhance
its statecraft and diplomatic efforts around the world.
As then-Secretary of State Kerry explained it in a recent
speech in South Korea:

> The internet is, among many other things, an instrument
> of freedom. . . . So of course, some leaders are afraid of it.
> They're afraid of the internet in the same way that their
> predecessors were afraid of newspapers, books, and the
> radio, but even more so because in this case, because of
> the interactivity that allows for a free-flowing discussion
> and the exchange of views—activities that can, and often
> do, lead to change.[35]

This discussion of the cyber domain as an avenue
to lead change is not simply hollow rhetoric coming
from senior-level U.S. leaders. The United States has
committed resources to supporting change agents in
regions it believes can most benefit. Between 2008 and
2012, the U.S. Department of State spent approximately
$100 million:

> to fund activities such as training digital activists in
> hostile environments and developing circumvention
> tools to bypass state-sponsored Internet filters . . . [and]
> in September 2015, U.S. ambassador to the United
> Nations Samantha Power announced a $10 million

venture-capital-like fund for the development of new circumvention technologies.[36]

Many of these "circumvention technologies" are aimed at getting around firewalls that are established by authoritarian regimes to limit their citizens' access to the unfiltered internet.

Domain's Influence on the Instruments of Information Power

The cyber domain's influence on the information instrument of power is mainly as a conduit for influence or information operations. As a matter of policy, the United States has a "stated interest in the free flow of information."[37] In three speeches between 2010 and 2011, former Secretary of State Hillary Clinton described information networks as a "new nervous system for our planet" and stated "users must be assured freedom of expression and religion online, as well as the right to access the Internet and thereby connect to websites and other people."[38] One expert has a starker view of information operations specifically related to U.S.-China interactions when he asserts:

> INFOOPS [Information Operations] plays a pivotal role in the unfolding 'cold war' between the United States and China for the domination of the Western Pacific. Both American and Chinese military doctrine builds heavily on INFOOPS.[39]

He continues with the warning that an information operation "is considered a basis for the growing Chinese capabilities to execute non-nuclear first strike against American and Allied military assets in the Western Pacific theatre of operations."[40] In this sense, the domain's influence on the information instrument of national power can have a direct influence on the military instrument of power.

Domain's Influence on the Instruments of Military Power

The cyber domain's influence on the military instrument of national power is arguably the most profound of the four instruments. Its emerging importance led one observer to note, "National and military presence in cyberspace has become vital to maintain presence in all other domains, putting its importance in supporting land and sea powers on par with air and space power."[41] An important aspect of the domain is that, while it is discussed and studied as a stand-alone domain, "it also affects the [military's] other four operational domains: land, air, sea, space."[42] Of particular significance is the fact that the U.S. military is reliant on not just critical military infrastructure but also critical civilian infrastructure to execute its missions. Forrest Hare of the George Mason University School of Public Policy notes:

> cyber-attacks that degrade the ability to command and control national security assets and attacks that disrupt critical infrastructure have direct implications to national security. This infrastructure may be civilian, military, or both.

He continues by stating that the "Department of Defense relies heavily on the nation's public and private cyber infrastructure backbone for communications purposes."[43]

Another example comes from a 2013 study conducted by the U.S. Defense Science Board entitled "Resilient Military Systems and the Advanced Cyber

Threat." In its report, the Board warned that the "benefits to an attacker using cyber exploits are potentially spectacular. . . . U.S. guns, missiles, and bombs may not fire, or may be directed against our own troops."[44] The report continued with:

> Resupply, including food, water, ammunition, and fuel may not arrive when or where needed. Military Commanders may rapidly lose trust in the information and ability to control U.S. systems and forces. Once lost, that trust is very difficult to regain.[45]

Not only can the domain influence military power through attacks and information manipulation, but also by enabling adversaries to gain advantages through cyber espionage. As one reporter notes:

> China's cyber-espionage is also of deep concern to the Pentagon, which fears Beijing is focused both on stealing plans for advanced armaments to build its own versions and on using that know-how to develop ways of countering high-tech American aircraft, drones, and other battlefield armaments.[46]

This cyber-enabled espionage allows our adversaries to counter potentially some of our most cutting-edge, sophisticated military technology without having to invest large amounts of resources in costly weapons systems research and development over many years. A *Washington Post* article stated that groups, including China's People's Liberation Army hackers, "stole information from over two dozen Defense Department weapons programs, including the Patriot missile system and the U.S. Navy's new littoral combat ship."[47] This theft of sensitive military information happens on both military and civilian industrial networks, highlighting the fact that the United States cannot simply secure its military networks to shield against the threat. A recent example is the potential loss of design and capabilities information of the F-35 Joint Strike Fighter. As Hare explains it:

> The information was stolen from private, proprietary industry networks (meaning no government access or frequent auditing), and it apparently contained several terabytes of design data on the future air defense capability for several nations.[48]

Because of incidents such as these, the U.S. military is investing scarce resources to counter the threat. The U.S. Air Force, for instance, is creating a "new, full-time office dedicated to protecting its weapons systems from cyber-attacks."[49] The organization, known as the Cyber Resiliency Office for Weapons Systems, was inaugurated with the acknowledgement that:

> even though a modern jet fighter is essentially a flying network of computing systems that's vulnerable to cyber threats, it's an exquisitely customized one that doesn't quite fit the procedures the government usually employs to protect its traditional IT [information technology] systems.[50]

Protecting U.S. military systems from threats in the cyber domain will require properly identifying threats and adequately allocating resources during the acquisition and budgeting processes. As General Ellen Pawlikowski, Commander, U.S. Air Force Materiel Command, recently noted, "getting weapons systems into a more cyber-secure condition would likely take another 5 to 7 years, partially because the military's budgeting process to date has not yet made it a priority."[51]

Finally, the cyber domain's influence on military power must be a consideration of multinational efforts with U.S. allies. Actions taken by adversaries against U.S. allies can have consequential outcomes for the United States. As the 2014 North Atlantic Treaty Organization (NATO) *Wales Summit Declaration* stated:

> We affirm . . . that cyber defence is part of NATO's core task of collective defence. A decision as to when a cyber-attack would lead to the invocation of Article 5 would be taken by the North Atlantic Council on a case-by-case basis.[52]

Domain's Influence on the Instruments of Economic Power

There is no doubt about the cyber domain's influence on the economic instrument of national power. Profitable businesses and sectors of the economy that offer cyber-enabled services have flourished, many without producing any physical product. As discussed earlier, much of the world's internet infrastructure resides in, or is routed through, the United States. This advantage is reflected in the U.S. position in the cyber related economy worldwide. One analyst describes the statistics this way:

> The Internet generates 6% of [U.S.] domestic economy. U.S. technology companies dominate the global Internet economy, with the United States accounting for 25% of global telecom revenue in 2015 and capturing close to 25% of the G-20's Internet economy. In India, nine of the top-ten websites are U.S.-based sites such as Google, Facebook, Twitter, and LinkedIn; seven of the top-ten sites in Brazil are run by U.S. companies. Google is the leader in search engines, and its Android operating system is on

over three-quarters of the smartphones being made in the world.[53]

The United States is not alone as a beneficiary of the cyber-enabled economy. China and some of its online businesses are also major beneficiaries. The Alibaba Group, owner of two of China's most popular online retailers, announced, "during the first 11 months of 2012, the total transactions of both shopping sites reached . . . $162 billion, the equivalent of [2] percent of China's total GDP."[54]

As can be expected, where there is this much potential wealth, there will be actors attempting to gain a competitive advantage through unscrupulous means.

> While there is no accepted measure of the size of cyber-enabled theft, it is assumed to significantly affect U.S. competitiveness. Former NSA head General Keith Alexander estimated the actual cost to U.S. companies at $250 billion in stolen information and another $114 billion in related expenses.[55]

As with much of the military-related cyber espionage, adversaries conduct industrial espionage through the cyber domain aimed at gaining a competitive advantage without having to dedicate significant resources to close the economic and technological gaps. Larry Wortzel, a member of the U.S.-China Economic and Security Review Commission, contends that:

> Chinese entities engaging in cyber and other forms of economic espionage likely conclude that stealing intellectual property and proprietary information is much more cost-effective than investing in lengthy R&D [research and development] programs.[56]

He further asserts, "these thefts support national science and technology development plans that are centrally managed and directed by the PRC [People's Republic of China] government."[57] The Chinese hackers in turn give the proprietary information and intellectual property to Chinese state owned enterprises, which gives those companies "an unfair advantage over their American competitors."[58] To address this growing problem, in September 2015, the U.S. and China agreed, in principle, to the U.S.-China Cyber Espionage Agreement that pledges, among other things, to:

> refrain from conducting or knowingly supporting cyber-enabled theft of intellectual property, pursue efforts to further identify and promote appropriate norms of state behavior in cyberspace within the international community, and establish a high-level joint dialogue mechanism on fighting cybercrime.[59]

An unfortunate outcome of China's cyber espionage against the United States for economic gain is that it is furthering strategic mistrust on both sides. As a recent discussion panel at the Carnegie-Tsinghua Center for Global Policy explained the downside, "it is the potential for distrust in the cyber domain to erode economic relations, which normally help to mitigate security tensions."[60]

U.S. AND CHINESE VIEWS ON CYBER DOMAIN

As stated earlier, "There is perhaps no relationship as significant to the future of world politics as that between the United States and China," and in that relationship:

> there is no issue that has risen so quickly and generated so much friction as cybersecurity. Distrust of each other's actions in the cyber realm is growing and starting to

generate deeply negative assessments of each country's long-term strategic intentions.[61]

In short, the United States and China represent the two most significant nations in the domain and their views of the domain are very different from one another.[62] Before addressing each nation's views of the domain, it is important to note an interesting observation from Segal and Tang regarding the U.S. and Chinese positions within the domain:

> The two countries are at different stages of technological development. All China does today is what the United States has already accomplished. China tends to learn and absorb U.S. best practices and lessons and has followed the U.S. model, which one might perhaps call a late-starting advantage. The United States, for its part, keeps a close eye on the measures China takes to improve its defense capabilities in the cyber domain and views these as a challenge. The root cause is absence of strategic trust between both sides.[63]

The sections below analyze how both the United States and China view the cyber domain. These views are significant to how each nation approaches behavior within the domain.

The United States has been involved in the cyber domain from its infancy. As early as February 2003, it published the *National Strategy to Secure Cyberspace*, the first national strategy of its kind.[64] In 2011, the Obama administration released the *International Strategy on Cyberspace* that declared that the United States would:

> work internationally to promote an open, interoperable, secure, and reliable information and communications infrastructure that supports international trade and commerce, strengthens international security, and fosters free expression and innovation.[65]

In 2015, former U.S. Secretary of State Kerry reiterated that strategy when he stated, "To begin with, America believes . . . that the internet should be open and accessible to everyone" and that "it matters to all of us how the technology is used and how it's governed. That is precisely why the United States considers the promotion of an open and secure internet to be a key component of our foreign policy."[66] He highlighted the differing viewpoints of the domain and tied the U.S. view to its national values when he said:

> We will have a lot of choices about technology among and between nations. Let me tell you something: How we choose begins with what we believe. And what we believe about the internet hinges to a great extent on how we feel . . . about freedom.[67]

This American notion of freedom pervades U.S. national institutions and is one reason for distrust of China's intent. As Lieberthal and Wang explain, Americans:

> tend to be deeply suspicious of countries that trample on the civil rights of their own citizens. For historical reasons, the fact that China is governed by a communist party in a one-party system inherently creates misgivings among many Americans, including high level officials, and makes it still harder to establish full mutual trust.[68]

Another difference is the U.S. viewpoint of conducting operations (either offensive or defensive) within the domain. As one expert observed:

> U.S. cyber-operations are extremely different from their Chinese equivalents. . . . When the U.S. military or intelligence community conducts cyber-operations, they are quiet, coordinated, exceptionally well targeted, and under the strict control of senior officers and government executives. Lawyers review every stage.[69]

He completed his explanation by reiterating, "The White House keeps a close hold on cyber-operations through senior executives, generals, and political appointees throughout the bureaucracy."[70] This tight control of operations is meant to prevent unintended consequences and miscalculations that could lead to escalation in the domain.

China's views on the cyber domain are quite different from the United States and, as addressed earlier, can be traced back to historical mistrust between the two nations dating back nearly 70 years. As a pair of experts reveal:

> Chinese distrust of the United States has persisted ever since the founding of the People's Republic of China (PRC) in 1949. In the 1950s and the 1960s, the PRC viewed the U.S. as the most ferocious imperial power and the gravest political and military threat.[71]

More recently, China saw the 2008-2009 world financial crisis as an indictment on U.S. economic and political systems.[72] The Chinese view the open, democratic, and laissez-faire approaches and policies of the United States as a structural cause of the global crisis.

As previously noted, China was not an early power in the cyber domain but has evolved into one. From the time that Chinese citizens first began going online, government officials and policymakers viewed the internet as a "double-edged sword—essential to economic growth and good governance but also the source of threats to domestic stability and regime legitimacy."[73] Even over 10 years ago, James Keith, a U.S. Department of State senior advisor on China and Mongolia, recognized that China's regulation of the internet was aimed at ensuring that "ideas that do not have the government's imprimatur or that challenge its authority do not take root in China."[74] Some Chinese analysts view U.S. efforts in the domain not only as a desire to maintain a strategic advantage, but also as a threat to the communist regime. These analysts "believe that the United States has soaked itself in Cold War and hegemonic thinking and wants to compete with China in all aspects of cyberspace, even wanting to jeopardize the current regime."[75]

Perhaps because of this viewpoint, in early 2014, Chinese President Xi Jinping began to elevate cyber issues in importance in the national security dialogue. He stated, "network and information security is a major strategic issue that relates to national security, development and the broad masses of working life" and that there is "no national security without cybersecurity."[76] A year-and-a-half later in July 2015, China passed a national security law which:

> viewed cybersecurity as an imminent and severe security risk that requires China to 'build an assurance system to protect network and information security, promote the defense capability, [and] safeguard sovereignty, security, and development benefits for the country in cyberspace'.[77]

This marked the first time that China codified the importance of cybersecurity in law.[78] While the United States seeks an open and secure internet, China seeks a secure regime. A recent National Bureau of Asian Research report asserts, "In the eyes of the Chinese government, the stability of the regime is the core security concern. Some scholars argue that Internet freedom is used as an excuse to intervene in China's internal affairs."[79] To address this security concern, "the Chinese government has built an Internet management system that has an external and domestic face. Offending material from outside China is filtered and blocked by a number of technologies colloquially known as the 'great firewall'."[80] This censorship can take the form of simply blacklisting certain terms or phrases and, "in extreme cases, whole regions can be removed from the Internet as happened for 10 months after riots in Xinjiang in 2009."[81]

SOVEREIGNTY: A KEY ISSUE IN THE DOMAIN

The differences in viewpoints noted above have profound effects on how the United States and China approach issues relating to the domain. This section addresses a few issues in the cyber domain and ends with a focus on a key issue in the domain—sovereignty. While the domain is increasingly important to overall U.S.-China relations, both countries:

> still have significant differences over the free flow of information and the openness of the Internet, cyberattacks and norms of behavior in cyberspace, Internet governance, and the security of supply chains and information and communications equipment.[82]

The result of these significant differences is that "each country is likely to see the other as an important, if not the main, competitor to the pursuit of its interests in cyberspace."[83]

At the heart of the disagreements is the question of who gets to determine the norms of the cyber domain.[84] In China, analysts believe "this authority belongs solely to the state, while the West incorporates multiple stakeholders, including technology companies and civil society."[85] One of the ways the United States and its allies are attempting to establish norms in the domain is through the NATO Cooperative Cyber Defence Centre of Excellence (NATO CCD

COE). This organization "has been addressing the subject of 'cyber norms' since its establishment in 2008," and has focused on "the question of how existing international legal norms apply to cyberspace by hosting and facilitating the Tallinn Manual process."[86] China has criticized the Tallinn Manual as an effort by the United States and its allies "to manipulate cyberspace through law."[87] In 2011 (revised in 2015), China, along with Russia, Kazakhstan, Kyrgyzstan, Tajikistan, and Uzbekistan — known collectively as the Shanghai Cooperation Organization (SCO) — introduced an alternative position to the Tallinn Manual to the United Nations General Assembly.[88] The common belief among the SCO countries is in "the primacy of the nation state, which should be carried over into cyberspace."[89] But, as Michael Schmitt and Liis Vihul note in a 2014 Tallinn Paper, "a 'code of conduct', like that proposed by the Shanghai Cooperation Organization, seldom qualifies as international law because it is aspirational or exhortational in nature, but not compulsory."[90]

A topic that has bearing on the issue of sovereignty in the cyber domain is that of borders. As Hare sets the stage, "Because actors in cyberspace enjoy relative anonymity and can threaten interconnected targets around the globe, there is considerable debate whether the concept of borders is relevant to the challenges of cyber security."[91] He concludes by stating, "Regardless the focus of the debate, the concept of borders is important because they define the territory in which national governments can employ sovereign measures."[92] Hare also relates the broader discussion of borders to the cyber domain when he argues that:

> whether the problem is addressed from the standpoint of criminal behavior like drug trafficking, or cyber-attacks in an interdependent, global domain, borders can be a

potentially useful construct to address cyber security issues and inform national policy decisions, regardless of the physical location of relevant nodes.[93]

Another topic with bearing on the issue of sovereignty in the cyber domain related to borders is whether or not the cyber domain is a global common. One expert notes that global commons are:

considered to be out of the jurisdiction of any state, international organization, company, or person, and to be fundamental in supporting human existence. The oceans, the atmosphere, space, and lately cyberspace are typically listed as part of the global commons, constituting the fabric or connective tissue of the international system.[94]

He further notes, "Many refer to cyberspace as a new 'global common' at its entirety."[95]

The U.S. position on cyber sovereignty is that actors within the domain should not take any actions to affect the openness or security of the domain. As one observer explains the differences between the United States and Chinese positions:

the United States believes that online content should flow freely across borders. China, in contrast, promotes a sovereignty-driven concept of cybersecurity, which gives governments the right to develop, regulate, manage, and censor Internet networks, as well as news, information, and data within their national boundaries.[96]

Another expert says simply, "The United States is committed to an open and global Internet, while China pushes a darker vision with strong national borders cutting out any objectionable material."[97] As outlined in the SCO alternative to principles found in the Tallinn Manual, "Russia and China both would like to see more government involvement in Internet governance and are pushing a . . . model of cyber sovereignty where, in effect, each country can maintain its own 'intranet'."[98]

As Mikk Raud writes in one of the 2016 Tallinn Papers:

> China is particularly sensitive in exercising its right to sovereignty in cyberspace and does not want it to be interfered with by any other state or international organization. . . . China does not see international law as the main regulator of cyberspace, but prefers each state setting its own rules.[99]

A recent Carnegie-Tsinghua panel of experts tied China's position on cyber sovereignty to "its long-standing policies advocating for noninterference in other states' domestic affairs."[100] In that statement, one can clearly identify similar Chinese complaints over U.S. "interference" in China's domestic affairs, specifically regarding Taiwan.

Another reason for China's position on cyber sovereignty is the threat it feels the domain poses to the security of the regime. As one Chinese expert notes:

> One of the main reasons why Beijing prefers sovereignty in cyberspace is stimulation from the actions launched by the [United] States in which the Internet served as the tools of US diplomacy, especially after 2009 when the term Internet Freedom has been produced to encourage NGO's to launch peaceful regime change all around the world.[101]

To support a secure regime, China's position on sovereignty even extends beyond its own citizens. Mikk Raud writes of China's position:

> the users of cyberspace, both domestic and foreign citizens within a state's territory, should be controlled

by the host state, a clear contradiction of the Western position which supports a liberal cyberspace respecting human rights. In China's political culture, maintaining social order is unquestionably more important than individual privacy.[102]

As outlined in the July 2015 National Security Law of China, "Cyber sovereignty occupies the central position of China's cyber security strategy," and the protection of sovereignty in cyber space is a critical national security task.[103] In 2014, Chinese President Xi detailed the components of cyber sovereignty that were the foundation for cyber sovereignty's importance in China's 2015 National Security Law:

> The first key part of cyber sovereignty refers to the sovereignty of the state to manage the information flow inside the territory; the second is that every single state has the power to make cyber related policy independently; the third is that every state should have roughly equalized rights to participate in the decision making process of the rules, norms, or code of conduct that governs global cyberspace; and the respect of sovereignty should be one of the most important guiding principles to deal with cyber related issues internationally.[104]

President Xi's version of cyber sovereignty is essential to enabling China to achieve its goal in the domain, namely, to become a cyber power.[105] At end-state, this goal will ensure that China:

> develops from an important actor to a great power in cyberspace which means China should not only effectively defend possible threats from/by cyberspace, but also become more influential in the building of the rules that govern global cyberspace.[106]

This vision of Chinese prominence in the cyber domain reflects the perspective of many leaders in China that "the shifting power balance between China and the United States is part of an emerging new structure in today's world." This is due in part to the outlook that "the United States is seen in China generally as a declining power over the long run."[107]

In order for China to achieve its goal of becoming a premier cyber power, one expert predicts that its main challenge will be:

> to provide a more precisely defined cyber sovereignty and develop a sophisticated national strategy on cyber security so that it would be taken as a workable guiding principle when China becomes more and more actively participatory in a creating process of code of conduct in the global cyberspace.[108]

From a U.S. perspective, it has concerns that China is attempting to undo its decades-long efforts to establish norms in the still immature cyber domain. A pair of experts summed it up this way:

> Moreover, the United States worries that China will push to rewrite the rules . . . by promoting 'an alternative to the borderless Internet embraced by Americans.' Preventing Chinese challenges to the U.S.-led cyber order is now a major task for the White House.[109]

These vastly different and competing positions on issues within the cyber domain and, more specifically, of the interpretation of sovereignty within the domain ultimately lead to a greater strategic mistrust between the two countries.

> The reasons for that distrust differ. On the Chinese side these doubts stem more from Beijing's application of lessons from past history, while on the U.S. side the doubts tend more to derive from Washington's uncertainties as to how a more powerful China will use its growing capabilities.[110]

Not helping matters is the fact that in this emerging, nascent domain with very few, if any, established norms of behavior, there is plenty of room for misjudgment and miscalculation by all actors operating within the cyber domain and that "neither the U.S. nor China clearly understands each other's red lines in this arena."[111]

Based on the information presented thus far, the final section of this project will propose some broad U.S. policy recommendations.

POLICY RECOMMENDATIONS

Although there are many issues facing the United States and China in the cyber domain, there are also areas where the countries can cooperate in an attempt to build some level of trust. As Segal and Tang identify, "Despite the wide ideological gulf between the two sides, both China and the United States have identified cyberspace as an area that requires cooperation."[112] There is also a cautious optimism that the two powers realize that they must work together on certain issues. As one analyst notes:

> Both sides have a pragmatic awareness of the issues on which they disagree, and both appreciate the importance of not permitting those specific disagreements to prevent cooperation on major issues where cooperation can be mutually beneficial.[113]

Common across all of these recommendations is the belief that maintaining open lines of communications at the highest levels of governmental and nongovernmental organizations is essential to signal the importance of the issues to the United States.[114] Additionally, the two sides must "ensure that discussions on norms of behavior in cyberspace continue at the highest level and are not suspended during times of tension."[115] It is these potential areas of cooperation on which this final section will propose recommendations with the hope of improving U.S.-China relations in not only the cyber domain but also the overall strategic relationship.

Perhaps one of the easiest areas of cooperation is where the United States and China already have an agreement. The United States should engage with Chinese leadership and actively follow-up on the September 2015 U.S.-China Cyber Espionage Agreement (described in the section on the domain's effect on the economic instrument of national power) with specific and actionable measures aimed at curbing cyber-enabled commercial espionage, theft of intellectual property, and cybercrime.[116]

The focus of early cooperation should be on shared interests and activities that both the United States and China view as harmful or criminal but that "do not have a significant political component to them."[117] Examples include cybercrime, intellectual property theft, supply chain security, and protection of critical infrastructure.[118]

One specific issue in the national interest of both the United States and China, and where both nations could benefit from cooperation, is the prevention of proliferation of cyber capabilities to violent extremist organizations and other nonstate actors. The two have already begun a cyber dialogue aimed at countering such actors. Two experts provide the concept that:

> the two sides agreed to work together to combat the posting on the Internet of instructions on how to build improvised explosive devices. As the discussions progress, the two sides could exchange intelligence on the capabilities of specific groups and share ideas on how

to disrupt the development and distribution of cyber weapons.[119]

Another recommendation is to increase what are known as people-to-people exchanges between the two countries. Exchanges of U.S. and Chinese citizens to conduct research at universities and in other technology related industries could help build shared understanding and trust at the lowest levels.[120]

A final recommendation is that the United States and China must further discussion of "red lines" in the cyber domain. A difficulty in these discussions is that, as outlined earlier, actions taken in the cyber domain can have near simultaneous effects in the other strategic domains. These cyber red lines are not isolated to the cyber domain. The discussion of red lines is essential to avoid miscalculation and misjudgment during crises that could lead to unintended escalatory actions on both sides.[121] Discussions could also lead to the development of norms and implementing measures that would take riskier actions off the table.[122] As one analyst related:

> From the United Nations to the ASEAN Regional Forum and the Organization for Security and Co-operation in Europe, there has been a growing interest in applying the concept of confidence building measures from the Cold War to the digital age.[123]

As the United States and China develop their relationship and enter into additional agreements, it will be important to have the backing of U.S. allies and partners in the region. In the advice of a recent task force from the Asia Society Center on U.S.-China Relations, "Expanding the scope of agreements beyond the bilateral relationship to multilateral organizations can help reinforce the Chinese government's commitments."[124]

All of the recommendations above are made with the desired end-state of expanding and strengthening the overall U.S.-China strategic relationship. Ultimately, improved relations will not end iniquitous actions or eliminate nefarious actors from the cyber domain, but will:

> put a framework in place that will not only help prevent disagreements in cyberspace from spilling over into other parts of the bilateral relationship, but also help both sides to get closer to an understanding of what constitutes strategic stability, i.e., peace, in cyberspace.[125]

CONCLUSION

The relationship between the United States and China in the cyber domain matters. From a cyber domain perspective, "Trust is currently a rare commodity in the Sino-U.S. bilateral relationship, and it is especially difficult to sustain in cyberspace."[126] That lack of trust in the domain matters because the consequences of a poor relationship affect more than just the cyber domain and more than just the two nations. From a broader perspective, this strategic mistrust holds an ominous potential if not improved. Lieberthal and Wang assess the potential this way:

> The United States and China are the two most consequential countries in the world over the coming decades. The nature of their relationship will have a profound impact on the citizens of both countries, on the Asia-Pacific region, and indeed on the world.[127]

The two nations must find ways to cooperate within the cyber domain to ensure strategic stability within all of the other domains.

ENDNOTES - CHAPTER 8

1. Travis Tanner and Wang Dong, "Introduction," in Travis Tanner and Wang Dong, eds., *NBR Special Report #57: U.S.-China Relations in Strategic Domains*, Seattle, WA: National Bureau of Asian Research, April 2016, p. v.

2. Ibid.

3. Sven Sakkov, "Foreword," in Anna-Maria Osula and Henry Rõigas, eds., *International Cyber Norms: Legal, Policy & Industry Perspectives*, Tallinn, Estonia: NATO CCD COE Publications, 2016, p. 7, available from *https://ccdcoe.org/multimedia/international-cyber-norms-legal-policy-industry-perspectives.html*, accessed January 18, 2017.

4. Ibid.

5. U.S. Joint Chiefs of Staff, *National Military Strategy for Cyberspace Operations*, Washington, DC: U.S. Joint Chiefs of Staff, December 2006, p. ix.

6. Viktor Nagy, "The Geostrategic Struggle in Cyberspace Between the United States, China, and Russia," *Academic & Applied Research in Military Science*, Vol. 11, No. 1, 2012, p. 14, available from *http://zmne.hu/aarms/docs/Volume11/Issue1/pdf/02.pdf*, accessed January 15, 2017.

7. Ibid.

8. Adam Segal and Tang Lan, "Reducing and Managing U.S.-China Conflict in Cyberspace," in Tanner and Wang, eds., p. 48.

9. Jason Healey, "China is a Cyber Victim, Too," *Foreign Policy*, April 16, 2013, available from *http://foreignpolicy.com/2013/04/16/china-is-a-cyber-victim-too/*, accessed January 15, 2017.

10. Ibid.

11. Forrest Hare, "Borders in Cyberspace: Can Sovereignty Adapt to the Challenge of Cybersecurity?" in Christian Czosseck and Kenneth Geers, eds., *The Virtual Battlefield: Perspectives on Cyber Warfare*, Amsterdam, The Netherlands: IOS Press, 2009, p. 92, available from *https://ccdcoe.org/publications/virtualbattlefield/06_HARE_Borders%20in%20Cyberspace.pdf*, accessed January 15, 2017.

12. Ibid.

13. Nagy, p. 13.

14. John Kerry, "An Open and Secure Internet: We Must Have Both," public speech, Korea University, Seoul, South Korea, May 18, 2105, available from *https://2009-2017.state.gov/secretary/remarks/2015/05/242553.htm*, accessed February 20, 2017.

15. Kenneth Lieberthal and Peter W. Singer, *Cybersecurity and U.S.-China Relations*, Washington, DC: Brookings Institution, 2012, p. iv, available from *https://www.brookings.edu/wp-content/uploads/2016/06/0223_cybersecurity_china_us_lieberthal_singer_pdf_english.pdf*, accessed January 15, 2017.

16. Ibid., p. viii.

17. Nagy, p. 17.

18. Hare, p. 88.

19. Ibid., p. 92.

20. Kerry.

21. Elias Groll, "U.S. Spy Chief: Get Ready for Everything to be Hacked All the Time," *Foreign Policy*, September 10, 2015, available from *http://foreignpolicy.com/2015/09/10/u-s-spy-chief-get-ready-for-everything-to-be-hacked-all-the-time/*, accessed January 15, 2017.

22. Tim Maurer, "The Future of War: Cyber is Expanding the Clausewitzian Spectrum of Conflict," *Foreign Policy*, November 13, 2014, available from *http://foreignpolicy.com/2014/11/13/the-future-of-war-cyber-is-expanding-the-clausewitzian-spectrum-of-conflict*, accessed January 15, 2017.

23. Yi Shen, "Cyber Sovereignty and the Governance of Global Cyberspace," *Chinese Political Science Review*, Vol. 1, Iss. 1, March 2016, p. 85, available from *https://doi.org/10.1007/s41111-016-0002-6*, accessed January 15, 2017.

24. Nagy, p. 15.

25. Ibid., p. 16.

26. Kenneth Lieberthal and Wang Jisi, *Addressing U.S.-China Strategic Distrust*, Washington, DC: Brookings Institution, 2012, p. 3, available from *https://www.brookings.edu/wp-content/uploads/2016/06/0330_china_lieberthal.pdf*, accessed January 8, 2017.

27. Maurer.

28. Nagy, p. 14.

29. Ibid.

30. Ibid., p. 16.

31. Ibid., p. 15.

32. Lieberthal and Wang, p. 31.

33. Segal and Tang, in Tanner and Wang, eds., p. 52.

34. Kenneth Geers, *Pandemonium: Nation States, National Security, and the Internet*, Tallinn, Estonia: NATO CCD COE Publications, 2014, p. 12, available from *https://ccdcoe.org/publications/TP_Vol1No1_Geers.pdf*, accessed January 18, 2017.

35. Kerry.

36. Segal and Tang, in Tanner and Wang, eds., p. 47.

37. Ibid.

38. Ibid.

39. Nagy, p. 22.

40. Ibid.

41. Ibid., p. 14.

42. Maurer.

43. Hare, p. 91.

44. Defense Science Board, "Task Force Report: Resilient Military Systems and the Advanced Cyber Threat," Washington, DC: U.S. Department of Defense, Office of the Under Secretary of Defense for Acquisition, Technology and Logistics, January 2013, p. 5.

45. Ibid.

46. Shane Harris, "U.S. Indicts Chinese Officials for Cyber-Spying," *Foreign Policy*, May 19, 2014, available from *http://foreignpolicy.com/2014/05/19/u-s-indicts-chinese-officials-for-cyber-spying*, accessed January 15, 2017.

47. Segal and Tang, in Tanner and Wang, eds., p. 48.

48. Hare, p. 91.

49. Jared Serbu, "Air Force Stands Up New Office to Shield Weapons from Cyber Attacks," Federal News Radio, January 10, 2017, available from *federalnewsradio.com/dod-reporters-notebook-jared-serbu/2017/01/air-force-stands-new-office-shield-weapons-cyber-attacks*, accessed January 16, 2017.

50. Ibid.

51. Ibid.

52. North Atlantic Treaty Organization, *Wales Summit Declaration*, Newport, Wales: North Atlantic Treaty Organization, September 5, 2014, available from *www.nato.int/cps/en/natohq/official_texts_112964.htm*, accessed February 22, 2017.

53. Segal and Tang, in Tanner and Wang, eds., p. 46.

54. Jing de Jong-Chen, "U.S.-China Cybersecurity Relations: Understanding China's Current Environment," September 15, 2014, *https://www.georgetownjournalofinternationalaffairs.org/online-edition/u-s-china-cybersecurity-relations-understanding-*

chinas-current-environment?rq=Jing%20De%20Jong-Chen, accessed January 8, 2017.

55. Segal and Tang, in Tanner and Wang, eds., p. 49.

56. Ibid., p. 51.

57. Ibid.

58. Harris.

59. John W. Rollins, Susan V. Lawrence, *Dianne E. Rennack, and Catherine A. Theohary, CRS Insight: U.S.-China Cyber Agreement*, Washington, DC: U.S. Library of Congress, Congressional Research Service, October 16, 2015, available from *https://fas.org/sgp/crs/row/IN10376.pdf*, accessed February 21, 2017.

60. Zhao Kejin, Charles Clover, Li Hengyang, Li Yan, and Wang Dong, "Establishing Cybernorms: Chinese and Western Perspectives," Carnegie-Tsinghua Center for Global Policy, May 31, 2016, available from *http://carnegietsinghua.org/2016/05/31/establishing-cybernorms-chinese-and-western-perspectives-event-5272*, accessed January 15, 2017.

61. Lieberthal and Singer, p. vi.

62. Ibid., p. iv.

63. Segal and Tang, in Tanner and Wang, eds., p. 57.

64. Piret Pernik, Jesse Wojtkowiak, and Alexander Verschoor-Kirss, *National Cyber Security Organisation: United States*, Tallinn, Estonia: NATO CCD COE Publications, 2016, p. 7, available from *https://ccdcoe.org/sites/default/files/multimedia/pdf/CS_organisation_USA_122015.pdf*, accessed January 18, 2017.

65. Barack Obama, *International Strategy for Cyberspace: Prosperity, Security, and Openness in a Networked World*, Washington, DC: The White House, May 2011, p. 8.

66. Kerry.

67. Ibid.

68. Lieberthal and Wang, p. 25.

69. Healey.

70. Ibid.

71. Lieberthal and Wang, p. 7.

72. Ibid., p. 8.

73. Segal and Tang, in Tanner and Wang, eds., p. 49.

74. Ibid.

75. Ibid., p. 55.

76. Ibid., p. 53.

77. Ibid., p. 54.

78. Ibid.

79. Ibid., p. 55.

80. Ibid., pp. 49-50.

81. Ibid., p. 50.

82. Ibid., p. 45.

83. Ibid.

84. Zhao et al.

85. Ibid.

86. Sakkov, "Foreword," in Osula and Rõigas, eds., p. 7.

87. Mikk Raud, *China and Cyber: Attitudes, Strategies, Organisation*, Tallinn, Estonia: NATO CCD COE Publications, 2016, p. 7, available from *https://ccdcoe.org/sites/default/files/multimedia/pdf/CS_organisation_CHINA_092016.pdf*, accessed January 18, 2017.

88. Ibid.

89. Ibid.

90. Michael N. Schmitt and Liis Vihul, *The Nature of International Law Cyber Norms*, Tallinn Paper No. 5, Tallinn, Estonia: NATO CCD COE Publications, 2014, p. 4, available from *https:// ccdcoe.org/sites/default/files/multimedia/pdf/Tallinn%20Paper%20 No%20%205%20Schmitt%20and%20Vihul.pdf*, accessed January 18, 2017.

91. Hare, p. 88.

92. Ibid.

93. Ibid.

94. Nagy, p. 15.

95. Ibid.

96. Asia Society, Center on U.S.-China Relations, "Task Force Report: US Policy toward China: Recommendations for a New Administration," New York: Asia Society, February 2017, p. 32, available from *http://asiasociety.org/files/US-China_Task_Force_ Report_FINAL.pdf*, accessed February 20, 2017.

97. Healey.

98. Asia Society, Center on U.S.-China Relations, p. 33.

99. Raud, p. 7.

100. Zhao et al.

101. Yi, p. 90.

102. Raud, p. 7.

103. Yi, p. 90.

104. Ibid.

105. Ibid.

106. Ibid.

107. Lieberthal and Wang, p. 9.

108. Yi, p. 91.

109. Segal and Tang, in Tanner and Wang, eds., p. 57.

110. Lieberthal and Wang, p. 34.

111. Ibid., p. 47.

112. Segal and Tang, in Tanner and Wang, eds., p. 57.

113. Lieberthal and Wang, p. 1.

114. Asia Society, Center on U.S.-China Relations, p. 32.

115. Segal and Tang, in Tanner and Wang, eds., p. 44.

116. Ibid.

117. Lieberthal and Singer, p. ix.

118. Segal and Tang, in Tanner and Wang, eds., pp. 57-59.

119. Ibid., p. 59.

120. Ibid., p. 44.

121. Tanner and Wang, "Introduction," in Tanner and Wang, eds., p. ix.

122. Lieberthal and Singer, p. x.

123. Maurer.

124. Asia Society, Center on U.S.-China Relations, p. 33.

125. Franz-Stefan Gady, "China-US Relations in Cyberspace: A Half-Year Assessment," *The Diplomat*, June 16, 2016, available from *https://thediplomat.com/2016/06/china-us-relations-in-cyberspace-a-half-year-assessment/*, accessed January 8, 2017.

126. Segal and Tang, in Tanner and Wang, eds., p. 61.

127. Lieberthal and Wang, p. 49.

PART III:
ECONOMIC INSTRUMENT OF POWER

CHAPTER 9

U.S. ECONOMIC REBALANCE TO THE ASIA-PACIFIC REGION: IS IT STILL POSSIBLE?

Jeffrey M. Zaiser

EXECUTIVE SUMMARY

With the abandonment of the Trans-Pacific Partnership (TPP), it is necessary to examine what, if any, mechanisms remain available for the U.S. Government (USG) to expand its economic engagement and integration with the TPP signatory countries and others, including the People's Republic of China (PRC), in the region. A "re-branding" of the TPP appears to be the "best second choice" for the United States to continue its economic engagement with countries in the region, to reassure our allies and partners that the United States remains committed to an increased economic integration, and to the avoidance of damaging trade wars.

If that is not possible, then the United States could negotiate and conclude bilateral free trade agreements (FTAs) and bilateral investment treaties (BITs) with TPP signatories and other countries in the region, hopefully in a relatively uniform and consistent manner. Additionally, the United States would need to encourage those countries to conclude similar bilateral agreements with each other, to build a network of non-conflicting bilateral agreements to replace the TPP.

At the same time, the United States should consider participation in some of the other Asian initiatives promoted by China. These include the Association of Southeast Asian Nations (ASEAN) and the Asia-Pacific Economic Corporation (APEC), including the Asia Infrastructure Investment Bank (AIIB), the "One Belt, One Road" Initiative, and the Regional Comprehensive Economic Partnership (RCEP). The latter would necessitate conclusion of an FTA with ASEAN, which probably is not feasible. Doing so could enable the USG to influence the policies and practices of those organizations in a positive way and to enhance U.S. business opportunities.

INTRODUCTION

On November 17, 2011, in Canberra, Australia, former U.S. President Barack Obama announced a "deliberate and strategic decision" regarding U.S. policy toward the Asia-Pacific region: "the United States will play a larger and long-term role in shaping this region and its future, by upholding core principles and in close partnership with our allies and friends." The President described the Asia-Pacific as "the world's fastest-growing region" that was "home to more than half the global economy" and was "critical to achieving my highest priority, and that's creating jobs and opportunity for the American people." To advance those economic goals for the United States, the President said he would pursue development of "an open international economic system where rules are clear and every nation plays by them." More specifically, for the Asia-Pacific region, he said the United

258

States, Australia, and other countries would soon complete the world's most ambitious trade agreement to date, the TPP.[1]

While Obama did not include the PRC in his TPP comments, he noted that the United States would "continue our effort to build a cooperative relationship with China" because the United States and other countries had "a profound interest in the rise of a peaceful and prosperous China." That said, however, the President clearly sought to create a new trading system "that is free and fair" and in an "open international economic system, where rules are clear and every nation plays by them." He also added that this system would have to include protections for workers' rights, intellectual property, and consumers, with "balanced growth," environmental protection, and good governance, and without manipulation of exchange rates, all implicitly but not explicitly referring to China.[2]

On October 5, 2015, the partners signed a final agreement on the TPP in Atlanta, GA. In his congratulatory note, Obama hailed the achievement that:

> when more than 95 percent of our potential customers live outside our borders, we can't let countries like China write the rules of the global economy. We should write those rules, opening new markets to American products while setting high standards for protecting workers and preserving our environment.[3]

On January 23, 2017, however, consideration of the merits and deficiencies of the TPP became moot when newly-elected President Donald Trump rejected the draft agreement, saying, "we're going to stop the ridiculous trade deals that have taken everybody out of our country and taken companies out of our country."[4]

ECONOMICS: THE WEAKEST PILLAR?

Despite the Obama administration's glowing assessments of the strong and growing economic importance of the Asia-Pacific region to the United States, the USG's ability to support that pillar of the rebalance:

> is arguably the most problematic instrument in the nation's repertoire, [and this] problem is especially acute among Asian governments . . . that still blame the United States for mismanagement of the 1997 Asian Financial Crisis and for causing the 2008 Global Financial Crisis.[5]

Over the past 2 decades, those same Asian nations have witnessed the rapid economic growth and development of China, with which they have become increasingly intertwined and interdependent. From their perspectives, they might agree, "Washington's military instruments dwarf its diplomatic, information, and economic instruments" while China "has economic resources that eclipse its other elements of power."[6]

WHAT WOULD THE TPP HAVE ACCOMPLISHED?

The USG intended the TPP to cement U.S. status as the leader of a global, rules-based economic system, which, over time, would have been extended to additional members able and willing to meet its new, higher standards for international economic activity within a reasonable time frame. The TPP negotiators sought to "create a 21st-century agreement" for the "increasingly globalized economy" that would "eliminate tariffs and nontariff barriers to trade in goods, services, and agriculture, and to establish or expand rules on a wide range of issues including intellectual property rights, foreign direct investment, and other trade-related issues."[7] As such, it was far broader in scope than typical bilateral or even multilateral FTAs or BITs, and it extended into areas not normally covered by those treaties, such as government procurement, intellectual property rights (IPR), state-owned enterprises (SOEs), labor, environment, and regulatory coherence. Perhaps more importantly, while the treaty clearly was intended to "strengthen and deepen trade and investment ties among its participants," the United States—and perhaps some other participants—also viewed it as a valuable means to advance non-economic "U.S. strategic interests in the Asia-Pacific region."[8]

Had it been realized, the TPP immediately would have become the largest U.S. FTA by trade flows, including $727 billion in U.S. goods exports and $882 billion in U.S. goods imports (2014 figures). The potential value of the agreement was greatly enhanced when Japan, which did not (and still does not) have an FTA with the United States, agreed to participate. Japan's potential membership reportedly attracted interest and support from a wide range of U.S. industries, including sectors like agriculture, automotive, and services. With the U.S. withdrawal from the TPP, it would be useful for the USG to translate Japan's comprehensive TPP agreement into a bilateral FTA, thus consolidating the TPP objectives between its two largest members.

CONSEQUENCES OF U.S. WITHDRAWAL

At the broadest level, U.S. refusal to ratify the laboriously negotiated TPP—which actually required major concessions by other members and very little change from the United States—may have undermined U.S. credibility in the Asia-Pacific region. The USG "expended serious political capital" with the other participants to negotiate the TPP in order to establish "U.S. rules and standards at the center of Asian trade."[9] It is likely that many Asian governments and people will link U.S. inaction on the strategic rebalance's economic pillar to the broader commitment of the United States to diplomatic, political, and security interests in the region. In other words, all aspects of the Obama administration's "strategic rebalance" to the region could be negatively affected by the collapse of the TPP. Within the United States, the business community broadly supported the TPP because it would have forced foreign competitors—including SOEs—to follow the same set of rules as U.S. companies. Some of those U.S. businesses now believe they have been undercut by Trump's decision to abandon the draft agreement and fear their future operations in Asia could be negatively affected. The Trump administration has not specified its concerns about the TPP, simply claiming that the agreement disadvantaged the United States by shifting production and employment to other countries.

By withdrawing from the TPP, the USG could encourage or even force some Asian countries to "take sides" and join alternative economic structures designed and dominated by China, rather than the stronger and more advanced U.S.-led system. During the TPP negotiation process, relatively progressive officials in some of those countries had been able to argue that the benefits of trade liberalization, including enhanced market access not only to the United States but also to other TPP members, outweighed the near-term costs of sweeping legislative, regulatory, and bureaucratic changes to their economic regimes. Without U.S. TPP participation, those marginal signatories are unlikely to implement all the reform measures to which they agreed, and may even be tempted to reverse the course of reform in some areas. In Vietnam, for example, negotiators "had hoped to use the deal to pressure sluggish state-owned companies to modernize and reform," which now may be deferred or not even take place.[10] Even Japan, a democratic ally with a modern capitalist economy that had endured a difficult internal political struggle to meet some of the agricultural market access requirements and other reforms required by the TPP, now may not be willing to implement those commitments.

Reform-averse officials in some TPP member nations, particularly the relatively less advanced and more state sector-dominated countries such as Burma and Vietnam, probably were relieved to see the agreement's demise, which in their view would have imposed burdensome requirements on their governments. They are likely to view the much less ambitious Chinese approach to regional economic architecture modernization, which generally focuses simply on trade in goods, as much "simpler and less controversial."[11] The collapse of the TPP in those countries could even cause governments to move backward in multiple respects: one Vietnamese labor activist recently said she feared her government would "use this [the U.S. withdrawal from the TPP] as an excuse to suppress the labor movement." A 10-page bilateral side agreement between the United States and Vietnam "would have required Vietnam to criminalize the use of forced labor and broaden enforcement to cases of debt bondage," both of which remain prevalent in that country. Furthermore, the TPP would have stipulated that workers "would be allowed to form their own grass-roots unions that could bargain collectively and lead strikes," a right not currently available in Vietnam.[12]

WHAT ABOUT CHINA?

The PRC was not one of the 12 TPP signatories, in part because it was widely viewed by the USG and others as being unable and/or unwilling to implement the sweeping changes in its economic structure and regulatory regimes to meet TPP standards within a reasonable time frame. The USG and other TPP country negotiators were also cognizant of China's historic modes of participation in the United Nations (UN) and other international organizations: "When it becomes a member of an international organization, China applies a high priority to national sovereignty and may therefore act as a brake on that organization," and would be "hostile to . . . any new and legally binding standard."[13] More fundamentally, at least one analyst also noted, "China will not be hasty to join the TPP, as the high standards and terms in [the] TPP are incompatible with China's economic reality."[14]

Throughout the TPP negotiation process, USG officials were careful to characterize the agreement as:

> primarily about increasing ties to Asia, not containing China, [and they emphasized that] building a constructive and productive relationship with China has been an important part of the Pivot ever since it was first announced.[15]

They also noted that if and when the PRC eventually joined the TPP, the agreement would prove "extremely beneficial" to that country, not only by generating "income gains of $800 billion over the next 10 years," but more fundamentally by pushing the Chinese government to implement wide-ranging reforms to its economic system.[16] At least some of the increasingly nationalistic Chinese leaders and citizenry, however, probably viewed their exclusion from the TPP process as part of yet another U.S. and Japan-organized plan to contain the rise of China; some observers even believe "China's attention to [the] TPP was piqued more by Japan than by the U.S."[17]

CHINA'S ALTERNATIVE PLANS

In recent years, believing the United States and some of its allies were rewriting the economic rulebook for the Asia-Pacific region without their participation or input, the PRC government has been "meticulously constructing an alternative architecture to the post-war Western order." Their developing system already includes the New Development Bank (a multilateral development bank founded by China and the other four BRICS nations [Russia, India, Brazil, and South Africa]), the AIIB, and the "New Silk Road Initiative" (also known as the "21st-Century Maritime Silk Road," the "Silk Road Economic Belt," or the "One Belt, One Road"). To achieve that end, "Beijing is using the strongest instrument in its soft-power toolbox: money," and has begun to "sign huge trade and investment deals, extend generous loans, and dole out hefty aid packages."[18] The U.S. response to these initiatives has been one of indifference (New Silk Road Initiative) or opposition (AIIB), a position that the USG should reconsider due to the demise of the TPP.

The most prominent of these new institutions is the AIIB, which the Chinese government announced officially in late 2013 as a "key arm of the New Silk Road Initiative."[19] China launched the AIIB over USG objections that it was redundant and would lack the "environmental, labor and procurement standards that are essential to the mission of development lenders." As China's economic power has grown rapidly in recent decades, it has become particularly unhappy with the Asian Development Bank (ADB): "although China is the biggest economy in Asia, the ADB is dominated by Japan; Japan's voting share is more than twice China's; and the bank's president has always been Japanese."[20] The PRC "insisted that AIIB will be rigorous in adopting the best practices of institutions such as the World Bank." The Chinese also noted that "Asia has a massive infrastructure gap" which even the ADB had estimated could be as much as $8 trillion, something which "existing institutions cannot hope to fill."[21] The USG has not disputed that need for investment, nor has it claimed that the ADP and World Bank could meet the demand for capital.

In addition to its own denunciations of the new AIIB, the USG also urged its allies and leading trading partners to resist participation in the new lending institution, for reasons noted above. These "clumsy efforts" to impede success of the AIIB, however, "gave the impression that Washington was indeed committed to constraining China's rise."[22] An (at least publicly) unstated concern for the USG and probably others, however, was that "China will use the new bank to expand its influence at the expense of America and Japan."[23] Despite USG efforts, approximately 50 countries, including the United Kingdom and other western European nations, decided to participate in the AIIB, something that seemingly "validates China's strategy of mixing international integration with its own shadow organization competing with the post-World War II Bretton Woods international institutions."[24]

While it may be too soon to evaluate the AIIB's performance, initial reports suggest that it is operating in a responsible and high-standard manner. China has opened its membership to European countries, recruited many U.S. and European professionals with World Bank backgrounds to manage its operations, and—perhaps most importantly—has not structured the AIIB's rules and procedures "to give it [China] an effective veto power over loan decisions."[25] Given the positive development of the AIIB since its inception, the USG could seek to participate in the institution in some way, thereby gaining influence in its decision making and reassuring regional allies of the continuing U.S. economic commitment to the region. Any Chinese resistance to U.S. participation would undermine China's professed openness to the widest possible foreign involvement in the AIIB.

China's New Silk Road Initiative—including both land-based and maritime components—was announced by PRC President Xi Jinping in Kazakhstan in September 2013. Since then, the Chinese government and Communist Party leadership has reaffirmed their support for the plan on multiple occasions. In addition to its foreign economic and security policy value, however, the New Silk Road initiative also is designed to "drum up development fever in the less developed regions in China" and to further "important internal development priorities." The overland route would extend from the relatively wealthy coastal cities of eastern and southern China through industrial centers in central and western China and continue on to central and south Asian destinations. Large Chinese state-owned enterprises, such as CITIC Bank and the Central Tourism Group, also would benefit significantly from the project and thus have supported it.[26]

Although to date, the USG has not commented publicly on the feasibility or usefulness of this initiative, cautious encouragement of U.S. companies to participate in the program could help ensure the infrastructure projects meet global standards and avoid creating a perception that the USG simply wants to prevent the PRC from advancing its own economic agenda.

THE ROLE OF ASEAN

In addition to these PRC-created organizations, Beijing also has supported ASEAN's plan for a Regional Comprehensive Economic Partnership (RCEP), which would include the 10 ASEAN member states as well as the 6 nations with which ASEAN already has FTAs (Australia, China, India, Japan, South Korea, and New Zealand). China "initially showed little interest in the RCEP . . . until Japan joined TPP, upon which point China spared nothing in cooperating with other Asian nations on the RCEP."[27] In actuality, however, some analysts believe "domestic support for RCEP is weak in China" and the plan primarily "was viewed as a counterweight to TPP."[28]

While negotiation of RCEP reportedly is close to completion, if and when it enters into force, it will be "far less ambitious [than the TPP], focusing on the basic business of cutting tariffs."[29] For that reason, it will be far easier for some ASEAN members to accept because it, like ASEAN in general, will operate under the prevalent "ASEAN strategy," which is more commonly described as the "principle of the lowest common denominator."[30] More specifically, RCEP would largely focus on "trade and investment promotion"[31] and would reduce or eliminate many tariffs, but it would provide a far less comprehensive and less far-reaching trade framework than the TPP, and it would not address a number of significant U.S. concerns in areas such as labor, food safety, the environment, and government procurement. Nevertheless, some governments that have been involved in both the RCEP and the TPP—including Australia, Brunei, Japan, Malaysia, New Zealand, Singapore, and Vietnam— view the two agreements as "complementary" rather than mutually exclusive, and believe conclusion of the RCEP could be useful.[32] The USG has not commented publicly on the merits or shortcomings of the RCEP, possibly because the United States does not have a Free Trade Agreement with ASEAN and is therefore not eligible to participate in the RCEP.

From the PRC's perspective, participation in ASEAN and its component structures has "incurred virtually no cost—in terms of national autonomy and discretion—for Beijing, while still providing her with significant benefits." More specifically, "joining ASEAN-led institutions did not require China to forfeit her freedom of movement on any of the issues considered important to Chinese interests," while at the same time "it was granted a de facto veto right on decisions and developments that Beijing might consider . . . adverse to its interests." Such status within ASEAN also gave the PRC "the possibility of playing on each country's eagerness to benefit from China's economic growth."[33] China also has used its ability to provide "no strings attached" loans and investments to ASEAN's poorer members, such as Cambodia, in return for which Beijing has received a "proxy" within ASEAN to prevent that consensus-bound organization from even issuing "statements that criticize China's expansive territorial claims in the South China Sea."[34]

The United States has the same observer status as China in ASEAN, and during the Obama administration, the USG significantly elevated its participation in ASEAN meetings, such as the ASEAN Regional Forum (ARF). At one of those meetings, in Hanoi, North Vietnam, former U.S. Secretary of State Hillary Clinton, together with most of the ARF membership, openly criticized Chinese behavior in the South China Sea, to the visible dismay of the PRC Foreign Minister.

CHINA'S DOMINANCE IN ASIA

As its economy has enjoyed high GDP growth rates over the past 3 decades, the PRC has become "the top trading partner for most other Asian nations," which in turn "has strengthened Beijing's ability to use its market power to reward its friends and punish those opposing its policies."[35] The interest of some of the smaller Asian countries in the TPP was at least in part based on their growing concern that "their significant dependence on China's economy exposes them to attempts at economic coercion by Beijing." This is a policy instrument that China in the past has employed "to pressure the Philippines over fruit, Japan over rare earths, Norway over fish, and even the U.S. over aircraft."[36]

The PRC's leaders are probably also aware that:

> unlike other leading countries, whose national strength emanates from the confluence of military, economic, social, and geopolitical vectors, Chinese power is inexorably tied to the expansion of the Chinese economy.[37]

In other words, China's "soft power" is a combination of "commercial diplomacy and the mutual benefit of partnership with China."[38]

Unfortunately, for China, some analysts believe the "halcyon days of China's unbridled economic growth are coming to an end," and China's leaders are "wrestling with how to translate the nation's economic clout into increased influence, especially in Asia."[39] While some would dispute that China's slowing GDP growth rate—from 8 to 10 percent annually to a still robust 6 to 7 percent—is cause for alarm in Beijing, most would agree that the Chinese government increasingly would have to devote attention and resources to serious internal social-political issues in the near future. These include rising labor costs that are eroding China's competitive advantages in lower-tech sectors, an aging population, enormous environmental destruction, and the potential for social discontent tied to any of those problems that could undermine the legitimacy of the ruling party and government. Were China's neighbors to perceive it and its economic growth model as faltering, then they might become less willing to tie their own future economic prospects to it. As long as the Chinese economy continues to grow at a respectable rate, however, those regional trading partners will continue to "wish above all for a stable China."[40] For at least the near term, however, China "has become the largest trade and investment partner of virtually every country in Central Asia and the largest trade partner of every country in East and Southeast Asia,"[41] and there is no imminent danger of that status diminishing.

CHINA: THE WORLD'S ECONOMIC ENGINE?

Most recently, PRC government officials have publicly promised to continue to pursue a more open global economic system. At the January 2017 World Economic Forum meeting in Davos, Switzerland, PRC President

Xi Jinping—the first Chinese president to attend this annual gathering of the capitalist world's political and business elite—announced that his country "will keep its door wide open and not close it" because "no one will emerge as a winner in a trade war."[42] That assessment almost certainly is correct: virtually all Western economists agree that trade wars are "no-win" situations for all participants, resulting in reduced economic activity and higher prices for consumers in the participating countries. Given the enormous volume of trade between the United States and China, a trade war between the two countries would be devastating to both economies and would have major negative repercussions on the global economy.

The Chinese government has said publicly that they "welcome continued participation by all countries for mutually beneficial outcomes" in their initiatives such as the "One Belt, One Road," the AIIB, and the Silk Road Fund.[43] Some Chinese officials also have said they plan to support the Free Trade Area of the Asia Pacific (FTAAP) negotiations among the 21 APEC member countries, including the United States, which would create an "even larger regional pact" than the TPP.[44] In 2010, APEC leaders agreed to push for the FTAAP as a "broad vision for the group,"[45] but its realization probably would require even more protracted negotiations and compromise than the TPP. Former U.S. Trade Representative Michael Froman previously stated, "the TPP could serve as a 'building block'" for the FTAAP,[46] but without the TPP, it is not clear if the FTAAP has any chance to be concluded in the near future. With the Trump administration's public comments against multilateral trade agreements, it is not likely that it would support any involvement in FTAAP negotiations.

CHINA AND THE UNITED STATES: INCREASINGLY INTERDEPENDENT

Despite their negative views regarding the existing international economic institutions and structures in the Asia-Pacific region, and their apparent belief that, in the longer-term, western (including Japanese) economic dominance will decline, China's leadership certainly is cognizant of their country's increasing economic interdependence with the United States. Some Chinese leaders and their economic advisors would acknowledge that their country's rapid economic growth and development since the late 1970s has been enabled and facilitated to a considerable extent by the existing, western-designed economic institutions—first the General Agreement on Tariffs and Trade (GATT), then the World Trade Organization (WTO)—even though the design of those agreements had been "fundamentally antithetical to closed societies and command economies."[47] The PRC had been able to transition from "one of the world's most isolated countries" in the late 1960s and to overcome the enormous "damage to the economy" inflicted by Mao Zedong during the 1966-1976 "Cultural Revolution" in large part through participation in that international economic system.[48] By 1986, as the benefits of state capitalist economic reform under the leadership of Deng Xiaoping were becoming apparent, even PRC President Li Xiannian—a product of the Marxist-Leninist-Maoist Communist Party system—publicly acknowledged that China's leaders "should have focused our forces more on economic development and reconstruction" rather than ideology.[49]

Even during the onset of the 2007-2008 global financial crisis, high-level Chinese economic and financial leaders frequently voiced the opinion that "we're in the same boat" with the United States and therefore needed to cooperate to resolve the crisis.[50] That interdependence has only grown since the crisis, to the point where China now is the second largest trading partner of the United States, which in turn is China's largest trading partner.[51] Despite that ever-increasing interdependence, however, for Beijing "sovereignty remains an absolute priority," and China has "balked at more convergence" in areas such as human rights, trade, or disarmament. One analyst characterized this behavior as a desire to keep "one foot in the international system and one foot outside."[52]

ALTERNATIVES FOR THE UNITED STATES

The U.S. withdrawal from the TPP obviously "removes the main economic plank" of the strategic rebalance to Asia and "leaves a gaping hole in the architecture of Asian commerce."[53] With the TPP off the table politically for the foreseeable future, the question becomes what could the USG offer as a viable economic component of the strategic rebalance (if the Trump administration decides to continue support for the rebalance in some form). This is a critical issue because the economic importance of the Asia-Pacific has not declined, and in all probability will only continue to increase both absolutely and relatively.

First, it should be emphasized that nothing else could fully replace the TPP. Some of the TPP's objectives could be achieved through bilateral mechanisms such as FTAs among Asia-Pacific countries; there already are 147 FTAs in force in Asia with another 68 at some stage of negotiation,[54] and the USG has FTAs with 6 of the other TPP countries (Australia, Canada,

Chile, Mexico, Peru, and Singapore).[55] Such a piece-meal system, however, would be "a jumbled, overlapping mess,"[56] also known as the "noodle bowl effect," of non-uniform or even incompatible arrangements that would not approach the TPP's comprehensiveness. Furthermore, such a conglomeration of bilateral arrangements would simply expand the current U.S. hub-and-spoke system with allies and partners, without addressing the economic arrangements among those other nations. Assuming the interested states then negotiated their own bilateral or regional agreements with their non-U.S. trading partners—some of which already exist or are under negotiation—there is no reason to believe that those new systems would be consistent with each other.

A better option, which at this time does not appear to be politically feasible in the United States, would be to re-brand and revise the existing draft TPP to address the criticisms levied against it by its U.S. opponents. Some key members of the U.S. Congress, including the Republican chairmen of the Senate Finance Committee and the House Ways and Means Committee, reportedly still "strongly support" the TPP, as do "many other members of Congress."[57] Since Trump took office on January 20, 2017, several well-reasoned pro-TPP arguments by both Democratic and Republican-affiliated authors have been published. In early January 2016, a study by a bipartisan group of former high-level USG officials detailed the benefits of a "cooperative U.S.-China relationship" but also the need for a "revitalized U.S. economic strategy" that would serve U.S. interests through a "trans-Pacific order supported by transparent institutions and rules." More explicitly, the study recommended that the USG should "complete the TPP," "take action to ensure that the U.S.-China relationship is mutually beneficial," and "update and uphold the Asia-Pacific economic architecture," none of which it viewed as mutually exclusive. By "revitalized," the group of former USG officials clearly meant that the USG needed to openly reassert—and then back up that assertion with concrete measures—its continuing interest in greater economic integration between the United States and Asia. The reference to "update and uphold the Asia-Pacific architecture" referred to the TPP as a replacement for the existing weak and haphazard arrangements.[58]

In early February 2017, another group of prominent former officials and academics published a list of political, economic, and security recommendations for the new U.S. administration's Asia and China policies. The authors explicitly stated, "our future prosperity depends on staying actively involved there" and that U.S. "economic and security interests in the region have long been intertwined."[59] They also noted that many Asian countries, including major U.S. trading partners such as India and Indonesia, "continue to pursue protectionist policies that limit opportunities for U.S. exporters and investors."[60] The authors explicitly addressed the "special opportunities and challenges" presented by China's rapid—but now slowing—economic growth and its emergence as a regional power willing and able to use its economic influence to further its interests. This nationalistic activism, said the authors, "has troubled neighboring countries" which were now "wary of overdependence and eager for the United States to play an active counterbalancing role."[61]

During China's rise over the past 2 decades, however, "Washington has been distracted and inconsistent in its approach to Asia while realities on the ground have not stood still."[62] With regard to economic policy, measures such as the TPP "have been left to languish" due to internal U.S. political differences. At the same time, U.S. responses to Chinese initiatives such as the AIIB at best have been ineffective and at worst, self-defeating; in retrospect, the USG clearly underestimated global interest in the AIIB and overestimated its ability to prevent other nations, including close allies, from joining that initiative. U.S. national interests would have been better served by U.S. participation in the AIIB from the outset.

Of the six priorities detailed in the paper, two were directly relevant to the economic component of the strategic rebalance. First, with regard to the Asia-Pacific region, the USG should focus on "rising concerns among allies and friends about the dependability and reliability of U.S. economic and security commitments in the Asia-Pacific region." Another priority was more directly linked to China: the United States should be "deploying effective tools to address the lack of reciprocity in U.S. trade and investment relations with China." The need for both these two and the other four priorities was based on four vital U.S. national interests: 1) "a fair and market-based global economic system" in which there is "deep U.S. economic integration with China"; 2) "a peaceful and stable Asia-Pacific region" supported by our "substantial security presence"; 3) "a liberal rules-based international order"; and, 4) "a positive and sustainable relationship with China."[63] To further these interests and address what they view as the priorities for the new administration, the authors strongly recommended a "revised Trans-Pacific Partnership treaty that can command bipartisan support in the U.S. Congress . . . and catalyze reform in China." If

China is not included in the new TPP, it "will not have a clear international standard for which to aim."[64]

Looking further into the future, some advocates of greater economic liberalization envision even greater changes to the Asia-Pacific economic architecture. They regard the TPP, the RCEP, and other modernizations as "way stations on the path to the ultimate destination, which is a massive though still distant agreement for the entire region, known as the Free Trade Area for the Asia-Pacific (FTAAP)."[65]

RECOMMENDATIONS

With the TPP off the table, at least during the current administration, the USG needs to identify and implement the next best option, to both avoid damaging trade wars and demonstrate its continuing economic engagement in the Asia-Pacific region. First, the United States could negotiate and conclude bilateral agreements—FTAs and/or BITs—with key countries in the region, while also encouraging those trade partners to negotiate similar and consistent bilateral agreements with each other. Second, the United States could participate in some of the other Asian initiatives promoted by China, ASEAN, and APEC, such as the AIIB, the One Belt One Road, and the RCEP (although the latter would necessitate conclusion of an FTA with ASEAN, which probably is not feasible). Taking some or all of these steps could help construct an improved rules-based economic architecture between the United States and its Asian partners, and also could promote U.S. exports and encourage Asian investment in the United States.

CONCLUSION

The TPP was the best option for comprehensive improvement to the economic system. It addressed not only trade but also environment, labor, the role of SOEs, and government procurement; it also pushed some Asian countries to commit to domestic reforms. As a multilateral agreement, it would have set identical standards for all participants, and it would have demonstrated the continuing U.S. engagement in the region. With the new administration's official and public affirmation that it would not join the TPP, the United States now needs to find other ways to improve the Asia-Pacific trading system and environment, support U.S. companies that are active in the region, and promote U.S. job creation and foreign investment in the United States.

ENDNOTES - CHAPTER 9

1. All quotes in this paragraph are from former President Barack Obama, "Remarks by President Obama to the Australian Parliament," Washington, DC: The White house, Office of the Press Secretary, November 17, 2011.

2. Ibid.

3. President Barack Obama, "Statement by the President on the Trans-Pacific Partnership," Washington, DC: The White House, Office of the Press Secretary, October 5, 2015.

4. Peter Baker, "Trump Abandons Trans-Pacific Partnership, Obama's Signature Trade Deal," *The New York Times*, January 23, 2017.

5. Douglas T. Stuart, *The Pivot to Asia: Can it Serve as the Foundation for American Grand Strategy in the 21st Century?* Carlisle, PA: Strategic Studies Institute, U.S. Army War College, August 2016, pp. 12-13.

6. Ibid, p. 56.

7. Ian E. Ferguson, coordinator, *The Trans-Pacific Partnership (TPP): Negotiations and Issues for Congress*, Washington, DC: Congressional Research Service, U.S. Library of Congress, March 20, 2015, p. 1.

8. Ibid, p. 5.

9. Kurt Campbell, *The Pivot*, New York: Hachette Book Group, 2016, p. 15.

10. "Trading Down: The collapse of TPP," *The Economist*, November 19, 2016, available from *https://www.economist.com/news/asia/21710287-big-free-trade-deals-demise-leaves-worrying-void-asia-trading-down*.

11. Campbell, p. 194.

12. Neil Gough, "Labor Abroad May Suffer as U.S. Turns Inward," *The New York Times*, March 1, 2017, p. B1.

13. Francois Godemont, *Contemporary China: Between Mao and Market*, Lanham, MD: Rowan and Littlefield, 2016, p. 149.

14. Min Ye, "China and Competing Cooperation in Asia-Pacific: TPP, RCEP, and the New Silk Road," *Asian Security*, Vol. 11, No. 3, December 8, 2015, pp. 206-224.

15. Campbell, p. 22.

16. Ibid, p. 195.

17. Ye, pp. 206-224.

18. David Shambaugh, "China's Soft-Power Push," *Foreign Affairs*, Vol. 94, No. 4, July/August 2015, pp. 99-107.

19. Ye, pp. 206-224.

20. S. R., "Why China is Creating a New 'World Bank' for Asia," The Economist explains, blog of *The Economist*, November 11, 2014, available from *https://www.economist.com/blogs/economist-explains/2014/11/economist-explains-6*.

21. Ibid.

22. John Pomfret, *The Beautiful Country and the Middle Kingdom*, New York: Henry Holt and Company, 2016, p. 626.

23. S. R.

24. Godemont, p. 226.

25. Jeffrey Bader, "A Framework for U.S. Policy toward China," Washington, DC: The Brookings Institution, October 10, 2016.

26. Ye, pp. 206-224.

27. Ibid.

28. Ibid.

29. "Trading Down."

30. Timo Kivimaki, "Power, Interest or Culture—Is There a Paradigm that Explains ASEAN's Political Role Best?" *The Pacific Review*, Vol. 21, No. 4, December 2008, pp. 431-450.

31. Ye, pp. 206-224.

32. Ferguson, p. 8.

33. Yves-Heng Lim, "How (Dis) Satisfied is China? A Power Transition Theory Perspective," *Journal of Contemporary China*, Vol. 24, Issue 92, 2015, pp. 18-19.

34. "The Giant's Client: Why Cambodia has cosied up to China," *The Economist*, January 21, 2017.

35. Orville Schell and Susan L. Shirk, chairs, "Task Force Report: U.S. Policy Toward China: Recommendations for a New Administration," New York: Asia Society, Center on U.S.-China Relations and University of California San Diego School of Global Policy and Strategy, 2017, p. 20.

36. Campbell, p. 195.

37. Bonnie Glaser and Matthew Funaiole, "Geopolitical Consequences of China's Slowdown," in Craig Cohen and Melissa Dalton, eds., *Global Flashpoints 2016*, Lanham, MD: Rowman and Littlefield, 2016, p. 58.

38. Godemont, p. 229.

39. Glaser and Funaiole, in Cohen and Dalton, eds., p. 58.

40. Godemont, p. 8.

41. Bader.

42. "The New Davos Man: Xi Jinping portrays China as a rock of stability," *The Economist*, January 21, 2017.

43. The State Council Information Office of the People's Republic of China, *China's Policies on Asia-Pacific Security Cooperation*, January 2017, available from *www.scio.gov.cn*.

44. "Trading Down."

45. Ferguson, p. 8.

46. Andy Morimoto, "Should America Fear China's Alternative to the TPP," *The Diplomat*, March 17, 2016.

47. Andrew Preston, "The Great Transition: From Geopolitics to Geoeconomics," in Lorenz M. Luthi, ed., *The Regional Cold Wars in Europe, East Asia, and the Middle East*, Stanford, CA: Stanford University Press, 2015, p. 116.

48. Preston, in Luthi, ed., pp. 153-156.

49. J. Simon Rofe, "Ends and Ends: The Cold War in International History at the Systemic and Subsystemic Levels," in Lorenz M. Luthi, ed., *The Regional Cold Wars in Europe, East Asia, and the Middle East*, Stanford, CA: Stanford University Press, 2015, p. 270.

50. Jeffrey M. Zaiser, experience as U.S. Treasury Deputy Financial Attaché at U.S. Embassy Beijing, 2008-2010.

51. Campbell, p. 231.

52. Godemont, pp. 211-212.

53. "Trading Down."

54. Ibid.

55. Ferguson, p. 8.

56. "Trading Down."

57. Robert J. Samuelson, "The TPP Lives—Maybe," *The Washington Post*, February 16, 2017.

58. Charlene Barshefsky, Evan G. Greenberg, and Jon M. Huntsman, Jr., cochairs, and the CSIS Asia Economic Strategy Commission, "Reinvigorating U.S. Economic Strategy in the Asia Pacific: Recommendations for the Incoming Administration," Washington, DC: Center for Strategic and International Studies, and Lanham, MD: Rowman and Littlefield, p. 2017.

59. Ibid., p. 1.

60. Ibid., p. 3.

61. Ibid.

62. Ibid., p. 4.

63. Schell and Shirk, pp. 16-17.

64. Ibid., p. 26.

65. Campbell, p. 193.

PART IV:
MILITARY INSTRUMENT OF POWER

CHAPTER 10

A NEW U.S. INDO-ASIA-PACIFIC SECURITY STRATEGY

Ryan M. Finn and David B. Moore

EXECUTIVE SUMMARY

If China is allowed to continue its systematic expansionist strategy, what some might term "coercive gradualism" in the South China Sea, its regional neighbors risk becoming increasingly indebted to China. Regional nations all have some degree of economic dependency on China, and when this dependency is coupled with an increasing military capabilities gap their ability to object to China's aggressiveness is further eroded. China is exploiting this situation to further leverage its economic and security dealings with these nations, and make it more difficult for them to balance against China by partnering with the United States.

U.S. forces are of the right size and composition to meet current challenges. However, while U.S. forces must be of the right quantity and postured appropriately, quality will increasingly take on special meaning when facing the transregional, multi-domain, and multifunctional (TMM) threat of the future. Furthermore, the United States must develop a national policy and cohesive joint military strategy to respond to regional actors in the Indo-Asia-Pacific who do not comply with the accepted world order, or be prepared to accept the erosion of the existing world order and the U.S. preeminent role in it. While the United States certainly has the means available, it lacks a comprehensive, joint vision on how to engage below the line of conflict, or in the "gray zone." In order to remedy this condition, the United States should do the following:

- The United States should continue to pursue and maintain an insurmountable technological edge over potential competitors that is focused on a qualitative, vice quantitative, advantage and focused on the TMM threat of the future.
- The United States must invite regional allies and partners, including China, into a broadened collective security architecture, and regularly exercise and demonstrate its qualitative advantage to allies and competitors.
- The United States must develop and implement responses to China's use of gray zone strategies. Failure to act will only allow the practice to propagate and continue to threaten U.S. vital interests in the region.
- The United States must unambiguously determine where the "redlines" are and clearly demonstrate the will and capacity to enforce them.
- The United States should increase unannounced Freedom of Navigation Operations in accordance with international laws and rulings.
- The United States needs to consider a cohesive joint strategy as it continues to redistribute military forces in the southern Pacific that will impose multiple strategic dilemmas against China's Anti-Access/Area Denial (A2/AD) efforts.

INTRODUCTION

> Over the past 70 years, America has not only helped
> heal the wounds of World War II. We've helped create
> the stability that has allowed people, economies, and
> countries throughout the Asia-Pacific to make incredible
> progress. . . . The rebalance—in a nutshell—is about
> sustaining this progress and helping the region continue
> to fulfill its promise.
>
> —Secretary Ashton Carter[1]

As former Secretary of Defense Ashton Carter so
aptly summarized, the world has enjoyed a historically
high degree of stability in Europe and Asia. The Amer-
ican-led world order, backed up by America's military
might, has largely enabled this remarkable stability.
The nation's policy goals are represented in military
procurements, deployments, and strategies. With the
resulting military advantage, the threat of action has
often been sufficient to compel acquiescence to international rules or norms. However, what happens when
compellence fails? If an adversary is not convinced of a
credible U.S. intent and the readiness to use the force,
it can be tempted to break the rules and practice military adventurism.

There are signs in the Indo-Asia-Pacific (IAP)
region that certain countries are pursuing this course
of action. Chairman of the Joint Chiefs of Staff General
Joseph Dunford has identified five strategic challenges
he termed the "4+1." These are Russia, China, North
Korea, Iran, and violent extremist organizations. Dunford further assesses that "future conflict with an
adversary or combination of adversaries is taking on
an increasingly [TMM] nature."[2] Therefore, while U.S.
forces are deployed worldwide, U.S.-led order must
be of the right quantity and postured appropriately,

quality will increasingly take on special meaning when facing this TMM threat of the future. Four of the 4+1 threats—China, North Korea, Russia, and violent extremist organizations—are present in the Asia-Pacific region, making the advance of U.S. interests there a significant challenge.

China's unprecedented economic growth over the last few decades, combined with its recent military growth, modernization, and innovations, have put it in a position to threaten U.S. influence, deny U.S. access, and weaken U.S. alliances in the Asia-Pacific region. China's rise has emboldened it to take assertive actions to strengthen its territorial claims in the East and South China Seas.

Of particular note is that China has employed "gray zone" tactics to pursue its objectives.[3] These Chinese assertive acts require a serious U.S. response. The United States must develop a national policy and cohesive joint military strategy to respond to regional actors in the IAP who do not comply with the existing rules-based international world order, or be prepared to accept the erosion of the existing world order and the United States' preeminent role in it.

STRATEGIC FOCUS

To study the role of the military in the IAP, one must start with an examination of the previous administration's strategic "pivot to the Pacific," or strategic "rebalance," as it became known. The term "rebalance" itself was adopted to indicate more accurately that the United States has always been deeply engaged in the Pacific region and is merely returning to a more historic posture following the wars in Iraq and Afghanistan. Indeed, it is important to remember that enduring U.S. interests in the region to ensure freedom of navigation and freedom from coercion date back to the post-World War II and Korean war treaty alliances with Japan, South Korea, and the Philippines.[4] In the early months of his presidency, George W. Bush began efforts at a "rebalancing" of his own, until the terrorist attacks of September 11, 2001 (9/11) diverted all attention to the Middle East.[5] Former President Barack Obama announced the rebalance as a distinct transition from focusing on the Middle East, to a post-war focus on America's economic interests in the vitally important Indo-Asia-Pacific region.

The objectives of the American policy toward the region are the maintenance of peace, prosperity, and stability, respect for international law, unimpeded lawful commerce, and freedom of navigation. The United States is committed to supporting its allies in the region to ensure peaceful resolution of disputes, in accordance with widely accepted rules, standards, and international laws. The United States, however, does not take a position on competing territorial claims over land features in the South China Sea.[6]

The United States asserts that the Western Pacific is a region with vital American interests, thus necessitating the strategic rebalance the Obama administration began.[7] First, more than half of the world's trade is shipped through the region. Second, by 2020, more than half the world's population will reside within the region.[8] Third, several regional actors, to include the Democratic Peoples' Republic of Korea and the Peoples' Republic of China, are acting in ways which contest accepted international norms. In China's case, this behavior jeopardizes not only U.S. interests, but also allies' interests and territorial claims.

Many of the atolls in this region hardly classify officially as islands, but their strategic significance is extraordinary. The United States Information Agency estimates that in these contested areas are 11 billion barrels of oil, 190 trillion cubic feet of natural gas deposits, and fisheries that account for 10 percent of the global total, $5.3 trillion in trade moving through annually.[9] The requirement to focus on the region, therefore, becomes evident, and in pursuing American interests, all elements of national power have been augmented in the region for a more robust capability. These rebalance initiatives prepare the United States to better respond to the broad range of anticipated requirements in the region, from assisting an ally or partner to countering a competitor.

The Problem

U.S. policies in the Asia-Pacific have been lacking in actual enforcement mechanisms. Many critics blast the Pacific "rebalance" as being overly militaristic, potentially causing the escalation of tensions between the United States and a rising China.[10] However, in fact, the military instrument has not been able to dissuade China from pursuing its increasing assertions to Nine-Dash Line claims, or even to its far more aspirant claims out to the Second Island Chain.

For example, in July of 2016, the Permanent Court of Arbitrations at The Hague (PCA) ruled against China's claims to disputed land features, "rocks," in the South China Sea, including the Scarborough Shoals. Yet, China has rejected this ruling and continues to maintain a Scarborough Shoals presence. The United Nations (UN) took no action to enforce the PCA ruling, and since China is a permanent member of the UN

Security Council, it never will. Moreover, since this period of peaceful prosperity is largely backed by U.S. military might, it seems to fall upon the United States to enforce this decision or see this world order begin to erode.

The threat that exists today in the region is largely from the same two actors that existed when the rebalance was designed in 2011, although several new developments have occurred. The North Korean threat will be examined extensively in subsequent chapters; therefore, this chapter will not address further policy options with regard to North Korea, but will focus on the military options to maintain deterrence and protection for regional allies in the South and East China Seas, and support other instruments of national power to achieve U.S. strategic objectives.

China has embarked upon a significant modernization effort to expand its military capabilities toward power projection in not only the East and South China Seas, but also worldwide.[11] Analysts suggest that China will continue its military expansion to allow not only the realization of its claims in the region, but also to project power world-wide as it seeks to offer an alternative to the current world order.[12]

China's assertiveness in the South China Sea has developed to the point of warranting a hard look at force posturing and strategy in the southern region. When the rebalance was announced in 2011, the Chinese began land reclamation activities on seven reefs in the Spratly Islands, creating several man-made "islands." China continues to assert its Nine-Dash Line claim that would give it sovereignty over the entire chain despite the objections of its neighbors and the international community.[13] China has promised non-military use of the man-made islands, offering humanitarian response, environmental protection, search and rescue, scientific research, and other types of international assistance as to their intended uses.[14] However, China's firm control of the islands and other forceful behavior in and around the Senkaku Islands in the East China Sea, Scarborough Shoals, Fiery Cross Reef, and other Spratly Islands in the South China Sea signal other intentions. Additionally, recent satellite images reveal runways and hangars suitable for military jets and bombers, radars, anti-aircraft artillery, anti-missile systems, ports and docks for naval shipping, and indications of potential for a naval base on Mischief Reef. Incidentally, Mischief Reef was specifically deemed to belong to the Philippines, according to the ruling of the Permanent Court of Arbitration on July 12, 2016. All of the islands have military facilities for housing troops and cement plants for future construction.[15]

All of this gives further indication of China's intent to become the regional hegemon, despite its stated intentions of peaceful prosperity. Besides building up islands from undersea features, China has created an Air Defense Identification Zone (ADIZ) that covers the Japanese Senkaku Islands.[16] There are indications that China intends to build on Scarborough Shoals as it has on seven other Spratly Islands. An ADIZ on that shoal would cover a large portion of the Philippines mainland, including Manila.[17] The type of intimidation that China has applied to the Philippines in the Scarborough Shoal situation is illustrative of how it sees its neighbors. If China is allowed to continue unimpeded in the South China Sea while it modernizes its military and grows economically, all while gradually gaining a buffer zone and edging out competitors, the rest of its neighbors will be indebted to China before long. Regional nations all have some degree of economic dependency on China; coupled with an increasing military capabilities gap, this further erodes their ability to object to China's assertions. China exploits these situations to leverage further economic and security dealings with these nations, and hedges them against similar partnerships with the United States as evidenced by Philippine President Rodrigo Duterte's recent stated intentions to push away from the United States.[18]

China utilizes classic gray zone tactics, conducting activities below a level which would prompt a military response from any claimant, and to which the United States has few response options. The Chinese strategic expansion in the South China Sea has thus been described as a very effective, "peacefully coercive . . . salami slice" strategy as it takes small, incremental steps that will not provoke a military response, but will "over time gradually change the status-quo regarding disputed claims in its favor."[19] This step-by-step expansionist strategy, or "coercive gradualism," whereby a nation expands its influence and control over the sovereign territories of others, or international waters, falls right in the heart of the gray zone, and has left neighbors and the United States perplexed and devoid of options.

Further, China seems prepared to escalate the situation, perhaps due to a lack of U.S. response to its moves. Regarding China's recent seizure of a U.S. Navy underwater drone, "Chinese political experts said China seized [the underwater drone] in the South China Sea . . . to send a strong warning to Trump not to test Beijing's resolve over the sensitive issue of Taiwan." Meanwhile, smaller countries in Southeast

Asia are watching the back-and-forth closely for signs that U.S. naval dominance might be diminishing.[20]

The Current Strategy

A key document created to execute the Obama administration's policy for the Asia-Pacific region, and nested under the *National Security Strategy* and *National Military Strategy*, is the Department of Defense (DoD) *Asia-Pacific Maritime Security Strategy*. Published in 2015, the strategy delineates the perceived threats and opportunities for the Asia-Pacific region and defines the military strategy to achieve U.S. goals. The *Maritime Security Strategy* represents a cornerstone in U.S. engagement in the region and is complemented by a series of classified theater strategy documents. It describes four regional challenges and calls for four lines of effort to overcome those challenges by deterring conflict and coercion and promoting international standards and adherence to the rule of law.

The *Maritime Security Strategy* describes the regional challenges:

"[1] Competing Territorial and Maritime Claims." The region is replete with a high number of territorial disputes that cover the East China Sea, South China Sea, and to a lesser extent, the Indian Ocean.[21] "[2] Military and Maritime Law Enforcement (MLE) Modernization." As the nations in the region advance economically and see their territorial claims unresolved, they have begun developing navy and coast guard-like capabilities to protect their interests. This build-up of capability, while having the potential to contribute to good order at sea, also increases the potential for escalation to conflict.[22]

"[3] Maritime Challenges" are described:

"Expanded Use of Non-Military Assets to Coerce Rivals."[23] Policies like China's "cabbage strategy" (coercive gradualism) are examples of activities the *Maritime Security Strategy* seeks to deter. The goal of the strategy is to assert China's sovereignty over these areas through a slow accumulation of small incremental changes, none of which in itself constitutes a casus belli but together substantiate China's claims of sovereignty over the long term.[24]

"Unsafe Air and Maritime Maneuvers." Attempts to intimidate ships or aircraft by maneuvering into their space and force them from their intended path.

"Land Reclamation on Disputed Features." China's reclamation of over 2,900 acres on features not recognized as anything more than rocks by international law demonstrates this point. Last summer's Permanent Court of Arbitration ruling clearly stated that China's claims of historic rights within the Nine-Dash Line were without legal foundation. The panel also concluded that China's activities within the Exclusive Economic Zones (EEZ) of other nations were illegal per international law.[25]

"[4] Dispute Resolution." Although multi-lateral negotiations for resolution are the preferred solution for other regional actors, China eschews multilateral fora for bilateral talks where it can more effectively coerce its opponent in order to achieve the outcome that benefits China.[26]

The Maritime Security Strategy describes the Lines of Effort (LOE):

LOE 1; strengthening military capacity to ensure the United States can successfully deter conflict and coercion and respond decisively when needed.

LOE 2; working together with allies and partners from Northeast Asia to the Indian Ocean to build their maritime capacity.

LOE 3; leveraging military diplomacy to build greater transparency, reduce the risk of miscalculation or conflict, and promote shared maritime rules of the road.

LOE 4; working to strengthen regional security institutions and encourage the development of an open and effective regional security architecture.[27]

LOE Analysis

The U.S. military, after the planned rebalancing is complete, will have the capacity to deter conflict and coercion, and respond when needed, if faced with the current threat. However, as China's A2/AD capacity increases in effectiveness, volume, and reach, the traditionally unfettered access of the United States is challenged and cannot be countered through an already lost quantitative matchup.[28] Further, due to the immense distances concerned, being in the right place if needed is key. The new distributed laydowns resulting from the rebalance should allow a more timely response and add to the deterrence factor.[29] The pre-rebalance force posture and basing was a post-World War II, post-Korean war laydown with a strong focus on the North West Pacific, enabling the United States to respond to potential Korean aggression.[30] As that situation remains relatively stabilized, and as other regional threats arise, it is prudent to seek a more distributed posture, as the rebalance does to some degree. However, the limited distribution of forces in the rebalance was one of required convenience more than it was a strategic decision.[31] The deterrence capacity is present in force numbers; what is lacking is the policy that uses said capacity to effectively deter unlawful behavior.

With the notable exception of Cambodia, which since 2013 has been strongly influenced by China, and the recent dramatic reversal of sentiment toward the United States in the Philippines, U.S. engagement appears to be achieving its goal.[32] The United States enjoys more access than it has since its bases in the Philippines were closed in 1991.[33] This access will assist the United States in its pursuit of continued regional security and stability. However, with China's growing influence in the region through economic enticements and forceful coercion, U.S. ready access and influence with allies and partners has become more complicated by their relationships with China.

The United States is falling short of the goal in the third LOE. One example of an attempt to reduce miscalculation is the creation of the Code for Unplanned Encounters at Sea (CUES), a standard set of signals used to communicate one's intentions clearly. Although there have been instances whereby the CUES was utilized, China is still conducting unsafe, unprofessional, and potentially escalatory actions.[34] This is evidenced by the recent People's Liberation Army-Navy (PLAN) shadowing of a U.S. destroyer and subsequent recovery of the undersea drone, by the 2001 collision of a Chinese jet with a U.S. EP-3C, and multiple collisions or near collisions of Chinese vessels with other nations' vessels in the East and South China Seas.[35]

Significant efforts have gone forth in LOE 4. The Maritime Security Initiative, aimed at developing a Common Operating Picture (COP) by outfitting regional allies with required equipment is a promising start toward a regional security architecture. Such a Maritime Domain Awareness (MDA) capability has application also to counter illegal fishing, transnational crime, and respond to natural disasters, and would help level the technological playing field between regional countries and China, enabling them to detect better gray zone tactics employed by Beijing, both individually and collectively. Funded at only $425 million over a 5-year period, opponents point out that, while it is a nice gesture, such low funding will scarcely produce such capability in reality. Other efforts have included helping the Philippines build a National Coast Watch Center; assisting Vietnam's establishment of a Coast Guard training center; and bolstering maritime surveillance and radar capabilities in Indonesia and Malaysia.[36]

The LOEs do an admirable job of attempting to combat the perceived threats within the constraints levied upon the current operational environment. There is a missing element, however, that will prevent successful continuance of the peace and stability of the past few decades. That element is the ability to contest the actions an opponent takes which fall below the current level of conflict. As Dunford stated before the Senate Armed Services Committee:

> these actors are advancing their interests through competition with a military dimension that falls short of traditional armed conflict and the threshold for a traditional military response. This is exemplified by Russian actions in Ukraine, Chinese activities in the South China Sea, and malicious cyber activities.[37]

As mentioned, regional actors, most notably China and North Korea, use these gray zone activities, furthering their national interests, often at the cost of U.S. and allied interests, without an overt response.

THE 60 PERCENT

There has been much focus on the right size of the military in the Asia-Pacific. In 2012, Secretary of Defense Leon Panetta first stated, "60% of the U.S. Navy will be homeported in the Pacific by 2024."[38] The new strategy calls for an allocation of 60 percent of U.S. Air and Naval forces to the Pacific region by 2020. There is a perception that the military instrument is disproportionately, and therefore unnecessarily, large in proportion to the diplomatic, information, and economic instruments of power, which can be attributed to the fact that the military is the most visible part of the rebalance, as Admiral Harry B. Harris, Jr., PACOM commander, has noted.[39]

One might question the calculus or factors that contributed to the arrival at the 60 percent number. It is a number based on quantities, not necessarily qualities, of forces, equipment, aircraft, ships, and vehicles. A detailed assessment of the regional threats in the Pacific and other regions led to the conclusion that 6 of the 10 operational aircraft carriers should be in the Pacific. This number was based upon multiple inputs, including size and scope of the regions covered, maintenance and training cycles, anticipated requirements, and level of perceived and expected threat.[40] Seven of the 10 would have undermined the ability to support the other combatant commanders, while a 5-5 split would not be commensurate to the requirement.[41] Navy force posture planners considered the remainder of the maritime fleet weighing the same factors. When the calculus was complete, planners had determined that 60 percent was a sustainable force posture requirement for the Pacific that would satisfy the strategic requirement. Under the rebalance, the Navy's plan was to increase the total number of ships in the region from about 150 ships to 180, which would equate to 60 percent. However, if sequestration cuts called for in the Budget Control Act of 2011 were to continue, that number would stay at 150, or roughly 50 percent, effectively canceling the rebalance.[42]

As with anything, the 60 percent number is costly on an already strained defense budget. According to Michael Green, a senior Asia advisor in the George W. Bush administration who is now with the Center for Strategic and International Studies, the sustainability of the 60 percent number is a significant question, given defense budget issues. According to an anonymous Senior State Department official, the rebalance intends to "take advantage of revenues that will be somewhat freed up" by the drawdown in Iraq and Afghanistan.[43] This is the scenario when a nation coming off a long period of war normally enjoys a "peace dividend," where it can refocus on domestic issues that have taken the back burner. In this case, that dividend is committed to the rebalance, and potentially at risk if other global requirements were to emerge or re-emerge.

There are also those who believe that a military ramp up in the form of the rebalance is not necessary, and might even damage efforts in other areas. John Kerry, during his confirmation hearing to become Secretary of State in 2013, noted, "I'm not convinced that increased military ramp-up [in the Asia-Pacific] is critical yet . . . that's something I'd want to look at very carefully."[44] The suggestion is that the United States would now focus more on diplomatic engagements in the region and avoid any provocations that an increase in military forces might bring. In addition, as the United States has been a Pacific power for more than a century and has played a key role in Asia's security and prosperity, Kerry was implying that a physical change in posture is not necessary. The new Secretary of Defense, James Mattis, tended to agree early in his tenure, stating that "there is no need right now at this time for military maneuvers or something like that, that would solve something that's best solved by the diplomats."[45] According to this position, it might actually damage current accomplishments and jeopardize future opportunities in the diplomatic and economic areas. A rebalance to the region is really more of a refocus on the world's most economically dynamic region.[46]

Mattis has seemingly reaffirmed the Trump administration's commitment to the rebalance, as evidenced by his first series of visits. He has visited the Republic of Korea and Japan, and has met with the Indian, Singaporean, and Australian Defense Ministers. In each case, he reaffirmed the U.S. commitment to each country and U.S. obligations in the region, promising continued security cooperation in the region.[47]

The magnitude of the military instrument of power, or "M," is more than just a number of forces, ships, or aircraft. The "M" pertains to military activities in the region, including Humanitarian Assistance/Disaster Relief Operations, training exercises with or without foreign partners, movement of supplies or forces, port visits, Freedom of Navigation Operations (FONOPS), or even just residing in regional homeports. Determining whether the "M" is too large or too small is a question of both the forces and associated activities in relation to the other instruments of power, and how it can assist or damage the achievement of U.S. strategic objectives in theater. Kerry and other State Department officials noted above have concerns that a military buildup could cause damage to U.S. interests. A military buildup would be damaging only if it is a temporary show of force that allies cannot depend on long term, or it generates feelings of containment by China resulting in provocations against regional allies. Therefore, regardless of the size of the "M," it is important to ensure that military diplomacy and diplomatic, or "D" efforts by State Department officials, are synchronized to reinforce the proper strategic message.

Today, the true significance of the 60 percent rebalance figure is the strategic message therein: the United States is focused on the region, and has permanently changed force allocations, deployment schedules, and strategic plans to reinforce the message. The informational aspect of a U.S. overbalanced focus to the region must synchronize with and reinforce the diplomatic and economic instruments. In fact, the recommendations posed later can be considered packaged in with these instruments of power. Furthermore, will 60 percent really bring the needed change to the region, or is something still missing in the rebalance?

THE REBALANCE BY SERVICE

The rebalance seeks to provide a joint force that is capable of responding to any threat in a suitable timeframe. In light of the transregional, multi-domain, multifunctional fight envisioned for the future, the United States faces serious challenges in this theater. The IAP is so vast that planners have coined the term "tyranny of distance" to describe the challenges one faces in responding to events. Consequently, one key element of the rebalance is force posture. Each service is attempting to increase their distribution from the focus on Korea to one that expands U.S. force presence across a larger share of the region.

Coupled with this distribution effort, the joint force seeks to maintain a qualitative advantage, as the United States cannot reasonably expect to maintain a long-term quantitative advantage. Thus, the services are deploying the newest technologies to the IAP region first, as U.S. competitors in this region are advancing most quickly to narrow the technology gap and bring that fight into the multi-domain, multifunctional fight. A brief synopsis of each service's post-rebalance posture will help lay the foundations for a means-informed discussion on possible strategic goals and achievable ends.

The Navy

The Navy's response to the rebalance is to employ 60 percent of its "battle force" vessels in the Pacific Command Area of Responsibility (AOR).[48] This is an increase from a pre-rebalance number closer to 50 percent.[49] To do this, the Navy has aggressively freed up capacity from other locations worldwide. For example, four destroyers now stationed at Rota, vice Norfolk, frees up six other destroyers for other worldwide applications.[50]

Another initiative the Navy has pursued is development and eventual deployment of new capabilities that will help deter or fight the particular threats anticipated in the region. Weapons systems including the F-35 Joint Strike Fighter (JSF), the P-8 Poseidon, and new nuclear submarines will field first to the Pacific theater. The most modern surface ships, with the most advanced capabilities have already begun entering the theater, allowing a more advantageous capability-to-threat posture if conflict is unavoidable. A focus on maintaining capabilities that best counter the perceived threat is exactly the right policy to pursue and must continue as regional actors continue to develop their own technologies.

Finally, emphasizing the importance of understanding the human element, the Navy has developed a program of regional experts. These sailors will be subject matter experts in their particular region, enabling a fuller understanding of the cultures, customs, and ways of thinking of the local populace. This will contribute significantly to preventing conflict and enabling dialogue that is more cooperative.[51]

The Marine Corps

The Marine Corps' response to the rebalance is more of a realignment of Marine forces within the Pacific. Much of the impetus for the realignment is the perpetual displeasure of the local Okinawan populace to a U.S. military presence dating back to World War II. Many Okinawans are vocal in their opposition to the Americans stationed there and have pushed the Government of Japan to request a reduction in U.S. troop presence on Okinawa.[52] The Marine Corps is in the process of reducing the troop strength on Okinawa from 20,600 to 11,500. In order to keep the desired number of Marines west of the International Dateline, the Marine Corps redirected 5,000 Marines to Guam, and 2,500 to Marine Rotational Force-Darwin in Australia, with the remaining 8,800 going to Hawaii.[53] The Marines took advantage of the requirement to constitute one additional rotational Marine Air-Ground Task Forces (MAGTF) for Darwin, and two additional MAGTFs based in Guam. Turning this requirement into operational capability, however, requires additional lift. The service plans to operate an unspecified number of MV-22B Ospreys for the Darwin MAGTF, and the Navy's plans for additional Amphibious Ready Group (ARG) shipping by 2020 will make the Guam Marines a viable responsive force.[54]

While pursuing this plan, the Marine Corps has also focused on resiliency of forces in light of the substantial A2/AD threat China poses to the first island chain currently. This resiliency features both a hardening of installations and an increase in their quantity, creating redundancy.

Another feature of the rebalance is the placement of emerging technologies in the Pacific theater. For instance, the Marine Corps is the first service to field the F-35 in the Pacific region, as their arrival in January delivers 5th generation capabilities to counter the advancing capabilities of regional actors.[55]

The last feature of the Marine Corps rebalance plan is the attempt to provide more partner access to high-end training to increase their capacity. This includes expanding the number of training areas for realistic, live fire amphibious assault training with partners and applicable activities allowed in regional training areas within the Northern Marianas Islands. This effort is commendable, but is currently subject to multiple bureaucratic delays, from environmental study concerns to foreign complaints, which stymie the process.[56]

The Army

The Army's rebalance measures are primarily a return of forces from Iraq and Afghanistan to their habitual bases in the Pacific region. Complementing the troop strength numbers, the Army created the concept entitled Pacific Pathways, which stresses the importance of rapid, scalable response to this vast region covering 14 time zones. The Pathways concept offers regional partners additional opportunity for engagement with the U.S. military and offers the Army more exposure to the region. This creates familiarity, enhances interoperability, and reassures select partners and allies in the region of U.S. commitment.[57]

Further, in its role as theater anti-missile defense, the Army is relocating its Terminal High Altitude Area Defense (THAAD) capabilities to the Republic of Korea. This is in an effort to negate the missile threat from North Korea, as the rogue nation threatens the region through continual advancement of its nuclear ballistic missile capability.[58] THAAD brings the additional benefit of offering a potential counter to China's growing A2/AD capability that will eventually threaten the second island chain.

Finally, the Army is expanding into the multi-domain fight. The Army is exploring ways to use ground-based weapons systems to exert control into other domains. For example, using missile and artillery batteries to extend control over adjacent sea-lanes is one course of action being explored, and ground control of air space is another.[59] Advances into the multi-domain fight would enhance the joint capabilities for the PACOM commander as the assets committed to counter these threats today are freed.

The Air Force

The Air Force has also committed to placing 60 percent of its strike aircraft to the Pacific theater. The rebalance is akin to that of the Marine Corps in that the Air Force seeks to disperse its current forces over a much wider geographic area.[60] Current Air Force posture focuses on Alaska, Hawaii, and Guam, but the rebalance is causing the Air Force to look south, to other allies in the region who might offer basing opportunities for both distribution and resiliency.

The Air Force is also focusing on force modernization and ensuring it deploys the most capable assets to the Pacific theater. This poses a significant challenge to the technology-focused Air Force, however, as that technology carries a high price tag and the post-sequestration budgetary environment is greatly influencing the Air Force's plans.[61]

Another key contribution the Air Force provides is intelligence, surveillance, and reconnaissance (ISR). The need for continued advances in this area is especially compelling in light of adversary advances to contest U.S. technological advantages and a growing A2/AD threat. "In particular, this means an increased emphasis upon stealth capabilities, unmanned systems and technologies which enable air platforms to succeed in highly challenged environments," said Lieutenant General Robert Otto, deputy chief of staff, ISR.[62]

RECOMMENDATIONS

While the United States has been focused heavily on other global commitments for nearly 2 decades, mired in political issues and challenged economically, China has taken full advantage of the period to turn its inward focus into a more overt, assertive one, enjoying a "period of strategic opportunity."[63]

Beijing has made clear that no one will stand in its way as it focuses on its core interests and claims of sovereignty. While great strides have been made in the region thus far in the rebalance, three things are apparent. First, U.S. allies either question our commitment to the region for the long term or feel that China is a more attractive ally. Second, the United States' will to employ its vastly superior military power as part of a compellence or deterrence strategy is in question by China and the region. Third, military response options to China's gray zone expansion through coercive gradualism given current U.S. policy and capabilities are non-existent. The new administration should update its military posture and strategy in the region, to nullify any capability that a regional actor may develop with significant overmatch, such that there is an unmistakably negative consequence to any action taken that goes against established international rules and norms.

No one will disagree that the United States has a clear technological and capability advantage across the globe. While there are close matches in any single capability by various military powers, there is no one superpower on the planet that is even close to matching U.S. capabilities and capacity in their entirety. Add to that the unmatched degree of experience in projecting power and operating as a synergistic joint or combined force across all domains in the swift achievement of military objectives, and the gap widens from the nearest competitor. Furthermore, U.S. defense industries are second-to-none, its private technological innovations are unsurpassed, and the two grow closer daily as our military leaders are beginning to understand the technological edge Silicon Valley has to offer in military innovation.[64] Topping it all off, there is no other nation on the planet that enjoys such an expansive network of allies and partners as the United States.[65]

In this theater, the United States faces a potential adversary in China that is making a strong attempt to gain ground militarily, but whose real advantage lays in its economic power and willingness to use that power to entice or coerce U.S. allies.[66] The question then becomes, how does the United States counter China's big "E" with a big "M"? The following recommendations focus the military instrument of power against that problem in an effort to reestablish a strong United States influence in the region in the attainment of policy objectives. For a summary of these recommendations, see Table 10-1.

	Recommendation:	Amplifying information:
1	Maintain insurmountable technological edge and lethality.	Focus on a qualitative, vice quantitative, advantage, focusing on the TMM threat without excluding the gray zone.
2	Bring allies and partners under this superior U.S.-provided collective security architecture.	Broadens deterrence of China's coercive activities while further reassuring allies/partners. Offer more Foreign Military Sales (FMS) agreements to enhance regional interoperability and compete with China's monetary enticements.
3	Compete in the gray zone.	Develop nonlethal technologies for use in maritime and aviation scenarios. Explore whole-of-government areas of leverage using other instruments of national power.
4	Exercise and demonstrate U.S. superior qualitative advantage with allies and partners through multinational exercises.	Focus on capacity building and interoperability, refinement of TTPs in collective defense/support scenarios while demonstrating superior capabilities.
5	Determine the "redlines" and clearly demonstrate the will and capacity to enforce them.	Determine unambiguous strategic objectives to defend; define adversary actions that cross clear redline thresholds; and predetermine escalation of force response options. This is paired with information campaign that demonstrates resolve while communicating soft power inclusivity with China.
6	Increase unannounced FONOPS in accordance with international laws and international rulings.	Remove bureaucratic obstacles and more frequently conduct FONOPS inside of 12 nautical miles from reclaimed land features that do not rate territorial waters according to international laws and rulings.
7	Distribute U.S. forces strategically across the region and develop strategies to expeditiously employ them as a joint/combined force.	Consider a cohesive, joint/combined strategy in securing rotational force agreements across the region that will impose multiple strategic dilemmas and frustrate China's A2/AD efforts.

Table 10-1. Summary of Recommendations.

First, the United States must maintain an unmatched technological edge and lethality. This does not mean entering into a Cold War-style arms race. In the simple counting of ships, aircraft, and military personnel in the Asia-Pacific region, the United States comes up quantitatively well short of what China already has in place. The amount of spending to compete quantitatively in that region would not be in the interest of the United States. As the economies of the United States and China are both global and interdependent upon one another, this type of expensive arms race could have an adverse effect on the world economy, not to mention the damage it would do to each country as they attempt to best the other. Furthermore, as the United States and its allies and partners widen their focus to include the gray zone tactic "du jour" to the TMM fight of the future, quantitative estimates of force numbers will be less relevant than qualitative ones.

Maintaining an unquestionable qualitative capability gap serves to either dissuade China's efforts at trying to match, or causes them to spend large amounts in wasted efforts to match. The United States should combine this dissuasion with immediate actions to bring to rapid production those technologies that are the closest to fielding, and those for which China has no immediate counter. An example is unmanned underwater vehicles (UUV) or non-lethal undersea capabilities.[67]

Second, allies and partners should be brought into this U.S. provided security envelope in the form of a collective security architecture. China already has the quantitative advantage in the region that will continue to widen, even when the assets of the United States and allies are combined.[68] Therefore, the key to effective balance in the region shared by all allies and partners will be to offer them the umbrella of protection by the United States — protection that they know is and will be technologically and qualitatively superior for the long term. Furthermore, China's ability to match competitors qualitatively is largely through copycatting those advances, whether in technology, doctrine, procedures, practices, or force structure. The United States has, and must maintain, this advantage. To implement, the United States should consider the collective security needs of the region, and individual security needs of partners, and negotiate individualized security and economic trade package deals across the region.

As stated earlier, China has had success in enticing long-standing allies, such as the Philippines, from alliance with the United States. China has given every indication that this will be their model at weakening U.S. influence with allies for the near future.[69] Again, U.S. diplomatic and information efforts must reinforce both a commitment to collective security, a clear technological military advantage, and the will to act on behalf of our allies and partners in defense of U.S. interests in accordance with treaty or security agreements, as well as international rules and norms. Much of that same technology can be delivered into the hands of U.S. allies and partners through Foreign Military Sales (FMS) agreements. Furthermore, Foreign Military Funding (FMF) arrangements could be made to offset defense-spending hardships, allowing allies and partners a method of financing these capabilities.

This initiative has several advantages. First, it directly competes with China's monetary offerings that serve to weaken the U.S. position with allies and partners. Second, FMS contracts with partners immediately increase joint and combined force interoperability in the region, an extremely beneficial aspect of this collective security strategy. Third, entering into FMS contracts with partners sends an immediate message of long-term commitment with that partner, as there is typically training and sustainment aspects to the contracts. Fourth, FMS contracts have the added benefit of supporting the U.S. domestic economy, encouraging overseas satellite cells of those industries, and reducing costs through economies of scale of the same equipment for the U.S. military by increasing the numbers of buyers. Fifth, the partner buys more security for less overall defense spending, as it brings them into a collective security arrangement that not only includes the distinct advantage of U.S. forces, but those of other regional partners. This would allow more of their remaining budget to be used for domestic expenditures.

Opponents argue that China's perception of U.S. containment of China further provoke unpredictable actions. The authors contend that the benefits listed above outweigh the risks and that an effective and supportive information strategy will also stress the security and stability being offered, not containment. The resulting increased commitment to regional allies can be used as leverage against China to compel them to align with international rules and norms.

Third, the strategy of late whereby large powers achieve their will or cause smaller powers to submit without triggering U.S. intervention is through mastery of the gray zone. Indeed, as Russia took Crimea with zero response through gray zone operations, China seems to write its own rules in the South China Sea. The United States needs to enter the gray zone.

One option for response to gray zone aggression is with non-lethal technology. These capabilities offer great promise in maritime escalation of force situations. The lack of response in enforcing international laws thus far has caused an erosion of U.S. strategy since the rebalance was announced. As mentioned previously, China continues to claim sovereignty over Scarborough Shoal, completely ignoring the international ruling in favor of the Philippines. Recognizing that U.S. strategy to date has been an ineffectual one that tends to appease China, even if the United States wanted to back the Philippines, there are few options short of escalating to acts of war to support our ally in this example. A solution could lie in non-lethal methods of escalation, such as the use of directed electromagnetic emissions or sound waves, to deter Chinese patrolling those waters.[70] The United States needs to continue development of these and similar technologies for use in maritime as well as aviation scenarios for use in the gray zone.

Other options for the gray zone include non-military, whole-of-government approaches. Ultimately, the United States needs to find areas of leverage that it can use to bring about more cost on the part of China than is caused to the United States, to include second and third order effects of such actions. Ideally, through economic and diplomatic outreaches to regional and worldwide partners, the United States can leverage the large advantage it enjoys over China in networks of international and regional partners to form coalitions in these approaches. Examples of areas to explore for leverage include student visas, trade, technology, and environmental sanctions.[71]

Fourth, the United States needs to exercise and demonstrate these capabilities with and among regional partners/allies. Annual U.S.-led multinational exercises focused on capacity building and training, training to real world combined scenarios, interoperability, as well as high-end technological, state of the art capability demonstrations such as forcible entry, Integrated Air Defense penetration strikes, counter-ballistic missile capabilities and counter A2/AD will accomplish many objectives. The first is the training of partners and the exercising of interoperability. This will not only serve to increase the capacity of partners, but it will also strengthen the web of collective security amongst allies and reassure them of continued U.S. commitment. Second, it allows all involved to refine tactics, techniques, and procedures in the use of collective defense scenarios. Third, this serves as a demonstration of capabilities inherent within the collective defense architecture. This will increase the confidence level of individual partners, build a sense of camaraderie among regional partners, and serve as a deterrent to potential adversaries. Finally, through a high-end, state of the art "culmination" demonstration, near-peer competitors get a yearly glimpse of exactly how far ahead the United States is in its innovative, technological edge. This serves as a clear strategic deterrence; as noted in the Center for a New American Security November 2016 report, "Counterbalance," Chinese leaders are "most likely to update their perceptions of the United States when Washington pairs clearly stated intentions with capabilities."[72]

Fifth, the United States and the international community need to unambiguously determine and communicate where the red lines are and clearly demonstrate the will and capability to enforce them. Lack of clarity on a specific defensive objective has been noted as a shortfall in U.S. efforts in the Western Pacific, perhaps leading to ambiguity. A suggestion from the "Counterbalance" article is for the United States to prevent Chinese control of the First Island Chain, thereby protecting U.S. allies and interests in the region.[73] This is in keeping with the historical U.S. strategic approach in the region while acknowledging China's growing capabilities. While the United States has no intent to fall back from this objective, despite China's touts of a U.S. strategic retreat, a clear signal of this as a strategic objective that supports the aforementioned policy objectives is much more unambiguous to regional allies and partners. While U.S. policy has been to avoid taking sides in conflict resolutions between opposing claimants, and to allow claimants to resolve disputes peacefully, there should be no question that the United States will enforce international laws and rulings, particularly in the defense of current and future allies and partners.[74]

Beyond more clearly defined strategic redlines the United States and the international community need more clarity in adversary actions that cross redlines. U.S. and partner actions need to be predetermined in escalation of force scenarios and ensure that those forces who would execute are empowered to do so.[75] In a collective security architecture, this might require combined action among partners and allies, depending on the situation. This will require close command and control among the combined force for coordination and to manage unnecessary escalation.[76] As actions and procedures are developed, consideration should be given to the fact that conflict might escalate from within the gray zone into actual armed engagements or standoffs.[77]

A renewed U.S. resolve to act in support of allies and partners and undeniably assert itself in the attainment of its interests will undoubtedly cause great alarm and suspicion on the part of China, as the regional power. While that is partly the objective, the other aspect is to create a path to peaceful coexistence. This will require a new information campaign that both demonstrates the new resolve and communicates inclusivity with China. Therefore, high-level diplomacy will be focused on this as well as reassuring U.S. allies and partners that the two powers will work together and do everything possible to avoid armed conflict. It is also important to communicate and demonstrate the two superpowers cohabitating in the region and cooperating militarily on as many soft power areas of common interest as possible. Several references note that this is a major interest of ASEAN nations, who do not want to be forced to take sides between the United States and China, and desire relations with both powers.[78]

Sixth, increase unannounced FONOPS, in accordance with international laws and international rulings. While PACOM strategy and numerous speeches highlight the fact that the United States will continue to "fly, sail, and operate wherever international law allows," the truth is that this is a very sensitive area with multiple bureaucratic obstacles.[79] In addition, it has been internationally recognized that not all of the reclaimed land features in the South China Sea rate an EEZ, and many do not even qualify as territorial waters. The United States has essentially condoned the illegal land reclamation and construction activities of China by remaining outside of 12 nautical miles (NM) from such features in the conduct of FONOPS. The bureaucratic obstacles to internationally legal FONOPS should be removed in order to facilitate their frequent execution, such that it is a regular enough occurrence to soften the sensitivities and make it the new (or renewed) norm. If these land features have been defined by a recognized, independent tribunal as nothing more than fixed objects in the open ocean, then treat them as such. The only way the United States can set the example of promoting international law and international rulings is to operate air and naval forces wherever international law allows, including inside 12 NM, and support or accompany allies and partners who do so.

Seventh, continue to distribute U.S. forces and develop realistic, resource-able strategies to utilize these forces across the range of military operations in rapid, expeditionary, joint and combined scenarios. Work out more rotational force agreements across the South Pacific, placing forces in a strategic manner and planning lift assets and logistics support in a way that supports rapid aggregation and disaggregation in accordance with emerging joint concepts. As alluded to previously, the re-posturing of forces that resulted after the rebalance was announced was largely reactive in nature, and executed as a result of pre-existing requirements (i.e., the Okinawa drawdown), and reallocations from the Global War on Terror (GWOT). Said another way, the United States militarily rebalanced forces from other commitments and opportunities, conveniently meeting a requirement to rebalance through happenstance instead of strategic realignment. In what could be termed a "next phase" of the rebalance, the United States needs to consider a cohesive joint strategy in securing rotational force agreements throughout the southern Pacific region that will impose multiple strategic dilemmas against China's A2/AD efforts.

CONCLUSION

While the United States has made great strides in its rebalance to the Pacific after 15 years of hard fought efforts in the GWOT, there is much room for improvement in the achievement of policy objectives in the region. In effect, if one were to look at the policy objectives—maintenance of peace, prosperity, and stability in the region; respect for international law; unimpeded lawful commerce; and freedom of navigation in the South and East China Seas—it is not difficult to conclude that, regardless of any progress that might have been made, overall, the United States is largely failing. True, out of these, commerce has continued unimpeded through this region thus far. How long, though, before China has the ability to become selective about which nations can conduct trade or military exercises with Asian nations as leverage against the international community? Through coercive gradualism, China slowly places its pieces throughout the region in an effort to gain this type of influence. The United States, with unmatched military power and a unique ability to project it wherever and whenever needed, runs its traditional plays, employing hope that good will ultimately prevail while seemingly unaware of what is happening right under its nose. Once a threshold is crossed, the United States will by that time have already been placed in an operationally unwinnable situation, or worse, be forced to become the offensive provocateur on the world stage; potentially a strategically unwinnable situation. To get ahead of the game that is being played, the United States needs to get in the game.

ENDNOTES—CHAPTER 10

1. Ash Carter, "Remarks on the Next Phase of the U.S. Rebalance to the Asia-Pacific (McCain Institute, Arizona State University)," As Delivered by Secretary of Defense Ash Carter, Tempe, AZ, April 6, 2015, available from *https://www.defense.gov/News/Speeches/Speech-View/Article/606660/*

remarks-on-the-next-phase-of-the-us-rebalance-to-the-asia-pacific-mccain-instit, accessed March 20, 2017.

2. "Posture Statement of General Joseph Dunford, Jr., USMC, 19th Chairman of the Joint Chiefs of Staff Before the 114th Congress Senate Armed Services Committee Budget Hearing March 17, 2016," Washington, DC: Senate Armed Services Committee, 2016, available from *https://www.armed-services.senate.gov/imo/media/doc/Dunford_03-17-16%20.pdf*.

3. Robert D. Blackwill and Ashley J. Tellis, "Revising U.S. Grand Strategy Toward China," Council Special Report No. 72, Washington, DC: Council on Foreign Relations Press, p. 19, available from *www.cfr.org/china/revising-us-grand-strategy-toward-china/p36371*, accessed December 20, 2016.

4. Idress Ali, "United States has 'enduring' interests in Asia-Pacific, defense secretary says," Reuters, December 6, 2016, available from *www.reuters.com/article/us-usa-japan-asiapacific-idUSKBN13W05U*.

5. Kurt M. Campbell, *The Pivot*, 1st Ed., New York: Hatchette Book Group, Incorporated, 2016, pp. 17-18.

6. U.S. Department of Defense, "The Asia-Pacific Maritime Strategy: Achieving U.S. National Security Objectives in a Changing Environment," Washington, DC: U.S. Department of Defense, August 14, 2015, p. 6, available from *https://www.defense.gov/Portals/1/Documents/pubs/NDAA%20A-P_Maritime_SecuritY_Strategy-08142015-1300-FINALFORMAT.PDF*.

7. Hillary Clinton, "America's Pacific Century," *Foreign Policy*, October 11, 2011, available from *http://foreignpolicy.com/2011/10/11/americas-pacific-century/*, accessed March 20, 2017; Blackwill and Tellis, p. 19.

8. Ibid.

9. Max Fisher, "The South China Sea: Explaining the Dispute," *The New York Times*, July 14, 2016, available from *www.nytimes.com/2016/07/15/world/asia/south-china-sea-dispute-arbitration-explained.html*.

10. Robert S. Ross, "The Problem With the Pivot," *Foreign Affairs*, November/December 2012, available from *https://www.foreignaffairs.com/articles/asia/2012-11-01/problem-pivot*.

11. David Tweed and Mira Rojanasakul, "The Great Asian Arms Buildup: China's Military Expansion, South China Sea to Dominate Shangri-La Dialogue," Bloomberg, May 31, 2016, available from *https://www.bloomberg.com/graphics/2016-shangrila/*, accessed March 21, 2017.

12. Ryan Pickrell, "Beijing Warns US 'Word Bombs' Won't Stop Chinese Power Projection," The Daily Caller, January 22, 2017, available from *dailycaller.com/2017/01/22/beijing-warns-us-word-bombs-wont-stop-chinese-power-projection/*, accessed March 21, 2017.

13. Steve Mollman, "The line on a 70-year-old map that threatens to set off a war in East Asia," Quartz, July 7, 2016, available from *https://qz.com/705223/where-exactly-did-chinas-nine-dash-line-in-the-south-china-sea-come-from/*, accessed March 21, 2017.

14. Daniel Russel, "Testimony of Daniel Russel Assistant Secretary of State Bureau of East Asian and Pacific Affairs U.S. Department of State Before the Senate Foreign Relations Committee Wednesday, May 13, 2015 Maritime Issues in East Asia," Washington, DC: Senate Foreign Relations Committee, 2015, available from *www.foreign.senate.gov/imo/media/doc/051315_REVISED_Russel_Testimony.pdf*.

15. Amanda Macias, "'This is militarization': We finally know what China's mysterious hexagonal structures in the South China Sea are for," *Business Insider*, December 16, 2016, pp. 857 224, available from *www.businessinsider.com/csis-satellite-hexagonal-south-china-sea-2016-12*, accessed December 18, 2016.

16. Zachary Keck, "China Imposes Restrictions on Air Space Over Senkaku Islands," *The Diplomat*, November 23, 2013, available from *https://thediplomat.com/2013/11/china-imposes-restrictions-on-air-space-over-senkaku-islands/*, accessed March 21, 2017.

17. Rear Adm. Michael McDevitt, "Is It Time for the U.S. to Take a Position on Scarborough Shoal?" USNI News,

July 19, 2016, available from *https://news.usni.org/2016/07/19/take-position-scarborough-shoal.*

18. "Duterte told: Ignoring sea row with China bad for PH, int'l law," ABS-CBN News, December 18, 2016, available from *http://news.abs-cbn.com/focus/12/18/16/duterte-told-ignoring-sea-row-with-china-bad-for-ph-intl-law*, accessed December 19, 2016.

19. Michael McDevitt, "The South China Sea: Assessing U.S. Policy and Options for the Future," *CNA Occasional Paper*, Arlington, VA: CNA's Center for Naval Analyses, November 2014, p. 33, available from *https://www.cna.org/cna_files/pdf/IOP-2014-U-009109.pdf.*

20. Nomaan Merchant, Associated Press (AP), "Drone seizure latest sign of tougher times between U.S., China," *Military Times*, December 19, 2016, available from *www.militarytimes.com/articles/drone-seizure-latest-sign-of-tougher-times-between-us-china*, accessed December 20, 2016.

21. U.S. Department of Defense, pp. 5-10.

22. Ibid., pp. 10-13.

23. Ibid., pp. 14-17.

24. Michael Spangler, "Rebalancing the Rebalance," *Parameters*, Vol. 44, No. 2, Summer 2014, pp. 11-21, available from *http://ssi.armywarcollege.edu/pubs/Parameters/Issues/Summer_2014/5_Spangler_Article.pdf.*

25. Euan Graham, "The Hague Tribunal's South China Sea Ruling: Empty Provocation or Slow-Burning Influence?" Council of Councils, August 18, 2016, available from *www.cfr.org/councilofcouncils/global_memos/p38227*, accessed January 29, 2017.

26. Spangler, p. 17.

27. Ibid., pp. 19-20.

28. George M. Gross, "The New Generation of Operational Concepts," *Small Wars Journal*, January 8, 2016, p. 2, available from *smallwarsjournal.com/jrnl/art/the-new-generation-of-operational-concepts.*

29. U.S. Department of Defense, pp. 5-10.

30. Felix K. Chang, "Sideways: America's Pivot and Its Military Bases in the Asia-Pacific," E-Notes, Philadelphia, PA: Foreign Policy Research Institute, April 16, 2013, available from *https://www.fpri.org/article/2013/04/sideways-americas-pivot-and-its-military-bases-in-the-asia-pacific/*.

31. An example is the redistribution of Marine forces to Darwin, Australia, Guam, and Hawaii. While this is a redistribution as described in this chapter, it was less a thoughtful strategic redistribution of forces and more a requirement to reduce force numbers in Futenma, Okinawa, that was a timely coincidence with the rebalance. The decisions to place them in Darwin and Guam were made out of convenience.

32. Veasna Var, "Cambodia: Between China and the United States," *The Diplomat*, May 20, 2015, available from *https://thediplomat.com/2015/05/cambodia-between-china-and-the-united-states/*, accessed March 21, 2017; Jane Perlez, "Rodrigo Duterte Gets Closer to China, and the Neighbors Notice," *The New York Times*, October 24, 2016, available from *https://www.nytimes.com/2016/10/25/world/asia/rodrigo-duterte-philippines-china.html*.

33. U.S. Department of Defense, pp. 5-10.

34. "Littoral Combat Ship USS Fort Worth (LCS 3) Completes South China Sea Patrol," Navy Recognition, May 14, 2015, available from *http://www.navyrecognition.com/index.php?option=com_content&view=article&id=2715*, accessed March 21, 2017.

35. Merchant, AP; AP, "US Navy destroyer conducts operation in South China Sea," Fox News, October 22, 2016, available from *www.foxnews.com/world/2016/10/22/us-navy-destroyer-conducts-operation-in-south-china-sea.html*; Mike Yeo, "US, Chinese aircraft in 'unsafe' encounter in South China Sea," *Defense News*, available from *https://www.defensenews.com/air/2017/02/10/us-chinese-aircraft-in-unsafe-encounter-in-south-china-sea/*, accessed February 13, 2017; Elisabeth Rosenthal with David E. Sanger, "U.S. Plane in China after It Collides with Chinese Jet," *The New York Times*, April 2, 2001, available from *www.nytimes.com/2001/04/02/world/us-plane-in-china-after-it-collides-with-chinese-jet.html*.

36. Prashanth Parameswaran, "America's New Maritime Security Initiative for Southeast Asia," *The Diplomat*, April 2, 2016, available from *https://thediplomat.com/2016/04/americas-new-maritime-security-initiative-for-southeast-asia/*, accessed March 26, 2017.

37. "Posture Statement of General Joseph Dunford, Jr., USMC, 19th Chairman of the Joint Chiefs of Staff Before the 114th Congress Senate Armed Services Committee Budget Hearing March 17, 2016."

38. Gregory Whitten and Erum Jilani, "Rebalance to the Asia-Pacific: A New U.S. Defense Strategy for the 21st Century," *Kennedy School Review*, June 28, 2014, available from *http://ksr.hkspublications.org/2014/06/28/rebalance-to-the-asia-pacific/*.

39. Terri Moon Cronk, "Pacom Commander: Rebalance to Asia-Pacific 'Being Realized'," DoD News, February 25, 2016, available from *https://www.defense.gov/News/Article/Article/673465/pacom-commander-rebalance-to-asia-pacific-being-realized/*, accessed December 20, 2016.

40. Interview with Navy planners, PACFLT, Pearl Harbor, HI.

41. Office of the Secretary of Defense, *Quadrennial Defense Review Report*, Washington, DC: U.S. Department of Defense, February 6, 2006, pp. 47-48, available from *http://archive.defense.gov/pubs/pdfs/QDR20060203.pdf*.

42. John Grady, "Locklear: U.S. 'Shouldn't Talk Ourselves Into' Conflict With China," USNI News, March 25, 2014, available from *https://news.usni.org/2014/03/25/locklear-u-s-shouldnt-talk-conflict-china*; John Grady, "U.S. Pacific Commander Defends 11 Carrier Navy," USNI News, March 6, 2014, available from *https://news.usni.org/2014/03/06/u-s-pacific-commander-defends-11-carrier-navy*.

43. Howard LaFranchi, "US 'pivot to Asia': Is John Kerry retooling it?" *The Christian Science Monitor*, February 20, 2013, available from *https://www.csmonitor.com/USA/Foreign-Policy/2013/0220/US-pivot-to-Asia-Is-John-Kerry-retooling-it*.

44. Ibid.

45. Phil Stewart, "Mattis says no need for dramatic U.S. military moves in South China Sea," Reuters, February 3, 2017, available from *https://www.reuters.com/article/us-usa-trump-southchinasea-mattis/mattis-says-no-need-for-dramatic-u-s-military-moves-in-south-china-sea-idUSKBN15J061*.

46. LaFranchi.

47. For the Asia-Pacific Rebalance, see "DoD Focus on the Asia-Pacific," U.S. Department of Defense, 2017, available from *https://www.defense.gov/News/Special-Reports/0415_Asia-Pacific-Rebalance*; for Mattis' remarks, see his comments Captain Jeff Davis, spokesman, "Readout of Secretary Mattis' Call with Japan Minister of Defense Tomomi Inada," Release No: NR-087-17, Washington, DC: U.S. Department of Defense, March 6, 2017, available from *https://www.defense.gov/News/News-Releases/News-Release-View/Article/1104289/readout-of-secretary-mattis-call-with-japan-minister-of-defense-tomomi-inada*.

48. Mr. Eugene Aiu, COMPACFLT N81 Force Posture, interview by authors, Pearl Harbor, HI, January 19, 2017.

49. Moon Cronk.

50. Press Operations, "The U.S. Defense Rebalance to Asia: As Prepared for Delivery by Deputy Secretary of Defense Ashton B. Carter, Center for Strategic and International Studies, Washington, D.C., Monday, April 08, 2013," U.S. Department of Defense Archives, April 8, 2013, available from *http://archive.defense.gov/speeches/speech.aspx?speechid=1765*.

51. Tuan N. Pham, "The Rebalance Requires BRAINS, Not Just BRAWN," *U.S. Naval Institute Proceedings*, Vol. 140, No. 4, April 2014, pp. 22-25.

52. Maki Kimura, "The anti-US military base struggle in Okinawa, Japan," openDemocracy, February 13, 2016, available from *https://www.opendemocracy.net/maki-kimura/anti-us-military-base-struggle-in-okinawa-japan*.

53. Mure Dickie, "US to move thousands of marines off Okinawa," *Financial Times*, February 8, 2012, available from *https://www.ft.com/content/f1e5389a-5266-11e1-a155-00144feabdc0*.

54. Michael Green, Kathleen Hicks, and Mark Cancian, "Asia-Pacific Rebalance 2025 Capabilities, Presence, and Partnerships: An Independent Review of U.S. Defense Strategy in the Asia-Pacific," Washington, DC: Center for Strategic & International Studies, January 2016, pp. 127, 204, available from *https://csis-prod.s3.amazonaws.com/s3fs-public/legacy_files/files/publication/160119_Green_AsiaPacificRebalance2025_Web_0.pdf*.

55. Brad Lendon, "US Marine F-35s to be 'cornerstone' in Japan, Pacific defense," CNN, January 13, 2017, available from *www.cnn.com/2017/01/12/politics/marines-f-35-stealth-jets-deploy-to-japan/index.html*, accessed March 11, 2017; "Lightning II Strikes Iwakuni, F-35B Arrives," The Official United States Marine Corps Public Website, available from *www.marines.mil/News/News-Display/Article/1052138/lightning-ii-strikes-iwakuni-f-35b-arrives/*, accessed March 11, 2017.

56. Dennis B. Chan, "Public hearing set for clean up of Chiget mortar range," *Saipan Tribune*, June 29, 2015, available from *www.saipantribune.com/index.php/public-hearing-set-for-clean-up-of-chiget-mortar-range/*.

57. Vincent K. Brooks, "U.S. Army Pacific And the Pacific Rebalance," *Army*, Vol. 63, No. 10, October 2013, pp. 121-122, 124, 126.

58. Jen Judson, "U.S. Army missile defense battery arrives in South Korea," *Defense News*, March 7, 2017, available from *www.defensenews.com/articles/us-army-missile-defense-battery-arrives-in-south-korea*, accessed March 11, 2017.

59. Sydney J. Freedberg, Jr., "Army's Multi-Domain Battle To Be Tested In PACOM, EUCOM Wargames," Breaking Defense, November 9, 2016, available from *https://breakingdefense.com/2016/11/armys-multi-domain-battle-tested-in-pacom-eucom-wargames/*.

60. Steven L. Basham and Nelson D. Rouleau, "A Rebalance Strategy for Pacific Air Forces: Flight Plan to Runways and Relationships," *Air & Space Power Journal*, Vol. 29, Iss. 1, January-February 2015, pp. 6-19, available from *www.dtic.mil/docs/citations/ADA622513*.

61. Deborah L. James and Mark A. Welsh, *USAF Posture Statement 2016*, Posture Statement presented to the 114th Cong., 2nd sess., Washington, DC: Department of the Air Force, February 10, 2016, available from *http://www.af.mil/Portals/1/documents/ airpower/FY16_AF_PostureStatement_FINALversion2-2.pdf*, accessed December 19, 2016.

62. Kris Osborn, "General: Air Force Must Rebalance ISR for 'Contested Environments'," Defense Tech, September 17, 2013, available from *https://www.defensetech.org/2013/09/17/ general-air-force-must-rebalance-isr-for-contested-environments/*.

63. Jacqueline N. Deal, "Prospects for Peace: The View from Beijing," *Parameters*, Vol. 46, No. 2, Summer 2016, pp. 9-10.

64. Ash Carter, "Remarks on 'Building the First Link to the Force of the Future' (George Washington University)," As Delivered by Secretary of Defense Ash Carter, George Washington University Elliott School of International Affairs, Washington, DC, November 18, 2015, available from *www.defense.gov/News/ Speeches/Speech-View/Article/630415/remarks-on-building-the-first- link-to-the-force-of-the-future-george-washington*, accessed October 18, 2016.

65. Gross, p. 3.

66. Douglas T. Stuart, *The Pivot to Asia: Can It Serve as the Foundation for American Grand Strategy in the 21st Century?* Carlisle, PA: Strategic Studies Institute, U.S. Army War College, August 2016, p. 56.

67. Mira Rapp-Hooper, Patrick M. Cronin, Harry Krejsa, and Hannah Suh, "Counterbalance: Red Teaming the Rebalance in the Asia-Pacific," Washington, DC: Center for a New American Security, November 14, 2016, p. 55, available from *https://www.cnas. org/publications/reports/counterbalance-red-teaming-the-rebalance-in- the-asia-pacific*, accessed December 18, 2016.

68. Robert Farley, "China's Military Has Nearly 3000 Aircraft. Here's Why That Matters," *The Diplomat*, May 17, 2016, available from *https://thediplomat.com/2016/05/chinas-military-has-nearly- 3000-aircraft-heres-why-that-matters/*, accessed January 8, 2017.

69. Rapp-Hooper et al., p. 52.

70. Raunek Kantharia, "18 Anti-Piracy Weapons for Ships to Fight Pirates," Marine Insight, January 18, 2013, available from *www.marineinsight.com/?p=25340*. Notable examples are the Active Denial System (ADS), which transmits directed E-M energy to cause a harmless heat sensation on the skin, or the Long Range Acoustic Device (LRAD), which uses a harmless pain inducing sound beam to achieve its effect.

71. Paul Mozur and Jane Perlez, "China Bets on Sensitive U.S. Start-Ups, Worrying the Pentagon," *The New York Times*, March 22, 2017, available from *https://www.nytimes.com/2017/03/22/technology/china-defense-start-ups.html?nytmobile=0*, accessed March 23, 2017.

72. Rapp-Hooper et al., p. 41.

73. Ibid., p. 55.

74. U.S. Department of Defense, pp. 5-7.

75. Rapp-Hooper et al., p. 56.

76. Ibid.

77. Ibid., p. 55.

78. Ibid., pp. 31-32.

79. U.S. Department of Defense, pp. 5-7.

CHAPTER 11

A DIPLOMATIC SOLUTION TO THE NORTH KOREA PROBLEM

Frazariel I. Castro

EXECUTIVE SUMMARY

Kim Jong Un is unlikely to give up his ballistic missile and nuclear weapons program in the current environment. The leader of the Democratic People's Republic of Korea (DPRK) has declared that the United States and South Korea are existential threats to North Korea and has sought to build a nuclear capability that he views as essential to defending his country.

The United States, under former President Barack Obama, pursued a policy of strategic patience in which the United States maintained an open hand to North Korea. The United States was prepared to welcome the country back to the international community as a participant in a rules-based international order as long as DPRK ceased provocations and committed to a change in behavior as a precondition for formal diplomatic discussions. This policy, however, has failed to produce the desired results. Given this fact, President Donald Trump should consider pursuing dialogue with Kim Jong Un and remove pre-conditions for a North Korean commitment of denuclearization in order to allow diplomacy to start. The United States and South Korea must attempt to change Kim Jong Un's mindset and strive to have him understand and publicly acknowledge that the United States is not seeking regime change. The United States should seek to first normalize relations, and then take nascent steps to limit Kim Jong Un's nuclear aims.

INTRODUCTION

The strength of the U.S. military supports a diplomatic option to address the persistent problems of ballistic missile testing, nuclear weapons development, and hostile provocation that the DPRK or North Korea has created on the Korean peninsula.[1] It is an option that removes the conditional requirement for Kim Jong Un, revered as North Korea's Great Successor, Supreme Commander, or Great Leader to commit first to denuclearization before any dialogue between the United States and North Korea occurs.[2] Both the Republic of Korea (ROK) or South Korea and U.S. forces stationed in South Korea are highly trained and ready to defeat any North Korean aggression. Armed with technologically superior equipment and weapons, they provide a formidable military deterrence while enjoying an overwhelming overmatch in capability over North Korean forces despite the size of the North Korean army. Moreover, the resolve of U.S. regional allies, South Korea and Japan, is unfaltering in their support for conflict resolution on the Korean peninsula. However, this alternate diplomatic option has neither been attempted nor advocated since Kim Jong Un came into power, and the North Korean threat lingers today. Indeed, Kim Jong Un ushered in 2017 and the new year with a buoyant proclamation to his people that North Korea had entered a final stage for the test of an intercontinental ballistic missile (ICBM).[3]

The message in Kim Jong Un's New Year's address continues the belligerent threats toward South Korea,

Japan, and United States. His proclamation for an ICBM test later this year is in line with North Korea's aggressive ballistic missile and nuclear weapons testing of 2016. Kim Jong Un also reflected that it was a year in which North Korea "achieved the status of a nuclear power, a military giant, in the East which no enemy, however formidable, would dare to provoke."[4] While Kim Jong Un begins the 6th year of his lifetime rule of North Korea, there is some political uncertainty ahead with regard to the leadership of his perceived enemies. The impeachment of South Korean President Park Geun Hye over allegations that she violated their laws by conspiring with an old friend to extort private companies for personal gain has left the country in transition as the citizens prepare to elect a new president.[5]

It remains to be seen how the impact of President Park's impeachment will change South Korean policy toward North Korea. In the United States, Trump assumed the office of president with the responsibility for shaping and developing U.S. foreign policy on North Korea. The current situation in Northeast Asia raises many questions and presents a few opportunities for consideration. How will U.S. policy change under Trump? How would Kim Jong Un respond to an offer of a different olive branch? What more can China do to help resolve the tension between its two southern neighbors?

This chapter argues for a U.S. approach beyond what was tried previously for resuming dialogue with North Korea in order to set conditions that will lead to formal diplomatic discussions and eventual talks to acknowledge and perhaps find options to meet each country's national interests.[6] This would include assuring North Korea that the United States does not pose an existential threat to either the Kim regime or the North Korean people.[7] The security, stability, and their return to the international community as a member of a rules-based society are in the best interest of all nations. With their security affirmed, this chapter further argues that, if these initial diplomatic talks are successful in convincing North Korea of U.S. good will, they would no longer have a need or justification for their nuclear weapons as a deterrent against the United States, South Korea, or Japan.

To better understand Kim Jong Un and North Korea today, it is necessary to understand their background and the foundation of their past. This chapter will first, briefly summarize critical periods of North Korea's recent history, starting with Japan's annexation of the Korean peninsula early in the 20th century. It focuses on North Korea's three prominent leaders, Kim Il Sung, Kim Jong Il, and Kim Jong Un, and how they established North Korea's national identity, framed its political culture, and developed its ideological belief that greatly contributed to its resilience.[8] Second, it will attempt to present Kim Jong Un's worldview and perceptions with which he rationalizes the methods he is pursuing to ensure his regime's survival. A review of the capabilities of North Korea's conventional military and the advancement and of its nuclear development will further highlight the current threat it poses to South Korea, Japan, and the United States. Third, it will assess previous and developing U.S. strategies and options used and considered to dissuade North Korea from pursuing its nuclear weapons program. This includes United Nations (UN) sanctions, with specific emphasis on UN Security Council Resolution (UNSCR) 2321. It also looks at the previous U.S. policy of strategic patience, current efforts at deterrence and assurance, and Trump's developing foreign policy.[9] Finally, a recommendation is out forward that diplomacy supported by the strength of the U.S. military is an option to consider for achieving peace through strength.[10]

BACKGROUND

A brief historical review beginning in the early 20th century provides necessary context for understanding both South Korea and North Korea. Having won its war with China in 1894-1895 and later was victorious over Russia in 1904-1905, Japan assumed control over the Korean peninsula in 1905, formally annexing the entire peninsula in 1910. The Korean people underwent a harsh and brutal existence under Japan's colonial rule until the end of World War II.[11] The Allied victory over Japan and the beginning of the Cold War between the United States and the Soviet Union brought forth the division between North Korea and South Korea.[12] As North Korea and its founding leader Kim Il Sung developed under Soviet communist influence, South Korea benefitted from western and U.S. assistance.[13] The Korean war, fought from 1950-1953, resulted in an armistice which brought an end to the fighting, but not the war.[14]

Kim Il Sung established the foundations for the Kim regime and North Korea's ideological and autocratic rule. He introduced the core concepts of *juche* (self-reliance) and *songun* (military first) politics.[15] Kim Il Sung remained in power until his death in 1994. His son, Kim Jong Il had already assumed control in 1980 but only formally became North Korea's Dear Leader when his father died.[16] Kim Jong Un inherited control and the current rule of North Korea when Kim Jong Il died in 2011.[17]

Identity

Kim Jong Un's rule, the family legacy of the Kim Regime, and the authoritarian state government are the foundation of North Korea's collective and national identity. North Koreans are culturally tied to and share a transnational identity with their South Korean neighbors. North Korea is often labeled as a hermit kingdom. Its population is quite homogeneous and reflects North Korea's regional identity.[18]

The North Korean government fosters a cult of personality in Kim Jong Un, and it is an essential element of its propaganda apparatus. Kim Il Sung and Kim Jong Il are immortalized with tributes and statues throughout the country, a strategy they used to solidify their power and position as leaders. They intertwined their background with their country's history and mythology.[19] It now appears Kim Jong Un is developing his own cult of personality as he, too, will be honored along with his father and grandfather in a monument that will be built on Mount Paektu, a sacred mythological point of origin site that links them to a bloodline that legitimizes their leadership.[20]

North Korea is an autocratic communist country. There is no democracy in the DPRK. Kim Jong Un has ruled with absolute power since he became the country's leader on December 17, 2011. Hence, North Koreans lack many basic freedoms. For example, the North Korean government does not allow its people to practice freedom of religion to include its traditional religions of Buddhism or Confucianism.[21] The North Korean government sponsors religious groups in order to create a façade that the country allows religious freedom. This is an example of North Korea's oppressive political culture.

Kim Jong Un is the leader of North Korea's major political party, the Korean Workers' Party (KWP). He ran unopposed during the country's last election held in March 2014. While there are two other minor political parties, the KWP controls both the Chondoist Chongu Party and the Social Democratic Party. Even the attempt to conduct elections highlights the hollowness of the North Korean government toward a democratic process. Likewise, the members of the Supreme People's Assembly, a unicameral legislative body, are really selected by the KWP. The KWP also chooses Supreme Court judges, although indirectly, as the Supreme People's Assembly designates the judges to their positions.[22]

The North Korean government maintains a state-run media. It includes the Korean Central Broadcasting Station and the Voice of Korea that are instrumental in communicating government propaganda to the masses.[23] The government prohibits independent media outlets from operating. The government takes steps to ensure radios and televisions are pre-tuned to the government stations. In addition, the government blocks foreign radio and television broadcasts to prevent outside influence.[24]

North Korea, notwithstanding its insulated national identity and its dictatorial political culture, has remained quite resilient. It appears that globalization has not had a great impact on North Korea and its people. As stated previously, North Korea's state-run media and propaganda contributes greatly to this desired state. North Korea has been surprisingly successful at keeping itself relatively isolated from the

international community. There are only a few priv-
ileged to have access to a fledging intranet, North
Korea's equivalent of the Internet. The ruling elite,
primarily those who live in North Korea's capital city
of Pyongyang, are among the 30 percent of the population that have routine access to electricity. They also
enjoy a better standard of living than the rest of the
population. In contrast, the majority of North Korea's
people have endured deprivation due to famine and
the shortage of food.[25]

North Korea's economic structure does not provide
them needed relief. The North Korean government centrally manages all aspects of its economy and receives
most of the revenue. There is no private enterprise.
China is North Korea's largest trading partner. North
Korea exports include coal, iron, iron ore, and weap-
onry. Its imports include petroleum, cooking coal,
textiles, and grain.[26] North Korea, at the expense and
labor of its people, also generates a significant amount
of revenue by maintaining an extensive workforce
employed abroad. Even with these limited business
and economic dealings, North Korea's engagement
with the rest of the world remains marginal.

However, it must also be noted that North Korea
does have formal diplomatic relations with select
nations. North Korea has a Permanent Mission to the
United Nations as well as in other countries. There is
no mutual diplomatic representation between North
Korea and the United States. The Swedish Embassy
in North Korea represents the United States. It serves
as its consular protecting power for American interests.[27] Even if North Korea wanted to seek diplomacy
and engage in dialogue with the international community, its continued ballistic missile and nuclear weapon
testing have impeded future opportunities. This is

apparent with the routine worldwide condemnation of North Korean provocations.

NORTH KOREA'S WORLDVIEW AND ITS PURSUIT OF NUCLEAR DETERRENCE

Kim Jong Un and the North Korean Government have espoused a view of the United States and South Korea as existential threats. They see themselves under a nuclear threat, and the annual joint U.S. and South Korean military training exercises, for example, are actually seen as wargames for a prelude to an attack on their nation.[28] They also see U.S. forces in South Korea as an aggressive interventionist and occupying force that is a challenge to North Korea's reunification goals.[29] Therefore, North Korea focuses its strategic policy on building up its self-defense capability. North Korea believes that having a nuclear force and pre-emptive strike capability is essential to defend their peace and security.[30] Additionally, the North Korean constitution, updated in 2012, makes tribute to Kim Jong Il's achievement in administering *songun* or "military first" politics which led to North Korea's successful achievement of becoming a nuclear state and an unchallengeable military power.[31]

The North Korean military is the source of power for Kim Jong Un and the country's ruling elite. They maintain control of the people through the military. With an estimated strength of 1.19 million active military personnel, North Korea has the third largest armed force in Asia.[32] China has the largest armed force with 2.33 million and India is second, with 1.34 million active personnel.[33] The Korean People's Army has an estimated 1.02 million service members, the navy has an estimated 60,000 personnel, the air force has 110,000, and the active paramilitary force (security troops including border guards and public safety personnel) is at 189,000. North Korea also has approximately 600,000 reservists and a 5.7 million reserve paramilitary force (provincial workers and peasant red guard).[34]

The number of personnel in North Korea's armed forces appears quite formidable. However, in order to offset its mostly aged and obsolescent equipment, North Korea would need a large armed force to counter the technologically superior military equipment of the United States and South Korean military.[35] North Korea also maintains a credible deterrent of its own with the thousands of artillery pieces it has positioned across the Demilitarized Zone (DMZ). This poses a great concern to the United States and South Korea as they have the range to reach Seoul and its millions of inhabitants.[36]

North Korea has four types of ballistic missiles that have been previously tested and deemed operational. The Hwasong-5 has a range of 300 kilometers (km) and the capacity to carry a 1,000 kilogram (kg) warhead. The Hwasong-6 has a range of 500 km and the capacity to carry a 700 kg warhead. The Rodong, capable of striking Japan, has a range of 1,300 km and the capacity to carry a 700 kg warhead. The Musudan has an even further range of 3,000 km and the capacity to carry a 650 kg warhead. The Taepodong-1, flight-tested but not deemed operational, has a range of 2,500 km and the capacity to carry a 500 kg warhead. Two potential ICBMs still under development and testing include the KN-08 and Taepodong-2. The KN-08 may have a potential range of 6,000 km and the capacity to carry a 750-1,000 kg warhead. The Taepodong-2 may have a potential range of 6,700 km and the capacity to carry a 700-1,000 kg warhead.[37] In addition to the platform based launched missiles, North Korea continues to develop its capabilities with mobile launchers and submarine-launched ballistic missiles.

North Korea has conducted five nuclear tests to date, two under Kim Jong Il and three under Kim Jong Un. Kim Jong Il's first test occurred on October 9, 2006, which had a yield of .48 kilotons and a 4.3 magnitude. For comparison, the atomic bomb dropped on Hiroshima yielded about 15 kilotons. On May 25, 2009, North Korea conducted a second nuclear test resulting in a 7-kiloton yield and a 4.7 magnitude. The three tests under Kim Jong Un occurred on February 12, 2013 (12.2 kilotons/5.1 magnitude), January 6, 2016 (11.3 kilotons/5.1 magnitude), and September 9, 2016 (17.8 kilotons/5.3 magnitude). During their respective periods of nuclear testing, Kim Jong Il launched 19 ballistic missiles, 7 in 2006 and 12 in 2009. Kim Jong Un, in stark contrast, launched 71 ballistic missiles from 2013 through 2016. Thirty-four of these launches occurred in 2016 alone.[38]

It is obvious that the technological advancement of the North Korea's ballistic missile and nuclear weapons program is a priority for Kim Jong Un. It is believed that North Korea may already have a nuclear arsenal inventory of 10 to 16 nuclear weapons.[39] Moreover, North Korea may have enough fissile material capable of producing an additional 35 nuclear warheads as early as 2020.[40] Fortunately, recent North Korean ballistic missile testing appears to indicate that North Korea has yet to perfect their technological advances.[41] While North Korea does not yet have a capable ICBM delivery system that can be armed with a miniaturized nuclear warhead, they continue to learn more and become bolder with every new test. Kim Jong Un will continue the aggressive development and testing of rocket engine and propulsion systems, missile re-entry, guidance targeting, and warhead miniaturization in order to attain a credible threat.

U.S. POLICY, INTERNATIONAL RESPONSE, AND DETERRENCE

Early in his first administration, former President Obama expressed a desire and willingness to engage in dialogue with North Korea. Rather than returning the sentiment, North Korea responded with provocative missile tests. Since then, the United States followed a policy of strategic patience. The United States maintained an open hand to North Korea and would welcome the country back to the international community as a participant in a rules-based world society as long as they ceased provocations and committed to a change in behavior, as a precondition for formal diplomatic discussions.[42] Obviously, this has not happened. Shortly after North Korea's fifth nuclear test in September 2016, then Director of National Intelligence James Clapper made the assessment that U.S. policy has failed and that North Korea would not willingly give up its nuclear program as it ensures their survival.[43] This would be a continuing problem for Trump and his administration to address.

Kim Jong Un managed to occupy much of Trump's attention during his first few months in office. On February 11, 2017, North Korea launched a medium- or intermediate range ballistic missile that flew for 310 miles before falling into the sea. This was North Korea's first missile launch of 2017 and the first challenge for Trump.[44] A few days later, on February 13, 2017, Kim Jong Un's half-brother, Kim Jong Nam, was killed in Malaysia. North Korea allegedly ordered the assassination.[45] On March 6, 2017, North Korea simultaneously launched four ballistic missiles. Three fell into the Sea of Japan and the fourth fell close to the waters of Japan's exclusive economic zone (EEZ).[46] On March 19, 2017, North Korea celebrated the testing of a rocket engine that could be further developed for an ICBM to reach the United States.[47] Although another missile launch on March 22, 2017, failed when the rocket exploded upon launch, the test occurring just a few days after a rocket engine test highlighted North Korea's increased technological capability in their ballistic missile program.[48] Despite all these events, the Trump administration reiterated U.S. unyielding support to South Korea and Japan against North Korean aggression.

Upon taking office, Trump spoke with the South Korean Acting President Hwang Kyo Ahn to assure him of the U.S. commitment to defend South Korea with all means to include extended military deterrence.[49] Immediately after the February North Korea missile launch, Trump, in a joint statement with Japanese Prime Minister Shinzo Abe, stated the security of Japan against the North Korean ballistic missile and nuclear threat remains crucial to the United States.[50] All three leaders agreed to sustain bilateral and trilateral cooperation in order to counter North Korea's confrontational and hostile actions.[51]

Secretary of Defense Jim Mattis also reaffirmed U.S. commitment to the security of South Korea and Japan, and emphasized the importance of the region by making his first overseas visit as Secretary of Defense to meet with these important allies in February 2017. In South Korea, Mattis cited the threat of North Korea's continued missile and nuclear weapons program development. He guaranteed the U.S. commitment for defending its ally, and pointedly remarked, "any attack on the United States or on our allies will be defeated and any use of nuclear weapons would be met with the response that would be effective and overwhelming."[52] In Japan, Mattis assured Prime Minister Abe that the mutual defense treaty between the United States and Japan held firm now and would remain so well into the future.[53] While Trump and Mattis echoed the U.S. long-standing commitment for the security of South Korea and Japan, it is through Secretary of State Rex Tillerson and his visit to the East Asia and Pacific region in March 2017 that perhaps a burgeoning U.S. policy toward North Korea may be seen as forthcoming.

At this point, it is prudent first to understand the basic underpinnings of Trump's direction for U.S. foreign policy. American interests and American national security are at the forefront of the Trump administration's America First Foreign Policy. Essential to this policy is the principle of "peace through strength," which "will make possible a stable, more peaceful world with less conflict and more common ground."[54] The policy highlights the defeat of the Islamic States in Iraq and Syria (ISIS) as the highest priority and requires the rebuilding of the U.S. armed forces in order to attain military dominance. In support of this, Trump, in a presidential memorandum, directed: "to pursue peace through strength, it shall be the policy of the United States to rebuild the U.S. Armed Forces."[55] Notably, foreign policy places emphasis on diplomacy. "The world must know that we do not go abroad in search of enemies, that we are always happy when old enemies become friends, and when old friends become allies."[56] Yet, diplomacy does not appear to be the primary approach voiced by either Tillerson or the U.S. Ambassador to the UN, Nikki Haley, in dealing with North Korea.

On his first official visit to Japan, South Korea, and China, Tillerson met with senior leaders from each country and reaffirmed Trump's commitment to strengthen alliances and partnerships, and to increase and improve U.S. security interests in the region.[57] During a press conference with Japanese Foreign Minister Fumio Kishida, Tillerson advocated for the development of a different approach to address the North Korean threat. He also extended indirect assurances to North Korea.

> North Korea and its people need not fear the United States or their neighbors in the region who seek only to live in peace with North Korea. With this in mind, the United States calls on North Korea to abandon its nuclear and ballistic missile programs and refrain from any further provocations.[58]

In addition, Tillerson believes that U.S. efforts toward diplomacy over the last 20 years have failed to change North Korea's nuclear ambitions. He stated a new approach is required to encourage North Korea to take a different path.[59] During his engagement with South Korean Foreign Minister Yun, Byung Se, Tillerson stated, "let me be very clear: the policy of strategic patience has ended."[60] The United States would keep all options, to include military, on the table while exploring new diplomatic, security, and economic measures to counter the escalating North Korean threat.[61] It is still too early to determine any specifics of how Trump's North Korean policy will differ from his predecessors, but the initial statements from Tillerson have not indicated anything new. On his last stop in China, which included a meeting with President Xi Jinping, Tillerson and Foreign Minister Wang Yi highlighted the mutual need for both countries to prevent any type of conflict on the Korean peninsula.[62]

Furthermore, Haley stated the United States is unwilling to revive and enter into Six-Party Talks. On engagement with North Korea, she acknowledged she does not interact with the North Korean envoy to the UN because North Korea has not yet displayed any positive action to address U.S. concerns. Rather, Haley outlined U.S. plans to engage China and Russia to become more involved in pressuring North Korea to stop its weapons development program.[63] Tillerson, on China's role to encourage North Korea to give up its nuclear weapons program, stated that "China is a major source of economic trade and activity with North Korea," and the United States expects the Chinese "to fulfill its obligations and fully implement the sanctions called for in the UN resolutions."[64]

With regard to economic sanctions, the United States has always led efforts to compel North Korea to stop its ballistic missile and nuclear weapons program. On November 30, 2016, the UN approved UNSCR 2321. This UN resolution approved additional economic sanctions against North Korea as a response to the fifth nuclear test it conducted on September 9, 2016. The sanctions were designed to eliminate significant sources of North Korean revenue such as its exports of coal, iron, and iron ore.[65] Time will tell if the UNSCR 2321 will be successful. Kim Jong Un and North Korea have weathered previous UNSCR sanctions imposed against their country. This is evidence of both the Kim Regime and North Korea's resiliency.

The United States also recognized China's influence, albeit waning, over North Korea. China supported

UNSCR 2321 and made it known to North Korea that it opposed its nuclear tests and ballistic missile launches. Moreover, in January 2017, the State Council Information Office of the People's Republic of China issued a white paper on China's policies on Asia-Pacific security cooperation. It recognized the nuclear issue on the Korean Peninsula as a destabilizing situation for the region. It also stated as its position that "China is committed to the denuclearization of the peninsula, its peace and stability, and settlement of the issue through dialogue and consultation."[66] Both the North Korean New Year's announcement of launching an ICBM and the U.S. counter of threatening to shoot them down prompted the Chinese Foreign Ministry to pronounce their concern and urged both sides not to intensify already heightened tensions.[67]

The strongest and most visible U.S. deterrence are the 28,500 U.S. armed forces personnel stationed in South Korea. The U.S. 8th Army strength is at 19,200 and the 7th Air Force is at 8,800 personnel.[68] South Korea has an active armed force of 655,000 personnel. Of that, 522,000 are in the army, 68,000 in the navy, and 4,500 are paramilitary. South Korea also has 4.5 million in the reserve and another 3 million as reserve paramilitary (Civilian Defense Corps).[69] In response to North Korea's September 2016 nuclear weapons test, the United States and South Korea conducted a show of force with a combined low-level flight with two B-1 strategic bombers that flew from Andersen Air Force Base, Guam. A South Korean F-15K fighter jet and U.S. F-16 fighter accompanied the B-1Bs during their flight over Osan Air Base on September 13, 2016.[70] This demonstrated U.S. resolve in support of its South Korean ally and its ability to respond to North Korean provocation.

As a deterrent, South Korea is also accelerating the deployment of a three-pronged defensive system developed to counter a North Korean nuclear attack. The three components of this defensive system are comprised of a pre-emptive strike system referred to as a Kill Chain, the Korean Air and Missile Defense (KAMD), and the Korea Massive Punishment and Retaliation (KMPR) plan. The Kill Chain, requiring surveillance satellites, cruise missiles, and air-to-ground missiles will target North Korean missile and nuclear weapons facilities if they pose an imminent threat. The KAMD will provide anti-ballistic missile defense. The KMPR response, using surface-to-surface ballistic and cruise missiles will target North Korea's military leadership. Originally planned for deployment in the mid-2020s, South Korea is taking steps to have all systems in place as soon as possible.[71] The South Koreans also have another deterrent focused on Kim Jong Un and his military elite. The South Korean Defense Ministry, as a signal to Pyongyang, also announced it would hasten plans to establish a brigade with a specific mission to target the North Korean command and control if wartime hostilities resumed. Often referred to as a "decapitation unit," if activated, their targets include Kim Jong Un and his military leaders.[72]

In July 2016, the United States and South Korea agreed to deploy a Terminal High Altitude Area Defense (THAAD) missile battery to South Korea as an added protective measure against any North Korea ballistic missile threats.[73] Former Secretary of Defense Ash Carter stated the North Korean "nuclear weapons and ballistic missile defense programs are a serious threat" and the United States, in order to defend the Korean peninsula, its friends and U.S. interests, would shoot down any missiles that threatened the United States or its allies.[74] Both China and Russia have opposed the introduction of THAAD onto the Korean Peninsula, stating it would destabilize the security in the region, increase the potential for conflict, and further an arms race.[75] China stated the deployment of THAAD would undermine efforts to maintain the peace and stability on the Korean Peninsula.[76] In light of this, what other options can the United States consider to address the North Korean threat?

RECOMMENDATION FOR AN ALTERNATE OPTION

Trump should consider pursuing dialogue with Kim Jong Un and remove pre-conditions for a North Korean commitment of denuclearization in order to allow diplomacy to start. The U.S. policy of strategic patience should not be continued. Kim Jong Un will not willingly give up his ballistic missile and nuclear weapons program. North Korean leaders will continue to opine the United States and South Korea are an existential threat. Kim Jong Un believes having a strong military and a credible nuclear capability allows him to counter this threat. The United States and South Korea must attempt to change Kim Jong Un's narrative and mindset and strive to have him understand and publicly acknowledge that the United States is not seeking regime change. Rather, the United States welcomes North Korea's return to the international community.

Although the United States has always maintained its willingness for diplomacy with North Korea, it has been contingent on North Korea's full commitment for denuclearization before dialogue could even begin. To date, this pre-conditional requirement has not led to effective talks with North Korea. While the United

States and South Korea maintain a formidable military deterrent, which likely keeps Kim Jong Un from going beyond brinkmanship displays and provocation, they have not changed North Korea's current path. Additionally, the UNSCR's imposing economic sanctions, as well as the unilateral economic sanctions imposed by the United States, South Korea, and Japan have yet to bring North Korea back to negotiations.[77] Of note, the belief that the Kim regime would simply collapse has long been hoped for by many, but has yet to materialize.

Initiating dialogue with the intent of beginning the normalization of relations and diplomacy should be pursued in order to reduce tension in this region. This does not weaken the U.S. position in any manner. To be sure, the United States has the military advantage and capability to execute a change in the North Korean regime if it so desired. However, diplomacy and direct engagement is the better approach. Furthermore, other western nations such as the United Kingdom have formal diplomatic relations with North Korea. This certainly warrants further investigation, and the United States should consider doing the same. In normalizing relations, it would allow all parties to understand their respective interests. The U.S. intent is not to overthrow the Kim regime, but rather to have North Korea return to the world community and participate in a rules-based society. If North Korea publicly acknowledges this U.S. position, North Korea would no longer have the argument to attempt to justify its own nuclear deterrent against the United States. Normalized relations may lead to an end to the Korean war.

CONCLUSION

It will not be an easy task to begin any type of dialogue with North Korea. This recommendation will not likely be a popular option for consideration particularly considering the North Korean withdrawal from the Six-Party talks in 2009. After all, for many years now, the United States has attempted to address the North Korean threat using an unsuccessful policy of strategic patience, international and unilateral economic sanctions that have not been enforced by all countries, and through strong military deterrence. Many are likely to argue that any negotiation without first attaining a North Korean commitment for denuclearization weakens the U.S. position. This is a fallacy. The United States has the military capability to destroy North Korean ballistic missile and nuclear facilities as well as the ability to essentially end Kim Jong Un's reign. This comes with significant risk. Therefore, the United States should seek to first normalize relations and then take nascent steps to limit Kim Jong Un's nuclear aims.

If the United States does not consider this recommendation, it will likely end up where it is presently heading. The United States and North Korea will not engage in dialogue or diplomacy, belligerent overtures and brinkmanship will continue, and Kim Jong Un will steadily increase his ballistic missile and nuclear weapons technology. It is plausible that, within the next 5 to 10 years, North Korea will attain the technological capability to launch successfully an ICBM armed with a nuclear warhead that can strike the United States. Minimizing options for diplomacy will lead the United States toward a path of increased tension, greater chances of miscalculation, and likely hostile military engagement that could reignite the conflict on the Korean peninsula. It is a future that must not come to fruition.

ENDNOTES - CHAPTER 11

1. Barack H. Obama, *National Security Strategy*, Washington, DC: The White House, February 2015, p. 10.

American diplomacy and leadership, backed by a strong military, remain essential to deterring future acts of inter-state aggression and provocation by reaffirming our security commitments to allies and partners, investing in their capabilities to withstand coercion, imposing costs on those who threaten their neighbors or violate fundamental international norms, and embedding our actions within wider regional strategies.

2. Victor Cha, *The Impossible State: North Korea, Past and Future*, New York: HarperCollins, 2012, p. 98.

3. Kim Jong Un, "Kim Jong Un's 2017 New Year's Address," trans. and pub. by The National Committee on North Korea, January 1, 2017, available from *http://www.ncnk.org/resources/news-items/kim-jong-uns-speeches-and-public-statements-1/kim-jong-uns-2017-new-years-address*, accessed January 5, 2017.

4. Ibid.

5. Ankit Panda, "South Korean Constitutional Court Unanimously Upholds Park Geun-hye Impeachment," *The Diplomat*, March 10, 2017, available from *https://thediplomat.com/2017/03/south-korean-constitutional-court-unanimously-upholds-park-geun-hye-impeachment/*, accessed March 22, 2017.

6. Obama, p. 2, Enduring national interests include:

1. The security of the United States, its citizens, and U.S. allies and partners;

2. A strong, innovative, and growing U.S. economy in an open international economic system that promotes opportunity and prosperity;

3. Respect for universal values at home and around the world; and

4. A rules-based international order advanced by U.S. leadership that promotes peace, security, and opportunity through stronger cooperation to meet global challenges;

Kim Jong Un. In his address, Kim Jong Un espouses North Korean interests for pursuing nuclear weapons.

> We will continue to build up our self-defence capability, the pivot of which is the nuclear forces, and the capability for preemptive strike as long as the United States and its vassal forces keep on nuclear threat and blackmail and as long as they do not stop their war games they stage at our doorstep disguising them as annual events. We will defend peace and security of our state at all costs and by our own efforts, and make a positive contribution to safeguarding global peace and stability.

7. Kim Jong Un. In his address, Kim Jong Un perceives hostile U.S. intent toward North Korea:

> We must put an end to the moves for aggression and intervention by the foreign forces including the United States that is occupying south [SIC] Korea and tries to realize the strategy for achieving hegemony in the Asia-Pacific region. . . . the United States must no longer cling to the scheme of whipping up national estrangement by inciting the anti-reunification forces in south [sic] Korea to confrontation with the fellow countrymen and war.

8. Jiyul Kim, *Cultural Dimensions of Strategy and Policy*, Carlisle, PA: Strategic Studies Institute, U.S. Army War College, May 18, 2009, pp. 9-10, available from *http://ssi.armywarcollege.edu/pubs/display.cfm?pubID=919*, accessed December 13 2016. This chapter uses the Analytical Cultural Framework for Strategy and Policy (ACFSP), which "identifies basic cultural dimensions that seem to be of fundamental importance in determining political and strategic action and behavior and thus are of importance in policy and strategy formulation and outcomes." The dimensions are identity, political culture, and resilience. "Identity: the basis for defining identity and its linkage to interests. Political Culture: the

structure of power and decision making. Resilience: the capacity or ability to resist, adapt, or succumb to external forces."

9. Cha, p. 296. Obama initiated "strategic patience" policy.

This policy essentially stated that the United States remains committed to diplomacy—that is, the United States seeks a peaceful diplomatic solution to the denuclearization of the Korean peninsula, and that it remains committed to the Six-Party Talks and to fulfilling its commitments in the denuclearization agreements of 2005 and 2007. However, in the face of the string of DPRK provocations in 2009 and 2010, Washington was willing to wait for a period of time in which Pyongyang could demonstrate some positive and constructive behavior and willingness to negotiate in earnest.

10. Donald J. Trump, "Presidential Memorandum on Rebuilding the U.S. Armed Forces," Washington, DC: Office of the Press Secretary, The White House, January 27, 2017, available from *https://www.whitehouse.gov/the-press-office/2017/01/27/presidential-memorandum-rebuilding-us-armed-forces*, accessed March 19, 2017. To pursue peace through strength, it shall be the policy of the United States to rebuild the U.S. Armed Forces.

11. Colin Mason, *A Short History of Asia*, 3rd Ed., London, UK: Palgrave Macmillan, 2014, p. 300.

12. Cha, p. 7.

13. Central Intelligence Agency, "North Korea," *The World Factbook*, Washington, DC: Central Intelligence Agency, updated November 14, 2017, available from *https://www.cia.gov/library/publications/the-world-factbook/geos/kn.html*, accessed December 11, 2017; Cha, p. 70.

14. Mason, p. 3.

15. Cha, pp. 37, 59.

16. Central Intelligence Agency, "North Korea."

17. Ibid.; Cha, p. 13.

18. Central Intelligence Agency, "North Korea."

19. Cha, pp. 72-73, 75.

20. Hamish Macdonald, "North Korea to erect first major monument to Kim Jong Un," NK News.org, January 12, 2017, available from *https://www.nknews.org/2017/01/north-korea-to-erect-first-major-monument-to-kim-jong-un/*, accessed January 13, 2017.

21. Central Intelligence Agency, "North Korea."

22. Ibid.

23. Cha, p. 85.

24. Central Intelligence Agency, "North Korea."

25. Ibid.

26. Ibid.

27. Ibid.; Cha, pp. 2-3.

28. Kim Jong Un.

29. Ibid.

30. Ibid.

31. *The Constitution of the Democratic People's Republic of Korea*, trans. text, and archived by The National Committee on North Korea, 2012, available from *http://www.ncnk.org/resources/publications/DPRK_Constitution_2012.pdf*, accessed January 8, 2017.

32. The International Institute for Strategic Studies, *The Military Balance: The Annual Assessment of Global Military Capabilities and Defence Economics*, 2015, London, UK: Routledge, 2015, p. 261.

33. The International Institute for Strategic Studies, *The Military Balance*, p. 486.

34. Ibid., pp. 262-263.

35. Ibid., p. 261.

36. Cha, pp. 11-12, 212.

37. Simon Scarr, Weiyi Cai, and Wen Foo, "Nuclear North Korea," Reuters Graphics, December 30, 2016, available from *http://fingfx.thomsonreuters.com/gfx/rngs/NORTHKOREA-NUCLEAR/0100316P2NM/index.html*, accessed January 17, 2017.

38. Ibid.

39. The International Institute for Strategic Studies, *Strategic Survey 2015: The Annual Review of World Affairs*, London, UK: Routledge, 2015, pp. 367-368.

40. Ibid., p. 368.

41. The International Institute for Strategic Studies, *The Military Balance*, p. 261.

42. Cha, p. 274. Cha wrote, "Obama promised no serious diplomacy until the North showed evidence of better behavior, ceasing provocations against the South and refraining from more missile and nuclear tests."

43. Geoff Dyer, "US spy chief admits North Korea policy has failed," *Financial Times*, October 26, 2016, available from *https://www.ft.com/content/1a2eb642-9b2c-11e6-b8c6-568a43813464*, accessed January 7, 2017.

44. Choe Sang-Hun, "North Korea Fires Ballistic Missile, Challenging Trump," *The New York Times*, February 11, 2017, available from *https://www.nytimes.com/2017/02/11/world/asia/north-korea-missile-test-trump.html?_r=1*, accessed March 20, 2017.

45. Joshua Berlinger, "Malaysia blames North Korea for Kim Jong Nam's death," CNN, March 8, 2017, available from *http://www.cnn.com/2017/03/08/asia/malaysia-north-korea-blame-kim-jong-nam/*, accessed March 20, 2017.

46. Ayako Mie and Jesse Johnson, "Abe says latest North Korean missile launch represents 'new level of threat'," *The Japan Times*, March 6, 2017, available from *https://www.japantimes.co.jp/news/2017/03/06/national/tokyo-says-north-korea-fired-three-four-missiles-came-japans-eez/#.WjF0lWZrzxj*, accessed March 20, 2017.

47. Barbara Starr and Ryan Browne, "US: North Korean rocket engine could go on long-range missile," CNN, March 20, 2017,

available from *http://www.cnn.com/2017/03/20/politics/north-korea-rocket-test-icbm/*, accessed March 20, 2017.

48. Ju-min Park, "North Korea missile test fails, U.S. and South say, as tensions simmer," Reuters, March 22, 2017, available from *https://www.reuters.com/article/us-northkorea-missiles/north-korea-missile-test-fails-u-s-and-south-say-as-tensions-simmer-idUSKBN16T07M*, accessed March 22, 2017.

49. Office of the Press Secretary, "Readout of the President's Call with Acting President HWANG KYO-AHN OF THE REPUBLIC OF KOREA," Washington, DC: The White House, January 29, 2017, available from *https://www.whitehouse.gov/the-press-office/2017/01/29/readout-presidents-call-acting-president-hwang-kyo-ahn-republic-korea*, accessed March 19, 2017.

50. Donald J. Trump and Shinzō Abe, "Remarks by President Trump and Prime Minister Abe of Japan in Joint Press Conference," Washington, DC: Office of the Press Secretary, The White House, February 10, 2017, available from *https://www.whitehouse.gov/the-press-office/2017/02/10/remarks-president-trump-and-prime-minister-abe-japan-joint-press*, accessed March 19, 2017.

51. Office of the Press Secretary, "Readout of the President's Calls with Prime Minister Shinzo Abe of Japan and Acting President Hwang Kyo-Ahn of South Korea," Washington, DC: The White House, March 6, 2017, available from *https://www.whitehouse.gov/the-press-office/2017/03/06/readout-presidents-calls-prime-minister-shinzo-abe-japan-and-acting*, accessed March 19, 2017.

52. "Remarks by Secretary Mattis and Defense Minister Han in Seoul, Republic of Korea," Washington, DC: Press Operations, U.S. Department of Defense, February 3, 2017, available from *https://www.defense.gov/News/Transcripts/Transcript-View/Article/1070902/remarks-by-secretary-mattis-and-defense-minister-han-in-seoul-republic-of-korea*, accessed March 21, 2017.

53. "Remarks by Secretary Mattis and Prime Minister Abe in Tokyo, Japan," Washington, DC: Press Operations, U.S. Department of Defense, February 3, 2017, available from *https://www.defense.gov/News/Transcripts/Transcript-View/Article/1070919/*

remarks-by-secretary-mattis-and-prime-minister-abe-in-tokyo-japan, accessed March 21, 2017.

54. "America First Foreign Policy," The White House, n.d., available from *https://www.whitehouse.gov/america-first-foreign-policy*, accessed March 19, 2017.

55. Trump.

56. "America First Foreign Policy."

57. "Travel to Japan, Republic of Korea, and China, March 15-19, 2017," March 15-19, 2017, Washington, DC: U.S. Department of State, available from *https://www.state.gov/secretary/travel/2017/t3/index.htm*, accessed March 21, 2017.

58. "Press Availability With Japanese Foreign Minister Fumio Kishida," Washington, DC: U.S. Department of State, March 16, 2017, available from *https://www.state.gov/secretary/remarks/2017/03/268476.htm*, accessed March 21, 2017.

59. Ibid.

60. "Remarks With Foreign Minister Yun Byung-se Before Their Meeting," Washington, DC: U.S. Department of State, March 17, 2017, available from *https://www.state.gov/secretary/remarks/2017/03/268501.htm*, accessed March 21, 2017.

61. Ibid.

62. "Remarks With Chinese Foreign Minister Wang Yi at a Press Availability," Washington, DC: U.S. Department of State, March 18, 2017, available from *https://www.state.gov/secretary/remarks/2017/03/268518.htm*, accessed March 21, 2017.

63. Eli Watkins, "Nikki Haley on North Korea talks: US has 'been there, done that'," CNN, March 16, 2017, available from *http://www.cnn.com/2017/03/16/politics/nikki-haley-north-korea/index.html*, accessed March 21, 2017; see also Erin Burnett, "Haley: North Korean threat is first priority," video, in Watkins.

64. "Press Availability With Japanese Foreign Minister Fumio Kishida."

65. "Security Council Strengthens Sanctions on Democratic Republic of Korea, Unanimously Adopting Resolution 2321 (2016)," United Nations Meeting Coverage and Press Releases, November 30, 2016, available from *https://www.un.org/press/ en/2016/sc12603.doc.htm*, accessed January 4, 2017.

66. The State Council Information Office of the People's Republic of China, *China's Policies on Asia-Pacific Security Cooperation*, January 11, 2017, available from *www.fmprc.gov.cn/mfa_eng/ zxxx_662805/t1429771.shtml*, accessed January 26, 2017.

67. Xinhua News Agency, "China warns against intensifying tensions in Korean Peninsula," Xinhuanet, January 9, 2017, available from *http://news.xinhuanet.com/english/2017-01/09/c_135967493.htm*, accessed January 16, 2017; "Meet the Press with Chuck Todd," NBC, January 8, 2017, transcript of video file, available from *https://www.nbcnews.com/meet-the-press/meet-press-january-8-2017-n704481*, accessed December 11, 2017.

68. The International Institute for Strategic Studies, *The Military Balance*, p. 267.

69. Ibid., pp. 263-266, 486.

70. "ROK-U.S. Alliance ready to meet mutual defense obligations," United States Forces Korea, September 13, 2016, available from *http://www.usfk.mil/Media/Press-Releases/Article/940461/ rok-us-alliance-ready-to-meet-mutual-defense-obligations/*, accessed January 10, 2017.

71. Jun Ji-hye, "3 military systems to counter N. Korea: Kill Chain, KAMD, KMPR," *The Korea Times*, November 1, 2016, available from *http://www.koreatimes.co.kr/www/news/ nation/2016/11/205_217259.html*, accessed January 14, 2017.

72. Joshua Berlinger and K. J. Kwon, "South Korea speeds up creation of Kim Jong Un 'decapitation unit'," CNN, January 11, 2017, available from *http://www.cnn.com/2017/01/05/asia/south-korea-kim-jong-un-brigade/*, accessed January 20, 2017.

73. "U.S. to Deploy THAAD Missile Battery to South Korea," DoD News, July 8, 2016, available from

https://www.defense.gov/News/Article/Article/831630us-to-deploy-thaad-missile-battery-to-south-korea, accessed January 7, 2017.

74. "Meet the Press with Chuck Todd."

75. "China, Russia Promise 'Countermeasures' To U.S.-Korean Defense System," Radio Free Europe/Radio Liberty, January 13, 2017, available from *https://www.rferl.org/a/china-russia-express-concern-us-south-korean-missile-defense-system-thaad-vow-countermeasures/28230460.html,* accessed January 17, 2017.

76. The State Council Information Office of the People's Republic of China, "China's Policies on Asia-Pacific Security Cooperation," China's position on THAAD deployment to South Korea. "Such an act would seriously damage the regional strategic balance and the strategic security interests of China and other countries in the region, and run counter to the efforts for maintaining peace and stability on the Korean Peninsula."

77. Choe Sang-Hun, "China Suspends All Coal Imports from North Korea," *The New York Times*, February 18, 2017, available from *https://www.nytimes.com/2017/02/18/world/asia/north-korea-china-coal-imports-suspended.html?_r=0,* accessed March 25, 2017. China's action to suspend all coal imports from North Korea may prove more crippling to North Korea. The decision came shortly after the assassination of Kim Jong Nam and North Korean ballistic missile tests.

CHAPTER 12

KOREAN PENINSULA: UPGRADING
THE DENUCLEARIZATION STATUS QUO

James L. Conner

EXECUTIVE SUMMARY

Despite years of concerted effort, the United States and the international community have been unable to persuade the Democratic People's Republic of Korea (DPRK or North Korea) to abandon its quest for nuclear weapons. To date, there is little to no progress toward denuclearization of the Korean peninsula, and the DPRK remains a key challenge for the global nuclear nonproliferation regime. It is time the United States and the international community admit that the current approach is not working. Rather than continue the policy of strategic patience, which is obviously inadequate, the United States must change course and pursue a three-pronged approach to dealing with North Korea that includes pressuring China to do more, enabling the South Koreans to have more military control, and applying new economic pressures to the North.

INTRODUCTION

For years, the United States has led international efforts to pressure the DPRK to abandon its nuclear weapon and missile development and stop its export of ballistic missile technology. These extensive efforts have not deterred the DPRK from further development and procurement of nuclear capabilities. Indeed, the DPRK carried out tests in 2006, 2009, 2013, and in January and September 2016.[1] To date, there has been little to no progress toward denuclearization of the Korean peninsula and the DPRK remains a key challenge to the global nuclear nonproliferation regime.[2]

Each successive North Korean experiment and test causes a greater potential for catastrophic results and failure. Further, the DPRK is developing an intercontinental ballistic missile (ICBM) with the capability to strike the Continental United States (CONUS). This development could further destabilize East Asia and enhance the risk of uncontrolled proliferation in and beyond the region. This potential reality may force the new U.S. president into an even more difficult decision concerning deterring the DPRK. Furthermore, the DPRK's ability to evade sanctions increases year after year. Even with the United Nations Security Council Resolutions (UNSCR) expanded legal authority, sanctions have had little to no effect on stopping the DPRK from further nuclear weapons research, development, and testing.[3] In short, the options available to the United States are narrowing and those available to the DPRK are expanding. Reversing these trends will require an urgent shift in U.S. policy.[4]

It should be clear that the status quo policy is not enough to achieve the goal of a denuclearized Korean Peninsula. The crucial question, therefore, is what are the requirements necessary for updating the current approach? Diplomatically, the United States must persuade China to take a tougher stance with its policies toward the DPRK. A denuclearized Korean Peninsula is accomplished through a renewed dialogue and collaboration with China. China, as the DPRK's number one supporter, must effectively engage the

DPRK through a series of collaborative steps designed to pressure the DPRK to abandon its nuclear weapons program. Militarily, the United States must accelerate the transfer of wartime operational control (OPCON) to South Korea. Doing so will ensure that the Republic of Korea (ROK) has the military it needs, assisted by U.S. enduring and bridging capabilities. Further, OPCON transfer will allow for U.S. strategic flexibility with its forces in the Korea Theater of operations and allows for a ROK-led unified Korea if the conditions permit. Finally, economically, the United States and the international community must do more in disrupting the DPRK's Royal Court Economy System. This system brings in millions of dollars of luxury goods for paying off the DPRK elite. Excessive sanctions and penalties for those who support this economic system may assist in eliminating DPRK's access to hard currency and luxury goods.

DIPLOMATIC EFFORTS: TAKING CHINA TO TASK

The United States and the international community have failed to meet their critical denuclearization objectives: to stop or end the DPRK's expanding nuclear weapons and ballistic missile programs and prevent it from proliferating nuclear weapon and missile technology to dangerous states around the world. The DPRK continues to refuse any risks to their nuclear weapons development by adopting political or economic reforms. Kim Jong Un's *byungjin* policy sets DPRK economic growth with nuclear development as equal priorities.[5] Despite the tensions paramount in this policy, the fear for regime survival discourages any kind of genuine North Korean rapprochement with the ROK.

China's reluctance to pressure the DPRK has allowed the regime to destabilize further a region critical to U.S. national security interests and to threaten the safety of U.S. allies. China has accounted for approximately half of the DPRK's overseas trade in the past decade. In 2014, bilateral trade between China and the DPRK amounted to $6.86 billion, and made up about 70 percent of the DPRK's external trade (exports $2.84 billion, imports $4.02 billion).[6] Since the early 1990s, China has accounted for almost 90 percent of the DPRK's energy imports and as much as 45 percent of its food imports. Mineral exports to China produce a major revenue stream for the DPRK; exports of anthracite, a higher-grade quality coal used for power generation, for example, have brought in more than one billion dollars annually since 2011.[7]

The diplomatic, economic, and military steps required to deter and contain the DPRK regime also threaten to aggravate U.S. tensions with China. Developments within the past year have altered the DPRK problem in many ways. Although China did consent to United Nations Security Council Resolution (UNSCR) 2321 to strengthen significantly the sanctions regime that restricts arms transfers and limits trade with the DPRK, China remains the DPRK's number one trading partner. Pyongyang's actions and Beijing's reluctance to support fully the UNSC resolutions in the past have provided incentive for closer military cooperation between the United States and the ROK. For example, the United States and the ROK have agreed to deploy the Terminal High Altitude Area Defense (THAAD) battery to strengthen missile defense on the peninsula.[8] To counter this alliance cohesiveness, the DPRK is accelerating the development of a capability to strike CONUS, as well as U.S. allies, with a nuclear capable warhead delivered by an ICBM. These developments present the United States with an exigent threat of a DPRK that can strike at the United States—but also with new opportunities to halt the cycle of provocation and prevent the DPRK from achieving this capability. China's policy toward the DPRK can critically affect change and the fate of the region. If China, the United States, and the international community can work together to pressure the DPRK to abandon its nuclear weapons program and mitigate its threatening military posture, a stable and prosperous Northeast Asia led by China and U.S. allies can emerge. If they cannot, the DPRK's recklessness will further strain the U.S.-China relationship and destabilize a region vital to both countries' interests.

For this reason, encouraging a transformation of China's policy toward the DPRK should be the administration's top priority in its relations with China. This transformation should be accomplished through a sequence of steps to increase gradually the pressure on China to support a cooperative approach, which, in turn, would pressure the DPRK to eliminate its nuclear capability. The United States, in collaboration with China, should present the DPRK with a sharper choice: seek a negotiated settlement to return to compliance with UN resolutions on nuclear weapons or face severe and escalating consequences. These steps should be sequenced carefully and deliberately so as to ramp up pressure incrementally on the DPRK. This will send a direct and credible signal to the DPRK that the United States and the international community will continually increase pressure until serious talks or negotiations resume. In addition, the United

States should also expand the trilateral U.S.-ROK-Japan cooperation to enforce sanctions on the DPRK and strengthen its joint deterrence profile.

On a parallel course, the United States and the international community should offer restructured negotiations that provide genuine incentives for the DPRK to participate in substantive talks in the face of the increased pressure discussed earlier through the strict enforcement of sanctions to include the new UNSCR 2321. Such incentives may include a multilateral security assurance arrangement. This arrangement could include an initiation of a diplomatic process toward normalization of DPRK's relations with the United States and other nations. It may also include removal of economic, trade, and investment sanctions. Doing so will target the DPRK's illicit activity, and encourages other nations in the region—including China—to join this effort. If the DPRK refuses this proposal, the United States should seek new multilateral sanctions to restrict the regime's funding sources and enact additional military measures, e.g., U.S.-ROK alliance show of force exercises to strengthen allied deterrence of military attacks. New nuclear tests or military attacks by the DPRK would definitely accelerate this timetable.

It is important to ensure that the DPRK does not use any talks or negotiations as a way of distracting attention from bad behavior, a tactic used in the past. Abrogation of the testing ban, new attacks, or stalled talks should result in their termination. The United States should also create a new approach to China. The objective is to enlist China in the effort to bring about a stable and nonnuclear Korean Peninsula. The United States should propose new dialogues on the future of the Korean Peninsula to demonstrate that it is in both countries' security interests to find a comprehensive resolution to the problem. A unified response to the DPRK stands the greatest chance of finding a lasting solution on the peninsula and of forging a stable and prosperous Northeast Asia, and is by far the preferable course of action. If the DPRK retains a nuclear weapons capability, the U.S.-China relationship will be strained.

MILITARY EFFORTS: ACCELERATE OPERA-TIONAL CONTROL (OPCON)

Combined Forces Command (CFC) was established on November 7, 1978. CFC is the ROK and U.S. warfighting headquarters with the role of deterrence or defeat, as necessary, of outside aggression against the ROK.[9] After almost 30 years in existence, the United States and ROK agreed in 2007 to disestablish CFC and replace it with separate United States and ROK military commands by April 2012.[10] This would allow the ROK to command ROK forces under wartime conditions with the United States as the supporting command.[11] Plans for this new command arrangement are referred to as OPCON (Operational Control) transfer. In 2010, the OPCON transfer was postponed to December 2015 after a series of provocations from the DPRK and concerns about the readiness of the ROK military on assuming responsibility. As 2015 grew closer, concerns again emerged about the timing and readiness of ROK forces. Reportedly, ROK officials worried that their military was not fully prepared to cope with DPRK threats and that Pyongyang might interpret OPCON transfer as a weakening of the alliance's deterrence.[12]

In October 2014, the United States and the ROK announced in a joint statement that the allies would take a conditions-based approach to OPCON transfer and determine the appropriate timing based on the acquisition and readiness of ROK military capabilities and the security environment on the Korean Peninsula. In 2014, the ROK Minister of National Defense (MND) reportedly announced that the goal was to transfer OPCON in 2023. The ROK MND stressed that the completion of the Korean Air and Missile Defense System (KAMD) by 2020 was an important step in the transfer process. To that effect, the ROK MND announced it would invest $1.36 billion in the KAMD system in 2017. The KAMD includes the establishment of the "Kill Chain," capable of immediate find, fix, target, and engage to prepare effectively for DPRK missile threats.

In testimony to Congress in April 2015, then-United States Forces Korea (USFK) Commander General Curtis Scaparrotti explained the three general conditions for OPCON transfer. South Korea must develop the command and control capacity to lead a combined and multinational force in high-intensity conflict; South Korea must improve its capabilities to respond to the growing nuclear and missile threat in North Korea; and OPCON transition should take place at a time that is conducive to a transition.[13] In order for a seamless and accelerated OPCON transfer, the United States must support the ROK with bridging capabilities and supplying "big-ticket" items allowing the ROK military to focus on improving command, control, communications, and computers, intelligence, surveillance and reconnaissance (C4ISR). These items include command and control platforms, ballistic missile defense, and precision munitions.

As DPRK provocation persists, it remains critically important that the United States continue to support the ROK military with these capabilities until the announced completion of the KAMD by 2020. Further, this allows U.S. forces to act as a deterrent against the

DPRK while allowing time for the ROK military to strengthen and reinforce its capabilities. Additionally, the ROK must share more of the burden of acquiring improved equipment and weapon systems that are compatible with U.S. systems. More resource spending is necessary for state of the art C4ISR. The ROK MND must stay committed to the ROK Defense Reform Plan of 2005 (DRP). This plan necessitated approximately $505 billion over the course of 15 years (9.9 percent military budget increase annually) for key C4ISR and missile defense spending. The average increase over those years remains at 7.2 percent.[14] The DRP is now dangerously underfunded and behind schedule. This becomes increasingly important as these resources become technologically advanced and expensive as time goes by. Further, the fact that DPRK nuclear weapons are involved makes the stakes much higher for cohesiveness in operations. The ROK military needs the capability to secure the weapons quickly and safely with U.S. supervision. Currently, the ROK military has not mastered operational planning or logistics for these types of nuclear-recovery operations. Nor has it mastered the ability to coordinate sufficiently with the civilian sector.[15]

Finally, OPCON transfer will allow the use of U.S. forces stationed in the ROK to be deployed for global contingencies and will transition USFK from leading to supporting the ROK military. Currently, U.S. forces in the ROK cannot deploy for purposes beyond conflicts on the Korean peninsula. OPCON transfer will allow for the strategic flexibility with the expansion within the pool of U.S. forces to support the Asia-Pacific or other global contingencies.[16] This strategic flexibility will not only address the DPRK problem but will also support security challenges within the entire

U.S. Pacific Command area of operations (USPA-COM AOR).[17] The OPCON transition will strengthen the U.S.-ROK alliance while ensuring the proper U.S. bridging capabilities, compatible ROK C4ISR, and increasing strategic flexibility for the United States.

These recommendations will result in a stronger and more self-sustaining ROK military. The key points as outlined will also prove to the ROK that the United States remains committed to South Korea's security, even when the United States no longer holds OPCON. The transfer will also require the United States to rethink its force structure in the region. This reevaluation will benefit U.S. force posture in preparation for support of other contingencies. Despite OPCON transfer, the Commander, United Nations Command (CDR UNC) will continue to serve as the commander of an international command responsible for maintaining the Armistice Agreement on the Korean Peninsula. His primary tasks will remain to provide strategic direction, guidance, and acceptance and integration of UNC member nations' forces during contingencies. This is essential in enabling access to the seven UNC bases in Japan.[18]

USFK must provide the Secretary of Defense (SECDEF) with recommendations to the ROK military's acquisition of the KAMD and assessments on the ROK's ability to counter weapons of mass destruction (WMD). Both the U.S. SECDEF and ROK MND must reevaluate the current conditions for a successful OPCON transfer to ensure the DPRK is deterred properly. Finally, the Presidents of the United States and ROK must agree upon the appropriate timing based on South Korean military capabilities and the security environment on the Korean Peninsula.

ECONOMIC EFFORTS: DISRUPTING THE DPRK'S ROYAL COURT ECONOMY SYSTEM

The Royal Court Economy, or the Kim Family Fund, is a slush fund for the Kim family's personal use, as well as to buy the loyalty of elites. To that end, the Korea Worker's Party (KWP) Central Committee Bureau 39 ("Office 39") plays a critical role.[19] Under KWP, the bureau reported directly to Kim Jong-il, who set up the office in 1974. It now reports directly to Kim Jong Un. The activities of Office 39 are not subject to the cabinet for central planning and control. Office 39 directs smuggling, counterfeiting, and trafficking in order to generate hard currency, while using sovereignty as a shield. The regime heads a state-sanctioned criminal organization used to generate revenue from abroad. Kim Kwang-jin, a North Korean defector and former "revolution fund" manager, estimates that this Royal Court Economy produces 200 times the foreign cash revenue of the centrally-directed economy.[20] The proceeds are used to support the opulent lifestyle of the Kim family, purchase luxury goods for the elites to obtain their support for the regime, and invest in the military including its nuclear weapons programs.

Despite UN sanctions on luxury goods imports, Kim Jong Un spent $645.8 million importing luxury goods in 2012. This far exceeded his father's, Kim Jong-Il, annual spending average of $300 million.[21] These luxury imports include $30 million worth of high-end alcohol, $37 million in electronic goods, and $8.2 million in luxury watches. While the regime spends hundreds of millions of dollars on luxury products for the Kim family and his elite, North Koreans continue to suffer from malnutrition and stunting, despite the

DPRK receiving international assistance for the past 20 years.

The Royal Court Economy is essential in sustaining the regime because it buys elite support. It also enables the DPRK's pursuit of a nuclear weapons program, which the regime considers a crucial card in regime survival. Since the Royal Court Economy is crucial to regime survival and has no benefits for the people, it is a prime target for sanctions. The UNSC and the international community should enforce measures to prevent the supply of revenues and luxury goods from reaching the DPRK. The mandatory inspection of cargo with any possible connection to DPRK, enacted in UNSC Resolution 2270, is a good example of such a measure.[22]

Targeting the DPRK's Royal Court Economy through excessive sanctions would assist in eliminating access to hard currency and luxury goods. Further, these targeted sanctions would assist in crippling upper echelons of the DPRK government and promote instability within the regime. Compliance becomes reality when targeted sanctions hurt the DPRK elite and lead to domestic and political instability.[23] A continual strain on Kim Jong Un's Royal Court Economy is a potential strategic lever that the international community can pull to negotiate an end to the DPRK nuclear weapons program.

CONCLUSION

The United States and the international community must continue to employ a full range of diplomatic, military, and economic responses to counter and put an end to Kim Jong Un's nuclear weapons development. Diplomatically, the United States and the international community must persuade China to place greater pressure on DPRK to dismantle their nuclear weapons program. Continued DPRK provocations, to include nuclear weapons testing and ICBM development that further destabilizes the region, should incentivize China to do more. Incentives such as the United States, ROK, and Japan working closer together (diplomatically and militarily) and increase in military capabilities to the region (deployment of the THAAD Battery) should also motivate China toward DPRK denuclearization. In the end, China can assist in getting the DPRK back to the negotiating table. Examples of China's assistance include withdrawing material support, enforcing sanctions, and applying diplomatic pressure.

Militarily, the U.S. and ROK alliance must review all options pertaining to the acceleration of OPCON transfer. This will ensure strategic flexibility for the USPACOM commander allowing for the employment of U.S. forces in place for the defense of the ROK to employ off the peninsula in support of other regional contingencies. Further OPCON transfer will allow the ROK to control its own forces should reunification of the Korean Peninsula occur. Finally, OPCON transfer will ensure the ROK has a credible and capable military through U.S. bridging and enduring capabilities that can deter further DPRK aggression.

Finally, the United States and the international community must continue to escalate economic pressure on DPRK's Royal Court Economy. Efforts such as financial measures taken against the Macao-based Banco Delta in 2005 are critical examples that have worked in the past, but are inconsistent unless the entire international community is involved. Severe economic pressure on the DPRK's Royal Court Economy is a necessary way to compel compliance with its nuclear, military, and human rights obligations to the UN and a central instrument of U.S. and international coercive power. However, sanctions prohibiting the DPRK's Royal Court Economy alone are not enough. The United States must with work with China and the international community to apply more assertive and consistent pressure to sanction the full range of DPRK illicit behavior. Implementation of multilateral sanctions from China and the international community should accompany U.S. financial sanctions that further apply escalating pressure to the DPRK's source of funding.

ENDNOTES - CHAPTER 12

1. "North Korea profile - Timeline," BBC News, August 17, 2017, available from *http://www.bbc.com/news/world-asia-pacific-15278612*, September 9, 2016, accessed December 14, 2016.

2. United States security interests for the Korean Peninsula include denuclearization and prevention of the proliferation of Weapons of Mass Destruction. Barack Obama, *National Security Strategy*, Washington, DC: The White House, February 2015, pp. 11, 24.

3. Security Council, The United Nations, "Security Council Strengthens Sanctions on Democratic Republic of Korea, Unanimously Adopting Resolution 2321 (2016)," The United Nations, November 30, 2016, available from *https://www.un.org/press/en/2016/sc12603.doc.htm*, accessed December 14, 2016.

4. President Obama's "Strategic Patience" policy involves the insistence of the DPRK to commit, to steps toward denuclearization as previously promised in the Six-Party Talks. The policy is intended to work closely with Japan and the ROK and attempts to convince China to take a tougher line on North Korea. Finally, it works through applying pressure on the DPRK through arms interdictions and sanctions. Ian E. Rinehart, *North Korea: U.S. Relations, Nuclear Diplomacy, and Internal Situation*, Washington,

DC: Congressional Research Service, U.S. Library of Congress, January 15, 2016, p. 6.

5. Greg Scarlatoiu, "Human Security in North Korea," *International Journal of Korean Studies*, Vol. XIX, No. 2, Fall 2015, p. 126.

6. Mikael Weissman and Linus Hagström, "Sanctions Reconsidered: the Path Forward with North Korea," *The Washington Quarterly*, Vol. 39, Iss. 3, Fall 2016, p. 64.

7. Ibid.

8. DoD News, US to deploy THAAD missile battery to South Korea, U.S. Army, July 11, 2016, available from *https://www.army. mil/article/171316*, accessed December 14, 2016.

9. "Mission of the ROK/US Combined Forces Command," United States Forces Korea, n.d., available from *http://www.usfk. mil/About/Combined-Forces-Command/*, accessed February 27, 2017.

10. Mark E. Manyin, Emma Chanlett-Avery, Mary Beth D Nikitin, Brock R. Williams, and Jonathan R. Corrado, *U.S.-South Korea Relations*, Washington, DC: Congressional Research Service, U.S. Library of Congress, October 20, 2016, p. 26.

11. Under peacetime conditions, the ROK has control of their own military. Steven Denney, *South Korean Politics Drive OPCON Transfer*, *The Diplomat*, October 28, 2014, available from *https:// thediplomat.com/2014/10/south-korean-politics-drive-opcon-transfer/*, accessed February 27, 2017.

12. Manyin et al., p. 26.

13. Ibid, pp. 26-27.

14. Shelley Su, "The OPCON Transfer Debate," in Jae-jung Suh, *dir., SAIS US-Korea 2011 Yearbook*, Baltimore, MD: U.S.-Korea Institute, The Paul H. Nitze School of Advanced International Studies, Johns Hopkins University, 2011, p. 163.

15. Ibid., p. 171.

16. Office of the Secretary of Defense, *Quadrennial Defense Review 2014*, Washington, DC: U.S. Department of Defense, March 4, 2014, p. V.

17. Ibid., p. 34.

18. "Advance Policy Questions for General James D. Thurman, USA Nominee for Commander, United Nations Command, Commander, Republic of Korea-United States Combined Forces Command, and Commander, United States Forces Korea," Washington, DC: U.S. Senate Committee on Armed Services, June 28, 2011, available from *https://www.armed-services.senate.gov/download/2011/06/28/james-thurman-testimony-062811*, accessed February 27, 2017.

19. Tara O, "Understanding the Nature of the North Korean Regime: A Foundation to Engagement and Coercion Discussions," *International Journal of Korean Studies*, Vol. XIX, No. 1, Spring/Summer 2015, p. 50.

20. Ibid.

21. Ibid.

22. Security Council, United Nations, "Security Council Imposes Fresh Sanctions on Democratic People's Republic of Korea, Unanimously Adopting Resolution 2270 (2016)," The United Nations, March 2, 2016, available from *https://www.un.org/press/en/2016/sc12267.doc.htm*, accessed December 14, 2016.

23. Daniel W. Drezner, *The Sanctions Paradox Economic Statecraft and International Relations*, New York: Cambridge University Press, 1999, p. 292.

PART V:
SOFT POWER CONSIDERATIONS

CHAPTER 13

PEOPLE-FOCUSED ACTIVITIES: A MEASURE TO PRESERVE AMERICAN STRENGTH

Joel M. Buenaflor

EXECUTIVE SUMMARY

People-focused activities provide tangible, convincing reassurance to foreign partner nations of security and other benefits that come with a relationship with the United States. These kinds of activities reinforce persistent impressions of the United States as a benevolent leader of a peaceful world order by delivering opportunity and assistance in improving human welfare. As China and other global competitors actively work to degrade the prevalence of the worldview that sees the United States in the lead, continued support for people-focused activities sustain the credibility of and respect for the United States as an engaged world power. Leveraging people-focused activities, however, requires employing a more diversified government approach in implementation and funding beyond reliance on just security and defense initiatives. Deep funding cuts planned for the Department of State and United States Agency for International Development (USAID) seem problematic in terms of how involved these entities are in implementing America's people-focused activities. Given the expected increase of Department of Defense (DoD) manning and resourcing by the Trump administration, the U.S. military should sustain and expand its own portfolio of people-focused activities.

The current administration's direction of planned budget cuts to diplomacy and increased spending in defense should be reconsidered to ensure appropriate and sufficient foreign policy advantage is available whether the situations at hand involve military force. The Chinese ability to bypass U.S. military advantages in achieving strategic goals should encourage additional investment in people-focused activities. Specifically, the United States should invest more into English language and education programs, humanitarian assistance and disaster relief, food security, and peacekeeping operations.

INTRODUCTION

With the People's Republic of China (PRC) increasing its defense spending and demonstrating a growing willingness to utilize the People's Liberation Army (PLA) as an assertive tool of its foreign policy, U.S. national and military strategies need to address how best to retain influence and initiative in the Asia-Pacific region. President Donald Trump has promised to revitalize the U.S. military with increases of funding and human resources.[1] In formulating a U.S. stance toward China, the current strategic context, particularly from a military perspective, seems to fall most easily into an adversarial Cold War-style calculation of battle lines delineated purely through a balance of hard military power, with each side accruing as much coercive military capability as possible. While potential to leverage traditional military force certainly plays an important role in today's regional balance of power in the Asia-Pacific, more unexpected and nuanced areas of competition appear to be emerging into which China is eagerly placing emphasis and resources. This chapter considers approaches for how some of these people-focused activities can best be utilized in response to China's strengthening posture in Asia.

China found, from recent foreign policy maneuvering, that its overreliance on hard power in the South China Sea triggered an arms-buying spree in Asia, caused Japan to loosen its self-imposed military use-of-force restraints, and generally deepened its competitors' military cooperation with each other.[2] As a correction to halt the momentum toward its isolation, China initiated a well-documented "charm offensive" that includes loans for infrastructure development, free trade agreements, sponsoring dialogs, and cultivating ties across a broad range of endeavors.[3] These reactive policies reveal a China "attempting to rebrand itself as a peaceful partner" and strengthening its case for being a desirable regional hegemon to supplant the United States.[4] For example, the remarks made by Chinese President Xi at the World Economic Forum at Davos, Switzerland, in January 2017 serve as an interesting data point of where and how this U.S.-PRC competition for acceptance as a hegemonic power is occurring. At this high-profile event attended by the world's economic leaders, Xi advocated for free trade and investment liberalization while demonizing protectionism—all appeals that traditionally would have been expected from an American leader, and which also notably contrasted quite starkly with the protectionist "America first" rhetoric instrumental to Trump's ascendance to the White House.[5]

Xi's comments, which usurped a narrative usually associated with American global economic influence, transcended the economic forum in which they occurred, and actually reveal a broader Chinese aspiration to compete with the United States as the world's preferred partner nation of choice. To attain this goal, however, the Chinese face an uphill struggle. Since many of the realities and systems of international interaction were shaped under American leadership in the post-World War II-era, decades of success and confidence on the world stage have made the United States a long-standing powerhouse in this courtship of international favor. On some level, however, projecting national power departs from just fostering diplomatic, military, and economic ties between formal, institutional collectives and begins to make connections between people. The United States enjoys a considerable lead and asymmetric advantage in the people-focused aspect of its foreign policy that deliberately and systematically should be preserved.

Simply put, for a nation to win over other nations requires a full spectrum of activities that create a strong affinity and attraction for the citizens of those other nations toward the nation looking for partnership, and the United States has traditionally excelled in doing so. Much of the gravitational pull exerted by America comes naturally from the domestic vigor of its society, economy, and political systems. The U.S. Government also rightfully nurtures America's appeal internationally as a foreign policy tool that wins admirers, friends, and influence. A whole-of-government approach—in which military contributions are effectively nested—toward conducting effective people-focused activities can sustain the U.S. lead in this area. Cultivating and preserving preference for assistance, opportunities, and self-determination championed by the United States would in turn retain respect for a U.S.-led world order and provide advantage for America remaining a capable, globally engaged superpower.

ENSURING AMERICA WEARS THE WHITE HAT

In the global competition to be the world's preferred partner nation of choice, victory goes to the country that most credibly establishes itself as the provider of the best available portfolio of benefits for the populations of its partner nations. Put another way, the leadership and citizens of nations around the world should be convinced that throwing their lots in with a given global hegemon would reliably yield the greatest good.

To substantiate such a claim in the eyes of world opinion requires that a global hegemon establish a proven track record as a responsible international player that can be trusted to serve the greater good; and people-focused activities provide a critical metric that allows the world to assess any would-be hegemon's trustworthiness in this regard. To characterize, people-focused activities are those undertaken by either China or the United States and its partners that aim specifically to deliver benefit to foreign people and populations as their immediate objectives (acknowledging that a strong component of self-interest drives these decisions, too). Such people-focused activities — specifically, the type, volume, and effectiveness of those that the United States and China choose to undertake — will shape the world's and the Asia-Pacific's views on which of these two nations has earned the right to hegemonic leadership.

In the post-World War II-era, the United States can clearly claim leadership, particularly while China was engulfed in the decades-long turmoil of its Communist revolution and the subsequent turbulence of its comprehensive social and economic reorganization.[6] America's willingness to enable post-war reconstruction, economic revitalization, and the establishment of collaborative multilateral means for promoting peace and stability (conspicuously, even with regard to its vanquished foes) undeniably cast a long shadow in modern world history and helped forge a positive perception of the United States in world affairs. Such a viewpoint drew credibility from the dynamic noted by Danny Quah, Director of the Saw Swee Hock Southeast Asia Center at the London School of Economics. He noted America's burgeoning power growth seemed to quicken counterintuitively the more the United States shared and spread power and resources, rather than reserving them all for itself, by creating an inclusive global order that welcomed others who shared democratic ideals.[7] Funding the Marshall Plan for Europe, facilitating the recovery of Germany and Japan, and choosing to support the United Nations (UN), which the United States itself was instrumental in establishing and funding, all represent major American government decisions that clearly reflect an American approach that cultivated state-level bilateral and multilateral partnerships. While many of the defining elements of post-war American foreign policy were not purely people-focused activities in and of themselves, they did serve as vehicles for people-focused activities that the United States sponsored to deliver their trademark benefits to foreign people and populations. These people-focused activities helped secure America its success in establishing a current U.S.-led world order whose rules, unsurprisingly, feature strong U.S. influence in their authorship and tacit or explicit acknowledgement of U.S. interests.[8]

From the early years of this Pax Americana, however, there are significant instances where U.S. activities ran aground of Chinese interests, first in the PRC's massive intervention on the side of North Korea in the Korean war, and again in the robust PRC support for North Vietnam during the Vietnam war. After the Central Committee of the Chinese Communist Party decided to liberalize its economy in 1978, Chinese wealth and international standing enjoyed explosive growth, which seems to have accelerated the increasing conflict of U.S.-PRC interests.[9] China borrowed liberally from economic models of the United States and its allies to foster its own growth and ultimately take international market share. Some of China's recent foreign policy showcases people-focused activities that programmatically mirror the approaches of the United States and its allies, appearing again to create a situation where Chinese gains would accrue at U.S. expense. Xi's recent statements at the World Economic Forum, for example, displayed clear people-focused elements when he said that economic philosophies should aim at ensuring "people have equal access to opportunities and share in the benefits of development."[10] In another more practical recent example, China's establishment of the Asian Infrastructure Investment Bank (AIIB) in 2014 created a PRC-led financial institution paralleling the World Bank that aimed to "lend money to build roads, mobile phone towers, and other forms of infrastructure in poorer parts of Asia."[11]

However, while Xi borrowing sound bites crafted in the American style and funding the AIIB to the tune of $50 billion make sensational news, the United States still currently has more leverage and credibility available than China in the realm of people-focused activities.[12] The luster of the Chinese narrative, after all, tarnishes somewhat when delivered by a one-party state with a track record of repression that clearly does not match its outward message.[13] The PRC's economic windfall and the advantage it enables play perhaps too outsized a role in China's elements of national power and cannot win the day on their own. In contrast, the United States has decades of credibility in the area of people-focused activities. English remains the primary language of economic opportunity and multilateral interaction. American higher education maintains its internationally recognized leadership and continues to attract students from around the world, including over 300,000 Chinese in the 2014-2015 school year, a 10.8 percent increase from the year prior. People around the world (again, including a sizable cohort of Chinese) still feel an intense attraction for becoming American citizens and enjoying a free and prosperous way of life.[14] The United States must acknowledge and exploit this asymmetric advantage over the Chinese in these and similar areas. America highlighting these attractive and distinct characteristics of its society and way of life and amplifying them in people-focused activities nested within its foreign policy could in their own way echo and remain consistent with the "America first" message preferred by the Trump administration, a significant positive policy element worth noting here.

THE ROLE OF EDUCATION AND ENGLISH IN THE AMERICAN "BRAND"

Much of the author's impetus for writing this chapter comes from experiencing first-hand during a recent assignment in Cambodia that demonstrated how durable esteem for America can be, even when subjected to an overwhelmingly well-funded Chinese campaign. The script for PRC-sponsored military assistance to Cambodia follows a course familiar to long-time observers of U.S. and Chinese foreign policies. In the wake of an egregious Cambodian human rights violation—in this case, returning Uighur refugees to China in 2010—U.S. military support to Cambodia abruptly halted among a political uproar within the United States. The Chinese stepped in 2 days later to sign deals estimated worth \$850 million to fill the military aid vacuum left by the United States.[15] Among the PRC efforts that poured resources into the Royal Cambodian Armed Forces, the Army Institute stands out as a particularly ambitious initiative, apparently the first of its kind for China, to stand up a large-scale military education institution in Southeast Asia.[16]

Cambodia's Army Institute, into which the Chinese poured resources for construction and whose operations they largely fund, prepares officers for entry into the Royal Cambodian Armed Forces.[17] The Cambodian Minister of National Defense has described its facilities as "luxurious"—a descriptor rarely applied to any kind of Cambodian military installation, and a word choice from a key Cambodian official that underlines the impact of the PRC investment there.[18] The student body at the Army Institute consists of approximately 1,000 young rising military leaders who study at the campus 50 miles outside Phnom Penh: 800 participate in a 4-year program, while another smaller cohort of 200 students attends a shorter 6-month program.[19] The 4-year program consists of not only courses at the Army Institute, but also conspicuously concludes with 6 months abroad studying in Chinese military institutions—an experience that one analyst characterized as containing a "significant political component aimed at forwarding China's foreign policy interests and building sympathy for China."[20] According to coverage by Reuters of the Army Institute graduation ceremony in 2015, the Cambodian Minister of Defense attended and thanked China "for understanding [Cambodia's] difficulties," ostensibly a reference to providing funding when the United States would not.[21] The same article noted that graduates of the Army Institute were now occupying positions of significant responsibility within the Royal Cambodian Army, to include brigade commands.[22]

While the Army Institute example provides proof that China is making inroads in Cambodia through the medium of funding educational opportunity, Chinese prestige in this field of endeavor actually still lags significantly behind that of the United States. Interviewing a Cambodian official about the program at the Army Institute revealed that when the Cambodian students spend their time abroad in China, the Chinese must actually provide their instruction in English, a reality imposed by the lack of Chinese language penetration among those able to translate a foreign language, particularly with specialized military content, into the Cambodian tongue.[23] This revealing footnote to the Chinese programs at the Army Institute exposes how much ground the Chinese have to make up before achieving parity with the United States in language acceptance and educational cachet. Further, despite the very high levels of foreign military aid investment by China in Cambodia and in spite of the PRC's foreign aid structure that appears calibrated to curry the favor of the Cambodian elite, these same elites dependably exhibit a marked preference for U.S., or at least Western, education that is conducted in English.[24]

No less than the Cambodian Prime Minister himself, whose successful consolidation of power has allowed him to control the reins of Cambodia for over 30 years, elected to send his eldest son to the United States Military Academy at West Point, New York.[25] That son, who graduated from West Point in 1999, already holds the rank of Lieutenant General, as well as the titles of Deputy Commander of the Army and Commander of the National Counterterrorism Special Force, roughly the Cambodian equivalent of U.S. Special Operations Command.[26] Given his family pedigree and predictably meteoric rise in the Cambodian power structure, some probability exists that this son might be the next Cambodian head of state. Mirroring the choices of the Cambodian Prime Minister, other Cambodians also seek a U.S. or similar Western, English-based educational background for their children. In fact, the prevalence of English proficiency among those holding key billets within the Royal Cambodian Armed Forces who attended the two annual Bilateral Defense Discussions held in 2015 and 2016—the highest level of military dialogues conducted between the Cambodian and U.S. militaries—was so high that the Cambodians elected to forgo using translators, thereby demonstrating their comfort level with English.[27]

The strong English skills among people of means in Cambodia reflect the larger reality of English being the single most preferred language for cross-cultural interaction both in Asia and worldwide.[28] The approximately 2 billion speakers of English around the world overwhelm the 1.1 billion speakers of Mandarin Chinese, who are also overwhelmingly concentrated in China.[29] Again revealing the strength of English as the dominant international language, China has approximately 330 million English speakers, "an estimated 1 million English teachers, as well as 125 million to 200 million school students and 6 million to 13 million university students learning English."[30] These numbers consequently also tip the scales in favor of English-based educational opportunities being the most desirable. This fact manifests itself in English being the common language of various international fora and organizations across a broad range of endeavors — for example, the Association of Southeast Asian Nations (ASEAN) and the international information technology and commercial aviation industries.[31]

The U.S. Government, to include the military, should deliberately work to preserve the current strength of English, relative to Chinese, as a means of international communication, which in turn has a ripple effect in strengthening the appeal and relevance across the board of U.S. international engagement activities. These kinds of efforts already exist in various programs sponsored by the U.S. Government. For example, the Young Southeast Asian Leadership Initiative (YSEALI) provides U.S.-based developmental opportunities for young Southeast Asians.[32] In a parallel effort, the Fulbright U.S. Scholar Program delivers U.S. experts to foreign countries to assist in English curriculum development, as well as various other education and developmental challenges.[33] Finally, American Corners offices serve as overseas outreach hubs providing access to English learning materials and U.S. scholarship opportunities for foreign audiences.[34]

The U.S. military plays a surprisingly robust role in propagating English and English-based education among Asian partner nations. English competence serves as a prerequisite for attending many of the seminars and courses that the U.S. military sponsors, particularly those featuring a mix of multilateral attendees requiring a common language among them, or those in which foreign partners are embedded within a group consisting of predominantly Americans. Given the unparalleled strength, reputation, and recent combat experience of the U.S. military, foreign militaries assign significant importance to one of their own being selected to take advantage of one of these opportunities, particularly one of the longer courses sponsored through the International Military Education and Training (IMET) program, and especially winning an appointment to attend one of the 4-year service academies. Former Philippine President Fidel Ramos, a graduate of West Point, and former Australian Secretary of Defence Duncan E. Lewis, a graduate of the U.S. Army War College, stand out as extreme examples of the ties U.S. military educational opportunities might foster.[35] While foreign heads of state graduating from American military institutions might be relatively rare precedents, they do illustrate how funding foreign partners to attend professional military education or other events sponsored by the U.S. military bring together the talent and the training for top-tier results.

The IMET, along with Foreign Military Financing (FMF), have initiatives to expand U.S. military outreach by supporting English training within partner nation militaries. Since eligibility to attend IMET courses requires prospective students to earn passing scores on a special English test administered at their nations' U.S. embassies, supporting English language training within partner nation militaries helps to grow the pool of personnel qualified to attend IMET courses.[36] Better English capabilities in a partner nation in turn increase engagement possibilities and potential for long-term impact, whereas low levels of English capabilities in a nation close the doors to attending many IMET courses, as well as many exchanges and multilateral engagements.

To address this issue, some IMET courses specialize in immersing foreign students in a tailored English learning environment at the Defense Language Institute English Language Center in San Antonio, TX, that prepares them to attend follow-on IMET courses as soon as they meet their required English proficiency benchmarks.[37] Taking a different approach to the problem, FMF can also be used to purchase both English language labs (servers, workstations, and software packages purpose-built to prepare students for English in a military training context) for installation in a host nation's educational institution and mobile training team (MTT) support to put qualified English instructors there to accompany them.[38] These foreign policy tools afford America the opportunity to shape the educational content and learning environment of a broadened cross-section of talented military leaders from partner nations—immersing them in English, familiarizing them with U.S. operational concepts, and exposing them to democratic values—that confers a tremendous amount of influence to the United States. As the members of that select group return to their own countries and assume leadership roles within their defense establishments after attending U.S.-sponsored programs, they will each bring a new set of life experiences upon which America will have left its fingerprints.

To the degree that education and travel can be transformative, these U.S. military programs have the potential to change their foreign participants' perspectives and outlooks, perhaps for as long and as far as their professional lives will take them. While the initial payback to U.S. policy by such programs may seem no more ambitious than just augmenting partner nation military expertise and interoperability with the United States, the long-term impact to U.S. interests might expand to other, far broader ramifications. For example, a specially curated catalog of IMET known as Expanded IMET focuses on:

> proper management of defense resources, improving military justice systems in accordance with internationally recognized human rights, understanding the principle of civilian control of the military, and contributing to the cooperation between police and military forces for counternarcotics.[39]

This Expanded IMET aims toward fostering not only improved defense institutions, but also advancing national governance and stability.

A generation of rising foreign military leaders experiencing first-hand various U.S. institutions and elements of American life—whether as lofty as democratic governance and freedom of the press, or as simple as having a basic command of English and a circle of American friends and colleagues—could have inestimable value to the potential for the United States to enjoy enduring shared vision and international partnership. As elevated as the dividends of such programs might seem, it is people-focused activities serving as the soil in which they grow. Without the people-focused activities that the U.S. Government funds and conducts for individuals to get better at their jobs, to become better leaders, and to become more familiar with English, the enticing follow-on effects for cultivating continued U.S. influence internationally will never develop.

DOES "AMERICA FIRST" REALLY PUT AMERICA FIRST?

Unfortunately, whatever the appeal of the current whole-of-government approach to propagating U.S. leadership through educational opportunities and support for widespread English usage just detailed in the last few paragraphs, inward-looking domestic federal budget priorities are threatening to weaken it significantly. As of early 2017, the proposed White House 2018 budget cuts funding for the State Department, which pays for much of the U.S. Government people-focused activity, by $10.1 billion or 28 percent from 2017 budget levels.[40] Trump's introductory letter for the budget proposal justifies these cuts by stating that they put "America first by keeping more of America's hard-earned tax dollars here at home."[41] To help contextualize the current risk to the programs described previously, however, consider that the Trump administration initially looked into eliminating the State Department's entire Bureau of Educational and Cultural Affairs. This bureau promotes overseas outreach for increasing English proficiency and access to American higher education opportunities, and whose programs encompass both the YSEALI and the Fulbright U.S. Scholar Program.[42] While the proposal to disband the Bureau of Educational and Cultural Affairs was tabled, the funding for its portfolio is expected to suffer a precipitous decline since an integral part of Trump's budget proposal consists of "deep cuts to foreign aid."[43]

Somewhat counterintuitively, the State Department's belt-tightening could also deeply affect military security cooperation. Funding for sending foreign military leadership to U.S.-sponsored professional military education, which seems solidly in the realm of DoD, actually comes from the State Department.[44] The International Security Assistance portion of the State Department budget contains both the funding lines for IMET, as well as the FMF that could be used to buy either more education and training opportunities from the IMET course catalog (to include English language training MTTs) or English language labs.[45]

Aside from wanting to keep U.S. tax dollars at home, the deep budget cuts to the State Department sought by the Trump administration also seek to underwrite "the rebuilding of our Nation's military without adding to our Federal deficit."[46] After a protracted focus on the Global War on Terror (GWOT), the need to fund defense modernization initiatives to reinvigorate U.S. capabilities to defeat near-peer competitors, along with investing to counter burgeoning threats in the cyber domain, suffice to make a strong case for an increased defense budget.[47] However, cutting the State Department's English and education programs to fund other priorities is too drastic. The quote from the current Secretary of Defense, Jim Mattis, during his tenure as U.S. Central Command Commander, "If you don't fully fund the State Department, then I need to buy more ammunition," neatly sums up the countervailing line of thinking to that of the White House.[48] A recent letter addressed to congressional leadership and signed by 121 retired three and four-star flag officers echoed the same sentiment. They cautioned, "that many of the crises our nation faces do not have military solutions alone" and acknowledged that the U.S. military "needs strong civilian partners in the battle against the drivers of extremism–lack of opportunity, insecurity, injustice, and hopelessness." They ultimately recommended, "that resources for the [State Department's]

International Affairs Budget keep pace with the growing global threats and opportunities we face."[49]

Given the current foundational text for Joint doctrine, Joint Publication 1, *Doctrine for the Armed Forces of the United States*, espouses the concept of Unified Action as one that "synchronizes, coordinates, and/or integrates joint, single-Service, and multinational operations with the operations of other USG departments [e.g., the State Department] . . . to achieve unity of effort." A nearly 30 percent budget reduction to the State Department coupled with promised increases to DoD funding might imbalance diplomatic and military efforts and inadvertently cut available funding for people-focused activities.[50] Though abilities to defeat near-peer foes might have atrophied during the GWOT, the military capability that arguable achieved its peak in the same time period was conducting Unified Action alongside State Department and USAID counterparts, whether through coordination with the massive U.S. embassies in Iraq and Afghanistan, or by working in or with one of the Provincial Reconstruction Teams. While government budgets are ultimately zero-sum games, it seems like a waste to dissipate whatever recent synergy might have developed between the Department of State and DoD by pitting them so starkly against each other in fiscal combat. The net result seems to pit the instruments of national power against each other, rather than seeking to maximize their aggregate effects through balance and synchronization.

CHINA'S GRAY ZONE ACTIVITIES AND WAY AHEAD RECOMMENDATIONS

The current U.S. administration's emphasis on hard power, coupled with its confusion between wanting to narrow its concerns to "America first" and wanting to maintain the mantel of global superpower, likely suits the PRC just fine. Since America's decisive Operation DESERT STORM victory in 1991, the Chinese have worried about what the ramifications are to them of the overwhelming U.S. military dominance demonstrated in that conflict.[51] The Chinese realized that the revolution in military affairs they had witnessed would necessitate a far-reaching reconsideration of their strategy.[52] In the wake of this strategic reassessment, the PRC has embraced a strategy of "gray zone" activities that successfully impose Chinese will on smaller Asian states, yet remain below U.S. and ally and partner nation thresholds for military action.[53]

Beginning in the 1990s and accelerating sharply in the late 2000s, China embarked on its most conspicuous example of gray zone activity by mobilizing all the elements of its national power to lay the foundations for its claims in the South China Sea.[54] China has implemented a range of policies and actions that successfully exert practical control over significant contested areas. These extend from early domestic legal revisions proclaiming offshore domestic territory to later informational narratives positioning the Chinese as economic developers uninterested in territorial conquest. They are followed by the employment of militiamen embedded in the fishing fleet and eventually to the construction of militarized outposts with the ability to enforce maritime and airspace claims.[55] By the estimate of analysts from the Naval War College and the Center for Strategic and Budgetary Analysis, China has "forced the region and the United States to live with a new and largely irreversible strategic reality" and "it's hard to see how such gains can be reversed short of open warfare."[56] These strategic maneuvers have allowed the Chinese largely to circumvent American conventional military superiority by utilizing methods that carefully avoided situations in which the United States or its allies would engage in armed conflict.[57]

The reality of this Chinese strategic success must shape future American employment of and investment across its own instruments of national power. The current administration's direction of planned budget cuts to diplomacy and increased spending in defense should be reconsidered to ensure appropriate and sufficient foreign policy advantage is available whether the situations at hand involve military force. The Chinese ability to bypass U.S. military advantages in achieving strategic goals should encourage additional investment in people-focused activities. As stated earlier, much of the strength of American appeal internationally stemmed from its credibility as a hegemon whose policies ultimately supported the international greater good from which partner nations would also benefit, and this concept should be embraced more deliberately and visibly.[58] The precedents of U.S.-sponsored people-focused activities provides a broad menu of options that greatly exceeds what this chapter covered, and new policy approaches can be formulated and executed. The hard work and difficult decisions lie in selecting which old and new approaches to take that are best suited to the changing political and operational environment and fit within resourcing parameters. In addition to the English language and education programs already displayed, Humanitarian Assistance/Disaster Relief (HA/DR), food security, and Peacekeeping Operations (PKO) stand out as three areas of exceptional potential.

The HA/DR exemplifies the strength of the people-focused activity approach. Natural disasters provide high-profile events that build unambiguous consensus regarding the need to act to relieve human suffering. HA/DR therefore provides a medium through which U.S. involvement in foreign affairs can unequivocally deliver on existing perception of a benevolent presence in the region. Whether HA/DR initiatives are civilian-led by the Office of Foreign Disaster Assistance at a U.S. Embassy, or consist of military-led efforts to deliver support in spite of damaged or destroyed civil infrastructure, the message is clear: America is a powerful, globally-engaged friend you want to have. As an example, U.S. HA/DR response to a tsunami that struck Indonesia in 2004, killing over 166,000 people, had a profound impact on U.S.-Indonesia relations.[59] Human rights issues that had previously strained relations between the two countries were immediately set aside and the imperative to aid Indonesian suffering opened the door for USAID and U.S. military assets to participate in the relief effort, thereby having a "dramatic and immediate impact on U.S.-Indonesia relations."[60] Similarly, the robust U.S. response to the 2011 Fukushima tsunami bolstered relations between the United States and Japan, highlighting the U.S. commitment to assist Japan and the benefits delivered by U.S. installations within Japan.[61] By being a people-focused activity intervening to benefit foreign populations when they are most in need and vulnerable, HA/DR can dramatically illustrate the U.S. benefits of U.S. presence and commitment to our allies and partners. The State Department funding line for International Disaster Assistance should be sustained to enable these operations.

An area that holds potential for countering PRC actions in the South China Sea is food security. Through USAID, the United States is already highlighting wild fisheries as an important element of the marine environment that provides a critical source of food and protein for communities in developing countries.[62] Like HA/DR, ensuring peoples' access to a livelihood and nutrition seems to serve as a firm foundation for consensus and conviction to act. This issue of food security relates strongly to Chinese actions in the South China Sea because they have precipitated an environmental catastrophe that is threatening a fishery collapse in key areas where they have been complicit in unregulated Chinese fishing and environmentally destructive land reclamation practices.[63] The ruling of the international tribunal on "Philippines vs. China, the case brought by Manila challenging China's claims and actions in the South China Sea" found "that China had 'violated its obligation to preserve and protect fragile ecosystems and the habitat of depleted, threatened, or endangered species' and 'inflicted irreparable harm to the marine environment'."[64] Going further, John McManus, professor of marine biology and fisheries and director of the National Center for Coral Reef Research at the University of Miami, spoke at a conference on the South China Sea held at the Center for Strategic and International Studies. He characterized the damage done by the Chinese as sufficiently grave to predict "a 'major, major fisheries collapse' if decisive action isn't taken."[65] These findings by the international tribunal and academia should be engaged by the United States through USAID as a people-focused activity highlighting an impending food security disaster created by China and threatening the welfare of civilians in the South China Sea. Taking the issue from the abstract disagreement regarding lines of maritime sovereignty to a people-focused issue should be explored to bring visibility and apply more pressure to this nagging foreign policy problem.

A final area to explore with respect to people-focused activities is PKO. While PKO may seem more aligned with military operations, it still merits consideration as a people-focused activity because its intent and impact delivers security and relief of suffering to an affected foreign population. In the frame of U.S. Government implementation, PKO parallels HA/DR in being a complex interagency effort in which military and civilian personnel will be enmeshed in intersecting approvals, logistics, and security concerns. However, while PKO seems to be among the most militarized of people-focused activities referenced so far, it might be the one that holds the most promise for defusing rising tensions between the United States and PRC. Again, as with HA/DR, PKO largely occurs when broad consensus exists that sufficiently horrific events are taking place that a dangerous and expensive intervention is required.

China has recently taken on significant responsibilities in this area by deciding to participate in PKO only under the auspices of the UN, but often being in the top 10 of all troop contributors to UN missions and committing the most troops out of all the permanent UN Security Council members.[66] This Chinese participation in PKO through the UN, one of the organizations with roots in a U.S.-led world order, presents a strategic opportunity for the United States, especially as Trump has expressed a desire for partners and allies to pay their fair share in shared security arrangements.[67] PKO holds potential as an area in which the United States and PRC could cooperate broadly (including militarily, which would be significant) over shared interests. The U.S. military should identify and resource some specific international PKO efforts for increased participation and deliberate cooperative outreach with the

PRC's military participants. Such an initiative could create some strong, mutually beneficial precedents in American and Chinese forces working together in support of a rules-based order, thereby helping counteract existing dynamics toward misunderstanding and conflict in these two nations' relationship.

CONCLUSION

People-focused activities provide tangible, convincing reassurance to foreign partner nations of the security and other benefits that come with a relationship with the United States. These activities reinforce persistent impressions of the United States as a benevolent leader of a peaceful post-World War II world order by delivering opportunity and assistance in improving human welfare. As China and other global competitors are actively working to degrade the prevalence of the worldview that sees the United States in the lead, continued support for people-focused activities has potential to sustain the credibility of and respect for the United States as an engaged world power. Leveraging the potential of people-focused activities, however, requires acknowledgement of needing a more diversified government approach in implementation and funding beyond reliance on just security and defense initiatives. Upcoming deep funding cuts planned for the Department of State and USAID seem problematic in terms of how involved these entities are in the implementation of much of America's people-focused activities. With the expected increase of DoD staffing and resourcing by the Trump administration, however, the U.S. military will still find itself in a position to sustain and perhaps expand its own portfolio of people-focused activities that support the preservation of American strength.

ENDNOTES - CHAPTER 13

1. Dan Lamothe, "Trump promises 'great rebuilding of the Armed Forces' while signing executive order at the Pentagon," *The Washington Post*, January 27, 2017, available from *https://www.washingtonpost.com/news/checkpoint/wp/2017/01/27/draft-executive-order-shows-how-trump-wants-to-grow-the-u-s-military-significantly/?utm_term=.fd4e08269eb8*, accessed May 7, 2017.

2. Paul J. Leaf, "China's Charm Offensive: A Temporary, Tactical Change," *The Diplomat*, December 17, 2014, available from *https://thediplomat.com/2014/12/how-long-will-the-veneer-of-chinas-charm-offensive-last/*, accessed March 17, 2017.

3. Ibid.

4. Ibid.

5. Ishaan Tharoor, "China plays the adult as Trump attacks the system," *The Washington Post*, January 18, 2017, available from *https://www.washingtonpost.com/news/worldviews/wp/2017/01/18/china-plays-the-adult-as-trump-attacks-the-system/?utm_term=.d47f2e58ff5c*, accessed March 20, 2017.

6. Colin Mason, *A Short History of Asia*, 3rd ed., New York: Palgrave Macmillan, 2014, pp. 222-224.

7. London School of Economics and Political Science, "American Decline: Global Power in the 21st Century," May 13, 2015, London School of Economics and Political Science YouTube Channel, video file, available from *https://www.youtube.com/watch?v=1_Eh_QXuw3A&t=304s*, accessed February 13, 2017.

8. Ibid.

9. Mason, pp. 227-228.

10. Tharoor.

11. S. R., "Why China is creating a new 'World Bank' for Asia," The Economist explains, blog of *The Economist*, November 11, 2014, available from *https://www.economist.com/blogs/economist-explains/2014/11/economist-explains-6*, accessed February 13, 2017.

12. Ibid.

13. Tharoor.

14. Bethany Allen-Ebrahimian, "Chinese Students in America: 300,000 and Counting," *Foreign Policy*, November 16, 2015, available from *http://foreignpolicy.com/2015/11/16/china-us-colleges-education-chinese-students-university/*, accessed February 14, 2017; London School of Economics and Political Science.

15. Aubrey Belford and Prak Chan Thul, "Chinese influence in Cambodia grows with army school, aid," Reuters, April 2, 2015, available from *https://uk.reuters.com/article/uk-cambodia-china-military/chinese-influence-in-cambodia-grows-with-army-school-aid-idUKKBN0MT0T220150402*, accessed February 14, 2017.

16. Ibid.

17. Ibid.

18. Ibid.

19. Ibid.

20. Ibid.

21. Ibid.

22. Ibid.

23. Interview with Cambodian official, Fall 2016.

24. Simon Denyer, "The push and pull of China's orbit: A rush to invest in Cambodia's infrastructure is part of a larger quest for regional influence," *The Washington Post*, September 5, 2015, available from *http://www.washingtonpost.com/sf/world/2015/09/05/the-push-and-pull-of-chinas-orbit/?utm_term=.6509c3d7160a*, accessed March 20, 2017.

25. Saing Soenthrith and Paul Vrieze, "Hun Sen's Second Son in Meteoric Rise Through RCAF Ranks," The Cambodia Daily, January 30, 2012, available from *https://www.cambodiadaily.com/archives/hun-sens-second-son-in-meteoric-rise-through-rcaf-ranks-1560/*, accessed March 20, 2017.

26. Ibid.

27. Author helped to coordinate and personally participated in the U.S.-Cambodia Bilateral Defense Discussions in 2015 and 2016.

28. Benjamin Herscovitch, "English is the language of the Asian century," ABC [Australian Broadcasting Corporation] News, September 12, 2012, available from *http://www.abc.net.au/news/2012-09-13/herscovitch-english-asia/4257442*, accessed May 7, 2017.

29. Ibid.

30. Ibid.

31. Ibid.; "Charter of the Association of Southeast Asian Nations," Jakarta, Indonesia: Association of Southeast Asian Nations, November 20, 2007, available from *http://asean.org/asean/asean-charter/*, accessed March 20, 2017; Joe Sharkey, "English Skills a Concern As Global Aviation Grows," *The New York Times*, May 21, 2012, available from *www.nytimes.com/2012/05/22/business/english-skills-a-concern-as-global-aviation-grows.html*, accessed March 20, 2017.

32. "Young Southeast Asian Leaders Initiative," U.S. Mission to ASEAN, n.d., available from *https://asean.usmission.gov/yseali/*, accessed March 20, 2017.

33. "Core: Fulbright Scholar Program," U.S. Department of State Bureau of Educational and Cultural Affairs, n.d., available from *https://www.cies.org/program/core-fulbright-us-scholar-program*, accessed March 20, 2017.

34. U.S. Advisory Commission on Public Diplomacy, "The New Diplomacy: Utilizing Innovative Communication Concepts that Recognize Resource Constraints," Washington, DC:

U.S. Advisory Commission on Public Diplomacy, available from *https://www.state.gov/documents/organization/22956.pdf*, accessed March 20, 2017.

35. See Fidel V. Ramos, Class of 1950, listed in "Notable Graduates," United States Military Academy West Point, n.d., available from *https://www.usma.edu/about/SitePages/Notable%20Graduates.aspx*, accessed March 20, 2017; Kareem Fahim, "Egypt General Has Country Wondering About Aims," *The New York Times*, August 2, 2013, available from *www.nytimes.com/2013/08/03/world/middleeast/egypts-general-sisi.html*, accessed March 20, 2017.

36. "English Comprehension Level Test: What is the ECL?" Defense Language Institute English Language Center, n.d., available from *http://www.dlielc.edu/testing/ecl_test.php*, accessed March 20, 2017.

37. "Frequently Asked Questions about Specialized English Training," Defense Language Institute English Language Center, n.d., available from *http://www.dlielc.edu/faq/set_faq.php*, accessed March 20, 2017.

38. Ira C. Queen, "The Value of Security Cooperation," *DISAM Journal*, Vol. 28, No. 3, 2006, p. 6, available from *https://www.discs.dsca.mil/Pubs/Indexes/Vol%2028_3/Queen_2_apr_2013_b.pdf*, accessed March 20, 2017.

39. "ESAMM Glossary: Expanded IMET," in Defense Security Cooperation Agency, *Security Assistance Management Manual Online*, Official Site of the Defense Security Cooperation Agency, April 30, 2012, available from *http://www.samm.dsca.mil/glossary/expanded-imet-e-imet*, accessed March 20, 2017.

40. U.S. Office of Management and Budget, *America First: A Budget Blueprint to Make America Great Again*, Washington, DC: U.S. Government Printing Office, 2017, p. 33.

41. Ibid., p. 1.

42. Carol Morello, "State Department's 28 percent cuts hit foreign aid, U.N., and climate change," March 16, 2017, *The Washington Post*, available from *https://www.washingtonpost.com/world/national-security/*

state-departments-28-percent-cuts-hit-foreign-aid-un-and-climate-change/2017/03/15/294d7ab8-0996-11e7-a15f-a58d4a988474_story. html?utm_term=.c9ec39070831, accessed March 20, 2017.

43. U.S. Office of Management and Budget, p. 2.

44. U.S. Department of State, "Congressional Budget Justification: Department of State, Foreign Operations, and Related Programs," Washington, DC: U.S. Department of State, p. 4, available from *https://2009-2017.state.gov/documents/organization/252179.pdf*, accessed March 20, 2017.

45. Ibid.

46. U.S. Office of Management and Budget, p. 1.

47. Senior U.S. Defense Official, lecture, U.S. Army War College, Carlisle, PA, Spring 2017.

48. Dan Lamothe, "Retired generals cite past comments from Mattis while opposing Trump's proposed foreign aid cuts," *The Washington Post*, February 27, 2017, available from *https://www. washingtonpost.com/news/checkpoint/wp/2017/02/27/retired-generals-cite-past-comments-from-mattis-while-opposing-trumps-proposed-foreign-aid-cuts/?utm_term=.465fa32703f6*, accessed March 20, 2017.

49. Ibid.

50. U.S. Joint Chiefs of Staff, Joint Publication 1, *Doctrine for the Armed Forces of the United States,* Washington, DC: U.S. Joint Chiefs of Staff, March 25, 2013, p. xiii.

51. Harlan W. Jencks, "Chinese Evaluations of 'Desert Storm': Implications For PRC Security," *The Journal of East Asian Affairs*, Vol. 6, No. 2, Summer/Fall 1992, pp. 455-456, available from *www. jstor.org/stable/23253951?seq=10#page_scan_tab_contents*, accessed March 27, 2017.

52. Ibid., p. 477.

53. James Holmes and Toshi Yoshihara, "Five Shades of Chinese Gray-Zone Strategy," *The National Interest*, May 2, 2017, available from *nationalinterest.org/feature/five-shades-chinese-gray-zone-strategy-20450*, accessed May 7, 2017.

54. Ibid.

55. Ibid.

56. Ibid.

57. Ibid.

58. Mason, pp. 222-224; London School of Economics and Political Science.

59. Anthony L. Smith, *Indonesia and the United States 2004–2005: New President, New Needs, Same Old Relations,* Special Assessment, Honolulu, HI: Asia-Pacific Center for Security Studies, February 2005, pp. 2, 7, available from *http://www.dtic.mil/docs/citations/ADA627444,* accessed December 8, 2017.

60. Ibid.

61. David M. Potter, "U.S.-Japanese Relations in Transition: The Case of Fukushima," *Norteamérica,* Vol. 8, No. 1, June 2013, available from *http://www.scielo.org.mx/scielo.php?script=sci_arttext &pid=S1870-35502013000100006,* accessed May 7, 2017.

62. Measuring Impact, *Fishing for Food Security: The Importance of Wild Fisheries for Food Security and Nutrition,* Washington, DC: U.S. Agency for International Development, April 2016, pp. 3-6, available from *https://rmportal.net/biodiversityconservation-gateway/resources/projects/measuring-impact/mi-project-resources/fishing-for-food-security-importance-of-wild-fisheries-for-food-security-and-nutrition-pdf/view,* accessed May 7, 2017.

63. Shannon Tiezzi, "South China Sea Ruling: China Caused 'Irreparable Harm' to Environment," *The Diplomat,* July 15, 2016, available from *https://thediplomat.com/2016/07/south-china-sea-ruling-china-caused-irreparable-harm-to-environment/,* accessed May 7, 2017.

64. Ibid.

65. Ibid.

66. Courtney J. Fung, "China's Troop Contributions to U.N. Peacekeeping," *Peace Brief,* No. 212, Washington, DC: U.S.

Institute for Peace, July 26, 2016, available from *https://www.usip. org/publications/2016/07/chinas-troop-contributions-un-peacekeeping*, accessed May 7, 2017.

67. Jacob Pramuk, "Trump aims to reassure allies about US support, but asks them to pay up more," CNBC News, February 6, 2017, available from *https://www.cnbc.com/2017/02/06/trump-tries-to-reassure-allies-about-us-support-but-asks-them-to-pay-up-more.html*, accessed May 7, 2017.

CHAPTER 14

DIPLOMACY UNDER THE STRATEGIC REBALANCE AND A LOOK FORWARD

Sandra Minkel

EXECUTIVE SUMMARY

This chapter examines the use of diplomacy under former President Barack Obama's "pivot to Asia" through the Diplomatic, Information, Military, Economic (DIME) construct to assess the effectiveness and soundness of diplomatic efforts under the rebalance strategy. It discusses successes and failures that form the basis of lessons-learned in order to provide recommendations for the Trump administration as it formulates its strategy for the Indo-Asia-Pacific region. The formulation and articulation of strategy is key to any administration. The process prioritizes foreign policy objectives and guides government officials as they strive to promote and protect U.S. national interests successfully through bilateral and multilateral negotiations with other sovereign states in a rules-based international order.

While the balance between the roles of diplomatic and military power under the Obama administration seemed right for the situation, the rising tensions in the South China Sea and on the Korean peninsula may demand an adjustment. Based on lessons learned, the following are recommendations to continue to support U.S. interests in the region.

- Continue face-to-face high-level (Presidential and Cabinet-level) exchanges through summits, dialogues, and participation in multilateral forums.
- Join the Asia Infrastructure Investment Bank (AIIB) as a member and support efforts through coordinated projects with the World Bank and the Asia Development Bank (ADB).
- After pulling out of the Trans-Pacific Partnership (TPP), quickly negotiate and enter into bilateral or multilateral trade deals that support U.S. economic prosperity and business opportunities abroad. Trump stated his preference for bilateral trade deals. However, consideration should be given to multilateral trade deals that support his economic agenda.
- Use various mediums to relay a consistent U.S. policy with explanations to the public as to its importance.
- Nominate personnel with appropriate regional experience to fill key positions within State, U.S. Agency for International Development (USAID), and the Department of Defense (DoD) to assist with policy formulation and ensure implementation of the policy in line with the new administration's priorities.
- Refrain from deep budget cuts in foreign assistance that allows the Department of State and USAID to deliver diplomatic and development exertions required to achieve national security objectives.

INTRODUCTION

In November 2016, the people of the United States elected Trump to be the 45th President of the United States. The new leadership will undoubtedly usher in different priorities, policies, and strategies, making this an ideal time to review Obama's strategic pivot or rebalance to the Indo-Asia-Pacific (IAP) and to look ahead toward the next 4 years. This chapter considers the Obama administration's use of diplomacy to achieve long-term objectives in line with national security interests in the IAP region. While traditional diplomatic negotiations are often not directly in the public eye or as newsworthy as military activities, they nevertheless occur on a constant basis across all governmental agencies. As Kurt Campbell, Assistant Secretary of State for East Asian and Pacific Affairs under Obama, wrote, "The personal dimension of American diplomacy is probably the least understood and most important facet of American power in Asia."[1]

Merriam-Webster defines diplomacy as "the art and practice of conducting negotiations between nations" and the "skill in handling affairs without arousing hostility."[2] Charles Freeman described diplomacy in his book, *Arts of Power: Statecraft and Diplomacy,* as the adjustment of relations between states by mutual agreement. It is the method and process by which foreign policy is pursued through peaceful means. He added that diplomatic strategy "must be judged by what it prevents as much as by what it achieves."[3] This chapter discusses successes and failures under the pivot to the IAP in the use of diplomacy in a whole-of-government pursuit of foreign policy objectives. It reviews aspects of the strategy through the DIME construct to determine whether the efforts in the region were sound. It contends that there was a mix of successes and disappointments. It then draws on these lessons learned to recommend actions under the Trump administration.

OBAMA ADMINISTRATION: REBALANCE TO THE INDO-ASIA-PACIFIC

In 2011, Obama declared to the Australian Parliament that he had "made a deliberate and strategic decision—as a Pacific nation" to seek "security, prosperity, and dignity for all" in the Asia-Pacific region. He clearly stated, "So let there be no doubt, in the Asia Pacific in the 21st century, the United States of America is all in."[4] While the United States has always been a "Pacific nation" and previous administrations have focused on emerging opportunities in Asia, many in the region felt that in recent years, U.S. presence waned. The wars in Iraq and Afghanistan, as well as the 2008 financial crisis, had diverted resources and attention. As a result, high-level U.S. officials did not always attend regional forums, leading Asian leaders to feel abandoned in their quest for regional stability.

Among the few visible gauges of traditional diplomacy, the "D" in DIME, are state-to-state and high-level engagements and meetings. In this regard, Obama backed up his pledge to "be all in." "Nine-tenths of success in diplomacy in Asia is showing up," said Michael J. Green, a key figure on Asian affairs on President George W. Bush's National Security Council, in a riff on a quote made famous by Woody Allen.[5] Obama definitely showed up—traveling to Asia 63 times, more than any president in history. A look at the records of four two-term presidents—Dwight Eisenhower spent 12 days in Asia; Ronald Reagan, 21 days; Bill Clinton,

52; and George W. Bush, 50—illustrates the increasing focus on the region over the last 24 years.[6]

Hillary Clinton also did her part to reinforce the U.S. reinvigorated interest in Asia. She broke from tradition when she became the first Secretary of State in 50 years to visit Asia on her first official trip—just 1 month after her confirmation.[7] Maintaining the enthusiasm for commitment to the rebalance, she went on to make more trips to the region than any previous Secretary of State—62, compared to Secretary Condoleezza Rice's 47.[8] In a 2015 speech at the Brookings Institute, Clinton called the rebalance policy a "response to the very real sense of abandonment that Asian leaders expressed to me,"[9] due to the U.S. focus on Afghanistan and Iraq. The sense was "we were just not paying attention to the developments in Asia."[10] Secretary Clinton reinforced the U.S. commitment by attending the first Association of Southeast Asian Nations (ASEAN) Regional Forum (ARF) Ministerial Meeting, where she signed ASEAN's Treaty of Amity and Cooperation (TAC) in July 2009. The TAC's language represents the foundational principles of ASEAN, and signing indicated a general acceptance of them for dealing with the 10 ASEAN nations. It also opened the door for expanded participation in other ASEAN-related forums. The United States became the first non-ASEAN country to establish a dedicated diplomatic mission, and in 2010 to appoint a resident ambassador to the ASEAN Secretariat in Jakarta.[11] The arrangement provided for continuous and consistent contact by a U.S. representative dedicated to ASEAN affairs.

Transition to a new Secretary of State, John Kerry in 2013, and the departure of Assistant Secretary for

East Asian and Pacific Affairs Kurt Campbell—one of the architects of the rebalance to Asia—sparked Asian doubts about the U.S. ongoing commitment to the region.[12] Meanwhile, disagreements at home over the debt ceiling added to concerns about U.S. stability and staying power. "Running the government of the world's mightiest power by sequestration and threats of going over a fiscal cliff," wrote Robert Hathaway, a Public Policy Fellow at the Wilson Center, "mystified those who look to the United States for leadership,"[13] and exacerbated doubts of U.S. commitment to the rebalance. Criticized for diverting attention to issues in Europe and the Middle East, Kerry and other administration officials nevertheless continued to engage substantively with Asia, making it a point to attend the ARF meetings, for example, and standing in for Obama at Asia-Pacific Economic Cooperation (APEC) and East Asia Summit (EAS) meetings. (APEC, comprised of 22 economies, is a forum for promoting economic cooperation and trade liberalization.)[14]

The partial U.S. Government shutdown in 2013, driven by sharp budget differences between congressional Republicans and the White House,[15] prompted Obama to cancel his attendance at an APEC meeting in Indonesia, an EAS meeting in Brunei, and a visit to Malaysia. Although the United States sent Kerry, along with U.S. Trade Representative Michael Froman and Commerce Secretary Penny Pritzker, the Asians were disappointed that Obama was not there to offer a high-level counter to the Chinese head of state, Xi Jinping.[16] In particular, key leaders were disappointed he was unable to use his personal influence to press for progress on the TPP,[17] an agreement connecting 12 countries and intended to expand economic growth with lower non-tariff barriers and higher standards to address intellectual property rights and state-owned enterprises.

Meanwhile, on the sidelines of APEC, Xi was pushing countries to commit to the Regional Comprehensive Economic Partnership (RCEP), an agreement between ASEAN and six other Asian countries—Australia, China, India, Japan, New Zealand, and South Korea—with which it has bilateral free trade pacts.[18] The United States and Russia had become full participants in the EAS in 2011. In an article for the East Asian Forum, John Pang wrote that the "single biggest influence on the direction of the EAS has been the consistent presence of Washington's 'Pacific President,' who shifted the EAS agenda towards geostrategic concerns."[19]

Public Diplomacy

The success of diplomacy requires clearly defined and articulated messaging, which gains buy-in and impels others toward common goals. In "America's Pacific Century," a 2011 article for *Foreign Policy*, Secretary Clinton included such phrases as "the United States stands at a pivot point," "efforts to pivot to new global realities," and, "this kind of pivot is not easy." Journalists latched onto the catch phrase to brand the new strategy.[20] Whereas the intent had been to articulate an integrated approach to focusing on a strategically important region in the 21st century, the phrase had the unintended impact of signaling a turning-away from Europe and the Middle East. Uncertainty regarding U.S. capabilities and the long-term U.S. commitment to those other regions grew. Asian allies became concerned that the United States could as easily turn away from them should a crisis arise in another region.

Though the policy would later be re-branded as a "rebalance," it was too late to repair the initial damage.

Kurt Campbell admitted to a poorly-handled roll-out of the rebalance, saying the administration "could have been more effective at communicating what the goals were," including its desire to "embed China in a regional strategy."[21] The branding itself detracted from the broader intent. While attempting to reassure the IAP region that it was a top priority for the United States, this phrasing—in widespread use until recently—made it seem as though the administration was shifting from, rather than extending the efforts of previous administrations.

In fact, the rebalance was nothing more than an elevation of a strategy conceived by previous administrations. Thanks to September 11, 2001 (9/11), the wars in Iraq and Afghanistan, and the global financial crisis of 2008, this earlier strategy had simply fallen off the radar. While his administration had focused on Asia from the start, Obama turned his attention to the financial crisis, as it was shaking nerves across the global community and calling into question the U.S. role as a world leader. China seized on this perceived weakening, becoming more assertive in its territorial claims in the South and East China Seas, as well as on the economic front.

The Obama administration also could have done a better job explaining its integrated strategy to the American people. A well-articulated and documented strategy in one central place might have assuaged confusion and uncertainty for stakeholders at home and abroad. The administration had captured top-level priorities, including a refocus on Asia and a whole-of-government approach to foreign policy, in the 2015 *National Security Strategy*, but the public knew little to nothing about it.

Bilateral Diplomacy

Fortified through various bilateral and multilateral diplomatic, economic, and security relationships, the IAP is of great importance to U.S. security and economy. The U.S. Department of Agriculture (USDA) estimates that, by 2030, the IAP region will contain the three largest economies after the United States (China, India, and Japan).[22] Five of the 10 most populous countries—Bangladesh, China, India, Indonesia, and Pakistan—are in Asia, and 7 of the 10 largest militaries are in the IAP.[23] Of these, the United States has bilateral defense treaties with Japan, South Korea, Australia, and the Philippines, strong partnerships with Singapore and New Zealand, and strengthened partnerships with Indonesia and Vietnam. The simple guiding goal of the pivot, as Campbell has explained, is to intensify its bilateral relationships with "nearly every Asian state, from India to Vietnam and from Malaysia to Mongolia, and to embed itself in Asia's growing web of regional institutions."[24]

In her *Foreign Policy* article, Secretary Clinton wrote that strengthening bilateral relations was among the six elements of the strategy that complement efforts through multilateral forums and institutions and regional security architecture.[25] Bilateral relationships and promotion of U.S. interests and values overseas are not new, but the number of high-level visits and face-to-face dialogues helped to build relationships. Under Obama, administration officials strengthened bilateral relationships across the IAP, promoting an international, rules-based order, adherence to international law, democratic values, and human rights. Nations long neglected by Washington (New Zealand, Indonesia, the Philippines, and small Pacific island states) received high-ranking U.S. official visits, as did India, and most notably, Burma and Vietnam.[26]

After signing the TAC in 2010, Secretary Clinton presented the U.S. "principled engagement" strategy toward Burma to ASEAN. The strategy represented a shift in policy, from sanctions imposed by previous administrations to engagement based on Burma's reform efforts toward democracy. When she visited a year later, Clinton became the first Secretary of State to do so in 55 years. A year later, the U.S. Government re-established full diplomatic relations with Burma—nominating Derek Mitchell as the first ambassador since 1990—and reopened a USAID mission there. In testimony to the House Foreign Affairs Committee, Deputy Secretary of State Antony Blinken highlighted efforts with Burma to "modernize and strengthen legal and regulatory regimes" in the country, "helping set the stage for major American companies to enter that market."[27]

Similarly, the engagement with Vietnam brought positive results. Since a bilateral trade agreement was signed in 2001, trade and investment opportunities have grown dramatically, and the country continues to take positive steps on human rights, including having authorized independent trade unions, a first in modern times. The 2013 U.S.-Vietnam Comprehensive Partnership has encouraged respect for the rule of law. After Obama visited the country in May 2016, in part to mark the 2015 anniversary of 20 years of bilateral relations (that year U.S. exports to the country increased by 23 percent), Vietnam signed the TPP. Still, challenges remain, particularly regarding labor standards; Vietnam has yet to pass laws that would bring it to the level required for participation in the TPP.[28]

Presidents Clinton, George W. Bush, and Obama all visited India, underscoring the growing importance of this bilateral relationship for mutual prosperity and security. The Bush administration committed to new cooperation on four highly sensitive fronts: civilian nuclear energy, civilian space programs, dual-use high technology, and missile defense.[29] The 2005 U.S.-India Civil Nuclear Cooperation Agreement "opened the doors to a new relationship with an emerging power," as Ashley J. Tellis put it.[30] In the years since, cooperation between the two countries has steadily increased, helping to offset China's growing expansion in the region. Obama highlighted the "strategic convergence" with India's Act East Policy and the U.S. "continued implementation of the rebalance to Asia and the Pacific" in the *2015 National Security Strategy*.[31] Similar to the U.S. rebalance, India actively seeks to engage with ASEAN and other Asian countries. India is the second largest contributor to the AIIB and is negotiating to join the regional trade agreement. In 2012, the United States and India created the Defense Technology and Trade Initiative, and the White House recognized India as a major defense partner, a level that the United States accords its close partners and allies.[32] This enables expanding defense trade and technology sharing with the country. With the rise of India's population and economy—Bloomberg reports that the USDA expects India to move ahead of Japan as the world's third largest economy by 2030[33]—it will continue to be a significant partner economically as well as militarily.

South Korea and Japan are both treaty allies with long histories of cooperation (and some historical tensions between the two) with the United States. These countries are integral alliance partners and coordinate closely with the United States on the denuclearization of the Korean peninsula and other economic and military issues in the region. The United States worked to modernize the treaty with Japan by modifying the Defense Guidelines with new and expanded forms of security cooperation in 2015 and a new 5-year package of host nation support for U.S. troops in 2016.

South Korea agreed last year to host the U.S. Terminal High Altitude Area Defense (THAAD) missile defense system as a way of defending against rising threats from North Korea. South Korea's hosting of THAAD threatens China, as it is perceived as a surveillance mechanism and soured South Korea's relations with China and created additional tensions in the region. Many Asian experts believe that Obama's approach of "strategic patience" toward North Korea has failed, and they are looking to Trump for a change in strategy. Secretary of State Rex Tillerson recently said that, after 20 years of failure to denuclearize the peninsula, "strategic patience is over," and that the new administration would most likely take a different approach.[34]

In 2014, the United States deepened long-standing security cooperation with the Philippines by signing the Enhanced Defense Cooperation Agreement. The agreement authorizes the U.S. military access on a rotational basis and allows the two nations' forces to conduct security cooperation exercises, joint training, and humanitarian assistance and disaster relief activities.[35] The United States is one of the largest foreign investors in the Philippines, and there is a strong bilateral trade relationship, though recent concerns about human rights abuses under the Duterte presidency and harsh statements made by Duterte about Obama raise questions about future long-term relations. Additionally, Duterte's balancing act between pleasing the United

States and China is a precarious situation fraught with the potential to anger either of the two large powers.[36]

China remains the most prominent player and the most complex of U.S. bilateral relationships in the region. Historians, political analysts, and academics have theorized about the "rise of China" as a great power and whether a transition from the United States as the status quo power and the rise of China as a great power might escalate to a military conflict (as has happened in 12 out of 16 such transitions over the last 500 years). Whether, in other words, the two rivals will avoid the so-called Thucydides Trap[37]—a reference to the author who chronicled the 5th century BC Peloponnesian War, pitting a rising Athens against the status quo power, Sparta, and the shift in the balance of power between them. In a 2015 article for *The Atlantic*, Graham Allison considered the key drivers behind the conflict: on one hand, "the rising power's growing entitlement, sense of its importance, and demand for greater say and sway," and on the other, "the fear, insecurity, and determination to defend the status quo this engenders in the established power."[38]

China says it strives for peaceful development, with win-win benefits for both nations, while the United States says it welcomes a peaceful rise of China as long as it adheres to multilateral norms and the rules of international law. "There is no such thing as the so-called Thucydides Trap," said Xi on a visit to Washington in 2015. "But should major countries time and again make the mistakes of strategic miscalculation, they might create such traps for themselves."[39] It will take diligence, dialogue, and understanding to avoid such miscalculations. After dealing with U.S. domestic issues, the Obama administration showed signs of improved partnership with China—following the line from the Bush administration to hold China accountable as a responsible stakeholder regarding global issues and increasing the number of high-level dialogues.

The Obama administration invested substantial resources in a growing set of bilateral forums, including the U.S.-China Strategic and Economic Dialogue, the Strategic Security Dialogue, and over 60 other issue-based and regional dialogues with Chinese government officials.[40] In 2013, Obama hosted Xi in California for an informal 2-day summit, just months after the new president had taken office, to deepen their personal relationship and seek a way forward on key issues. The leaders discussed North Korea, cyber-theft and espionage, maritime territorial disputes in the East and South China Seas, and U.S. arms sales to Taiwan.[41] These informal summits, the Security and Economic Dialogues, and other forums increase understanding and cooperation and yield results. Arguably, the mutual commitment to the Paris Agreement on climate change is a great sign of willingness to address global challenges. However, any momentum toward growing trust and cooperation established during the Obama administration has been lost with the Trump administration's decision to pull out of the Paris Agreement.

While the agreement on climate change and high-level dialogues delivered many positive benefits, there is still much to do to reduce the level of mistrust on both sides. China claims it strives for peaceful development with win-win benefits while protecting its core interests. The United States says it welcomes a peaceful rise of China as long as China adheres to the norms of international law and multilateral norms. The relationship will continue to be problematic as long as the core interests of each country are not in closer alignment.

Multilateral Arrangements

The United States uses a whole-of-government approach to work through bilateral as well as multilateral institutions in order to promote its interests of peace, security, and respect for international law. Aside from the long-standing and largely U.S.-led Bretton Woods institutions, the most significant multilateral achievement under the rebalance was the U.S. signing of the ASEAN TAC, which resulted in the United States playing an active and influential role in ASEAN forums such as the ARF, EAS, and ASEAN Defense Ministers' Meeting-Plus (ADMM-PLUS). In addition, the United States is a member of several other regional organizations such as the Asia-Pacific Economic Cooperation (APEC), the Lower Mekong Initiative, and is an observer to the Pacific Islands Forum and the Conference of Interaction and Confidence Building in Asia.

Geopolitical changes are forcing many multilateral organizations to reevaluate their memberships and voting rules to reflect better the growing influence of countries such as China and India. In 2010, the International Monetary Fund's (IMF) executive board approved a plan to increase the voting share of the aforementioned members and to double the amount of permanent funding available to the Washington-based fund.[42] While the Obama administration made several efforts to obtain legislative approval of the changes, the proposal languished in Congress for 5 years.[43] Edwin M. Truman, a former assistant secretary of the U.S. Treasury, warned that failure to act would compel other nations to work around the United States at the IMF.[44] Congress finally approved the proposal in 2015; 5 years after the IMF had submitted it.

Analysts have posited growing frustration with Washington and U.S.-led international organizations prompted China to create the AIIB. In an article for *The Pacific Review*, Xiao Ren wrote that slow-moving reforms and resistance to accommodation of China's growing status in the IMF, World Bank, and ADB frustrated the Asian powerhouse.

> China's push for a regional institution within which it would be dominant or at least have considerable impact was a reflection of Beijing's frustration over the Western, especially American, dominance of the existing international multilaterals.[45]

Some call Washington's reaction to the AIIB a "diplomatic disaster."[46] Not only did the United States show no interest in joining the AIIB, it actively lobbied its allies to stay away, suggesting that the new bank would not have the same high standards of creditworthiness and transparency as the other multilateral banking institutions. The United States also feared that the AIIB would increase China's ability to use infrastructure financing to influence countries toward a pro-China stance. Some have argued that China might have invested in one of the existing banks in order to achieve the same purpose, but its frustration had reached a peak. Since then, several allies and other countries rushed to join the AIIB, a situation that suggests the United States is losing influence.

In a March 2015 issue of *The Economist*, the editors wrote that the United States is not wrong to question the existence of the AIIB, but that it would have more influence working from within the structure. They also pointed out that, while the ADB and the World Bank are focused on poverty alleviation and healthcare, the focus of the AIIB is large-scale infrastructure programs. "The continent's relentless urbanization requires at least $8 trillion of infrastructure spending in this decade, according to ADB,"[47] adding that the AIIB complements existing development bank programs.

Economic Diplomacy

Under the rebalance, the United States intended to focus on economic statecraft and strengthening economic leadership[48]—the "E" in DIME. At the heart of this portion of the strategy was the ambitious TPP, a comprehensive trading network encompassing 12 countries on 4 continents. The Obama administration negotiated an agreement that sought to lower barriers, raise standards, and address intellectual property rights and state-owned enterprises, and that would have covered 40 percent of the world's trade. It would have fortified the U.S. status as the leader of a global, rules-based economic system that would have expanded to trading partners in the region with North America and South America. The ability to invest in the development of the Asian economies and to sell goods and services to their growing middle classes was to power U.S. growth for decades to come.[49]

While Obama signed the negotiated agreement in 2016, Congress still needed to draft a bill to implement the agreement, which would have served as U.S. ratification of the trade deal.[50] The U.S. business community largely supported the TPP—it would level the playing field and open markets for export—but there was not sufficient political will for ratification. The Obama administration's efforts to conclude the TPP were laudable, but its inability to submit the agreement to Congress before the beginning of a contentious U.S. election cycle put the entire project at risk. In the end, both candidates for president denounced the agreement—though one had worked on it as Secretary of State—and the new administration was clear that it would take TPP no further.

Military Diplomacy

The military initiated its portion of the pivot by shifting 60 percent of the force to the Asia-Pacific to protect U.S. interests while strengthening and modernizing bilateral relationships with treaty allies Japan, South Korea, Australia, and the Philippines. North Korea's continued efforts to acquire and test long-range nuclear missiles that will reach the United States destabilizes the region and threatens the security of the United States and its allies. China's aggressiveness on territorial claims and its militarization of the South China Sea, combined with a staggering build-up and modernization of its forces, threaten security and freedom of navigation in the South and East China Seas. John Pomfret chronicled a confrontation between Secretary Clinton and Chinese Foreign Minister Yang Jiechi in Hanoi in 2010, just months prior to the announcement of the rebalance. In response to her assertion that claims to maritime space should be directly tied to legitimate claims to land features, Yang said, "China is a big country and other countries are small countries, and that's a fact."[51] This statement may be interpreted two different ways. On one hand, China reacted to harsh criticism from Secretary Clinton and others, because it felt that the United States was unfairly joining with the ASEAN countries to contain the rising power from exercising its rightful claims, and that the United States was meddling in regional affairs. On the other hand, the outburst may be interpreted as China's true intent—to use its economic might and growing military to coerce the "smaller countries" to gain its goals. While the majority of Asian nations welcome the shift in U.S. forces, China and North Korea view it as a threat to their national interests and security. China consistently voices concerns about the United States trying to contain it, but this shift was largely intended as a signal to reassure allies of the U.S. commitment to provide stability in the region.

Over the last 6 years, the United States has participated in the ADMM-Plus and the ARF in order to build regional trust, cohesion, and civil-military cooperation and integration. In 2015, Assistant Secretary of Defense for Asian and Pacific Security Affairs David Shear said that, "leveraging defense diplomacy to build greater transparency, reduce the risk of miscalculation or conflict, and promote shared maritime rules of the road"[52] would assist in reducing gaps and building trust. Participation in ASEAN-related forums augments the bilateral relationships that DoD maintains. The DoD will seek to expand trilateral and quadrilateral defense discussions with key partners. ASEAN-centered relationships are of growing utility in a region affected by frequent natural disasters, the threat of terrorism, rival maritime claims, illegal fishing, food security challenges, environmental degradation, and other shared interests that require a multilateral response. However, it must be inclusive of China, as too much emphasis on force posture and alliance building to counter China is another unintended sign that the U.S. strategy is strictly a counterbalance to China's growing power as opposed to a supportive peaceful development. Former Secretary of Defense Ash Carter characterizes China as self-isolationist. In his view, the

Chinese are raising the barriers to working in unison by "erecting a Great Wall of self-isolation."[53]

Renewed and modernized defense agreements with the Philippines, Japan, and Australia allow forward deployment of forces on a rotational basis. Moving forward, they will allow the military to respond quickly to potential conflicts as well as to provide security in the region and an increased number of combined partner exercises, and assure freedom of navigation and air space.

The Obama administration has also expanded trilateral cooperation. Bush initiated the most productive of these, the U.S.-Japan-Australia Trilateral Strategic Dialogue. The Obama administration expanded the cooperative reach through a U.S.-Japan-India trilateral in 2015. Another trilateral dialogue formed between Japan-India-Australia in 2015. This signals the increased importance of various countries coordinating and cooperating on a range of security issues in every configuration. The shift represents an elevated number of joint exercises between allies as well as bilateral China-U.S. cooperative maneuvers. The latter consists mostly of military school visit exchanges, dialogues, and recently the inclusion of China in the multinational Rim of the Pacific exercise.

The increased multiple partner exercises assist in mitigating the potential for miscalculations. In relation to the complicated territorial disputes in the South China Sea, to which the United States is not a claimant, Secretary James Mattis recently said that, "these territories which are contested need to be addressed politically through a legal framework consistent with international law."[54] This represents the long-standing view of the administration to lead with diplomacy and statecraft and use military hard power as a last resort.

The presence of the U.S. military is itself a show of military diplomacy, with an aim toward protecting U.S. interests, regional stability, and freedom of navigation. It is doubtful that any parties want to choose between the United States and China, and elevating diplomacy across all levels of statecraft, including military, will help to achieve stability.

A LOOK AHEAD TO THE TRUMP ADMINISTRATION

Although the Trump administration has not yet published a comprehensive foreign policy strategy, there are signs that the President is placing some importance on Asia. In a press briefing, Acting Assistant Secretary of State for East Asian and Pacific Affairs Susan A. Thornton clearly stated that, while the pivot or rebalance is over, the new administration will remain engaged and active in IAP as the region is very important to global economic prosperity and growth as well as security. She said the U.S. policy approach seeks to level the playing field for U.S. interests and promote fair and balanced economic opportunities.[55]

Regarding China, Trump has significantly softened the tough rhetoric of his campaign, during which he threatened to name China as a "currency manipulator" and stated that trade deals between the countries were "lopsided" in China's favor. As president-elect, Trump accepted a congratulatory phone call from Taiwanese President Tsai Ing-wen. In an interview with *The Wall Street Journal*, he said that the long-standing U.S. "One-China policy" was negotiable.[56] The policy remains essentially as first articulated in a 1972 Shanghai Communiqué: "The United States acknowledges that all Chinese on either side of the Taiwan Strait maintain there is but one China and Taiwan is a part of China."[57] Trump subsequently talked with Xi in February 2017 and acknowledged that he will honor the decades-long U.S. "One China" policy.[58]

Meanwhile, Tillerson talked with the leaders of Australia, Japan, and South Korea in February and "reiterated the Administration's intent to strengthen our military alliances, our economic partnerships, and our diplomatic cooperation."[59] In March, he met with Chinese Foreign Minister Wang Yi at the G20 Summit in Germany, urging Beijing "to help rein in North Korea."[60] Tillerson also traveled to Japan, South Korea, and China to continue discussions on dealing with North Korea and negotiated an April 2017 meeting between Xi and Trump at Mar-a-Lago.[61] This sends a message that North Korea's recent actions are a high priority, and the United States will remain engaged in the region.

After the heated debates and messages from the campaign trail, it is imperative for the United States to delineate a clear vision and strategy for the next 4 years. To assist in formulating strategies and policies toward the IAP and globally, the Trump administration should nominate people to fill the multiple vacant positions in State, DoD, and USAID. According to the nonpartisan Partnership for Public Service, as of April 11, 2017, the White House formally nominated 24 people to fill 553 politically appointed positions across all government agencies that require Senate approval. Of the 24 nominations, 22 have been confirmed.[62] The administration would benefit from nominating people with extensive Asia experience to fill the key positions that deal with this region, in particular to assist with formulation of strategy and policy in accordance with the new administration's approach. This will also assist high-level decision-makers in the formulation of a comprehensive, whole-of-government strategy toward the IAP.

Another concern that will affect diplomatic efforts is the President's budget request. Asked how cuts to the State Department budget might affect the U.S. military and its activities around the globe, Office of Management and Budget Director Mick Mulvaney replied, "Make no mistake about it, this is a hard-power budget, not a soft-power budget. That is what the president wanted, and that's what we gave him."[63] The United States has one of the largest development assistance programs in the world (roughly 25 billion in absolute dollars), but one of the smallest as a share of gross national income (.018 percent), according to the Organization for Economic Cooperation and Development.[64] Cuts to eliminate positions and support programs will drastically shift government efforts from a whole-of-government balanced soft power approach to an emphasis on use of military force: hard power. The foreign assistance budget has historically received bipartisan support. Senior Republican Senator Lindsay Graham said the Trump budget is "dead on arrival" and added that such drastic cuts would be "a disaster." Senator Marco Rubio had similar statements: "Foreign Aid is not charity," and it is "less than 1 percent of our budget and critical to our national security."[65] Over 120 retired generals signed a letter urging Congress not to drastically cut foreign assistance as proposed, since "elevating and strengthening diplomacy and development alongside defense are critical to keeping America safe."[66]

CONCLUSION AND RECOMMENDATIONS

Diplomacy plays a key role in implementing foreign policy objectives across all agencies in the government and in the wise use of the military instrument as a deterrent. Obama and his administration should be lauded for increased travel to and consistent presence in the IAP and for peacefully furthering bilateral and multilateral relationships in the region. This all could have been accomplished without the distraction of a "pivot" that created confusion and left various partners around the world wondering if the United States had the ability to respond to its security commitments worldwide. His use of a whole-of-government approach and use of other soft power tools to prevent the need for military confrontation is applauded, as is his recognition of the requirement for active behind-the-scenes efforts to build diplomatic relations gradually. Obama's inability to shepherd the TPP through its ratification process, however, and the decision not to participate in and to lobby allies against the AIIB will continue to have negative effects on the economic front.

While the balance between the roles of diplomatic and military power under the Obama administration seemed right for the situation, the rising tensions in the South China Sea and on the Korean peninsula may demand an adjustment. Based on lessons learned, the following are recommendations to continue to support U.S. interests in the region.

- Continue face-to-face high-level (Presidential and Cabinet-level) exchanges through summits, dialogues, and participation in multilateral forums.

- Join the AIIB as a member and support efforts through coordinated projects with the World Bank and ADB.
- After pulling out of the TPP, quickly negotiate and enter into bilateral or multilateral trade deals that support U.S. economic prosperity and business opportunities abroad. Trump stated his preference for bilateral trade deals. However, consideration should be given to multilateral trade deals that support his economic agenda.
- Use various mediums to relay a consistent U.S. policy with explanations to the public as to its importance.
- Nominate personnel with appropriate regional experience to fill key positions within State, USAID, and DoD in order to assist with policy formulation and ensure implementation of the policy in line with the new administration's priorities.
- Refrain from deep budget cuts in the foreign assistance that allows State and USAID to deliver diplomatic and development exertions required to achieving national security objectives.

Formulation and articulation of strategy is key to any administration. While Obama had a sound strategy, the commotion in naming it as a pivot or rebalance detracted from the intended outcomes. The administration's missteps in messaging combined with the inability to implement the economic portion of the rebalance were damaging. However, the new administration received a stronger regional security architecture to assist with potential issues with North

Korea and the South China Sea. The Trump administration should draw on mistakes and successes not only from the Obama administration, but also from all previous administrations. Recent years indicate that a whole-of-government approach, led by soft power first and hard power as a last resort, will yield dividends— because no one "wins" because of a war.

ENDNOTES—CHAPTER 14

1. Kurt M. Campbell, *The Pivot: The Future of American Statecraft*, New York: Hatchette Book Group, Incorporated, 2016, p. 326.

2. "Diplomacy," in *Merriam-Webster Dictionary Online*, updated November 28, 2017, available from *https://www.merriam-webster.com/dictionary/diplomacy*, accessed December 8, 2017.

3. Charles W. Freeman, *The Arts of Power: Statecraft and Diplomacy*, Washington, DC: United States Institute of Peace Press, 1997, p. 72.

4. Barack Obama, "Remarks by President Obama to the Australian Parliament," The White House Office of the Press Secretary, Canberra, Australia, November 17, 2011, available from *https://obamawhitehouse.archives.gov/the-press-office/2011/11/17/remarks-president-obama-australian-parliament*, accessed April 27, 2017.

5. Michael J. Green, quoted in George E. Condon, Jr., "Air Force One's Pivot to Asia," *National Journal*, May 26, 2016, available from *https://www.nationaljournal.com/s/626967/air-force-ones-pivot-asia*, accessed December 23, 2016.

6. Condon, Jr., "Air Force One's Pivot to Asia."

7. Ibid.

8. Ibid.

9. Catherine Putz and Shannon Tiezzi, "Did Hillary Clinton's Pivot to Asia Work?" FiveThirtyEight, April 14, 2016, available

from *https://fivethirtyeight.com/features/did-hillary-clintons-pivot-to-asia-work/*, accessed February 19, 2017.

10. Ibid.

11. The White House Office of the Press Secretary, "Fact Sheet: Unprecedented U.S.-ASEAN Relations," Washington, DC: The White House, February 12, 2016, available from *https://asean.usmission.gov/fact-sheet-unprecedented-u-s-asean-relations/*, accessed January 25, 2017.

12. Center for a New American Security, "Secretary Kerry and the Future of the U.S. Rebalancing to Asia," Center for a New American Security, March 22, 2013, available from *https://www.cnas.org/press/in-the-news/secretary-kerry-and-the-future-of-the-u-s-rebalancing-to-asia*, accessed January 25, 2017.

13. Robert Hathaway, "Kerry in Asia: Fleshing Out the Rebalance," Asia Program Research, Wilson Center, April 12, 2013, available from *https://www.wilsoncenter.org/article/kerry-asia-fleshing-out-the-rebalance*, accessed January 15, 2017.

14. Ibid.

15. Murray Hiebert, Noelan Arbis, and Kyle Springer, "The 2013 APEC Leaders' Meeting and East Asia Summit," Washington, DC: Center for Strategic and International Studies, October 11 2013, available from *https://www.csis.org/analysis/2013-apec-leaders%E2%80%99-meeting-and-east-asia-summit*, accessed December 27, 2016.

16. Ibid.

17. Ibid.

18. Ibid.

19. John Pang, "The East Asia Summit: a platform for confidence building," East Asia Forum, November 12, 2016, available from *www.eastasiaforum.org/2016/11/12/the-east-asia-summit-a-platform-for-confidence-building/*, accessed December 27, 2016.

20. Hillary Clinton, "America's Pacific Century," *Foreign Policy*, October 11, 2011, available from *http://foreignpolicy.com/2011/10/11/americas-pacific-century/*, accessed October 17, 2016.

21. Campbell, pp. 6-7.

22. Jeanna Smialek, "These Will Be the World's 20 Largest Economies in 2030," Bloomberg, April 10, 2015, available from *https://www.bloomberg.com/news/articles/2015-04-10/the-world-s-20-largest-economies-in-2030*, accessed January 10, 2017.

23. UN News Centre, "UN projects world population to reach 8.5 billion by 2030, driven by growth in developing countries," Sustainable Development Goals, blog of the United Nations, July 29, 2015, available from *www.un.org/sustainabledevelopment/blog/2015/07/un-projects-world-population-to-reach-8-5-billion-by-2030-driven-by-growth-in-developing-countries/*, accessed February 7, 2017.

24. Campbell, p. 14.

25. Clinton, "America's Pacific Century."

26. David Shambaugh, "Assessing the US 'Pivot' to Asia," *Strategic Studies Quarterly*, Vol 7, Iss. 2, Summer 2013, pp. 10-19.

27. Antony J. Blinken, "Testimony before the House Foreign Relations Committee on the Obama Administration Policy in the Asia Pacific," Washington, DC: U.S. Department of State Archives, April 28, 2016, available from *https://2009-2017.state.gov/s/d/2016d/256694.htm*, accessed November 17, 2016.

28. Bureau of East Asian and Pacific Affairs, "Fact Sheet: U.S. Relations with Vietnam," Washington, DC: U.S. Department of State, December 11, 2017, available from *https://www.state.gov/r/pa/ei/bgn/4130.htm*, accessed December 12, 2017.

29. Ashley J. Tellis, *Opportunities Unbound: Sustaining the Transformation in U.S.-Indian Relations*, Washington, DC: Carnegie Endowment for International Peace, January 7, 2013, pp. 5-6, available from *http://carnegieendowment.org/2013/01/07/opportunities-unbound-sustaining-transformation-in-u.s.-indian-relations-pub-50506*, accessed January 14, 2017.

30. Ibid., p. 6.

31. Barack H. Obama, *National Security Strategy*, Washington, DC: The White House, February 2015, p. 25.

32. Ash Carter, "The Rebalance and Asia-Pacific Security," *Foreign Affairs*, November/December 2016, p. 68.

33. Smialek.

34. Rex W. Tillerson, "Press Availability with Japanese Foreign Minister Fumio Kishida," Washington, DC: U.S. Department of State, Tokyo, Japan, March 16, 2017, available from *https://www. state.gov/secretary/remarks/2017/03/268476.htm*, accessed March 18, 2017.

35. "Enhanced Defense Cooperation Agreement between the Philippines and the United States," *Official Gazette*, Republic of the Philippines, April 29, 2014, available from *http:// www.officialgazette.gov.ph/2014/04/29/document-enhanced-defense-cooperation-agreement/*, accessed April 5, 2017.

36. "Philippines President Walks Trademark Tightrope Between US, Chinese Interests," Sputnik International, April 18, 2017, available from *https://sputniknews.com/ asia/201704181052739893-philippines-president-duterte-policy/*, accessed April 19, 2017.

37. Graham Allison, "The Thucydides Trap: Are the U.S. and China Headed for War?" *The Atlantic*, September 24, 2015, available from *https://www.theatlantic.com/international/archive/2015/09/ united-states-china-war-thucydides-trap/406756/*, accessed December 21, 2016.

38. Ibid.

39. Xi Jinping, "Full Text of Xi Jinping's Speech on China-U.S. Relations in Seattle," CRI English, September 24, 2015, available from *http://english.cri.cn/12394/2015/09/24/3746s897214.htm*, accessed December 21, 2016.

40. Bates Gill, "The Pivot, Past and Future," *The Diplomat*, December 1, 2016, available from *https://thediplomat.com/2016/12/ the-pivot-past-and-future/*, accessed January 24, 2017.

41. Richard C. Bush, "Obama and Xi at Sunnylands: A Good Start," Up Front, blog of The Brookings Institution, June 10, 2013, available from *https://www.brookings.edu/blog/up-front/2013/06/10/obama-and-xi-at-sunnylands-a-good-start/*, accessed January 7, 2017.

42. Andrew Mayeda, "Congress Approves IMF Change in Favor of Emerging Markets," December 18, 2015, available from *https://www.bloomberg.com/news/articles/2015-12-18/congress-approves-imf-changes-giving-emerging-markets-more-sway*, accessed January 5, 2017.

43. Gerald F. Seib, "How Congress's Inaction on IMF Reform, Trade Hinders the U.S.," Washington Wire, blog of *The Wall Street Journal*, March 31, 2015, available from *https://blogs.wsj.com/washwire/2015/03/31/how-congress-inaction-on-imf-reform-trade-hinders-the-u-s/*, accessed February 26, 2017.

44. Ibid.

45. Xiao Ren, "China as an institution-builder: the case of the AIIB," *The Pacific Review*, Vol. 29, No. 3, 2016, p. 436.

46. Shannon Tiezzi, "America's AIIB Disaster: Are There Lessons to be Learned?" *The Diplomat*, March 18, 2015, available from *https://thediplomat.com/2015/03/americas-aiib-disaster-are-there-lessons-to-be-learned/*, accessed January 15, 2017.

47. "China on the world stage: A bridge not far enough," *The Economist*, March 19, 2015, available from *www.economist.com/news/leaders/21646746-america-wrong-obstruct-chinas-asian-infrastructure-bank-bridge-not-far-enough*, accessed February 26, 2017.

48. Hillary Clinton, "Delivering on the Promise of Economic Statecraft: Remarks, Hillary Rodham Clinton Secretary of State, Singapore Management University, Singapore," U.S. Department of State Archives, November 17, 2012, available from *https://2009-2017.state.gov/secretary/20092013clinton/rm/2012/11/200664.htm*, accessed November 30, 2017.

49. Aaron L. Connelly, "Congress and Asia-Pacific Policy: Dysfunction and Neglect," Sydney, Australia: The Lowy Institute, September 24, 2015, available from *https://www.lowyinstitute.org/*

publications/congress-and-asia-pacific-policy-dysfunction-and-neglect, accessed February 4, 2017.

50. Muftiah M. McCartin and Kaitlyn McClure, "What's Next for TPP: Will Congress Ratify in 2016?" Global Policy Watch, January 21, 2016, available from *https://www.globalpolicywatch. com/2016/01/whats-next-for-tpp-will-congress-ratify-in-2016/*, accessed April 27, 2017.

51. John Pomfret, "U.S. takes a tougher tone with China," *The Washington Post*, July 30, 2010, available from *http:// www.washingtonpost.com/wp-dyn/content/article/2010/07/29/ AR2010072906416.html*, accessed April 27, 2017.

52. Jim Garamone, "U.S. Outlines Asia-Pacific Maritime Security Strategy," U.S. Pacific Command, August 21, 2015, available from *http://www.pacom.mil/Media/News/News-Article-View/ Article/614504/us-outlines-asia-pacific-maritime-security-strategy/*, accessed February 6, 2017.

53. Carter.

54. Fred Dews, "Joint Chiefs Chairman Dunford on the '4+1 framework' and meeting transnational threats," Washington, DC: The Brookings Institution, February 24, 2017, available from *https://www.brookings.edu/blog/brookings-now/2017/02/24/joint- chiefs-chairman-dunford-transnational-threats/*, accessed March 3, 2017.

55. Susan A. Thornton, "A Preview of Secretary Tillerson's Upcoming Travel to Asia," U.S. Department of State Foreign Press Center Briefing, Washington, DC, March 13, 2017, available from *https://fpc.state.gov/268444.htm*, accessed March 17, 2017.

56. "Trump, China Diverge on New World Order," *The Wall Street Journal*, video file, January 17, 2017, available from *http://www.wsj.com/video/trump-china-diverge-on-new-world- order/0F2860E5-DC74-4B43-BF7F-EC0478E5D299.html*, accessed March 13, 2017.

57. "Joint Statement Following Discussions With Leaders of the People's Republic of China," Document 203, in Steven E. Phillips, ed. and Edward C. Keefer, gen. ed., *Foreign Relations of the*

United States, 1969–1976, Volume XVII, China, 1969–1972, Washington DC: U.S. Government Printing Office, 2006, digital archive from Office of the Historian, U.S. Department of State, available from *https://history.state.gov/historicaldocuments/frus1969-76v17/d203*, accessed March 30, 2017.

58. Ben Blanchard and Steve Holland, "Trump changes tack, backs 'one China' policy in call with Xi," Reuters, February 9, 2017, available from *https://www.reuters.com/article/us-usa-trump-china/trump-changes-tack-backs-one-china-policy-in-call-with-xi-idUSKBN15P0ED*, accessed March 13, 2017.

59. Office of the Spokesperson, Mark Toner, Acting Spokesperson, "Readout of Secretary Tillerson's Phone Calls with Foreign Minister of Australia Julia Bishop, Foreign Minister of Japan Fumio Kishida, and Foreign Minister of the Republic of Korea Yun Byung-se," Washington, DC: U.S. Department of State, February 7, 2017, available from *https://www.state.gov/r/pa/prs/ps/2017/02/267487.htm*, accessed February 14, 2017.

60. L'Agence France-Presse, "N. Korea to top agenda on Tillerson Asia visit: reports," Yahoo News, March 3, 2017, available from *https://www.yahoo.com/news/n-korea-top-agenda-tillerson-asia-visit-reports-045853391.html*, accessed March 4, 2017.

61. Office of the Spokesperson, "Previewing Secretary Tillerson's Travel to Japan, South Korea, and China," Washington, DC: U.S. Department of State, March 10, 2017, available from *https://www.state.gov/r/pa/prs/ps/2017/03/268355.htm*, accessed March 13, 2017.

62. Nancy Cook, Josh Dawsey, and Andrew Restuccia, "Why the Trump administration has so many vacancies," *Politico*, April 11, 2017, available from *https://www.politico.com/story/2017/04/donald-trump-white-house-staff-vacancies-237081*, accessed April 13, 2017.

63. Louis Nelson, "Mulvaney justifies budget: We can't ask a coal miner to pay for the Corporation for Public Broadcasting," *Politico*, March 16, 2017, available from *https://www.politico.com/story/2017/03/mick-mulvaney-trump-budget-priorities-236117*, accessed March 17, 2017.

64. Gordon Adams and Richard Sokolsky, "Savaging State and USAID Budgets Could Do Wonders for Results," *Foreign Policy*, March 9, 2017, available from *https://foreignpolicy.com/2017/03/09/savaging-state-and-usaid-budgets-could-do-wonders-for-results-tillerson-development-diplomacy-cuts/*, accessed March 9, 2017.

65. Sylvan Lane, "GOP senator: Trump budget dead on arrival," The Hill, February 28, 2017, available from *http://thehill.com/policy/finance/321576-gop-senator-trump-budget-dead-on-arrival*, accessed March 2, 2017.

66. Yeganeh Torbati, "Retired U.S. military officers urge Congress to fully fund diplomacy, aid," Reuters, February 27, 2017, available from *https://www.reuters.com/article/us-usa-trump-budget-foreignpolicy/retired-u-s-military-officers-urge-congress-to-fully-fund-diplomacy-aid-idUSKBN1661YK*, accessed March 2, 2017.

ABOUT THE CONTRIBUTORS

PROJECT EDITORS

DAVID LAI is Research Professor of Asian Security Studies at the Strategic Studies Institute (SSI) of the U.S. Army War College (USAWC). Dr. Lai joined SSI in 2008. Before then, he was on the faculty of the U.S. Air War College, Maxwell AFB, Montgomery Alabama. Dr. Lai's research and teaching interests cover U.S.-China and U.S.-Asian security relations. He has also made special contributions to the study of Chinese strategic thinking and military operational art, receiving acknowledgements from Dr. Henry Kissinger, General (U.S. Air Force Ret.) Steve Lorenz, Dr. Joseph Nye, Jr., Dr. Graham Allison, and many in the U.S. diplomatic and defense communities.

JOHN F. TROXELL is currently serving as Research Professor of National Security and Military Strategy, with the SSI, USAWC. He served as an economics instructor with the Department of Social Sciences, at the United States Military Academy from 1982 to 1985, and prior to assuming his current position he was Professor of National Security Affairs with the Center for Strategic Leadership as a member of the Strategic Decision-making Exercise team. Prior to that, he served as the Director of National Security Studies, Department of National Security and Strategy, USAWC. He is also an adjunct faculty member of the Baltic Defense College. In addition to his research activities with SSI, for the past 14 years he has taught an elective course on the economics of national security and has widely lectured on related topics. Colonel (U.S. Army Ret.)

Troxell earned a bachelor's degree from the United States Military Academy in 1974 and a master's degree from the Woodrow Wilson School, Princeton University in 1982. He is also a 1997 graduate of the USAWC.

FREDERICK J. GELLERT is Professor of Resource Management at the USAWC. He served at U.S. Army Pacific as the Chief of Force Management and then the Deputy Chief of Staff for Operations G-3/5/7 from 2008-2011. He teaches courses and lectures on strategic leadership, defense management, and Asia-Pacific regional studies. Colonel (U.S. Army Ret.) Gellert holds a bachelor's in physics from Wayne State University, a master's in astrophysics from Rensselaer Polytechnic Institute, and a Master's of Strategic Studies from the USAWC.

PROJECT RESEARCHERS

ROBERT R. ARNOLD, JR., is a U.S. Army Colonel and a recent graduate of the USAWC, 2016-2017. He is currently deployed to Afghanistan and serves as Senior Advisor to the Deputy Minister, Security, Afghan Ministry of the Interior. He has held various command and staff positions throughout his 26 years of military service. Most recently, he served as Commander, 504th Military Police Battalion, and Secretary of the General Staff, I Corps, Joint Base Lewis-McChord, WA. Colonel Arnold supported humanitarian relief in Florida following Hurricane Andrew, deployed to Bosnia-Herzegovina in support of Operation JOINT ENDEAVOR, to Kosovo in support of Operation JOINT GUARDIAN, to Iraq and Afghanistan in support of an operational assessment for the Army Battle Command System, and twice to Iraq in support of Operation IRAQI

FREEDOM. Commissioned through Officer Candidate School at Fort Benning, GA, in 1995, Colonel Arnold holds a Master of Science in Strategic Studies from the USAWC, Carlisle, PA, a Master of Science in International Relations from Troy State University, Troy, AL, and a Bachelor of Science in Elementary Education from Trenton State College, Trenton, NJ (1990).

ROMEO S. BRAWNER, JR., is a Colonel in the Philippine Army. He graduated from the Philippine Military Academy in 1989 at the top of the list of graduates joining the Army. He joined the Special Forces Regiment (Airborne) as a Company Commander, Regimental Operations Officer and Battalion Commander. He was also the spokesperson of the Philippine Army and later of the Armed Forces of the Philippines. Colonel Brawner has a Master of Science degree in Information Management, a Master of Business Administration degree, and a Master of Strategic Studies from the USAWC. In 2013, Colonel Brawner was the recipient of the Ten Outstanding Philippine Soldiers award.

JOEL M. BUENAFLOR is a U.S. Army Colonel. He has had extensive experience in the Pacific region including service as the Chief, Office of Defense Cooperation in Cambodia, Strategy Branch Chief with Pacific Command, Southeast Asia Desk Officer with the U.S. Army Pacific, and a tour of duty in Korea. He is currently serving on his second tour to Afghanistan. Colonel Buenaflor holds a Master of Science in Strategic Studies from the USAWC, Carlisle, PA, a Master of Arts in English from Texas A&M University, and a Bachelor of Science in Philosophy from the United States Military Academy.

TODD D. CARROLL is a Commander in the U.S. Navy. He has served as a Naval Flight Officer who has made four deployments in support of Operations IRAQI FREEDOM, ENDURING FREEDOM, and NEW DAWN. He has accrued over 2,500 hours in the F/A-18F. Prior to his arrival at USAWC, he was the Strike Operations Officer on USS *Gerald R Ford* (CVN-78) and is currently a placement officer at Navy Personnel Command. Commander Carroll holds a BS in industrial engineering from the University of Wisconsin, Madison, and a Master of Strategic Studies from the USAWC.

FRAZARIEL I. CASTRO is a U.S. Army Colonel and Logistician. He was commissioned through the Reserve Officers Training Corps in the Transportation Corps with a branch detail to Air Defense Artillery. Colonel Castro's current assignment is Deputy Director, HQDA G-46, Logistics Information Management Directorate at the Pentagon, Washington, DC. Previous assignments include Commander, 68th Transportation Company (Line Haul), 28th Transportation Battalion at Mannheim, Germany; and Commander, Army Field Support Battalion-Korea, 403rd Army Field Support Brigade at Camp Casey, Republic of Korea. Colonel Castro most recently served as the Transportation Organizational Integrator, HQDA G-3/5/7 (Force Management), at the Pentagon. Colonel Castro holds a Bachelor of Arts in politics from the University of San Francisco, a Master of Arts in management and leadership from Webster University, and a Master of Strategic Studies from the USAWC.

JAMES L. CONNER is a U.S. Army Colonel. He was commissioned into the U.S. Army Chemical Corps through ROTC in 1995. He has spent more than 8 years in various assignments in the Republic of Korea, including service as the Battalion Commander for USFK Special Troops Battalion, in Yongsan. In addition to a deployment to Afghanistan, he has also had several assignments in the Pentagon, with the Joint Staff, J34 Anti-Terrorism/Force Protection CBRNE Branch, and with the Army Staff, G-3/5/7 Operations Division for Readiness as the Joint Operations Branch Chief. He is currently assigned as the Eighth Army-Director, G-34 Operational Protection Directorate, in Seoul, Korea. Colonel Conner holds a B.S. in criminal justice from Fayetteville State University, a master's degree in public policy administrative management from Georgetown University in Washington, DC, and a Master of Strategic Studies from the USAWC.

WILLIAM P. DONNELLY is a Lieutenant Colonel in the U.S. Marine Corps. He has served as a U.S. Marine for more than 20 years in multiple operational and instructional training assignments. In addition to his operational experience, he has served the Marine Corps as a staff officer in several capacities. He is currently serving with the U.S. European Command in Stuttgart, Germany. Lieutenant Colonel Donnelly holds a Bachelor of Science degree in history from the U.S. Naval Academy, a Master of Business Administration degree from the Naval Post Graduate School, and a Master of Strategic Studies from the USAWC.

RYAN M. FINN is a Lieutenant Colonel in the U.S. Marine Corps. He has deployed to Iraq and Afghanistan, as well as several tours of duty with Marine

Forces Pacific. Lieutenant Colonel Finn holds a Bachelor of Arts in biology from Ithaca College, a Master of Military Art and Science from the Marine Corps Command and Staff College, and a Master of Strategic Studies from the USAWC.

SANDRA K. MINKEL is a career Foreign Service Officer with the United States Agency for International Development (USAID). Her current position is as the USAID Senior Development Advisor to the U.S. Pacific Command (PACOM) in Hawaii. She joined USAID in 2000 and has more than 16 years of progressive experience in financial management and international development, with extensive experience in Zimbabwe (2011-2016), Iraq (2010-2011), Nepal (2008-2010), Republic of Georgia (2006-2008), and Hungary (2001-2006). In addition, she has experience through advisory and technical assistance within USAID, host governments, and the private voluntary and non-governmental organization communities in the Balkans, Caucasus, Nepal, and Zimbabwe. She has served in a variety of civic and charitable organizations providing domestic community service and as a team leader for the National Civilian Community Corps in South Carolina. She was also a U.S. Peace Corps Volunteer in Kitale, Kenya (1991-1993). Ms. Minkel holds a Bachelor of Science in business administration from Central Michigan University, and a Master of Strategic Studies from the USAWC.

DAVID B. MOORE is a Lieutenant Colonel in the U.S. Marine Corps. He is a Marine Cobra pilot who has served in the U.S. Marine Corps for more than 20 years. His current assignment is with the United States European Command. He has deployed three times to the Asia-Pacific region as part of the Unit Deployment Program and the 31st Marine Expeditionary Unit (MEU) out of Okinawa, Japan, and has served in combat tours to Iraq in 2003 and 2007 and Afghanistan in 2013. He served in staff billets with Second Marine Aircraft Wing, Forward (2dMAW Fwd) in Afghanistan and with Headquarters Marine Corps, Department of Aviation in Washington, DC. He served as the Marine Aircraft Group 29 (MAG-29) Headquarters Squadron Commanding Officer from July 2014 until January 2015 and as the Commanding Officer of Marine Light Attack Helicopter Squadron 467 (HMLA-467) from January 2015 until June 2016. Lieutenant Colonel Moore holds a master's degree in military studies from the U.S. Marine Corps Command and Staff Course in Quantico, and a master's degree in strategic studies from the USAWC.

NEIL J. OWENS is a Lieutenant Colonel in the U.S. Marine Corps with extensive experience in the Asia-Pacific region. In addition to multiple operational, instructor, staff, and headquarters billets, he has had several opportunities to serve with international militaries, to include Operations Advisor to the Afghan National Army, an exchange officer with the United Kingdom Royal Marines, and as a student at the Australian Command and Staff College. He has conducted multiple deployments to Iraq and Afghanistan and has deployed to Okinawa, Japan, three times. His last assignment was as Commanding Officer of 3d Battalion, 12th Marines, and an artillery battalion in Okinawa Upon graduation from USAWC, he will be assigned to the III Marine Expeditionary Force in Okinawa. Lieutenant Colonel Owens holds a Bachelor of Arts in history from George Washington University, a

Master of Strategic Studies degree from the University of New South Wales, Australia, and a Master of Strategic Studies from the USAWC.

STEVEN M. PIERCE is a U.S. Army Colonel and has served more than 22 years in the Army. His assignments include in airborne and armored units through the division level, on a Combined Joint Task Force staff and at the Headquarters, Department of the Army. He has deployed twice in support of Operation IRAQI FREEDOM and once in support of Operation ENDURING FREEDOM. His next assignment is as a Liaison Officer for the Combined Joint Task Force Horn of Africa at U.S. African Command. Colonel Pierce's military education includes the Combined Arms and Services Staff School, Joint Firepower Course, Joint Air Operations Command and Control Course, and Command and General Staff College. He holds a Bachelor of Science degree from the University of North Carolina-Greensboro, and a Master of Strategic Studies degree from the USAWC.

DERIC K. WONG is a career civil servant currently assigned to the Joint Force Development directorate of the Joint Staff (JS J-7) and serves as the Chief, Policy Integration Branch for joint force training. In this role, Mr. Wong ensures Department of Defense policy guidance and pronouncements are integrated into military policy and guidance issued on behalf of the Chairman of the Joint Chiefs of Staff. He also provides program evaluation expertise to the Department's joint exercise program. Mr. Wong entered the civil service as the Manager, Theater Security Cooperation program for Headquarters, Pacific Air Forces (HQ PACAF) in 2000 eventually becoming Chief, International Affairs branch supervising seven political/regional affairs specialists and overseeing PACAF's foreign military sales program. Prior to his assignment to the Joint Staff, Mr. Wong served on the Air Staff of the U.S. Air Force and was an operational planner on the staff of the Air Force District of Washington (HQ AFDW). Mr. Wong holds a Bachelor of Science degree in physics from Oregon State University, a Master of Business Administration degree from Rensselaer Polytechnic Institute, a Master of Arts degree in economics from the University of Oklahoma, and a Master of Strategic Studies degree from the USAWC.

ERIC W. YOUNG is a U.S. Army Colonel, commissioned in 1993 from Purdue University in West Lafayette, IN. Previous assignments include: Executive Officer, U.S. Army Legal Services Agency, Fort Belvoir, VA; Chief, Active Component Career Management Branch/Lieutenant Colonels Assignments, Personnel, Plans and Training Office, Office of The Judge Advocate General, Washington, DC; Deputy Staff Judge Advocate, U.S. Pacific Command, Camp H.M. Smith, HI; Professor, International Law, U.S. Naval War College, Newport, RI; Deputy Staff Judge Advocate, CJTF-101/101st ABN DIV (AASLT), Bagram, Afghanistan; Command Judge Advocate, Combined/Joint Special Operations Task Force-Afghanistan; and Group Judge Advocate, 3rd Special Forces Group (Airborne), Fort Bragg, NC. Colonel Young holds a Master of Arts (MA) with Highest Distinction in national security and strategic studies from the U.S. Naval War College, Newport, RI; a Master of Laws (LL.M) from The Judge Advocate General's Legal Center and School, Charlottesville, VA; a Juris Doctor (J.D.) from Marquette

University Law School, Milwaukee, WI; and a Master of Strategic Studies degree from the USAWC.

JEFFREY M. ZAISER is a career Foreign Service Officer. He has served primarily in East and Southeast Asia, including U.S. Embassies and Consulates in South Korea, the People's Republic of China, Vietnam, Thailand, and Hong Kong, as well as at the American Institute in Taiwan. More recently, he spent 4 years in the Middle East region (Iraq and Jerusalem). Mr. Zaiser holds a bachelor's degree from the University of Virginia, studied economics at the graduate level at the University of Stockholm, and holds a master's degree from the USAWC.